THE STRUGGLE FOR INFLUENCE

The Impact of Minority Groups on Politics
And Public Policy in the United States

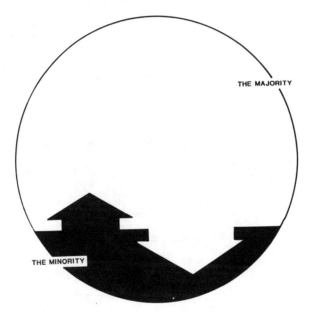

Michael C. LeMay

Frostburg State College

UNIVERSITY
PRESS OF
AMERICA

LANHAM • NEW YORK • LONDON

Copyright © 1985 by

University Press of America,® Inc.

4720 Boston Way
Lanham, MD 20706

3 Henrietta Street
London WC2E 8LU England

Library of Congress Cataloging in Publication Data

LeMay, Michael C., 1941-
  The struggle for influence.

  Bibliography: p.
  1. Minorities—United States—Political activity.
  2. Political participation—United States. 3. United
  States—Politics and government—1945-   . I. Title.
  E184.A1L44   1985   323.1'73   85-6105
  ISBN 0-8191-4653-6 (alk. paper)
  ISBN 0-8191-4654-4 (pbk. : alk. paper)

All University Press of America books are produced on acid-free
paper which exceeds the minimum standards set by the National
Historical Publications and Records Commission.

DEDICATION:

To CLARKE, who served as my original

inspiration and constant role model,

and

To PATRICIA, who makes it all worthwhile.

ACKNOWLEDGEMENTS

As can be seen by even a brief glance at the bibliography, this author owes a great debt to the numerous scholars in the field who have published works which have shaped his thinking. Sources quoted directly are, of course, cited in the text. Moreover, when I paraphrased or drew specific illustrative data from a given source, even though not directly quoting it, that source is cited in the text. Other references used more generally for a given chapter are listed in the additional readings section at the end of each chapter. A special mention should be made of several sources which were especially useful: Milton Gordon and Richard Schermerhorn for their pioneering theoretical efforts; Edgar Litt for the political conceptual framework; Mark Levy and Michael Kramer for their efforts in ethnic voting behavior analysis; William Davison and John Uhran for the systems dynamic model approach; and Stanley Lieberson for his application of sociological data to an empirical analysis of varying rates of assimilation.

Several of my colleagues read various drafts of these chapters and provided useful suggestions to improve them, most notably: Anthony Crosby and Maureen Connelly, Stephen Simpson and John Bowman, and John Wiseman. Two of our librarians, Gary Paul and Sean Maloney, were helpful above and beyond the call of duty in assisting me in getting various data and books I needed for this research. My colleagues Kathy Lese, Helene Baldwin and Dennis Gartner provided some highly useful editing and proof-reading of the various drafts of several of these chapters. Professor William Winter, of the University of Colorado, read the entire manuscript in rough draft and provided very useful suggestions which strengthened and improved the final edition.

Several student assistants helped me in compiling data over the years, most notably: Wanda Prince, Kevin Lillian Carter, David Sevinsky, and Richard Marino. And, of course, the many students who have studied ethnic politics with me over the years deserve mention for their serving as a captive audience and individuals with whom I could test various concepts and methods of presenting this material. The papers they have submitted for the course also proved useful to me in acquiring a grasp of the vast body of relevant literature on this complex subject.

v.

My daughter, Mrs. Jane Truly, gave invaluable assistance by helping to type some of the draft material of the manuscript. Mrs. Anna Mae Alexander helped type the final manuscript, without whose assistance I could not have completed this task on schedule.

Any errors of fact or interpretation contained herein are, of course, solely the responsibility of the author.

CONTENTS

LIST OF FIGURES

LIST OF TABLES

PREFACE

In The Uprooted, his Pulitzer-prize winning study of immigration to the United States, Oscar Handlin wrote: "Once I thought to write a history of the immigrants to America. Then I discovered that the immigrants were American History." To paraphrase Handlin, this book is about minority group politics in America, but to understand that is to grasp American political behavior. One cannot begin to understand the latter without a firm grasp of the former, of their struggle for influence. It is a perennial struggle. Indeed, ethnic politics display a surprising persistence and a richness of styles and techniques. They cannot be understood simply as the old-style urban political machine.

During the past two decades, newspapers, periodicals, and literally hundreds of books have examined the topic of ethnic or minority groups and their problems. This recent literature has been more extensive and varied than the "group studies" of previous decades. Interest in minority politics and the "ethnic revival" itself reflect in great measure the impact of the civil rights movements of the past two decades, particularly those of the Blacks and the Spanish-speaking minorities, but also those of the American Indian and of the Gay Rights and Feminist Movements. These movements have impressed upon American society an acute awareness of the presence within that society of discontented minority groups. We are all painfully aware of their struggle for influence.

Popular culture reflects that awareness. Consider, for instance, the remarkable success of the book and miniseries, Roots, or the popularity of "ethnic" TV shows such as Chico and the Man, The Jeffersons, and the like. So too, public policy reflects that awareness. In June of 1972 Congress passed the Ethnic Heritage Studies Bill. The law establishes special Ethnic Heritage Centers to support ethnic and immigration studies and ethnic activities in culture and the arts.

The recent Bicentennial celebrations often highlighted the special contributions to our culture of various ethnic groups. Demands for bilingual education, for revisions in the American Indian reservations school system, for affirmative action plans and the like reflect a changing public policy awareness regarding the value of American pluralism.

Indeed, the explosive decades of the 1960´s and 1970´s laid to rest the myth of the melting pot. The earlier works of social scientists which raised expectations of more or less complete assimilation as the processes of industrialization and urbanization reduced the salience of ethnicity have been re-examined and rejected. New studies have demonstrated the richness and complexity of the assimilation process and the persistence of racial and ethnic status and its relevance for political, social, and economic behavior.

As the various minorities developed into interest groups struggling to get "their fare share of the pie," it has become increasingly necessary for the perspectives of all the social sciences to be used to study the ethnic question. The perspectives of the political scientist, the sociologist, the historian, the psychologist can all add to our theoretical knowledge of the problem. An integration of those perspectives will also provide a better insight into how public policy may promote a healthy pluralism in our society. This, in turn, may limit minority group conflict, either between such groups or between them and American society as a whole.

Public policy in the 1980´s and beyond will increasingly shape the nature of that new pluralism. Will bilingualism be emphasized, thereby promoting a wide variety of ethnic patterns in our society? Will structural pluralism be stressed--in which primary group relationships among differing subcultures are kept separate, but society recognizes a positive value in these subcultures and allows them to remain? Will the American Indian, the Chicano, the Gay, the Gray, and the Women´s Rights movements be able to apply the model of the Black Civil Rights Movement´s protest style of politics with equal success? Will these political developments further revive the white ethnic groups´ collective consciousness, perhaps resulting in a white backlash voter reaction? Will new coalitions of realigned minority or ethnic blocs bring about a new array of political party affiliations? Will new limits on immigration and refugee policies be enacted? How will the new pluralism work to resolve such policy concerns as affirmative action, de facto segregation, school busing for racial integration, the removal of barriers to minorities in housing, employment, political participation, or police relations, or establishing community control via neighborhood school districts or little city halls? These policy areas have particular impact upon minority groups who are, by definition, less powerful. As such, they are all the more susceptible to the ravages of inflation, unemployment, and recession.

In order to better understand these pressing public policy issues and concerns, we need to understand the history, contribution, and special problems of minority groups in our society. In short, we need to understand the how and why of their struggle for influence.

This book, then, has several goals. It seeks to describe, primarily through an historical approach, how the United States came to have its rich mixture of various minority subcultures and how they criss-cross with class status to form persistent patterns. It attempts to apply a multi-faceted analysis to racial and ethnic minorities in order to better grasp their similarities and differences. It investigates social mobility in the United States, attempting to develop a systems model of assimilation which will enlightened and further our understanding of the wide variety of factors which interrelate and influence the rate, degree, and types of assimilation of the various minorities struggling within American society. It examines various public policy areas, describing how such policy is used by the majority to control or channel access and routes of assimilation open to the various minorities. It describes how policy can be used to ascribe social status to various groups. It shows, in turn, how various minorities use the struggle for influence over public policy to change their role and status in our culture, to cope with the problems resulting from ascribed minority status, or to influence the nation's foreign policy vis-a-vis their "other nation" loyalties. It seeks to describe and explain the degree to which various groups have assimilated. In short, it seeks to show the degree of their success in the struggle for influence.

A decade of teaching a course entitled American Ethnic Politics has led me to attempt to integrate a wide variety of sources of data and insights into a single and cohesive book. In the past I have used many books to teach the course. I have found, however, that when an instructor adopts three or four books many students often unduly struggle with the material because of the authors´ differing styles and approaches. Hopefully, this book loses none of the richness of insight into and understanding of the various perspectives that political science, sociology, history, and psychology can bring to bear upon the complex topic of racial and ethnic minority group relations in the political processes of the United States, while providing coherence and consistency of style of a single author.

Chapter One presents the basic concepts and themes of the book. Key terms are defined and explained. Chapter Two begins exemplifying those concepts by describing the minority groups based upon nationality, focusing on the Germans, Irish, Scandinavians, Italians, Greeks, Slavs, and Jews.

Chapter Three is devoted to religious-based minority groups, exemplifying particularly the experiences of Catholics, Jews, and Mormons. Chapter Four concerns the various Hispanic groups, particularly the Chicano, the Puerto Rican, and the Cuban. Chapter Five deals with racially-based minority groups, the Asian-Americans, Black Americans, and the American Indian, focusing on the "Black Protest Model" which now predominates among minority groups struggling for influence.

Chapters Six and Seven return to more theoretical discussions. Chapter Six presents a systems model of assimilation while discussing the various theories of assimilation. Chapter Seven is devoted to the various strategies employed by minority groups in coping with their minority status. An instructor adopting this text for a course with advanced undergraduate students who have some familiarity with racial and cultural minority studies may desire to have the students study Chapters One, Six and Seven together, discussing the theoretical concerns and perspectives before moving on to specific groups which exemplify those concerns. A decade of teaching experience, however, has led this author to employ the sequence presented here.

Chapters Two through Five provide most undergraduate students, who frequently lack familiarity with the extensive body of literature synthesized here, with the data base and exemplary material necessary to grasp the theoretical points discussed in Chapters Six and Seven. The instructor adopting this text can use whichever sequence seems most appropriate to the type of students using it.

Chapter Eight discusses "other" bases of minority status: gender, sexual preference, and age. It also devotes a brief discussion to the special problems of our "newest" immigrant minority groups--those coming in large numbers since the end of World War II, or special "refugees."

Chapter Nine closes the book with a discussion of public policy and minority status. It treats both the topic of how public policy is used by the majority to keep minorities in their lower status, and how minorities, in turn, struggle to influence public policy for their benefit. Particular emphasis is placed on the major policy areas affecting minority/majority relations: education, employment, foreign policy, housing, law enforcement, and political participation.

THE STRUGGLE FOR INFLUENCE

CHAPTER ONE: BASIC CONCEPTS

For any field of study a fundamental problem is the definition of basic concepts used in that field. In the case of minority groups, this is especially problematic as common usage and even scholarly discussions of certain key terms have somewhat muddied the waters. A wide variety of scholars, for instance, have offered differing definitions of the concept of assimilation. All of us, moreover, are members of either a majority or a minority group. As such, we carry emotionally charged attitudes regarding the basic concepts with which this chapter is concerned: "prejudice," "discrimination," "majority," "minority," "minority group," "ethnic group," "racial group," "acculturation," and "assimilation." A common understanding of these basic concepts and some analytical distinctions about the manner in which they will be used is essential to grasp the complexity of minority group politics in the United States.

A clear focus of these basic concepts is needed because much of the practical political behavior of the American system reflects prejudice, discrimination, or the reactions to them by the minority groups in our system. A great deal of American political behavior reflects, too, the majority's attempt to deal with the presence of so many and varied minorities within our system's bounds.

Prejudice

In our everyday use of the terms, prejudice and discrimination are often treated as if they were synonymous. Such usage, however, obscures important analytical distinctions between these concepts. These distinctions have significant impact on public policy. They will help us to have a clearer understanding of political behavior generally. Arnold Rose defines prejudice as "a set of attitudes which causes, supports, or justifies discrimination (Rose, 1951: 5)." G. W. Allport, in his classic The Nature of Prejudice, rather simply defines it as "an antipathy based upon a faulty and inflexible generalization (Allport, 1958: 10)." Simpson and Yinger feel it is "an emotionally rigid attitude, or predisposition to respond to a certain stimulus in a certain way toward a group of people (Simpson and Yinger, 1965: 10)." The social

1

psychologist Barry Collins has summarized the various definitions of prejudice as all having the following features: prejudice is an <u>intergroup</u> phenomenon, involving a <u>negative</u> orientation towards a group, established as a firmly set <u>attitude</u> (Collins, 1970: 249).

As we will use it herein, then, <u>prejudice</u> will be understood as a sort of mind-set whereby an individual or group accepts the negative social definitions that the majority society forms in reference to some minority as valid, and is predisposed to apply those negative social definitions to all individuals who are perceived as belonging to the group simply on that basis. Prejudice is an emotionally charged attitude towards an outgroup (that is, majority members may be prejudiced against minority members, <u>and vice-versa</u>) of some kind that is directed in negative and stereotyped terms based upon a social definition of the group. A person is hated, feared, shunned, despised and avoided merely because that person is seen, not as an individual to be judged on his or her own merits, but as a member of that outgroup.

We may distinguish types of prejudice based on micro- and macro-analyses. In terms of micro-analysis, prejudice is an attitude or mind-set of an individual towards others. An individual internalizes the values implicit in negative stereotyping and thereby fears or hates or despises another solely on the basis of that other person manifesting a certain characteristic or set of such held to be common to all members of a certain rejected group. The stereotyping triggers an automatic response in the emotional/attitudinal mind-set.

A person may learn or acquire these prejudicial attitudes at an early age, often at a preconscious or subconscious level. One has virtually no control over the attitudes since they are deeply ingrained and often connected with very primary feelings or emotions. Given a certain stimulus, the individual will react unconsciously in a given--that is, prejudicial--way. A person may fear or dislike another solely on the basis of some stereotyped trait without ever showing that fear or dislike in his or her overt behavior. Such an individual, in other words, may be prejudiced but does not discriminate.

2

In terms of macro-analysis, prejudice can become so widely accepted that it begins to underlie the values or institutionalized. The prejudicial values become structured to the detriment of some for the benefit of others. Blacks may be forbidden from joining certain labor unions, for example, thus cutting off their access to certain occupations. This may benefit the employers of blacks by tending to hold down the pay scales for those jobs they are allowed to enter. It benefits some whites by allowing them to hold disproportionately the desirable occupations.

A racist society, or one in which the prejudice underlies a caste system, is one which has prejudicial attitudes permeating the norms and values of that society. Such prejudice will, of necessity, be manifested in behavior, since the societal values determine the norms of behavior of persons within that society.

Among students of prejudice, the psychological attitudes common to all these definitions contributed to a concern with the psychological causes of prejudice. Many early studies tried to find a simple, single-factor explanation of prejudice. That focus shifted in later studies as it became increasingly clear that groups differ in the degree and direction of the prejudice they exhibit, and that the target groups for prejudice may shift over time and/or place within a society. Kitano, in reviewing the literature on the causes of prejudice, specifies four categories of how prejudice develops: exploitation, ignorance, racism/ethnocentrism, and symbolism (Kitano, 1974: 21-29).

Exploitation concerns theories that one group dominates another sexually, economically, and socially. The "inferior" group must be kept in its place in order that the "superior" group can continue to enjoy advantages of better employment, social status, and life-styles. Thus, for instance, through subtle or even overt means, a particular nationality group may be forced to take certain jobs to ensure employers of a large group of cheap labor, or so that certain necessary but socially undesirable tasks will be performed. A classic example of such an explanation is Marxian theory.

Ignorance is often viewed as a simple explanation of prejudice. Lack of information and knowledge leads to stereotyping. Stereotyped images, in turn, are projected through the mass media and permeate the popular culture of a society. The process of selective perception often works to reinforce such stereotyping by basically validating the attitudes. A group may be labelled as "overly avaricious," always concerned with making a buck. If a member of a minority seems to fit the stereotyped image (and often the society generates subtle pressures on persons which induce them to behave in ways which fit the stereotypical pattern), then the majority group member sees evidence to confirm the stereotyped image. A minority group member's behavior which does not conform to the image is ignored. Or the prejudiced person will make exceptions, such as "but he doesn't act like one of them," which, in effect, does nothing to upset the basic prejudice.

Ethnocentrism, or the belief that one's own group is unique and right, is seen as being almost universal. This concept is used to explain prejudice as a weapon in group conflict. Ethnocentrism serves the group in power. An example would be a racist society which develops an ideology of white supremacy based upon a biblical and/or "scientific" theory which proports to justify the white supremacy, thereby justifying slavery.

Symbolic explanations view prejudice as a symptom or symbolic by-product stemming from other concerns. Freudian theory, for example, views all behavior as psychically determined. Prejudice is seen as a symptom reflecting a deeper intra-psychic phenomenon. Social psychological theory, following this perspective, emphasizes frustration and aggression as critical variables behind prejudice. Frustrated persons feel hostility. Often they are blocked from directing this anger towards the true source of that frustration. In such instances, the frustrated person deals with his hostility by directing it at a more convenient target--a scapegoat. Minority groups, because of their relative powerlessness in society, become convenient scapegoats. In Czarist Russia, for instance, the peasantry could not take out their aggressions on the nobility and upper classes who exploited them, so they turned their aggression against the Jews. Studies have shown, moreover, that the very ineffectiveness of the frustration/hostility/scapegoat cycle can lead to further prejudice. The very guilt and anxiety that the

4

frustrated individual feels about his displaced hostility leads to further displacement and hostility towards the scapegoat, thus reinforcing the vicious cycle (see, for example, Dollard, Doob and Miller, or Brewton Berry). This perspective would also include such theories as those of Adorno et al, who describe The Authoritarian Personality. They view prejudice as being the result of improper socialization, leading to the development of a "sick" or "defective" personality-type.

A more sociological perspective is advocated by other scholars of racism and prejudice, such as Robert Park, or Raab and Lipset. This view sees prejudice as being "caused" by social change. The more diverse and changing a society, the greater its prejudice. The more static the society, the less its prejudice. This theory views prejudice as an attempt to conserve or preserve the existing social order. Thus, anti-Semitism or anti-Black prejudice would rise in the United States whenever we have periodic economic turmoil, such as a severe recession or a depression, or during periods of rapid social change brought on, for example, by the country's involvement in a war.

This view represents a shift in focus which recognizes the distinction between attitude and behavior. They note that prejudiced attitudes do not predetermine prejudiced behavior. An individual's behavior may be determined more by the social situation at any particular time than by that person's pre-existing attitudes. In other words, both attitude and behavior are highly susceptible to situational change.

Their view places a new focus on how prejudice (as a person's attitude set) is learned. In their view, prejudiced behavior (an act of discrimination) shapes and alters prejudiced attitudes. The learning of prejudice is affected by the kinds of social situations in which people live. The complex of prejudicial practices within a given community provides the family and similar traditional and peer groups with the frame of reference that perpetuates these practices and sustains or even extends prejudice. Jim Crow legislation in the South, then, is viewed as being a necessary legal underpinning of societal norms designed to enforce the continuation of the existing social order. And to the contrary, if a society wishes to change or reduce the degree of prejudice within it, such a society must begin by changing such institutional bases of prejudice.

5

How a society might employ public policy in an
attempt to reduce or at least deal with prejudice is
primarily shaped by which of these perceptions is
accepted as the prevailing viewpoint. The "cure" is
designed to fit the perceived "illness." If one
believes that prejudice is caused by ignorance, for
instance, than the policy options to deal with it would
involve various forms of education designed to alleviate
that ignorance by overcoming or refuting the stereotyped
images. If one accepts prejudice as being caused by
exploitation, by contrast, than a far different set of
public policy options is suggested. In that case,
affirmative action programs or some sort of "quota"
system to end systematized occupational prejudice would
result. The alternative sources of prejudice are summed
up in Figure One, below.

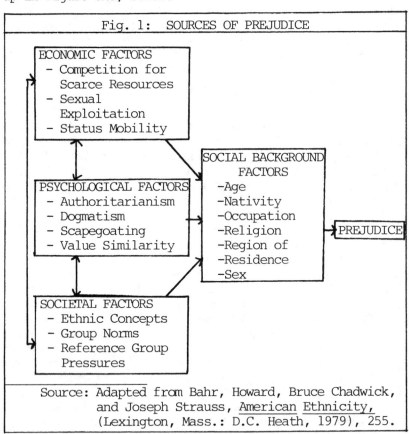

Fig. 1: SOURCES OF PREJUDICE

ECONOMIC FACTORS
- Competition for
  Scarce Resources
- Sexual
  Exploitation
- Status Mobility

PSYCHOLOGICAL FACTORS
- Authoritarianism
- Dogmatism
- Scapegoating
- Value Similarity

SOCIETAL FACTORS
- Ethnic Concepts
- Group Norms
- Reference Group
  Pressures

SOCIAL BACKGROUND
  FACTORS
-Age
-Nativity
-Occupation
-Religion
-Region of
-Residence
-Sex

PREJUDICE

Source: Adapted from Bahr, Howard, Bruce Chadwick,
        and Joseph Strauss, American Ethnicity,
        (Lexington, Mass.: D.C. Heath, 1979), 255.

Discrimination

Discrimination is analytically distinct from prejudice although the two are often confused in common usage. Yet clearly, a person may have a prejudiced attitude without exhibiting discriminatory behavior. Likewise, an individual, given a certain social milieu, may routinely behave in a discriminatory manner even if that person does not possess the relevant prejudicial attitudes. A bigoted person may dislike Jews, but in a given social setting where Jews are accepted or are in a position of power over that person, he or she may refrain from ever manifesting that bigotry. Likewise, a non-bigoted person may move into an area where a prevailing prejudice has become so institutionalized that he or she may behave according to the prejudicial norms without having internalized those prejudicial attitudes. A man raised in Sweden, for instance, may have migrated to the southern part of the United States during the early 1900´s. Even though he had been raised with absolutely no prejudice against blacks, that person may start a business and conform, in his hiring and employment practices, to those current anti-black norms of the South.

Merton distinguishes four types of persons based upon this prejudice/discrimination distinction. He discussed the following types: (1) the Unprejudiced Non-discriminator, or the All-Weather Liberal, a person who neither has personal prejudices nor behaves in a discriminatory way because of social norms or pressures; (2) the Unprejudiced Discriminator, or Fair-Weather Liberal, a person like the Swedish-American example used above, who does not have the prejudiced attitudes, but gives in to societal pressures and discriminates, often without thinking of it or being consciously aware of the discriminatory behavior he or she is exhibiting; (3) the Prejudiced Non-discriminator, or Fair-Weather Illiberal, such as the timid bigot described above; and (4) the Prejudiced Discriminator, or All-Weather Illiberal, the classic "red-neck" or Archie Bunker type of bigot who manifests his prejudice in discrimination almost instinctively and consistently. Kitano develops a similar schema regarding racist behavior: (1) the overt racist, (2) the aversive racist, and (3) the institutional racist (Kitano:121-123. See also, Berry: 9-126).

In short, we may define <u>discrimination</u> as overt or behavioral prejudice in which the antipathy an individual feels towards members of an outgroup is acted out or institutionalized into public policy or norms thereby ascribing the group to minority status by subordination of their economic, political, and social rights. Therefore, while both majority and minority members can, and usually do, develop prejudices, only the majority group members are able to translate those prejudices into discrimination.

Kinloch applies these two concepts to race relations:
> In general, then, racial prejudice refers to attitudinal acceptance of racist criteria, while racial discrimination reflects the societal translation of these norms into the form of a racial caste system. In the case of America, whites, blacks, chicanos, Indians, and the Chinese are examples of major racial groups. Anti-black or anti-Indian attitudes and associated stereotypes reflect racial prejudice, while residential segregation of and occupational discrimination against these groups are examples of discrimination (Kinloch, 1974: 55).

Types of Discrimination

Discrimination is typically manifested in a number of ways. The majority will try to <u>control the numbers</u> of the minority--the better to ensure their remaining a powerless minority. Discrimination may be manifested <u>economically</u>: for example, by barring the minority members from unions or professional associations, or by otherwise excluding them from certain occupations, or by regularly making them the last hired and the first fired among those occupations they are allowed to enter. Discrimination is often manifested in <u>education</u>, demonstrated in a reluctance to educate "inferiors," or at least, in providing them with inferior education. Discrimination is usually seen in restrictions placed on their <u>political participation</u> through such disenfranchisement devices as the white primary, the grandfather clause, the poll tax, literacy tests, or in the inequality in the application of registration and residency requirements. <u>Social</u> discrimination is typically seen by restrictions in minority's use of hotels, restaurants, public transportation, and public facilities like parks, pools, and libraries. Churches are often closed to them. Intermarriage is at least socially limited, and often legally restricted. The minority group may be socially isolated. The Jim Crow laws of the South, for example, were designed to segregate blacks in all areas of social life. Ghettoization of blacks and Jews, and the forcing of Indians into reservations, exemplify the use of public policy to enforce geographic segregation intended to isolate a minority group.

Thus, the distinction between prejudice and discrimination is an important one. When critics of social reform legislation argued that "you can´t legislate morality," or that "you can´t write laws to make people like niggers," they show their confusion of these two concepts. Granted, one cannot legislate attitudes. But a society can modify the social situations which support discriminatory behavior. And as Raab and Lipset have stated, attitudes are shaped by the social situation, by the behavioral norms of the society. If you change the behavioral pattern over time, therefore, you will change attitudes. As they point out:

> ...an attitude is not a thing; it is a process; it is an interaction. It is an interaction involving not only the person and the object, but all other factors that are present in the situation (Raab and Lipset: 366).

It is the majority society´s patterned behavior of unequal treatment--discrimination--which creates the need for minority-group politics.

When persons within the minority group find themselves subjected to discrimination, they must react in some manner. They cannot ignore the behavioral norms which institutionalize patterns of discriminatory behavior. Berry discusses four ways that minority groups will react to discrimination. One pattern is acceptance of their status, in which they typically develop some sort of ideology which explains and psychologically mitigates their minority status. During the period of slavery, for instance, many blacks developed mechanisms for dealing with that slave status. Another pattern is avoidance, in which the minority attempts to restrict as much as possible its contacts with the majority. The Amish tried to isolate themselves in rural areas and avoid contact with the

9

majority society except in the most limited and basic economic exchanges necessary for life. Yet another pattern involves assimilation, in which the minority accepts the values of the majority and attempts to merge into that society. The German or Scandinavian immigrants, for example, manifested this pattern. A final pattern is aggression, in which the minority group conflicts--in varying degrees from non-violent to violent behavior--with majority society. The minority attempts to change the values of majority society or at least reduce the incidence and the impact of discrimination (Berry:382-403).

We may also distinguish some typical reactions of the majority group to the presence of a minority subculture within that society. Gordon suggests four types of society with regard to their ethnic orientation: (1) racist, in which the minority suffers a severe restriction and segregation, based upon an elaborate system of structured discrimination; (2) assimilationist, in which the minority is expectrd to become like the majority; (3) liberal pluralist, in which the minority is allowed to maintain its own subculture with little or no discrimination against it; and (4) corporate pluralist, in which the minority is granted structural or institutional bases for maintaining their subcultural identities (in Glazer and Moynihan: 106).

A more complete discussion of the strategies employed by minorities will be dealt with in chapter seven. Suffice it to say here that minority groups will typically react in one or more of these ways to their being ascribed minority status.

The Majority

The group which determines the differential treatment is, by definition, the dominant group. The group which has the power--one which is superordinate in superordinate/subordinate relationship--is the group which does the discriminating. It need not be a numerical majority; it simply must have sufficient power to determine the values and norms of society, to set public policy. Such a group, by definition, is the "discriminator" rather than the subject of such discrimination.

10

In American society that group is the WASP--the White Anglo-Saxon-Protestant majority. It was out of the colonial era, during the last quarter of the seventeenth century, that the Anglo-American emerged as the dominant group along the Atlantic seaboard region becoming the "host" or "native" group in the United States. They replaced the native American Indian and surpassed in influence all other western-European immigrant groups. English language, customs, and their ideas regarding commerce, law, government, and religion predominated. By 1700 the Anglo-Americans had replaced--by killing or driving ever westward--the Indians as the "native" stock. By 1815, Anglo-conformity had become dominant and unchallenged.

This emergence came during a time when intellectual credence, based upon biblical and pseudo-scientific support, was increasingly given to the concept of white supremacy; that is, to the belief that the military and economic success of the whites were the result of biologically inherited differences among racial groups. Anglo-conformity held that the more nearly a person approximated the Anglo-American model, the more nearly American that person was judged to be. In the words of one scholar:

> From this standpoint, an American is someone who fits exactly (or closely resembles) the pattern of life and racial type preferred by the members of the Anglo-American ethnic group in colonial America. He or she should speak American English without a "foreign accent," be of a Protestant religious persuasion, be of the so-called white physical type, English surname, and prefer the customs and manner of the Anglo-American way. Viewed in this light, assimilation is a process of inclusion through which a person gradually ceases to conform to any standards of life that differ from the dominant-group standards and, at the time, learns to conform to all of the dominant group standards. Assimilation is complete when the foreigner merges fully into the dominant group (McLemore: 33-34).

In short, various immigrant groups that later came to the United States could be graded as more or less desirable according to how closely they resembled the Anglo-American pattern at the outset, how rapidly they departed from their own cultural patterns, and how successfully they became socially invisible within the newly emerging WASP-American society.

11

Any group which was either unwilling or unable to neatly fit into the developing American majority pattern was viewed as a problem group. Either a group´s clannish refusal to accept the "superior" way of life of the majority, or their possession of some undesirable physical trait which made it difficult or impossible to become "WASP-like," was sufficient to brand such a group as being in some way deficient, and hence such a minority group was ascribed to lower social status and subjected to discrimination.

Minority and Minority Group

Common usage emphasizes the numerical aspect of the concept of minority. Webster´s defines minority, for instance, as "the smaller in number of two groups constituting a whole," or "a group having less than the number of votes necessary for control (Webster´s Seventh Collegiate Dictionary, 1971:540)."

For our purposes, however, minority is a political concept simply referring to a power relationship. It is a group which is on the subordinate end of a superordinate/subordinate relationship, subjected to differential treatment.

The blacks of South Africa are a "minority" even though they comprise about 80 percent of the population. Women are a minority in the United States, although they constitute just over fifty-two percent of the population. The concept of minority is a power status concept. Relationships between dominant and minority groups are not determined by numbers but rather by the distribution of power. As Louis Wirth so aptly expresses it:

> We may define a minority as a group of people, who, because of their physical or cultural characteristics, are singled out from the others in the society in which they live for differential and unequal treatment, and who therefore regard themselves as objects of collective discrimination. The existence of a minority in a society implies the existence of a corresponding dominant group with higher social status and greater privileges. Minority status carries with it the exclusion from full participation in the life of the society (in Linton, 1945: 347).

12

Graham Kinloch stresses the group's self-image as well as the negative treatment:

> Minority group may be defined as any group that views itself and/or is defined by the dominant power elite as unique on the basis of perceived physical, cultural, economic, and/or behavioral characteristics and is treated accordingly in a negative manner (Kinloch: 50).

This emphasis upon the self-image is an important distinction in understanding American minority group politics since many "groups" did not become such with a self-conscious group identity until they arrived in the United States and found themselves being treated differentially. The immigrant arriving from Dublin, Ireland in 1848, for example, may not have thought of himself so much as an "Irishman" than as a "Dublinite." But after being treated here in an unequal manner—for instance, being refused jobs on the basis of "No Irish Need Apply" signs—simply because of his national origin, he _then_ began to think of himself as an "Irishman," or "Irish-American." His group identity grew in response to the discriminatory treatment he experienced.

In a sense, the majority "creates" the minority as a group by deciding to treat all persons evidencing a certain characteristic as being "different" from them and subjecting all such persons to differential treatment on the basis of basis of that perceived difference. What characteristic is singled out as constituting a significant "difference" varies from society to society and even from time to time or place to place within a society. In the United States there have been a variety of characteristics upon which minority status has been been based, as will be discussed more fully below.

The concept of "group" itself is not a simple one. When does a collection of individuals constitute a group? In Whyte's view a group consists of persons of varying status whose behavior is determined by the expectations of the other members. While all members follow the expected behavioral norms, the group is in equilibrium. If some are forced or allowed to deviate from their accustomed pattern, equilibrium is broken down, and the group no longer exists as a group. The very existence of the group means that the behavior of each member is influenced by his or her belonging to the group (in Wilson: 14-60). In Professor Truman's words:

...the patterns of action and attitude among individuals will differ from one another in large measure according to the clusters of group affiliations that the individuals have (Truman: 16).

We can further distinguish types of groups. Ethnic groups are primary groups, those characterized by intimate face-to-face association and cooperation. A primary group involves a sense of mutual identification for which "we" is the natural expression. The very essence of a primary group is that sense of "we-ness" that develops among the members (see Truman: 17).

Groups can also be viewed from an internal versus external perspective. The external tradition is by far the most common one, employed by most sociologists. This perspective views the group as a whole. It stresses the group's relationship to other groups and to the total society. But we can also view groups from an internal perspective. Groups are assemblages of individuals. This view stresses the factors of solidarity or anomie. It focuses on the pressures, the positive or negative rewards, which induce persons to comply with the group's wishes, to form social relationships strengthen group solidarity. The forces of anomie are those factors which induce one to avoid social relationships and to behave independently of one another.

Such feelings of interrelatedness are the key aspect of group life. The group depends on the inter-action of its members, on their acceptance of the norms and goals of the group and a common perception of membership. The group develops a status and structure and fosters cohesiveness. Indeed, the group interaction is even more crucial than is their shared characteristic (Truman: 24).

Some further distinctions regarding belonging to a group might usefully be made. We may view persons in the degree to which they feel a sense of "belonging" to a given group, or are visibly discernible with regard to the trait(s) which society uses to categorize persons as belonging to a certain group. That is, we may analytically distinguish persons on the basis of a "group-relatedness" typology.

A Group-Relatedness Typology

Individuals within any group vary in the degree to which they identify with that group. For some members, their belonging to that group becomes central to their own identity. For others, their social and patterned behavior and most of their internalized values are deeply dependent upon the group. Still others may be but tangentially involved in the group, and internalize that connection only weakly.

Joseph Fichter developed a useful typology for members of a religious group (a parish) which can be equally well adapted to any minority group and will help us to understand the person's relations to the group. This typology will be useful to grasp the dynamics of intergroup relations and why some groups vary in their rates of acculturation and assimilation. Fichter specifies four types of persons in terms of their group-relatedness: (1) nuclear, (2) modal, (3) marginal, and (4) dormant (Fichter: 29-79). A nuclear member of a group is one whose self-identity is totally involved in the group. Such an individual would exhibit all of the norms, values, and physical or cultural traits associated with that group. Applying this concept to a nationality group, for example, we could describe our hypothetical nuclear member of the Italian-American minority as, for instance, the seventy-two year old Italian grandmother who immigrated to this country at age sixteen. She has been widowed for many years but still dresses in black every day. She attends mass daily, praying the rosary often. She speaks almost no English, and that with a heavy Italian accent. She lives in an Italian-American neighborhood, let us say in South Boston, above a little Italian-American delicatessen store that she and her husband operated for some thirty years. All of her friends (really acquaintances) are Italian-Americans. Her personal social life revolves totally around her parish and her family. Her married children still come over every Sunday for a big family meal. She eats Italian food three times a day, every day. You could pick her up and deposit her in some village in Italy and she would hardly notice except for the absence of her family and friends. She is, in short, more Italian than American.

The modal type, that is, one who accepts most of the norms and values of the group and who manifests all of the physical or cultural traits of the group, would be--for this hypothetical case--her fifty-five year old son. He speaks Italian fluently. But having been born in the United States, he also speaks English as a native language. He married an Italian-American girl from the neighborhood, a childhood sweetheart. He owns and operates an Italian-American restaurant, which he and his wife and several of his children and other relatives all run. He is a practicing Catholic, attending mass on Sundays and all Holy Days. He eats Italian style food at least once per day. His social life, too, revolves around his family and the parish, although he does have a few close "anglo" friends from when he served in the U.S. army. His clothing and physical features are such that nearly any stranger seeing him would likely guess him to be an Italian-American. You could pick him up and drop him in Italy and he would survive and adjust fairly well. He is, in short, still more Italian than American. He would, moreover, think of himself as an Italian-American.

His twenty-five year old son might exemplify the marginal type; that is, one who manifests only a few traits or internalizes only some of the norms and values of the group. He has left home and the neighborhood and attended college, majoring in business administration. He recently joined a large corporation as a personnel manager, and they have stationed him at a branch office located in a small midwestern town where there are few Italian-Americans. Before joining the firm he legally anglicized his surname. He married a non-Catholic and non-Italian girl (let us say of Swedish nationality background). He no longer practices Catholicism regularly, attending church only a few times per year (at Christmas, Easter, and for weddings and funerals); he usually goes along with his wife to a Lutheran Church, unless he is back home visiting with his family. He still harbors guilt feelings, however, about that fact. He speaks little Italian, and that with a heavy American accent. He can understand it much better than he can speak it, but he reads it poorly. He now rarely if ever uses it, as there are so few opportunities to do so in that small town. He only occasionally eats Italian food. He dresses like the other rising young junior executives of the company. A stranger might guess him to be of Italian heritage, judging from his physical features, but not necessarily so. If asked to do so, he would probably describe himself as an "American of Italian descent."

16

His daughter, who will grow up with a non-Italian sounding name and acquire yet another upon her marriage, and who was raised in a non-Italian family environment, exemplifies the dormant type. That is, she would be a person exhibiting few, if any, of the physical characteristics typical of the group and would have internalized in a latent manner only a few of the norms and values of the group. By adulthood, she will be a person who recognizes some Italianness in her background, but she will speak about as much Italian as the typical American can--that is, only a few phrases picked up from the popular culture. She will not practice Catholicism at all and will attend the service of another denomination only rarely. She also grows up to marry a non-Catholic, let us say of German-American background. Italian, of course, is never spoken around the home, nor can she understand or read it. She knows, of course, that her grandparents on her father´s side are Italian-Americans. She loves them dearly, but has really only been with them on a few occasions for a week or so at a time when they took family vacations to visit her father´s family in Boston. She has some emotional ties as a result, however, and they are strongly though largely subconsciously held. Given the right stimulus, they do surface. She does, for instance, react strongly to any "dumb Italian" or "cowardly Italian" jokes. If asked to do so, she would describe herself as an "American of Swedish and Italian descent."

Although these examples employ a generational gap to illustrate the differing degrees or types of group-relatedness, the reader should understand that such a time continuum is not essential. A person could be an immigrant stepping off the ship and be, psychologically speaking, a marginal type. The type of group relatedness depends upon the person´s internalized self-identity with the relevant group. A third-generation Greek-American, in these terms, might behave as a modal or even nuclear type. Witness the Black-American who discovers his roots and goes "Afro." Religious groups, in fact, often provide good examples of this effect. An adult convert to a particular religious group is often more nuclear or modal in his or her behavior than are many persons who have been "born and raised" in a given denomination.

These distinctions are useful because they help us to understand the effects of acculturation patterns on rates of assimilation. As a group develops more and more marginal members, its assimilation rate will speed up. Thus, factors which cause a particular group to experience higher rates of marriage outside the group (and marriage to a person of any "outgroup" will do, even if such a person is not of the majority group), let us say due to a frontier setting, will accelerate that group's rate of assimilation into majority society. On the other hand, a group which is concentrated within a ghetto and which socially enforces marriage only within the group will tend to assimilate, all other things being equal, more slowly. This typology helps us in understanding why so many nationality groups assimilate more readily than do racial groups. Often the most marginal persons in a given nationality are among the first to emigrate and seek entrance into a new country or culture. The marginal nature of their attachments to the "old" culture enables them to acculturate and thereafter to assimilate quickly. Thus, if the entire group quickly develops many marginal or dormant types, then the entire group will quickly assimilate. And to the contrary, if a group maintains most of its members as nuclear or modal types, then it will acculturate and thereby assimilate more slowly.

This aspect of marginality is related to the members of a group developing a sense of affiliation with some other group--an overlapping membership. And as Truman notes, such overlapping membership affects the cohesion and both the internal and external politics of the group.

> The internal political situation of a group is affected by the extent to which its membership overlaps that of other groups because of the varying effects that such overlapping has, and can have, upon cohesion. Cohesion, in turn, along with the related factor of size and those of organization, financing and techniques--is a crucial determinant of the effectiveness with which the group may assert its claims (Truman: 159).

Racial and Ethnic Minority Groups

Although the United States exhibits minority groups on the basis of many characteristics, the two primary bases have been race and ethnicity. This distinction,

18

too, is important since the differing base for minority status affects the manner in which the group copes with the problem of being ascribed minority status. It also affects the manner in which the majority will accept or not and will channel the options open to that minority group for coping with its status.

The ethnic basis presents us with some conceptual problems, as the term "ethnic group" is another one about which there is considerable confusion. Several attempts have been made to define the concept of "ethnic group" and can be briefly summarized here.

An ethnic group is a self perceived group of people who hold in common a set of traditions not shared by others with whom they are in contact. Such traditions typically include "folk" religious beliefs and practices, language, a sense of historical continuity, and a common ancestry or place of origin...The ethnic identity of a group of people consists of their subjective symbolic or emblematic use of any aspect of culture, in order to differentiate themselves from other groups (DeVos and Romanucci-Ross: 15).

Milton Gordon defines an ethnic group more succinctly as "any group which is defined or set off by race, religion, or national origin, or some combination of these categories (Gordon, 1964:27)." And Arnold Dashefsky, elaborating on Gordon defines ethnic group as follows:

An ethnic group may be defined as a group of individuals with a sense of shared peoplehood based on presumed shared sociocultural experiences and/or similar physical characteristics. Such groups may be viewed by their members and/or outsiders as religious, racial, national, linguistic and/or geographical. Thus, what ethnic members have in common is their ethnicity, or sense of peoplehood, which represents a part of their collective experience (Dashefsky: 3).

Racial Groups

Racial groups are in a sense a sub-category of ethnic groups in that racial identity can be and usually is a basis for "commonly shared cultural traditions" or

19

a sense of "peoplehood." Yet a distinction between the two is analytically worth making since racial groups often experience special barriers.

As with our previous concepts, racial group needs a more precise definition than the common use of the term. A social definition of race is provided by Van den Berghe:

> ...a human group that defines itself and/or is defined by other groups as different from other groups by virtue of innate and immutable physical characteristics. These physical characteristics are in turn believed (by the racist society) to be intrinsically related to moral, intellectual, and other non-physical attributes or abilities (in Kinloch: 51).

A key aspect of this definition is its emphasis upon the reciprocal social definition of race, which is based upon perceived physical differences that both groups view as being significant.

In contrast to Van den Berghe's views, Gordon describes race as "differential concentrations of gene frequencies responsible for traits which, so far as we know, are confined to physical manifestations such as skin color or hair form; it has no intrinsic connection with cultural patterns and institutions (Gordon, 1964: 27)."

Gordon's definition, however, may slight the fact that there is a connection--even if not an intrinsic one--between the physical characteristics and cultural or institutional forms. The connection is a social one. And for understanding differences in American political behavior between, for example, ethnic groups based upon national origin and ones based on race, those social connections are the truly significant ones.

Implications for Political Behavior

The presence of so many and so varied minority subcultures within American society has had a profound impact upon the political behavior of both individuals and groups within the majority and the minority subgroups. As Professor Lowi notes in The Politics of Disorder:

The history of the United States is not merely
one of mutual accommodation among competing
groups under a broad umbrella of consensus.
The proper image of our society has never been
a melting pot. In bad times, it is a boiling
pot; in good times, it is a tossed salad. For
those who are in, this is all very well. But
the price has always been paid by those who
are out, and when they do get in they do not
always get in through a process of mutual
accommodation under a broad umbrella of
consensus (Lowi: 53. His italics.).

Ultimately, this entire book is devoted to a
discussion of those implications. It seems useful to
simply highlight a few of those implications here; in a
sense this section will preview the considerations
discussed more fully in later chapters.

The need to absorb so many millions of persons of
various subcultural patterns and deal with the "other-
group" loyalties has had a significant impact upon the
majority. Elite groups within the majority have
attempted to influence public policy in various ways in
direct response to the influx of minorities. The
majority, itself, has split into factions depending on
how differing viewpoints about the best policy for
dealing with "problem minority groups" have affected
those factions. Some have gravitated towards the
nativist reactions. They have formed groups which have
pushed for restrictive policy, for instance the Know
Nothing Party. Or they have attempted to severly
restrict groups by violence or to socially segregate
them. An example of this reaction would be the Ku Klux
Klan and its campaign of passing Jim Crow laws or the
use of informal social norms or even violence against
disliked minorities.

By contrast, other elite factions have reacted in
just the opposite way. They have reached out to and
sought such groups, advocating an open-door policy or
even lobbying to spend public monies to recruit minority
people to come to the United States. Generally,
however, this elite has been mixed in its pro-minority
position. It usually has actively sought some "desired"
minorities, such as some of the nationality-based
groups, while being less enthusiastic about certain
religious or racial groups.

21

This latter elite faction, nonetheless, has often been among the better off economically, and usually the more politically powerful. Their views have usually prevailed with respect to the public policies actually adopted by government. Sometimes they have acted upon economic policy through non-public institutional forms: railroads, steamship lines, or corporations, for example, which hired immigration agents. Others have acted through public policy, especially the leaders of several political parties. The Republican and Democratic parties became the dominant ones, establishing the two-party system in American politics, primarily because they did reach out to the immigrants, forming their parties as coalitions of voting blocs of various groups.

The minority groups, too, were greatly influenced in their political behavior by their minority status, and continue to be so today. Most groups exhibit at least an initial period of relatively low political participation. How long that period lasts varies considerably from group to group. Generally, nationality groups become politically active to a higher degree and more quickly than do racially-based minorities. Many religious factions, likewise, reject participation for a long period. The minority's reaction is in large measure influenced by the majority's stance towards them. The period of inaction is typically followed by a stage in which they use politics very consciously to seek social and economic gains and/or to reduce and mitigate the effects of discrimination against them.

Party identification becomes linked to ethnic loyalties, and groups display a persistent pattern of bloc voting. Nationality groups tend to develop this linkage more quickly than do racial groups because the former groups see a faction of the elite seeking and rewarding their behavior, which it is more reluctant to do for racial minorities. Those political parties which responded to the opportunity afforded by blocs of voters who could be manipulated on the basis of ethnic loyalties survived and became dominant. Those parties which rejected building such coalitions quickly declined and disappeared. Note, for example, the fate of the Whigs, the Know-Nothing, or the American Party.

Both majority and minority groups tend to become political interest groups who seek to influence public policy (Truman: 37.) Policy questions take on ethnic relevance. The majority develops factions, as stated above, which seek to pass restrictive immigration laws or to legally force certain racial groups into geographic or social isolation through such means as the reservation policy, the anti-Chinese land laws, the ghettoization of Blacks and Jews, and Jim Crow legislation. Other majority factions seek public policy to end those very restrictions. Some factions of the elite quickly learn that stands on public policy issues of both domestic and foreign policy can become convenient means by which they can politically manipulate large blocs of voters.

Minority groups respond to domestic legislative proposals which will reduce discrimination or otherwise socially and economically benefit them as a group. Often the mere psychological benefit accrued by simple recognition--the naming of a school or public park after some ethnic hero, for example--is enough to cement the loyalty of a minority to a particular political leader or party.

Minority groups, too, become keenly interested in foreign policy to the extent such policy can influence the nation or foreign government to which they feel an ethnically-based loyalty or antipathy. The "Greek" or "Jewish" lobbies, for instance, are significant forces attempting to influence U.S. foreign policy vis-a-vis Greece, Cyprus, and Israel respectively.

As we shall see in greater detail later, minority groups develop a strategy for dealing with minority status which shapes the degree and manner of their political participation. Each strategy exhibits various tactics employed in the pursuit of that strategy. A given minority group may be factionalized and engage in more than one strategy at a given time, just as the majority splits into factions over how to deal with the presence of a minority within its culture. Edgar Litt suggests that all minorities will respond in one of three ways or strategies: (1) accommodation, which may be primarily economic or political; (2) separatism, which may be either geographic or psychological; or (3) radicalism, which may be either of the "old- style" or the "new-style" type (Litt: 60-110). Black Americans, for example as exemplified by Booker T. Washington, have

23

advocated accommodating to racial discrimination by attempting to find an economic niche for themselves which would be non-threatening to the white majority such that, over time, they could eventually move into middle-class status and be accepted. Other blacks, such as Marcus Garvey's "Back to Africa" Movement, or the Black Muslims, have preached separatism. Still others, such as W.E.B. DuBois or Dr. Martin Luther King, Jr., have advocated a radical approach by attempting to change the basic value system of majority society. Each of these strategies will be discussed more fully in chapter seven. It is important to understand that all minority groups must develop some means for dealing with their status. Such a strategy is determined not only by their values and resources, but by the majority's reaction to them as a group. Such strategy will, moreover, inevitably involve them in what we understand as minority group politics--in a struggle for influence.

As Professor Gamson notes in The Strategy of Social Protest:

> From time to time, previously unorganized groups begin to find a political voice. Vague dissatisfactions begin to crystallize over some more specific claim or demand for change, be it incremental or revolutionary. These challenging groups vary in the responses they experience. Some collapse quickly without leaving a visible mark, some are destroyed by attack, some have their programs preempted by competitors, some are given the formal trappings of influence without its substance, some die and rise again from the ashes, some shove their way, yelling and screaming, into the political arena and become permanent fixtures, some walk in on the arms of well-placed sponsors, and some wander in unnoticed and remain in by fait accompli (Gamson: 11-12).

The Bases of Minority Status

A variety of characteristics may be singled out by any given society as being "significantly different" from the majority's self-image so as to provide a basis for ascribing minority status to some groups in that society. Such bases vary from society to society and from time to time or place to place within any given society. 24

One of the leading scholars of ethnic relations, R. A. Schermerhorn, has argued persuasively that how a minority becomes such is critically important to our understanding of such factors as the degrees of pressure applied against them, the avenues open to them, the resources they have to deal with such status, and the like. He distinguishes five inter-group sequences. The first is the emergence of pariahs, such as the Eta or Buraku in Japan or the "Untouchables" in India. A second sequence is the emergence of indigenous isolates; for example, certain tribes in African nations which remain in traditional life-styles while the dominant elite, usually some other tribe, moves the rest of the nation towards modernization. A third sequence results from annexation, which may be either due to military force such as conquest, or due to economic means such as treaty purchase. A fourth sequence is due to migration, which may be of several types: slave transfer, movements of forced labor, contract labor (e.g. the coolie system), displacement of persons, or voluntary migration. A fifth sequence is that of colonialization (Schermerhorn: 92-163).

R. A. Park posited a much simpler cycle of race relations which he implies is characteristic of all groups and is unidirectional. His sequence consists of four states: contact between the two cultures, leading to competition between them, leading to accommodation, usually more by the minority culture than by the majority, but involving some adjustments by both, finally leading to the eventual assimilation of the two cultures into one (Park: 150).

Within the United States, the bases upon which minority status has been ascribed include the following: (1) national origin, (2) religion, (3) race, (4) gender, (5) sexual preference, and (6) age. It is important to remember, also, that prejudice against groups may be cumulative; that is, it will generally be stronger against groups exhibiting two or more such characteristic bases. The more visible the traits or characteristics upon which the status is determined, moreover, the more severe the discrimination against the group is likely to be and the more complex and lengthy will be the route to assimilation. It is to those processes we next turn our focus.

Acculturation and Assimilation

Two more basic concepts, again often confused in common use, remain to be discussed. The various ethnic or minority groups mentioned above have all found themselves to be in contact with a majority culture which has ascribed them to minority status, using discrimination to keep the group in a lower socioeconomic level. The minority must react to this situation. The interaction is inevitable. It is the quality or type of interaction which characterizes minority group politics.

Acculturation may be defined as the process by which a member of a minority subculture gradually absorbs the norms, values, and life-styles of the majority society, or that portion of the majority culture within which it operates.

Assimilation refers to the subjectively-felt or psychological identification with the majority. In total assimilation, the (former) minority member feels a part of the majority, and the majority accepts him/her as such.

Whenever two differing cultural groups come into sustained contact with one another, some degree of acculturation necessarily takes place. The minority member who thus acculturates, however, does not lose all feelings of marginality or minority-group status as that individual gradually acculturates. It is only with total assimilation that all status distinctions based upon ethnicity are lost or are no longer made by either the (former) minority member or the host community.

Acculturation is thus viewed as a kind of assimilation--cultural assimilation. The best and most extensive theoretical discussion of acculturation and assimilation is that of Milton Gordon. Gordon distinguishes seven kinds of assimilation, or what he refers to as seven assimilation dimensions or variables: cultural or behavioral, structural, marital, identificational, attitude receptional (the absence of prejudice), behavioral receptional (the absence of discrimination), and civic (the absence of value and power conflict).

26

He goes on to make certain hypotheses about the relationships among these dimensions: (1) that in majority/minority contact, cultural assimilation or acculturation will occur first; (2) that acculturation may take place even when none of the other types of assimilation has occurred and that the situation of "acculturation-only" may continue indefinitely; and (3) that if structural assimilation occurs along with or subsequent to acculturation, the other types of assimilation will inevitably follow (Gordon, 1964: 71, 84-85. Also in Glazer and Moynihan: 84-110).

Prejudice and discrimination will disappear from a society only when civic assimilation has been achieved. Obviously, that stage has not, and maybe never will be, achieved in American society. Indeed, a good deal of cultural assimilation has taken place in the United States, but only some degrees of structural assimilation is as yet evident with the Euro-American minorities. Little structural assimilation has yet occurred with respect to our racial minorities.

The capacity of a specific minority to achieve the more advanced dimensions of assimilation, according to Gordon, is determined by what he labels as competitive power, the ability of individuals to compete in the reward system of society, and by pressure power, that is, the power to effect change in society in a collective fashion. Such power pressure may be manifested in one of two ways: political pressure involving actions appropriate to the standard political behavioral norms of that society, for instance, actions via voting, litigation in the courts, lobbying the legislature and the like; or disruptive pressures, involving acts which disrupt normal and expected routines of social intercourse, ranging from peaceful but unconventional demonstrations on up to the extreme of violence, such as revolution.

Three broadly accepted models of assimilation processes are anglo-conformity, the melting-pot theory, and cultural pluralism. Gordon popularized the anglo-conformity model. Basically, it describes the process of new immigrants accepting and conforming to anglo standards. It fits best the white European immigrant experience, which involved acculturation but little structural assimilation. Both the majority and the minority desire to interact to some extent, so acculturation takes place. But minority members are not allowed to enter the more intimate circles of the majority society (Gordon, 1964: 55).

27

The melting pot theory was especially popular during the early twentieth century. It envisions a unique American character emerging out of the intermingling of different people in this new environment. It assumes structural assimilation takes place. The term itself comes from a 1908 play produced by Israel Zangwill entitled The Melting Pot. While the concept is a noble one, it never accurately depicted minority experience in the United States.

Gordon and Kallen have both described the perspective of ultural pluralism. In this perspective, ethnic groups adapt to particular regions and preserve much of their own culture, language, religion, and communal institutions. But they also exhibit a good deal of acculturation: they learn English, communicate readily with majority society members, and participate in varying degrees within the overall political and economic life of the nation (Gordon, 1964: 111).

Additional Readings

Allport, C. W. The Nature of Prejudice. New York: Doubleday, 1958.

Bahr, Howard M., Bruce Chadwick and Joseph Strauss. American Ethnicity. Lexington, Mass.: D. C. Heath, 1979.

Banton, Michael. Race Relations. New York: Basic Books, 1967.

Blalock, Hubert M. Towards a Theory of Minority Group Relations. New York: John Wiley and Sons, 1967.

Daniels, Roger and Harry Kitano. American Racism: Exploration of the Nature of Prejudice. Englewood Cliffs, N.J.: Prentice- Hall, 1965.

Dinnerstein, Leonard and David M. Reimers. Ethnic Americans. New York: Harper and Row, 1975.

Glazer, Nathan and Daniel Moynihan (ed.). Ethnicity: Theory and Experience. Cambridge, Mass.: Harvard University Press, 1975.

Gordon, Milton. Assimilation in American Life. New York: Oxford University Press, 1964.

Kinloch, Graham. The Dynamics of Race Relations. New York: McGraw-Hill, 1974.

Kitano, Harry L. Race Relations. Englewood Cliffs, N.J.: Prentice-Hall, 1974.

Litt, Edgar. Ethnic Politics in America. Glenview, Ill.: Scott, Foresman, 1970.

Park, Robert E. Race and Culture. New York: The Free Press, 1950.

Raab, Earl and Seymour M. Lipset. Prejudice and
    Society. New York: B´Nai B´rith, 1959.
Schermerhorn, R. A. Comparative Ethnic Relations. New
    York: Random House, 1970.
Van den Berghe, P. Race and Racism. New York: John
    Wiley and Sons, 1967.

CHAPTER TWO: NATIONALITY-BASED MINORITIES

The United States is unique in that no other nation has experienced as many and as varied an influx of various ethnic groups. From 1820 to 1930 the United States absorbed an estimated 42 million immigrants, some 37 million of whom came from the European continent alone. The arrival and amalgamation of those millions is one of the most significant factors in shaping the development and political behavior of the country. One cannot understand American politics, let alone American minority group politics, without grasping that fact.

National origin was among the first and most important bases upon which minority status was ascribed to groups in the United States. The patterns of behavior of these "hyphenated Americans" established the model of minority group behavior which predominated in majority/minority relations until the 1950's. These patterns of political participation were extremely influential in the development of the American two-party system.

This chapter deals with the nationality-based minorities: how and why they came to the United States; how they acculturated and began the assimilation process; in short, how they coped with minority status. For the sake of convenience, these minorities will be categorized into two commonly employed groupings: the "old" and the "new" immigrants.

The "old" immigrants came mainly from the northern and western countries of Europe and include the Germans, the Irish, and the Scandinavians. Arriving most heavily during the 1820 to 1880 period, they came in two great waves: 1845 to 1854, dominated by the Irish and Germans; and 1865 to 1875, when the British and Scandinavians also figured heavily with the Irish and German groups.

The "new" immigrants, who came from southern and eastern Europe and from Asia, include the Italians, the Greeks, and the Eastern Europeans (principally the Slavs and the Jews). Their major immigration occurred between 1880 and 1920.

31

An overview of the total immigration to the United States from 1820 to 1980 is provided in Table One. It lists, in rank order, the various immigrant groups by their country of origin, numbers, and peak periods of immigration.

Perhaps a word should be said about the accuracy of the numbers used in the table. Although a very specific number is listed based on the most recent Immigration Service Report, for most countries that number should be understood by the reader as a rough approximation. Thus, while Germany is listed as sending 6,991,504 persons, it should be understood as about 6 3/4 million. Data from the 1820-1867 period represented alien passengers who arrived from a given country; such passengers may or may not have been actual residents of that country. Also, for dates prior to 1906, data relate to country from whence the alien came; after 1906, it represents the last permanent residence. For several European countries, the boundaries changed. Even the lists of countries the Immigration Service recorded changed, so that data is not uniform nor consistently accurate throughout the 1820-1980 period. Poland, for example, is recorded separately from 1820 to 1898 land from 1920 to 1980. From 1899 to 1919, during its actual peak period, Poland is included variously with Austria-Hungary, Germany, and Russia. While the table lists Poland at 523,084 other sources more accurately estimate the number of Polish immigrants at more than three million.

TABLE 1: RANK ORDER OF IMMIGRATION TO THE U.S. FROM NATION OF ORIGIN, 1820-1980			
RANK/NATION OF ORIGIN:NUMBER:		TIME SPAN:	PEAK DECADE:
1. Germany (1)	6,991,504	1830-1930	1881-1890
2. Italy	5,305,854	1880-1930	1901-1910
3. United Kingdom(2)	4,963,527	1820-1970	1881-1890
4. Ireland	4,691,954	1820-1920	1841-1850
5. Austria-Hungary (1,4)	4,317,897	1890-1920	1901-1910
6. Canada, Newfoundland(7)	4,138,647	1840-1960	1921-1930
7. U.S.S.R.(4,5)	3,385,776	1880-1920	1901-1910
8. Mexico(8)	2,232,886	1900-1970	1961-1970
9. West Indies	1,831,126	1840-1970	1961-1970
10.Other Asia(13)	1,696,015	1880-1970	1951-1960 1970-1980
11.Sweden(3)	1,273,457	1840-1930	1881-1890
12.Norway (3)	857,315	1840-1930	1881-1890
13.France	755,234	1820-1960	1921-1930
14.South America	738,456	1901-1970	1961-1970
15.Greece	665,527	1890-1920	1901-1910
16.China(14)	567,629	1850-1900	1881-1890
17.Poland(4)	523,084	1890-1930	1921-1930
18.Portugal	460,830	1870-1970	1921-1930
19.Japan(6)	415,159	1890-1910	1901-1910
20.Turkey	389,094	1890-1930	1901-1910
21.Denmark	365,042	1840-1930	1881-1890
22.Netherlands	361,994	1840-1930	1881-1890
23.Central America	351,540	1901-1960	1961-1970
24.Switzerland	350,590	1840-1930	1881-1890
25.Spain	264,715	1850-1960	1911-1920
26.India	204,930	1901-1980	1970-1980
27.Belgium	203,490	1880-1930	1921-1930
28.Romania(11)	173,984	1890-1930	1921-1930
29.Africa	157,252	1901-1960	1951-1960
30.Czechoslavakia(10)	138,574	1920-1940	1930-1940
31.Australia, N.Z.	123,193	1870-1960	1941-1950
32.Yugoslavia(9)	117,509	1920-1960	1921-1930
33.Other Americas	109,462	1940-1960	1951-1960
34.Bulgaria(9)	68,142	1901-1930	1901-1910
35.Other Europe	55,919	1911-1960	1921-1930
36.Finland(10)	34,081	1840-1960	1881-1890
37.Pacific Islands	24,855	1880-1960	1881-1890
38.Lithuania(10)	3,936	1930-1970	1931-1940
39.Luxemberg(12)	2,932	1930-1970	1951-1960
40.Latvia(10)	2,622	1930-1970	1931-1940
41.Albania(10)	2,611	1930-1970	1931-1940
42.Estonia(10)	1,157	1930-1970	1931-1940

| ALL COUNTRIES | 49,655,952 | TOTAL AMERICAS | 9,452,117 |
| TOTAL EUROPE | 36,339,257 | TOTAL ASIA | 3,272,827 |

Source: INS,1980 Statistical Yearbook.

Notes:
1. Data for Austria-Hungary was not reported until 1861. Austria and Hungary have been reported separately since 1905. From 1938-1945, Austria included in Germany.
2. United Kingdom: England, Scotland, Wales, and N. Ireland.
3. From 1820-1868 figures for Norway and Sweden were combined.
4. Poland recorded separately 1820-1898, and since 1920; otherwise Poland included in Austria, Hungary, Germany or Russia.
5. From 1931-1963 U.S.S.R. broken down into European and Asian U.S.S.R., since 1964 total has been reported in Europe.
6. No record of immigration from Japan until 1861.
7. Prior to 1920, Canada and Newfoundland recorded as British N. America. From 1820-1898 figures include all British N. American figures.
8. No record of immigration from Mexico from 1886-1893.
9. Bulgaria first recorded in 1899, reported separately since 1920. Since 1922 Serbs, Croats, and Slovenes recorded as Yugoslavia.
10. Countries added to list since W. W. I.
11. No record until 1880.
12. Figures for Luxemberg are available since 1925.
13. Beginning in the year 1952, Asia includes the Philippines. From 1934-1951, Philippines are included in Pacific Islands.
14. Beginning with the year 1957, China includes Taiwan.

The Germans

German immigration reached approximately seven million, making Germany the single largest source of immigrants to the United States after the combined British Isles. Roughly 40 million Americans today claim some German ancestry. Although Germans immigrated steadily and in a heavy flow throughout U.S. history, three major currents within that flow are commonly distinguished: the colonial period when Germans immigrated primarily for religious and economic reasons;

34

from 1848 to the Civil War period when they came for political and economic reasons; and the post-Civil War period when they came for economic opportunity, often having been actively recruited by various state governments, the railroads, several major industries, and friends and relatives already living here. The German-American case is instructive for understanding the immigration patterns of many of the nationality-based groups both in terms of their responses to being ascribed to minority status and of their impact upon politics and policies.

In one sense, the German immigrants were never one nationality--their distinctive "Germanness" developed here when they were treated alike, as German-Americans. Until 1870 there was no single German nation, only a loose federation of many German states. Indeed, for most of their modern history, the Germans have been a hybrid people from the German-speaking states of Central Europe and from Austria, Hungary, Luxembourg, Switzerland, Poland, Czechoslovakia, and Russia. In America they were all treated alike, and often categorized for immigration purposes based on their common language. Although the native stock viewed them as a single people, they were a fairly diverse group splintered by regional strife and along religious lines.

During the colonial period German-American immigration patterns were distinguished by the movement of entire communities bound together by religious creeds not accepted in their homeland. They sought out and cultivated some of the richest farmland in colonial America. Their grainaries served as the "breadbasket" for the Revolutionary Forces. Scattered thinly among the total population, they were united only by their language, had little political clout and not much interest beyond their local and private affairs. They tended to intermarry with the Anglo-Saxon native stock more readily than in later periods, thus facilitating their relatively rapid assimilation. Geographically, they came from Europe as Palastines, Salburgers, Wurttenburgers, and Hanoverians. Religiously, they were Mennonites, Dunkers, Lutherans, Calvanists, and a few Jews.

The outbreak of the Revolutionary War changed that. Though widely scattered, they still comprised the single largest nationality group in the United States after the British. They felt no special loyalty to the British crown and were often unfriendly to the Tories who favored continued union with England. While at first the German immigrants refrained from taking part in colonial politics, they did become easy converts to the cause of independence. Several German regiments were raised and fought prominently and well in the war.

Their war service was widely recognized and helped to develop a spirit of mutual respect. Several states, for instance, passed laws which translated their statutes and other governmental proceedings into German. Because of their wartime contributions, Germans farming on the frontier no longer were ignored by the native stock. The war became their first major step towards assimilation.

As their general social and economic conditions improved, they began to take a more active part in public affairs. In party politics they tended toward affiliation with the Democrats. Being small farmers, they were never at home with the eastern seaboard establishment.

During the 1830's and 1840's, Germans emigrated for different reasons. The agricultural revolution hit central Europe, especially the southeastern area of Germany. The inheritance laws required agricultural lands to be divided equally among all children, and many farmers were forced off their land because their farms became too small for even subsistence living. Families turned to manufacturing clocks, tools, and the like, but even this left them overly vulnerable to economic change. When the potato famine which plagued Europe in the 1840's struck, their choice was to emigrate or starve.

Fortunately, this coincided with the opening of the American midwest. Texas, the Great Lakes region, and the Ohio River Valley all became homes to these new settlers. As midwestern cities exploded in population, they all attracted large German migrations. With such places as Chicago, Detroit, Milwaukee, Cincinnati, and St. Louis heading the way, a section of land some two hundred miles wide stretching across the northern tier of states from New York down to Maryland to the Mississippi River became known as the "German belt."

The political turmoil and the 1848 revolutions led many German intellectuals to flee to America. The "forty-eighters," as they became known, made significant contributions to the liberal movement in the states where they settled. Although they numbered only about 10,000, they wielded influence far beyond their numerical strength. They started German language newspapers, reading societies, theatres, and similar cultural activities. Although the full extent of their influence is still a debated question(2), the forty-eighters did provide important leadership in the American labor movement, especially from 1880 to 1910. They were also instrumental in the nation´s conservation movement. Forty-eighter Carl Schurz led the drive to save virgin forest land and became the Secretary of the Interior in 1877.

They were also prominent in the anti-slavery movement and were instrumental in the founding of the Republican Party. They took credit--undoubtedly an inflated claim--for the election of Lincoln, who had wisely invested in a German language newspaper (3).

During and after the Civil War German immigrant labor filled the desperately needed slots in the northern industrial labor force opened by the war. The booming economy drew immigrant labor into the areas of high demand. This became a major factor in their rapid absorption into the mainstream of American life. The largest waves of German immigration came after the Civil-War period. The Homestead Act of 1862 provided the beacon of free land to the overcrowded population of the homeland. Western states advertised for German farmers who had a reputation for being hard working and highly productive. The state governments were joined by the railroads who also sent agents seeking to induce German immigrants to settle and develop the abundant railroad lands. An additional draw was that America became a haven from the military conscription during the years of the German wars of unification.

German immigrants did face some opposition, of course, most notably the Know Nothing Party of the 1850´s. They also came into conflict with the Irish. German Catholics immigrated at the same time as the large wave of Irish Catholics. The latter dominated the clergy and hierarchy of the Catholic Church in the United States until the early 1900´s when the German hierarchy finally began to fill some leadership roles in the Church. 37

World War I acted as a temporary setback on German-American assimilation because of their initial opposition to the War, but once the nation was formally involved such opposition largely ceased, and the German-American community gave its support to the war effort.

Another issue which united the German-American community was their opposition to Prohibition. The importance of beer to their cultural heritage, plus the fact that America's brewing industry was nearly exclusively in their hands, accounted for their opposition. Prohibition threatened the brewers with financial disaster.

In 1916 Congress established the Council of National Defense, designed to speed up the assimilation of German and other nationality groups. While of debatable direct impact, when the act was extended to the states, several mid-western state legislatures enacted comparable statutes granting the state, local, and county councils sweeping legal powers, including subpoena and punishment for contempt. These state councils forbade the use of German language in schools, churches, over the telephone, and in semi-public places. This banning of German probably sped up the process of acculturation.

Post-War isolationism reflected a phobia against everything foreign. Isolationist voting was strongest among those states with heavy German-American populations. Perhaps the disillusion after World War I turned them inward.

After President Roosevelt's 1936 election, his administration adopted a distinctly anti-German foreign policy. This policy shift triggered substantial defections of German-Americans from the Democratic Party at all levels. While as a group they demonstrated their loyalty to the United States by their sons' conduct in the war effort, in the secrecy of the ballot box they voted anti-Roosevelt. Upon his death they came back to the Party fold in the 1948 election in significant numbers, contributing to President Truman's surprise victory.

After World War II the German-American bloc vote largely disappeared. Today, German-Americans are part of the Anglo-Teutonic white stock which comprises the majority. Their assimilation is virtually completed.

The Irish

Today, approximately thirteen million Americans claim Irish descent, representing about 6.5 percent of the total population. Approximately two-thirds of those Irish-Americans reside in the east, concentrating in New York, Massachusetts, Pennsylvania, and New Jersey.

Irish immigration can be traced back to the colonial period, when they settled mostly in Pennsylvania and Maryland. By 1790 the Irish comprised about two percent of the nation's total population of just over three million, their numbers and Catholicism generating the first strong and overt discrimination. After 1830, as the Irish were fleeing the political and religious persecutions under British rule, Irish immigration became a flood.

The potato famine of the late 1840's instigated a massive migration when the choice was often to emigrate or to starve. Between 1847 and 1854 approximately 1.2 million Irish immigrated to the United States. The wave peaked in 1851 when almost a quarter million reached our shores. This famine-induced emigration was particularly important because it created a sudden and quite literal deluge of Irish immigrants into the eastern urban areas and activated existing prejudice. Their sheer numbers, their Catholicism, their obvious poverty, and their openly anti-British feelings all contributed to the native stock's antagonism towards the Irish. Perhaps equally important, because of their poverty, the millions arriving here from rural backgrounds were trapped in the nation's seaboard cities.

Their high rates of illiteracy and lack of job skills forced them into unskilled work. They acquired lower class status precisely at the time when the United States was developing a class consciousness (4). They were viewed as a special threat, a great concentration of "indigent foreigners," and a lower class of people who formed the first huge pool of manual labor (O'Grady, 1973: 65). Consequently, the Irish were the first minority group to face overt job discrimination. Job advertisements in Boston, New York, and other eastern cities for some time included the line, "No Irish Need Apply." Irish immigrants accepted whatever work was open to them--unskilled jobs such as stevedores, teamsters, ditch diggers, dokers, and terriers. They formed construction gangs which razed or erected the buildings of an explosively expanding city. They built the roads, canals, and railroads connecting the east with midwest and beyond. Much to their dismay, not only were the streets of America not paved with gold, those streets were unpaved and the Irish would do much of the paving!

Such jobs were periodic or seasonal, low-paying, and subject to constant threat of job competition. Labor competition was, at least partially, a factor that led to the beginnings of problems in race relations—the Irish regarding the Blacks and the Chinese as a special menace to their own very precarious position.

They also became trapped in an existence which was depressing and grim. Social barriers and meager and unsure incomes forced them to live in slums. Many "escaped" through alcoholism, thereby contributing to the stereotyped image of the entire group being excessive drinkers.

To break out of that vicious cycle and move up from the lowest rung of the socioeconomic ladder, involvement in the beginnings of the American labor movement and the use of politics to enter the local governmental bureaucracies became the routes "chosen" by Irish; more realistically often the only routes left open to them. While few Irish immigrants had experience in labor union affairs, their economically precarious position led them into many labor associations. They were the early leaders in the formation of unions from New York to San Francisco, which included the gambit from skilled craftsmen to tailors, bricklayers, shoemakers, carpenters, long shoremen, and simply "unskilled laborers." In the 1850´s these unions operated solely at the local level, but by the 1860´s they began to appear at the national level. In 1861 Martin Burke helped form the American Miners Association. By the late 1870´s a second-generation Irish-American, Terrance Powderly, gained control of the first truly effective national-level labor union, the Knights of Labor. Peter J. McGuire, the "Father of Labor Day," helped form the American Federation of Labor in 1886 (O´Grady: 163).

The tens of thousands who poured into America during the 1840´s and 1850´s led to the burgeoning of America´s cities. This massive urbanization required rapidly increasing local governmental work-forces, especially police departments. The incoming Irish immigrants were quick to join, and some rose to levels of responsibility quite rapidly. By 1863 a John A. Kennedy led New York City's police force. In the 1870's, a New detective, Michael Kerwin, became Police Commissioner.

The police job was particularly attractive to the Irish immigrant. The status of the uniform and the steady employment were magnets. So, too, was the power potential of such a position. In Ireland, they had been oppressed by the police—evicted, taxed, seized for questioning, imprisoned, and even killed. In America, they exercised such power.

> The Irish policemen exercised wide discretion in apprehending violators and as upholders of the law, they interpreted the law with a latitude and flexibility appropriate to their interests and those of the politicians they served, and the political morality they inherited justified this practice (Levine: 123).

Since politicians controlled the appointments to the force, the Irish immigrants realized that job security depended upon the success of the growing urban machine's slate at primaries and the party's victory on election day. The Irish-dominated police departments became the mainstays of the ward and district organizations of the party.

Ultimately, politics set the pattern of immigrant minority group/majority society relations that served as the model for most of the "new" immigrant groups. It was the route which served as the prototype for many subsequent groups, none of whom were able to employ it as successfully because conditions of society changed by the time those later groups attempted to emulate the Irish model.

By the 1870's the Irish had gained control of the Democratic Party machine in Brooklyn. Irish-Americans served as mayors in Richmond, Memphis, Baltimore, Wilmington, and Scranton. In 1871, an Irishman entered Congress as a Representative from New York; in 1876 another won a seat from Pennsylvania. The highly influential Irish Catholic Benevolent Union (I.C.B.U.) sent several of its most prominent members to seats on the City Council of Philadelphia during the 1870's, one

41

of whom—William Harrity—served as Chairman of the
Philadelphia Democratic City Committee. He later served
as Chairman of the Democratic National Committee during
President Cleveland's 1892 campaign, setting the
precedent for a long tradition of Irish Democratic
National Committee Chairmen. The I.C.B.U. also provided
eight men who held judgeships during the 1870's, and by
1880 its founder, Dennis Dwyer, won a seat on New York
State's Supreme Court. This type of success appeared in
various parts of the nation, but Irish-American
political clout reached its zenith in New York City
through their fifty-year control of Tammany Hall. As
Daniel Patrick Moynihan so aptly describes it:

> Dick" Connolly and "Brains" Sweeney had shared
> power and office with Tweed, as had any number
> of their followers, but with few exceptions
> the pre-1870's Irish had represented the
> canaille. With the dawning of the Gilded Age,
> however, middle-class and upper-class Irish
> began to appear; thus ranging across the
> social spectrum, the Irish appeared to
> dominate a good part of the city's life for
> half a century. They came to run the police
> force and the underworld; they were as evident
> on Wall Street as on the Bowery; Irish
> contractors laid out the subways and Irish
> laborers dug them. The city entered the era
> of Boss Croker of Tammany Hall and Judge Goff
> of the Lexow Committee which investigated him;
> of business leader Thomas Fortune Ryan and
> labor leader Peter J. McQuire; of reform Mayor
> John Purroy Mitchel and Tammany Mayor "Red
> Mike" Hylan. It was a stimulating miscellany,
> reaching its height in the Roaring Twenties
> with Al Smith and Jimmy Walker (in Fuchs:79-
> 80).

Scandinavian-Americans

Scandinavians were among the first European people
to explore America—the Viking explorations and minute
settlements going back to the period of 800 to 1050. In
the mid-1600's several settlements from the region were
established in Delaware. A few immigrants continued to
come to America from Norway, Sweden and Denmark, but
their numbers were not substantial until after the Civil
War. From then on, motivated by such factors as
religious dissension, voting disenfranchisement, crop

42

failures, and related economic factors, Scandinavians emigrated in large numbers. Total Scandinavian immigration to the United States was approximately 2.5 million. The Swedes hit their peak period in 1910, the Norwegians in the 1920´s.

Although the Norwegians, Swedes, and Danes came from countries with diverse governments, traditions and spoken languages, their physical similarities and tendency to settle together in the United States led to the use of the term "Scandinavians" to refer to all three groups. As Babcock (1914) describes it:

> The common use of the term Scandinavian to describe Swedes, Norwegians, and Danes in a broad and general way is one of the products of commingling of these three peoples on the American side of the Atlantic. The word really fits even more loosely than does the word British to indicate the English, Welsh, and Scotch. It was applied early in the history of the settlements in Wisconsin and Illinois, to groups which comprised both the Norwegians and Danes on the one hand, or Norwegians and Swedes on the other hand, when no one of the three nationalities were strong enough to maintain itself separately, and when the members of one were inclined to resent being called by the other names... The Scandinavian Synod of the Evangelical Lutheran Church, organized in 1860, included both Norwegians and Danes...The use and acceptability of the word grew steadily; the great daily paper in Chicago took the name Scandinaven in 1889...the term has become a household word universally understood in the sense in which we here use to to designate the three nationalities (:15-16).

On the whole, Scandinavians were a very successful group of immigrants. As was true of virtually all immigrants, they were willing to work hard. Moreover, they arrived in better financial shape than most groups which enabled them to escape the poverty and slums (and the accompanying social stigma) of the eastern seaboard cities. By 1880 the average Scandinavian immigrant brought approximately $60 to $70 with him. These sums often enabled them to reach the Midwest where they could take advantage of the cheap land and put their farming skills to use. Farming was not, however, their only trade. They went into business, commerce, manufacturing, finance, and the professions. In the frontier settlements they successfully established their own stores, shops, factories, and banks.

Before the 1890's they tended to settle in the Midwestern states whose soil and climate reminded them of their homelands, and their successive settlements attracted others. Minnesota, Wisconsin, Iowa, Illinois, and the Dakotas all saw dramatic rise in their populations due to this influx.

Beginning in the 1890's, however, they were increasingly attracted to the industrial opportunities in the Northeast and Middle Atlantic states, and to the lumber industry of the Pacific Northwest. By 1920 Chicago had the largest number of Swedes of any city but Stockholm, and more Norwegians than any city but Oslo.

Scandinavian assimilation proved comparatively easy. Unlike the Irish, they did not use politics to advance themselves but entered majority society largely through the economic path. Their political involvement generally followed economic and social success.

Several factors account for the relative ease of the acculturation/assimilation. They did not have to overcome the stigma of some "undesirable" trait which hampered so many of the other immigrant groups. They were Caucasian and thereby escaped racial prejudice. Strongly Protestant, they avoided the anti-Catholicism of the area. Thirdly, by coming in relatively small numbers compared to the Irish and Italian waves numbering in the millions, the Scandinavians escaped the scapegoat effect. The anti-immigrant hatred was directed toward Irish and Italians who were feared as job competitors and "papists." By arriving in smaller groups with sufficient money and job skills to reach the Midwest, the Scandinavians were not viewed as threats to native-American labor.

Another element in their escaping the anti-immigrant wrath was the fact that they worked hard at becoming Americans. Strongly desiring to assimilate, they worked to master English as quickly as possible. Schools were very important in their settlements, and they insisted on schools which could teach English.

44

Since Scandinavians were overwhelmingly Protestant, their religion gave them something in common with the majority. They were primarily Lutherans and were more devout and strait-laced than the Germans. Their stern faith frowned on drinking, dancing and levity and stressed piety and the work ethic. Many Scandinavians, moreover, were anti-Catholic and were accepted more readily by the native stock since they shared a common enemy. They also tended to fragment their synods into fairly small segments. Unlike the Irish and Italian groups whose loyalty to a unified Catholic Church kept them tied to their old country and customs earning them the suspicion and enmity of many of the Protestant native stock, the Scandinavians formed numerous new churches often based on American ideas, which greatly eased their assimilation.

Financial success helped them become more socially accepted. The Homestead Act of 1862 provided them with cheap land, so they became established without going heavily into debt. Their standard of living was soon comparable to that of most of the native stock frontier settlers. Describing Norwegian settlers in the Dakotas, a writer in 1889 said: "Most of them came with just enough money to buy government land and build a shack. Now they loan money to their neighbors...Every county has Norwegians worth $25,000 to $50,000, all made since settling in Dakota" (Dinnerstein and Reimers: 97-98).

By 1870 the typical Scandinavian immigrant had a fairly clear understanding of American-style politics with its numerous points of access: elections, representation, constitutions, and fragmented political power distributed among many local governments. As a group, they tended to be very patriotic. They organized political groups to get information on laws and elections. They often learned the rules of American politics through organizing new townships, working the town machinery, carrying on local elections, levying and collecting taxes, and laying out new roads. In the early stages of political development, sometimes more than one-fifth of the men participated in the administration of town affairs. This ratio decreased with the growth of the towns.

As with other immigrant groups, Scandinavian political activity was initially centered on local offices. The first Scandinavian-born politician to enter state-level politics was a Norwegian, James

Reymert, who represented Racine county in the second constitutional convention of Wisconsin in 1847. After the Civil War, however, Scandinavians became visibly involved in state-level politics, at least as measured by their electoral success. Norwegian-born Knute Nelson was the first governor of a state with many Scandinavian immigrants. He was elected in succession to the legislatures of Wisconsin and Minnesota, to the United States Congress, and finally, to the Governorship of Minnesota on the Republican ticket in 1892. By the 1890's many Scandinavians served in the Wisconsin, Minnesota, and Dakota state legislatures.

The great majority of Scandinavian immigrants became strong Republicans. When they first came to the United States, the slavery question aroused them, and they quickly indoctrinated new-comers to the anti-slavery issue. Bound together by their strong feelings against slavery, they stuck together on other political questions. Using their religious ideas to help them decide many of their political issues, they allied themselves as a large voting bloc with the Republican Party. They considered the G.O.P. as the party of the "moral ideas" and seldom defected from it. On the Greenback vote in Wisconsin, for example, only 3 percent of the Scandinavian vote went Democratic, and only 2 percent went so in Minnesota. That was the first time the Scandinavians "broke" with the Republican Party, small though that break was seen. They broke several more times in relation to issues such as agriculture, education, and election reforms. Each break resulted in fewer returning to the flock, but for the most part Scandinavians are still strongly Republican.

By the 1930's Scandinavians had ceased to be thought of as a foreign ethnic group that was different and therefore subject to discrimination. By the 1950's, 60's and 70's, the third-generation Scandinavians were considered to be fully a part of the WASP majority in the United States. "By appearance, by democratic attitude, by ambition, and by religion, the Scandinavians took root quickly in America (Bakin: 27)." Since the 1970's only a few thousand have emigrated from the Scandinavian countries to the United States. Today's immigrants come as professionals, highly skilled craftsmen, or prospective business executives. They tend to assimilate quickly and painlessly. They are less likely than those of the past to have feelings of ethnic community.

"Other" Older Immigrant Groups

Several other immigrant groups arrived in sufficient numbers during the 1820-1880 period. The Chinese, the Dutch, the French, the Scots, Scotch-Irish, and Welsh are usually grouped among the "old"immigrants. Most exemplify patterns similar to those discussed above. One group, the Chinese, showed a considerably diverse pattern, but they will be dealt with in Chapter Five.

The Dutch

Total immigration from the Netherlands for the 1820-1980 period was over 350,000. Although more than half of that total occurred from 1880 to 1920, they are generally grouped among the "older" immigrant groups because they came in significant numbers during the earlier period and their greatest impact on American society was during the colonial period. Dutch influence was most strongly felt in New Jersey and New York. Brooklyn, the Bowery, and the Bronx, for example, all take their names as derivatives of Dutch words. The Dutch language remained a major one in the area for some time, still being spoken as late as 1950 among older people in Ramapo Valley, New Jersey.

Religious dissenters from the Netherlands founded colonies in Michigan and Iowa in 1846. Their departure coincided with the potato blight and economic depression which hit their Dutch homeland and much of Northeastern Europe in the mid to late 1840´s. These religious separatists established a settlement which became Holland, Michigan. It served as the prototype for a new wave of immigrants who settled in Wisconsin and Illinois, as well as Michigan and Iowa, because the soil and climate were so favorable.

The uniting force among these settlements was religion rather than national identity. Subsequent schisms resulted in the formation of the Dutch Reformed Church, the Christian Reformed Church, and the Netherlands Reformed Church. The Holland, Michigan, settlement was particularly successful. They achieved a high social status, in part reflected by the establishment of Hope College. The Christian Reformed Church, a more conservative group, emulated their example by founding Calvin College in Grand Rapids.

Dutch settlers, whether urban or rural, generally achieved middle-class status in income and occupations at a fairly rapid rate. As Parrillo summarizes their experience:

> Although most of the Dutch immigrants have come to the United States during the same period as the southern, central, and eastern Europeans, they have not encountered ethnic antagonism and they have assimilated more easily. Their physical features, their religion, their comparatively small numbers, and their more urbanized backgrounds have enabled them to both adapt and to gain approval from the dominant society more easily than other groups (:127.).

The French

France has been the source of a large and rather continuous flow of immigrants to the United States. French-Americans fall into three distinct subgroups, each with a somewhat different pattern of immigration/assimilation: 1) immigrants from France itself; 2) French Louisianans, or "Cajuns," who were expelled from Acadia French Canada by the British in 1755; and 3) French Canadians who settled primarily in New England. The total number of immigrants from France during the 1820-1980 period was over 738,000.

The colonial-era immigrants from France were dominated by the Huguenots, Protestants, who were fleeing religious persecution. Most of them readily converted to the Anglican Church here, and that fact, coupled with their rapid adoption of English, eased their assimilation. They did experience some antagonism, however, due to the comparatively frequent hostilities between England and France spilling over into animosities in the colonies. Such antagonism, however, was generally short-lived. Their marginal status did encourage them to anglicize as quickly as possible by changing their names and customs, and by learning English. Full assimilation into American life was clearly a desired goal of this group. When the Revolutionary War made France an ally against Great Britain, their assimilation was greatly facilitated. Indeed, it was a French diplomat, De Crevecoeur, who first used the concept of the United States as the asylum for the poor of Europe and who first popularized the concept of America as being "the melting pot" (Rischin: 24; Parrillo: 128).

48

By contrast, the French Revolution led to thousands of French aristocrats immigrating to the United States. Unlike their earlier compatriots, this group kept to themselves and avoided the native stock whom they felt were socially inferior. They rejected assimilation and citizenship. Most returned to France after the fall of Napolean. The French Revolution also briefly aroused anti-French immigrant feelings here as Americans began to fear and detest the excesses of that revolution. This sentiment was particularly strong among the Federalist Party members.

The Louisiana French, who became part of the United States by absorption in the Louisiana Purchase in 1803, afford yet another pattern. They have exhibited an exceedingly strong and persistent subculture that has absorbed other ethnic groups in the area, largely through intermarriage and their matriarchical socialization process. Also, the strong influence of the French Catholic priest and the appeal of the French way of life may account for the persistence of this distinctive ethnic subculture even though the French language has been declining in the area.

The French Canadians exhibit another persistent subculture. Overpopulation at home and the diminishing size of agricultural land which had been subdivided for generations finally led many to start migrating in the 1830's. Their peak periods were between 1860 and 1900, when an estimated 300,000 emigrated, settling for the most part in the mill and factory towns of New England. Other substantial settlements can be found in New York, Michigan, Illinois, and Wisconsin. Parrillo estimates the total French-Canadian influx at a half-million. Like their compatriots in Louisiana, the family and church structures seem to account for their persistent subculture and slow rate of assimilation (Parrillo: 131).

The Scots, Scotch-Irish, and Welsh

The Scots, Scotch-Irish, and Welsh all exhibit similar patterns. They all started their immigration during colonial times and all have assimilated rather easily. Their religious preferences for Presbyterianism, Episcopalianism, and Anglicanism helped to promote their reputations for following a strict moral code, the "Protestant work ethic," and a wide-spread reputation for frugality and honesty which made them easily accepted by Calvanist New Englanders.

49

They settled heavily in Pennsylvania, the Carolinas, and New England. They worked frequently as farmers or miners. In the latter occupation they were often desired as skilled workers who served as superintendents and foremen.

They did experience some ambivalence and anti-immigrant feelings. Since they often settled in larger numbers in what was then the frontier regions, the native stock sometimes feared they might become the dominant group. The native labor force perceived of them as an economic threat, because their job skills made them highly desired workers by some of the native elite. The discrimination they experienced led two scholars to characterize the Scots, Scotch-Irish, and Welsh as one of America's first immigrant "minority groups" (McClemore: 36; Hansen: 49).

Nativist Political Reaction

The successive "waves" of "old" immigrants did not go unnoticed by the native majority. Many WASPS (White Anglo-Saxon Protestants) accepted and welcomed the immigrants. Numerous state governments and some businesses, particularly the railroads, industrial and manufacturing concerns which were just beginning, and the transatlantic shipping lines welcomed, if not actively recruited, immigrants. But not all of the native stock reacted so favorably.

The massive influx of immigrants in the 1830's and 1840's gave rise to a nativist movement reflected in several organizations. The American Party, founded on July 4, 1845, was a specific anti-immigrant party whose main platform was a rejection of the foreigner. The party depended upon the xenophobia, a fear of what is foreign, which swept the east coast during the 1840's. In their declaration of principles, the party stated:
> The danger of foreign influence which threatens the gradual destruction of our national institutions has not failed to arrest the attention of the Father of His Country. Not only in rendering the American system liable to the poisonous influence of European policy--a policy at war with the fundamental principles of the American Constitution, but also its still more fatal operation in aggravating the virulence of partisan warfare--has awakened deep concern in the minds of every intelligent man from the days of Washington to now (O'Connor: 122).

The most prominent nativist movement became known as the Know Nothing Party. Originally called the Order of the Star Spangled Banner, the party had its beginnings as a secret patriotic society founded in New York in 1849. It achieved its earliest successes in Massachusetts and Pennsylvania. In the 1854 elections it added striking successes in Rhode Island, New Hampshire, Connecticut, Delaware, Maryland, Kentucky, and Texas. The party also wielded a strong influence in Virginia, Georgia, Alabama, Mississippi, and Louisiana (Smith: 141; and Nevins: 329).

In the 1856 elections the Know Nothing Party ran a presidential candidate, former President Millard Fillmore. However, its platform was too narrowly based on an anti-immigrant, anti-Catholic stance. It was silent on the slavery issue altogether and merely played the role of spoiler. Fillmore received 874,534 votes and carried only one state, Maryland .

Deep-rooted feelings caused many natives to oppose the immigrants by joining the new militantly nativist party. The massive immigration following the potato famines aroused fear and hostility among the native stock which fed the movement and contributed so significantly to the rapid rise and temporary success of the Know Nothing Party. The slavery question, which ultimately contributed to the demise of the party, loosened ties so that many voters who were unwilling as yet to cast their lot with either the pro-slavery Democrats or the anti-slavery forces forming the Republican Party, found a home in the Know Nothing Party.

In order to join, a person had to be a native-born American and a Protestant. He had to swear an oath to vote for whomever or whatever the party told him to vote. If asked their goals or stands or a position, they were instructed to reply, "I know nothing," which gave rise to the party's popular name. On occasion some party members would close one eye and place a thumb and forefinger over the nose. This signified "eye nose nothing" (Bailey: 135).

The party attracted the working-class natives who feared their jobs would be taken and the institutions and order of society would be undermined. They feared the increasing political threat as the electoral clout of the immigrant bloc vote became increasingly evident

51

in the beginnings of the urban machines.   These fears,
of course,   were not entirely unfounded.   The new
immigrants   were   flocking to the   cities   causing
unbelievable overcrowding and providing a massive and
cheap labor pool.   Employers were quick to determine
that the new immigrants would do almost any job for very
low pay.   It was widely felt that this led to overall
low pay rates and deplorable working conditions.

Many native Americans rose up "...to burn Catholic
convents,   churches and homes,   assault nuns, and murder
Irishmen,   Germans and Negroes" (Beals: 9).   A violent
hate campaign was unleashed in many cities where the
immigrants were concentrated.   In Brooklyn, for example,
mobs of Irish and Know Nothing members clashed,   leaving
two dead.   In Newark, an estimated 2,000 Protestants and
Irish squared off, leaving one dead, many wounded, and a
Catholic Church burned down.   In 1855 Know Nothings and
Germans in Louisville clashed in an intense riot that
left twenty dead and many injured.   In Baltimore, where
the Know Nothing Party was especially strong,   numerous
clashes took place,   including a riot in 1854 in which
eight were killed (Hofstadter and Wallace: 93, 313).

Obviously, not all Americans reacted so negatively.
Ralph Waldo Emerson attacked the growing xenophobia and
the nativist movement by stressing what he considered to
be the advantages of what he called the "smelting-pot
theory.

I hate the narrowness of the Native American
Party.   It is the dog in the manger.   It is
precisely opposite to true wisdom...Well, as
in the old burning of the Temple of Corinth,
by the melting and intermixture of silver and
gold and other metals, a new compound more
precious than any, called Corinthian brass,
was formed; so in this continent--asylum of
all the nations--the energy of Irish, Swedes,
Poles, and Cossacks, and all the European
tribes,--of the Africans, and of the
Polynesians, will construct a new race, a new
religion, a new state, a new literature, which
will be vigorous as the new Europe which came
out of the smelting-pot of the Dark Ages, or
that which earlier emerged from the Palasogic
and Etruscan barbarianism (in Orth and
Ferguson: 299-300).

Obviously, however, many native Americans were afraid of just that. Those to whom the nativist movement appealed did not want a new race, nor a new religion, nor a new language, state or literature.

The party experienced a rapid decline. Its 1855 convention split wide-open over the slavery issue. Its northern members were anti-slavery; its southern wing would not budge from its pro-slavery stand. Attempted reconciliations failed, signaling serious trouble for the party. After the 1856 election, the party essentially disintegrated, with its southern wing going Democratic (and later sessionist), and the northern members joining the Republicans.

The "New" Immigrants

Although immigrants from the south/central/eastern European nations had arrived in the United States during colonial times and throughout the 1820-1880 period, their numbers and influence were comparatively small until after the 1880´s. Indeed, 1896 represents the turning point--at which time the numbers of immigrants from SCE Europe exceeded those from northern and western Europe.

Because these newcomers were far different in their physical and cultural features than previous groups and, of course, the majority, their arriving in sufficient numbers to preserve their cultural and social identities in the various ethnic enclaves within America´s burgeoning urban centers worked to increase the prejudice and discrimination they experienced. Their religion was yet another barrier. They also were arriving just as racial theories which questioned their ultimately being able to assimilate were becoming popular. The social and economic unrest engendered by World War I eventually led to the passage of restrictionist immigration policy clearly aimed primarily at these new immigrants.

The substantial nativist fear of "Rum, Romanism, and Rebellion" was exacerbated by the great influx of Catholics during the 1880-1920 period. Catholics were only one percent of the population in 1790 and seven percent in 1850; by 1900, however, 12 million Catholics comprised 16 percent of the total, and they were growing at what was perceived to be an alarming rate.

A substantial portion of the newcomers were of religious affiliations considered by the WASP majority to be even more suspect than Catholics--namely, the Orthodox Christians from Greece or Russia, and the Jews. Of the estimated two million Jews who fled eastern Europe, over 70 percent were from Russia and approximately 90 percent came to the United States. Jewish population in the United States soared from an estimated 250,000 in 1877 to over 4 million in 1927 (Dinnerstein and Reimers: 37-38).

What compelled these "new" immigrants to leave? Millions came from southern Europe--from Italy, Portugal, and Greece. Millions more fled central Europe--from Austria-Hungary, Poland, Czechoslavakia, and what became Yugoslavia. Still millions more fled eastern Europe--from Bulgaria, Rumania, and Russia. Some 27 million Europeans made their way to the United States during the 1880 to 1930 period! Both "push" and "pull" factors were apparent in this vast migration of peoples.

The major push factors included the urbanization and industrialization revolutions which were spreading across SCE Europe which engendered severe political, social, and economic disruptions. This led to political unrest and repression. Governments had to cope with these pressures brought on by high unemployment, population growth, high birth rates, chronic poverty, epidemics, the decline of feudalism with its resulting social and economic dislocations, and the economic shift from agrarian to industrial concerns. Emigration was an expedient policy to deal with these problems so governments greatly encouraged the waves of emigration.

Unrest in Czarist Russia contributed to another push factor--the Jews becoming the scapegoats for all the country's ills. Government-sponsored pogroms, which began in 1881 with the assassination of Czar Alexander II and continued for thirty years, forced many Jews to flee. Those brutal campaigns of beatings, killings, and looting were exemplified by the 1903 pogrom in Kishineff. Some 2,750 families were affected: 47 persons were killed, another 424 wounded. Scores of Jewish homes were burned and their shops pillaged (Ibid: 38).

A number of "pull" factors were also involved. Transatlantic travel via the steamship lines eased the hardships of the journey. Letters from friends and relatives in the United States induced many to come. Finally, the promise of the "golden opportunities" afforded by America was the beacon that drew millions to our shores.

Once here, they often found themselves trapped in the teeming cities. From 1815 to 1855 the slum-bred cholera epidemics nearly doubled the mortality rate in New York. The half-million tenement slum dwellers in New York's East Side comprised the world's most densely populated district, exceeding even the density of Old London. Jacob Riis (1957) describes such overcrowding:

And yet experts had testified that, as compared with uptown, rents were from twenty-five to thirty percent higher in the worst slums of the lower wards, with such accommodations as were enjoyed, for instance, by a "family with boarders," in Cedar Street, who fed hogs in the cellar that contained eight or ten loads of manure; or "one room 12 X 12 with five families living in it, comprising twenty persons of both sexes and all ages, with only two beds, without partitions, screen, chair or table (p. 8).

The successive waves of immigrants caused the nation's cities virtually to explode upward and outward. By 1920 immigrant groups comprised 44 percent of New York, 41 percent of Cleveland, 39 percent of Newark, and 24 percent of Pittsburgh, Detroit, Boston, Buffalo, and Philadelphia (Lieberson: 24).

The Italian-Americans

Italian-American immigration is a phenomenon which occurred almost exclusively after the 1870 period. The 5.3 million immigrants make Italy second only to Germany in the number of immigrants who came to the United States.

There was a little colonial and pre-Civil War immigration from Italy. As early as the 1620's the Virginia colony had Italian winegrowers. Pre-Revolutionary War immigration by Italians was lightly scattered among Virginia, Georgia, the Carolinas, New York and Florida. In addition, some political

55

repression in Europe during the 1780's caused a number of Italian intellectuals and revolutionaries to come here.

Although very small in number, the pre-1880 Italian immigrants, who were almost exclusively from the northern provinces of Italy, had a considerable impact on the areas within which they settled. They founded the floundering opera in the United States during the 1830's and 1840's. From the 1820's to 1870's Italian artists were brought in by the national government for commissioned artwork such as frescos, murals, busts and statues. By 1848 two Italian immigrants had been elected to the Texas state legislature. A year later in New York, Secchi de Casali founded L'Eco d' Italia, a prominent Italian-language newspaper which supported the Whig Party and later the Republicans (Iorizzo and Mandello: 26).

By the 1850's there was an Italian settlement in Chicago where they served as saloon keepers, restauranteurs, fruitvenders, and confectioners, as well as common ditchdiggers and commissioned artists. At the same time they were also lured California by the gold rush. Instead of mining, however, most of these immigrants became wine growers, vegetable farmers, and merchants, giving rise to "...the Italio-American folklore that, 'the miners mined the mines, and the Italians mined the miners...'"(Ibid: 13).

The early Italian-Americans were often skilled craftsmen who were of middle and upper class backgrounds and who came seeking better economic opportunity. This changed radically after 1870.

The "Risorgimento," which resulted in the unification of Italy in 1870, also sparked a mass exodus which saw nearly nine million Italians cross the Atlantic to both North and South America seeking the socio-economic betterment denied them by the movement which they had supported at home. The trickle of Italian immigrants, largely from the north, became a flood from the South. From 1881 to 1910 more than three million Italians came to the United States. Most of them settled in the cities of the industrial northeast. By 1930 New York's Italian American immigrants numbered over a million and comprised 15.5 percent of the city's total population (The Italians of New York, p. viii). Today an estimated 7.2 million Italian-Americans comprise about 3 1/2 percent of the population of the United States.

This flood of immigrants was by no means a static bloc, as is often the popular image. A good deal of mobility was shown by the group after they arrived here. They moved back and forth between Italy and America, and they moved within the enclaves or "Little Italy" settlements here. Data from 1908 to 1914 shows that about half of the Italians who immigrated to the United States returned, at least for a time, to Italy. Until the passage of the quota law made it impossible, many Italian immigrants moved back and forth annually, spending winters at home in Italy, and working the remainder of the year in America. Nelli´s study showed they often moved within their enclaves as well (Nelli: viii).

As with other groups, several push and pull factors influenced these immigrants to leave Italy and undertake the arduous and uprooting migration to America. Most immigrants were motivated by economic factors: they left Italy to be free from the shackles of poverty. The contrast in wages was considerable. During the 1890´s agricultural workers in Italy were payed 16 to 30 cents per day, and during the winter season that fell to 10 to 20 cents per day. Italian miners worked for 30 to 56 cents a day. General laborers received $3.50 for a six-day work week compared to $9.50 for a 56 hour week in the United States. Carpenters in Italy received 30 cents to $1.40 a day, or $1.80 to $8.40 per six-day week; that same worker received an average $18.00 for a 50 hour week in the United States! (See:The Italian-Americans,: 43-44; The Italians of New York: 36-49).

Other push factors which compelled many to leave Italy were the problems of floods, volcanic eruptions, and earthquakes which plagued the country and contributed to the bleak agricultural outlook, particularly in the South. That region was also especially hard hit by phylloxera, a disease which killed off agricultural plants on a scale similar to the Irish potato blight of the 1840´s. Southern Italy was further troubled by frequent and severe epidemics of malaria. Others fled military service.

Far more important were the pull factors. The development of the steamship lines made the journey cheaper, faster, and easier. The glowing reports of relatives and village acquaintances about the wealth of opportunity drew others. Returning "Americani," some of whom made the trip back and forth, had sufficient money

57

not only to return temporarily to Italy for brides, but also to attract many others to emulate their "success" in America. State governments, such as those of Illinois, New York, Pennsylvania, California, and Louisiana hired agents to contract for laborers to come.

From 1890 to 1914 Italians came in excess of 100,000 per year, and during 1900 to 1914 a total of three million came. So massive was the migration that:

> One author told the humorous and probably apocryphal tale of a mayor who greeted the Prime Minister of Italy then touring the provinces: "I welcome you in the name of five thousand inhabitants of this town, three thousand of whom are in America and the other two thousand preparing to go (The Italian-Americans,: 48).

Perhaps as important for subsequent acculturation patterns as the massiveness of this migration was the fact that the Southern Italian was more often a sojourner in his mentality, undoubtedly associated with the social and cultural background of the peasant as opposed to the background of his earlier Northern-Italian counterpart. For historical reasons, the "Mezzogiorno" (the South) was more traditional, backward and poor than the north. The "contadini" (peasants) were at the bottom of a still largely feudal society. Oppressed and exploited by signori and borghesi alike, they were despised as "cafoni" (boors). Illiterate, unschooled, lacking self-confidence, the peasantry was preindustrial in culture and mentality. Not a very good preparation for grappling with the life in America's tenement slums!

In emigrating, the motive of the contadini was not simply to escape the grinding poverty; rather it was to improve their family's lot by earning money with which to buy land back in their village. Thus, most came with the intention to work, save, and return after several years with a few hundred dollars. Like the Chinese, to whom they were often compared, the Italians were sojourners. The predominantly male and youthful character of the immigration reflected that purpose.

Of the millions who emigrated, about half in fact did return to their villages, some having accomplished their mission, others having met defeat. But even those who remained in America often continued to nourish

58

thoughts of the day when they would go back to their paese. The persistence of that mentality was an important condition affecting their adjustment. Why learn English, why become a citizen, why Americanize, if one were going back to the old country, if not this year than next? In the villages of southern Italy today one finds these "Americani" who after fifty years returned to live on their social security benefits (Dinnerstein and Jaher: 202).

In the states, most Italian immigrants settled in the teeming central cities. They managed to find jobs in a wide variety of occupations. Many were common laborers on the railroads, or they dug the canals and waterways then under construction. In the cities they dug the sewage systems and laid pipes for the water supply. Many took up fruit vending and vegetable truck farming, psychologically appealing after their disastrous agricultural experiences in Italy had taught them, by contrast, that truck farming was a good investment. Match and shoe factories recruited laborers and soon found that the "chain" migration was so effective that they no longer needed agents to recruit the laborers who were drawn by word of mouth or by letters from friends and relatives who had preceded them.

Some did settle in more rural settings and occupations. In San Francisco they dominated the fruit and vegetable truck farming business, and in California they were so prominent in that market that "Del Monte" became a household word. In 1881 the Italian-Swiss colony established at Asti in Sonoma County sparked the development of the wine industry. A smaller but comparable role was played in the growing wine industry in upstate New York. Other important agricultural settlements included Vineland and Hammonton, New Jersey, and Geneoa, Wisconsin. In 1850 Louisiana had more Italians as laborers in the cotton fields than any other state, and New Orleans had a larger proportion of Italians than any other city. By 1920, however, New York City led the nation with its more than one-half million Italian residents.

The Italian immigrants arrived by the hundreds of thousands precisely when America was experiencing an economic downturn. The turbulent socio-economic unrest following the Panic of 1873 and the subsequent crippling depression led to rising anti-Semitism, emerging Jim

59

Crowism, and growing antipathy towards European immigrants. The latter were viewed by the native stock as radicals and criminals who filled the ever-growing slums, fueled class conflicts, and contributed to the developing urban machine and its blatant political corruption.

They did seem to be filling the cities. According to the 1910 census, first and second generation Italian immigrants accounted for 77 percent of Chicago's foreign inhabitants, 78 percent of New York's, and 74 percent of Boston's, Detroit's, and Cleveland's (Italians in Chicago: xi).

The late 1880's and 1890's witnessed depression-induced violence that swept the nation and was frequently directed at Italians. Table Two summarizes the lynchings, murders, and mob violence directed against Italian-Americans during the 1870-1920 period.

TABLE 2: MOB VIOLENCE AGAINST ITALIAN-AMERICANS		
DATE:	LOCATION:	NUMBER AND CONDITION:
12/17/1874	Buena Vista, Pa.	4 killed
3/28/1886	Vickesburg, Miss.	1 lynched
3/14/1891	New Orleans, La.	11 lynched
7/2/1893	Denver, Colo.	1 lynched
3/21/1894	Altona, Pa.	200 driven from city
3/12/1895	Walsenburg, Colo.	6 murdered by a mob
8/11/1896	Hahnville, La.	3 lynched
7/20/1899	Tallulah, Miss.	5 lynched
7/11/1901	Erwin, Miss.	2 lynched, 1 wounded
11/18/1901	Marksville, La.	4 driven from city
5/14/1906	Marion, N. C.	2 killed, 5 wounded
9/20/1910	Tampa, Fla.	2 lynched
10/12/1914	Willisville, Ill.	1 shot and killed
6/12/1915	Johnson City, Ill.	1 lynched

Source: Adapted from Iorizzo and Mondello, The Italian-Americans, New York: Twayne, 1971): 223.

Another result of the intense discrimination against Italian-Americans was in their living conditions. Nearly 90 percent lived in the nation's urban areas, mostly in "Little Italy" sections of major cities. Conditions there were grim. Jacob Riis

60

describes the slums in and around "The Bend," "Bandit's Roost," and "Bottle Alley," which characterized the Mulberry Street-Mulberry Bend area that was New York's first Little Italy section. He described one such visit to the area as follows:

> Half a dozen blocks on Mulberry Street there is a ragpicker's settlement, a sort of overflow from "the Bend," that exists today in all its pristine nastiness. Something like forty families are packed into five old two-story and attic houses that were built to hold five, and out in the yards additional crowds are, or were until very recently, accommodated in shacks built of all sorts of old boards and used as drying racks by the Italian stock (Riis: 49).

Nor were those conditions atypical. Other studies showed comparable conditions. One survey taken found that 1,231 Italians were living in 120 rooms in New York, while another report stated they could not find a single bathtub in a three-block area of tenements. In In Chicago, a two-room apartment often housed an Italian family of parents, grandparents, several children, cousins and boarders. A 1910 survey in Philadelphia noted that Italian families had to cook, eat, and sleep in the same room, while most t shared outhouses and a water hydrant--the only plumbing facility available-- with four or five other families. In addition, many Italians kept chickens in their bedrooms and goats in their cellars (see Dinnerstein and Reimers: 48).

However, these Little Italy colonies did help the immigrants to cope. One form of help was the "padroni" system. Although probably exaggerated as to its exploitive nature and extensiveness, the "boss" system was nonetheless an important mechanism for the immigrant. The padroni, the bosses, knew individual employers, spoke English, and understood American labor practices. They were invaluable to American business in need of gangs of laborers. The newcomers depended on them for jobs, and other services--such as collecting wages, writing letters, acting as a banker, supplying room and board, and handling dealings between workers and employers.

Although the Foran Act of 1885 forbade contract labor, the golden era these padroni was from 1890 to

61

1900. The conditions of poverty in which so many families lived often forced the young to forgo school and start to work at very early ages. In 1897 an estimated two-thirds of the Italian workers in New York City were controlled by padroni (Dinnerstein and Reimers: 45).

Although the padroni system did exploit the immigrants, it also helped them to find jobs and eased the acculturation process. After 1900 it rapidly declined in importance as others began providing some of the social services previously done only by the padroni. In addition, railroad and construction officials began to investigate and became aware of the worst abuses and were able to find laborers without use of the padroni. Finally, the sheer massiveness of the numbers of immigrants that poured in from Italy from 1900 to 1920 was more than the padroni system could adequately handle. The later immigrants moved into more stable settlements, were thus less dependent on bosses for jobs, housing, and persons to assist them with English or with contacts with government and labor officials.

One mechanism they used to assist their rise in the employment area was their involvement in the American labor movement. Their role was rather a mixed one. Initially they were used as scabs and strikebreakers. This gave rise to the commonly accepted view that they were anti-union or hard to organize because they were too conservative. In places where they were barred from union membership and activity, they often did play such a role. Where unions were open to them,however, and where such organization looked likely to succeed, they often provided a significant number of members and local leadership. By the early 1980's, Italians ranked second only to Poles in percentage of white ethnics belonging to blue-collar, working-class, organized-labor jobs.

Unlike the Irish, the Italian-Americans found the church less useful in their assimilation process. Their anti-Irish attitudes often spilled over into their relations with the Church, which exhibited an Irish-dominated hierarchy. Gradually, however, Italian-American priests were ordained who could better meet their needs, and some inroads into the upper levels of the hierarchy were achieved by the 1930's. After the 1920's the Church did prove useful as a means of their assimilation.

Perhaps even more influential in assisting them to adjust to life in America was the wide variety of mutual aid or benevolent societies. These self-help organizations were founded fairly early in the Italian-American experience. San Francisco, for instance, had an Italian Mutual Aid Society in 1858. The Society of Italian Union and Fraternity was started in New York in 1857. By 1912 there were 258 mutual aid groups in New York City alone, including the nation's most influential, the Society for Italian Immigrants, begun in 1901 (The Italian-Americans: 95). By 1919 there were 80 such societies in Chicago, the most noted of which was the Union Sicilian, the Columbian Federation, and the Order of the Sons of Italy in America (Nelli: 172). These organizations often began as burial societies or as groups to help them find housing and jobs. They soon developed into a wide variety of organizations providing insurance, a host of social services, and became the basis of the social life for many of the immigrants.

To a degree, the mafia and crime-related organizations emerged in a similar fashion. The mob violence and discrimination directed against them contributed to a rise of criminal activities, in part as self-protective associations. Careers in crime became a "curious ladder of social mobility" (Vecoli: 205). When the urban machines and crime organizations linked in the 1910 to 1930 period, crime organizations provided a linkage to political clubs and party activity. It provided a source of political leadership, especially in Chicago, where Colosimo, Torrio, and Al Capone emerged (Nelli: 113-114). Crime became a source of the derogatory stereotyping of all Italians as criminals. That image, plus the 1913 Depression, undoubtedly played a part in the revival of anti-Italian immigrant fervor by such groups as the Ku Klux Klan in the early 1900's, and to a resurgence in the use of pejorative terms like "wop" and "dago."

Wars had an impact on Italian-American assimilation as well. Although to a lesser degree than was the case with the Irish, Italian-Americans saw some initial, if short-lived, benefits on their image and acceptability to Anglo-America by their service in the Civil War. New York City sent a regiment—the Garibaldi Guard—to fight for the Union forces. Their war record was substantial. In addition to the Guard, 100 Italians from New York served with Union forces, and three reached the rank of general. The effects of W.W.I., when some 300,000 Italian-Americans served, were also profound (The Italian-Americans:30).

63

In politics, they used the Irish model but less successfully so. They moved into political activity more slowly than did the Irish and often came into conflict with the Irish politicians who had "arrived" before them and were reluctant to share power or move over to make room for the newcomers. Such Irish-Italian conflict was common, often severe, and occasionally violent.

Initially, Italian-Americans emerged from various political clubs. They ran as Democrats, Republicans, Socialists, Independents, and Progressives. The Progressive and Republican parties, however, were the more popular among them. Before the 1920's most of their political activity was at the local level. They often supported machine candidates. In New York, political activity included the creation of the Italian Federation of Democratic Clubs and the founding, in 1925, of the Fascist League of America. Political leadership emerged out of the padroni system as well. In upstate New York these included several notable leaders with connections to the Republican Party: Marnel, D'Angelo, Lapetino, Gualtieri, and later LaGuardia in New York City (The Italian-Americans: 138-158). In Chicago, a varied pattern was evident. The first state-level Italian-American politician in Illinois was a Democrat, Charles Cois, who was elected to the State House in 1918. At the same time, on the Republican ticket, Dr. Camille Volini was elected County Commissioner and Bernard Barasa a municipal judge. Nationally, they at times supported and worked with the Democratic machines, but as often as not they clashed with the Irish leadership of the party. In Chicago, for example, they had a running battle against ward boss John Powers (known to them as Johnny De Pow and Gianni Pauli).

In the words of Oscar Durante, the election of 1828 equalled a declaration of war against Gianni Pauli on the part of the 19th Ward Italians. More than any other ethnic group they resisted his blandishments and supported Jane Addams...and the Progressive Reform movement against him (Nelli: 99).

In 1912, anti-Wilson views swung many of them away from the Democrats. In New York, Republican Fiorello LaGuardia emerged as their political leader. He was elected to the U.S. House of Representatives in 1915

64

and, after a distinguished war service, again in 1918. In 1920 he won the seat vacated by Al Smith. In 1933 he was elected the "reform" mayor of New York. During the 1920´s, Italian-Americans split their votes, most of which went to the Republicans, but with their usually voting "wet" over "dry" no matter what the candidate´s party affiliation. In 1932, and basically ever since, they returned solidly to the Democratic fold, with a 60 percent vote for Roosevelt.

During the 1930´s the increasingly prominent Italian-American politicians were working themselves up to state-wide and even national-level offices. By 1937, for instance, three Italian-American judges served on New York´s Supreme Court. Angelo Rossi, LaGuardia, and Robert S. Maestri were, respectively, the mayors of San Francisco, New York, and New Orleans. Three U.S. Congressmen from New York were prominent Italian-Americans: Vito Marcantonio, James Lanzetta, and Alfred Santangelo. Through judicious "behind the scenes" politics, and his own business acumen, another Italian-American stood at the pinnacle of success in American business: Amadeo Peter Giannini, Chairman of the Board of the Bank of America. By 1945 his bank had surpassed the Chase National Bank of New York as the largest commercial bank in the world (The Italian-Americans: 193-210).

During the inter-war years some of them flirted with Fascism, although both pro- and anti-fascist groups emerged within the Italian-American communities. In part, Il Duce became a source of ethnic pride, reflecting a sort of communal hero-worship. Nelli cites a "strongly anti-Fascist Italian-American girl," who said, despite her opposition to Mussolini and his program, "You´ve got to admit one thing: he has enabled four million Italians in America to hold up their heads, and that is something. If you had been branded undesirable by a quota law, you would understand how much that means (: 241)."

As with the Irish, politics became a source of economic betterment. Political connections enabled Italian-American businessmen to evade bothersome city and state laws. Political advertisements were a source of income to Italian-language newspapers. Patronage provided many of them with jobs on the cities´ swelling bureaucracies. Even the ethnic politician or their corrupt business ally could become a source of ethnic pride:

65

Italians might complain of the fame and fortune enjoyed by their leaders and might feel they were secured at their expense. But they might also be proud. Their own kind had made it. The Marnells, Gualtieris, and Lapetinos were from common stock...The success of the peasants´ alter egos obscured the fact that their advancement was not secured in the classical form of individual success, but through the increasing power and status of the ethnic group as a whole. This helps to explain the plethora of monuments which Italians erected throughout the country. This was one way, they felt, to establish that Italians belonged in America. Many educated Italians looked upon such statuary as wasteful of talent, energy and money. They were quick to condemn their countrymen for failing to undertake more useful projects, but slow to understand the psychological need of Italians for hero worship (The Italian-Americans: 158).

Since W. W. II they have remained aligned with the Democratic Party, when measured by national, and especially Presidential, voting behavior. Despite an occasional notable Republican politician of Italian heritage, such as Volpe in Massachusetts, they remain overwhelmingly Democratic. They will cross party lines to vote for one of their own. Thus, while 85 percent of the Italian-American voters in Massachusetts supported Kennedy for President in 1960, 50 percent crossed over to vote Republican for Volpe in his gubernatorial bid (Levy and Kramer: 178-179).

Republicans have made some very concerted efforts, particularly the two Nixon Presidential campaigns, to woo the Italian-American voter. Their results have been far from re-aligning. Two-thirds of Italian-Americans identify themselves with the Democratic Party, significantly above the rate for the general public. In the 1976 election, the Carter/Mondale ticket received an estimated 55 percent of the Italian-American vote (Siegel: 48).

Italian-Americans are showing sufficient political clout, and enough independence from any guaranteed bloc voting, to make themselves an attractive group of voters to be sought by leaders of both political parties. As Levy and Kramer put it:

Italians are beginning to recognize the political muscle inherent in the elections just reviewed. They are openly following the black lead, organizing unabashedly through whatever vehicle is most readily available, regardless of the efforts of outsiders to taint those organizations, and generally preparing to emerge not as Republicans, and perhaps not even as Democrats, but surely as a cohesive ethnic political force no politician will safely ignore (:189).

The Greeks

Greeks have been coming to America since colonial times--a scattering of explorers, sailors, cotton merchants, gold miners, and the ill-fated New Smyrna colony in Florida in 1768 (Moskos: 3-5). They did not arrive in any significant numbers, however, until after the 1880's. Between 1900 and 1920 they reached their peak of immigration when some 350,000 arrived. Although they came from all parts of Greece, the majority were young, unskilled males from the villages in the Penoponesus.

As with other SCE European groups, various push and pull factors led to their migration. Although political persecution played a role, economic conditions were the primary push factor. The rapid rise in the Greek population resulted in an excess that the land simply could no longer support. By 1931, for instance, even after rather heavy emigration, there were 870 persons for every square mile of cultivated land (Thernstrom: 431).

Another push factor was the ongoing state of war between Greece and Turkey. The Balkan War of 1912-1913 occurred during the peak period of Greek immigration to the United States. Many fled the compulsory military service in what they considered to be a Turkish tyranny.

Many Greeks, like the Italians and the Chinese, came as sojourners. Young men came intending to earn enough money to provide substantial doweries for the prospective brides in their families. The fact that about 95 percent of the Greek immigrants were young males meant many returned home for brides.

67

The opportunity for better jobs in America was the single most important pull factor. The flood of Greek immigrants who arrived during the 1880 to 1920 period followed one of three major routes: 1) Greeks going to the West to work on railroad gangs and in the mines; 2) Greeks going to New England to work in the textile and shoe factories; and 3) Greeks settling in New York, Chicago, and other large industrial cities who worked in factories or served as busboys, dishwashers, bootblacks, and peddlers.

Like the Italians, the Greeks used and were exploited by a padrone system. As with the Italian padroni, the padrone found jobs for the immigrants, helped with language problems, and settled disputes. Frequently, the padrone's "clients" were young boys sent directly to the padrone, who arranged for their room and board and a small wage. The wage was pre-arranged and agreed to by the parents. What the parents did not know were the conditions under which the boys lived--squalid and crowded basement rooms in the heart of the tenement slums, working 18 hour days with no time set aside for lunch.

This system was highly profitable for the padrone, who made an average of $100 to $200 per year per boy, and in some cases made as much as $500 per year per boy. The boys themselves would receive about $100 to $180 per year in wages. Theodore Soloutos describes it as "a modernized version of the indentured servant system of the late seventeenth and early eighteenth centuries" (:48).

Although the majority of Greek immigrants were young and unskilled, some educated and skilled Greeks also emigrated. Many of these men met with unforeseen problems. Greek lawyers could only practice law after learning English, studying for one year in an American law school, and passing a bar examination. Greek physicians had it a bit better; they were able to take qualifying exams in Greek. However, unless they were able to master a reasonable amount of English, their practice was confined to Greek-Americans. Many college graduates caught the emigration fever, but had few opportunities to proceed in their various interests. For the educated Greek it was difficult to find employment equal to their educations, and they felt it was beneath their dignity to work as unskilled laborers.

68

A fairly sizable number of Greek immigrants did manage to start their own businesses. They concentrated on confectionaries, candy stores, and restaurants. After World War I, for instance, there were an estimated 564 Greek restaurants in San Francisco alone. After World War II there were 350 to 450 Greek-American confectionary shops and eight to ten candy manufacturing concerns in Chicago (Parrillo: 207; Moskos: 17-20).

As with the Italians, many Greeks did return back and forth to Greece; many making the trip several times before finally staying in the States. This back-and-forth migration pattern undoubtedly slowed their acculturation/assimilation rate. It led to a mutual lack of understanding and often severe conflict.

In 1904 in Chicago, for instance, a strike broke out in the diesel shops of the city. The heated union/city management conflict left the city in a bad situation. Unaware of the conditions of the strike, inexperienced Greek immigrants served as strike-breakers. Since they broke the strike, the Greeks were considered by the strikers to be the enemy. A wave of anti-Greek hysteria and a period of severe anti-Greek press followed. Eventually the strike ended with the regular employees returning, but at the cost of a wave of anti-Greek sentiment. In the West, a virulent nativist reaction directed at the Greek immigrants, whose numbers made them more visible, erupted. In McGill, Nevada, for instance, three Greeks were killed in an anti-foreign riot in the summer of 1908. In Utah, the Mormons seemed to be particularly anti-foreign and anti-Greek. Greeks were characterized in the Utah press at the time as "a vicious element unfit for citizenship," and "ignorant, depraved and brutal foreigners." In 1917 a Greek accused of killing Jack Dempsey's brother was almost lynched in Salt Lake City. In 1923, in Price, Utah, local citizens rioted and attacked Greek stores, forcing the American girls who worked in them to return to their homes. The Ku Klux Klan was especially active in Utah in the early 1920's, and Greeks were singled out as special targets (Moskos: 17). In Omaha, in 1909, a sizable Greek community of seasonal workers led to a strike-breaking situation. During the period of heightened tensions, a false-arrest incident involving a Greek immigrant led to a scuffle in which the policeman died. An ugly riot the next day caused thousands of dollars of damage to the Greek section of the city (Burgess: 162-163).

69

Incidents such as these contributed to a growing anti-Greek sentiment. Even supposedly scholarly work, such as that of sociologist Henry Pratt Fairchild, reflected this negative image. His work stereotyped the Greek immigrant, like the Italian, as being disproportionately of the "criminal type," and he despaired their ever being able to assimilate (Fairchild, 1911).

And indeed, their assimilation did appear to proceed slowly. Greek immigrants tended to live in small colonies where they could socialize with one another and practice their religion. Since the church and state are not separate in Greece, almost every Greek immigrant was a member of the Greek Orthodox Church, one of the fifteen different parts of the Eastern Orthodox Church. An unwillingness to practice their faith with others—even with other branches of the Eastern Orthodox Church—tended to isolate Greeks from the mainstream of religious society, reducing their interaction with non-Greek groups and slowing their acculturation rate.

Greek social life also tended to isolate them. Dinnerstein and Reimers describe the role played by the community council and the coffee house, two major aspects of Greek-American social life:

In the Greek community, the kinotitos, or community council, was the governing body of the people. It provided for the establishment of churches and schools, hired and fired priests and teachers, and exerted a constant influence on Greek affairs. One could almost always gauge the feelings of the group by the actions of the kinotitos. For recreation, the Greeks flocked to their kuffenein, or coffee houses. These served as community social centers where men smoked, drank, conversed, and played games in what became literally a place of refuge after a hard day of work or an escape from dank and dreary living quarters. No Greek community was without its kuffenein, and one chronicler reported that in Chicago before World War I, "every other door on Bolivar Street was a Greek coffee house" (:54).

The Greek Church, the Greek-language press, such as the Atlantis, and the more than 100 Greek societies all encouraged cohesiveness. The largest and most notable of the Greek societies, the American Hellenic Educational Progressive Association (Ahepa), was founded in 1922. Its purpose was to preserve the Greek heritage and to help the immigrant understand the American way of life.

Greek family life was close-knit and stressed education, particularly advanced education into the professions. Law and medicine were especially stressed, as they were the most prestigious fields in Greece. Although education affected the children most immediately, the impact was felt on the whole family. Greek children went to two schools: the public school and the Greek-language school. Mandatory for most children, the purpose of the latter was to maintain communication between the parent, the child, and the church and to help preserve the Greek heritage in the new land. These schools usually were taught by priests, to insure the church's influence on the new generation. Children went to public school until mid-afternoon, then they would attend the Greek school, which usually lasted until early evening. This process of a dual education made it impossible for the Greek children to participate in after-school activities of the public schools, thereby having a slowing effect on their assimilation and that of their families. In 1978 there were some 400 Greek-language schools still operating here (Moskos: 31-32).

The beginnings of their change from sojourners to Greek immigrants to Greek-Americans can be traced to the 1920's when the Congress first passed restrictive immigration policies. The quota system established by the Reed-Johnson Act of 1924 set the Greek quota at 100 immigrants per year! This number contrasted sharply with the 28,000 Greeks who arrived in the United States in 1921, the last year of open immigration. In 1929 the Greek quota was raised to 307, where it stayed for the next thirty years. Nonquota immigration, however, as a means of re-uniting families, allowed a yearly average of about 2,000 to enter between the years of 1924 and 1930. The closing of the door had a profound impact on Greek-America. Initially, there was a scramble to acquire citizenship, for only naturalized citizens could bring over family members or be assured of returning here if he visited Greece. Also, without the continued arrival of new immigrants, the American-born Greeks soon became the majority, and their ascendancy was inevitable. The new immigration policy set in motion forces that affected both individuals and demographic forces which shaped the entire Greek-American community (Moskos: 49-50).

Another important event was the impact of World War II. Italy´s invasion of Greece in 1940 brought Greece into the war. The initial and heroic success of the Greek army in throwing back the Italian invasion had an exhilarating effect on the Greek-American community. Very favorable coverage of the "Greek heroism" by the American mass media allowed Greek-Americans to bask in unaccustomed glory. A Greek-American War Relief Association was immediately formed. It raised some five million dollars in five months, contributing towards saving an estimated one-third of the Greek population. When the United States entered the war on December 7, 1941, Greek-American support of the war effort was overwhelming. With Greece and the United States united in the struggle against the Axis powers, Greek and American interests came together as they had never before done. Ahepa joined the Treasury Department´s drive to sell war bonds and eventually sold a half-billion dollars worth! One Ahepa member, Michael Loris, was named U.S. Champion War Bond Salesman in 1943 for selling 24,142 individual bonds. The famed Andrew Sisters, whose "support our boys" tunes made them the most popular singing group during the war years, were second-generation Greek-Americans. World War II became a sort of watershed in Greek-America: the war effort became a matter of Greek pride combined with American patriotism (Moskos: 50-51).

The war effort, plus American involvement in the civil war in Greece which broke out after the war, deepened the tie. The 1947 Truman Doctrine capped a number of foreign policy initiatives that brought Greece into the American sphere and made President Truman a hero within the Greek-American community. At a White House ceremony in 1948 Truman became the only President to be initiated into Ahepa, and in 1963 the Ahepa erected a statue in Athens memoralizing Truman.

The changed attitude among Greek-Americans was reflected in a changed attitude within majority society towards them as well. Today few negative comments about Greek-Americans are heard. Indeed, when they are

72

singled out it is often to serve as a model of a nationality group that has been accepted, has achieved economic security, and has become Americanized while retaining a strong pride in their heritage. The post-war years saw increasing numbers of Greek-Americans enter the middle-class, with a majority of them in white collar and professional occupations.

The post-war years also witnessed renewed efforts to change the limited quota, which generally failed until the 1953-1954 legislation which allowed non-quota Greeks to enter as displaced persons or through preferences given to close relatives. In the mid-1950's, 17,000 non-quota Greeks came to the United States, and by additional "borrowing on future quotas," some 70,000 Greeks came here between 1945 and 1965. The Immigration Act of 1965 abolished the quota system and led to a new influx, which probably contributed to a lingering of Greek ethnic consciousness and towards maintaining a pluralistic adaptation to American life.

Today's Greek-American community is estimated at about 1,250,000. Overwhelmingly urban, 94 percent of all Greek-Americans reside in urban areas (as compared to 73 percent of the total U.S. population). Over half of them live in or near about a half-dozen cities: New York, Chicago, Boston, Detroit, Los Angeles, Philadelphia, Cleveland, and Pittsburgh.

The central Greek-American institution today remains the Orthodox Church. Remarkably, the American-born generations are in many ways more Greek Orthodox than their contemporaries among the middle class youth in urban Greece. The introduction of English into the service exemplifies a process of Americanization of the Church, which is also reflected, to a lesser degree, in new architectural designs and other aesthestic aspects, and in the changing role of women in the church, and finally in the number of non-Greeks joining the church through marriage. In the 1960's, for example, mixed-marriage couples accounted for three out of ten church marriages, but by the 1970's that figure was about half of all such marriages. The Greek Orthodox Church stands midway between an ethnic religion and mainline status. Its ethnicity is self-evident, but its striving for mainline status is also apparent in its acceptance of the legitimacy of other religions, an acceptance based not on sufferance or tolerance but as a tenet of its own religion in the pluralism of America (Moskos: 66-116).

73

A similar picture emerges regarding Greek-American political involvement. By the 1940´s most Greek-Americans voted for the Democratic Party. First the New Deal, then Roosevelt´s and Truman´s foreign policies during and after World War II solidified Greek-American loyalty to the Democratic Party.

Some inroads were made by Republicans during the 1960´s with a weakening hold of the Democratic urban organizations, the movement of the Greek-American middle-class into the suburbs, and the appearance of Spiro Agnew on the national ticket in 1968 and 1972. But second and third generation Greek-Americans still vote Democratic at a greater rate than one would expect based solely on economic indicators of class status. Greek-Americans self-identify their political party affiliations as follows: 48 percent Democratic, 24 percent Republican, and 29 percent Independent; which reflects almost exactly the party identification of the population nationally (Siegel: 48).

Greek-American impact on American politics, however, comes not so much from its electoral strength as from the visibility of second-generation Greek-Americans in relatively high electoral office. Though the mainstream Greek-American group is socially conservative, some prominent Greek-American politicians have emerged from the liberal wing of the Democratic Party. Maryland, for example, elected Paul Sarbanes to the United States Senate in 1976, and he was comfortably re-elected in 1982. Senator Sarbanes, the son of a Greek immigrant cafe owner, is a graduate of Princeton University, holds a law degree from Harvard Law School, and was a Rhodes scholar. In 1978 he was joined in the Senate by Paul Tsongas, a Massachusetts Democrat, who is the son of a Greek tailor. Senator Tsongas graduated from Dartmouth and received his law degree from Yale.

The ninety-sixth Congress had five Greek-Americans holding seats in the House: John Brademas (D., Ind.), the majority whip who was also a Rhodes scholar; Gus Yatron (D., Pa.); Nicholas Mavroules (D., Mass.), the son of Greek immigrants who worked in the mills and who was later elected mayor of Peabody; L. A. Bafalis, a conservative Republican from Florida; and Olympia Snowe (R., Maine), who in 1978 was the youngest woman ever elected to the House of Representatives. Other Greek-Americans who held seats in the House during the 1970´s were Peter Kyros (D., Maine), and Nick Galifianakis (D., N.C.), a recently unsuccessful candidate for the Senate.

74

Several Greek-Americans are noteworthy at the state
level. Democrat Michael Dukkakis served as Governor of
Massachusetts from 1974 to 1978. Three others ran for
governor of their respective states in the 1970's:
Republican Nicholas Strike of Utah in 1972, Democrat
Harry Spanos of New Hampshire in 1976, and Democrat
Michael Bakalis of Illinois in 1978. Many Greek-
Americans have served in various state legislatures and
on state judicial benches. Several dozen have been
elected mayors of their cities, including some prominent
ones such as George Christopher of San Francisco, Lee
Alexander of Syracus, New York, George Athanson of
Hartford, Connecticut, Helen Boosalis of Lincoln,
Nebraska, and John Roussakis of Savannah, Georgia.
Scores more have been elected mayors of the small mill
towns of New England (see Moskos: 116-122).

This electoral record is all the more impressive
since, with few exceptions, none of these cities has a
truly sizable Greek ethnic voting bloc on which to build
a base for their electoral success. All have had to
pitch their campaigns to the general electorate. They
have received substantial contributions, however, from
the Greek-American community. Senator Sarbanes, for
example, raised several hundred thousand from Greek-
American contributors across the nation for his
successful bids to the Senate, accounting for about one
fourth of his total campaign budget.

Perhaps the lack of a sizable ethnic bloc allows
them to remain unconstrained by a parochial ethnic base
and they run without special appeal to an "ethnic"
loyalty. Such was the case of former Vice-President
Spiro Agnew. Emerging rapidly from a school board
chairmanship to become Governor of Maryland on the
Republican ticket, the relatively unknown Agnew burst
upon the national scene at the 1968 Republican National
Convention. His Vice-Presidential election in 1968 and
re-election in 1972 made him the leading contender for
the 1976 Presidential nomination until his resignation
in disgrace in 1973 ended his political career.

Agnew exemplifies the case of an assimilated
ethnic. Greek-American on his father's side, his name
was anglicized from Agagnostopoulos. Spiro spoke no
Greek and was an Episcopalian rather than Greek
Orthodox, but his father had been the owner of a small
lunchroom, an active member of Ahepa, and a pillar of
Baltimore's Greek-American community. Not only could he

be called a Greek, Agnew articulated how most of them felt about law and order, family integrity, and upward social mobility based on one's own efforts. His was an "up-by-your-own-bootstraps" mentality. He personified the 1968 and 1972 Republican Party strategy of appealing to the white ethnic vote.

His resignation after pleading no contest to charges of income tax evasion shocked the Greek-American community. But a survey of that community shortly after revealed an ambiguity of opinion typical of ethnic minority groups when confronted with examples of corruption among their "own." Some retreated to the rationale that he never was really a Greek anyway. Others responded with: "He may be an S.O.B., but at least he's our S. O. B." Most, however, acted with dismay at his betrayal of his middle-class constituency. In any event, Agnew quickly became a non-person within the Greek-American community (Moskos: 118-120).

Any inroads the Republicans may have made into the Greek-American community during the Nixon years were reversed during the Ford years due to the Cyprus crisis. In July, 1974 a Greek-led coup overthrew President Markarious of Cyprus. Turkey responded by invading Cyprus. By August, after numerous cease-fire agreements had failed, Turkey gained control of about 40 percent of the land area, displacing about a third of the nearly 180,000 Greeks on the island. Greek-Americans organized a huge relief effort. Angered by the Ford/Kissinger "tilt" towards Turkey and by the Turkish invasion of Cyprus, the Greek-American community was politically mobilized as never before. Led by the Greek-Orthodox Archdiocese and the Ahepa,they exerted great influence on Congress. The press began covering them as one of the most effective lobbies in Washington, D. C. Congress did respond by imposing an embargo of arms to Turkey in February, 1975, although restrictions were later modified. The incident led to the emergence of the American Hellenic Institute-Public Affairs Committee (AHI-PAC). An association to promote trade between Greece and the United States, the PAC operated as the lobby arm on the Cyprus question and sought to activate the Greek-American community to become politically involved. Also active were the United Hellenic American Congress headquartered in Chicago and linked to the Archdiocese which served as its umbrella organization to coordinate Greek-American political efforts, and the Hellenic Council of America, a New York-based

76

organization which enlisted professional and academic Greek-Americans for the cause. The issue united the Greek-Americans to a degree unprecedented since the Greek War Relief efforts of World War II. These efforts reflected the political maturation of Greek-Americans. It demonstrated to them the value of working within the American political system. The political mobilization, staunchly "anti-Ford/Kissinger," led them to back whomever the Democrats nominated. Greek-American organizations, including normally Republican-oriented Greek-American newspapers, endorsed Carter. An estimated 87 percent of the Greek-American vote went to the Carter/Mondale ticket. The effectiveness of their lobbying now rivals the reputation of the Jewish lobby:

> In Greek-American discussion it is common to contrast the perceived weak Greek influence of foreign policy with that of strong Jewish influence in support of Israel. Indeed, the Jewish precedent was frequently cited as the appropriate model for Greek-American efforts in behalf of Cyprus in Washington. It was thus something of a reversal to read a 1977 letter in the New York Times defending the Jewish pressure against Carter's Middle-East policies: " We (American Jews) were only acting in the American tradition, just as the American Greeks attacked American foreign policy on the Cyprus issue." Such a testament is a fitting footnote on the Greek-American entrance into the political system (Moskos: 122).

The Slavic Peoples

Immigrating overwhelmingly in the late nineteenth and early twentieth centuries, the various Eastern European groups traditionally discussed as "the Slavic peoples" were often treated alike and experienced many similarities in their emigration, acculturation, and assimilation patterns. They can be grouped into three regions of nations: the Eastern Slavs, the Western Slavs, and the Southern Slavs. The Eastern Slavs included the Russians, White Ruthenians, and Ukranians. The Western Slavs include the Poles, Czechs, Slovaks, and Lusatian Serbs. The Southern Slavs located in southwestern Europe, primarily in the Balkan Peninsula, are Slovanians, Croatians, Montenegrins, Serbs, Macedonians, and Bulgarians.

77

Although a few came after the Civil War, their migration is almost completely a phenomenon of the post 1870´s. Increasingly large numbers arrived from 1890 until 1921, when the Immigration Act of that year sharply curtailed their influx. During colonial times a few Slavic settlers reached the New Amsterdam and New Sweden colonies, and some Moravians joined the Quaker colony in Pennsylvania. The earliest Russian colonists date back to 1747 when a group settled in Alaska´s Kodiak Island. Some colonial-period Ukranians were missionaries in California. Polish-Americans proudly stress the role of Generals Pulaski and Kosciusko as heroes of the American Revolutionary War.

Slavic immigrants who came after 1880 tended to settle in the industrial centers of the northeast, some 80 percent of whom located in an area bound roughly from Washington, D. C. in the southeast to St. Louis in the southwest and to the Mississippi River, Canada, and the Atlantic Ocean. Two-thirds of them can be found in New York, New England, Pennsylvania, and New Jersey, with sizable numbers also in Illinois and Ohio. The major cities they settled in are New York, Chicago, Detroit, Cleveland, Boston, Philadelphia, Milwaukee, Buffalo, Baltimore, Pittsburgh, Providence, San Francisco, and Los Angeles.

Occupationally, the Slavic immigrants tended to replace German and Irish immigrants in the mines and factories of Pennsylvania and the midwest, and in the slaughterhouses of Chicago. Like the Italians and Greeks, the Slavic immigrants were often sojourners, comprising the majority of the more than two million aliens who returned to Europe between 1908 and 1914.

They all experienced severe segregation, frequently manifested in ghettoization and considerable economic hardship. The fact that their young boys began work at a young age, typically for a six-day, 10 hour-per-day work week meant that they all evidenced a slower rise up the socioeconomic ladder. Their peasant backgrounds, longer periods of economic deprivation which led to child labor, and therefore lesser formal educational achievements among the second generation, are all factors which contributed to their slower assimilation rates. This chapter will briefly review the experiences of four major Slavic groups: the Hungarians, the Poles, the Russians, and the Ukranians. The chapter will conclude with a discussion of Eastern European Jews.

The Hungarians

An estimated two million Hungarians came to the United States between 1871 and 1920, but about half returned home before World War I. About 30,000 entered the United States with the status of "special refugees" after the Hungarian Rebellion of 1956. Hungarian immigrants settled in large numbers in New York, New Jersey, Ohio, Pennsylvania, Indiana, and West Virginia. The two greatest concentrations were in New York City and Cleveland. By 1920, for example, 76,000 Hungarians resided in New York City, making it the city with the third largest Hungarian population in the world. Cleveland´s Hungarian population was sufficiently large for it to be referred to as "an American Debucan," and it grew remarkable fast:

> Between 1900 and 1920, Cleveland´s Hungarian immigrant population jumped from 9,558 to 42,134. From roughly 8 percent of Cleveland´s foreign born in 1900, increases in immigration pushed the Hungarian share of the city´s foreign born to 18 percent by 1920 (Weinberg: 174-175).

They emigrated primarily for economic reasons. Predominately male and single, many returned to their homeland after only a few years here. Where they settled they created an ethnic enclave with a surprisingly strong and lasting subculture. They viewed their life here in terms that suggest the persistence and transcendent importance of Hungarian cultural traditions, values, and norms. Their community, called Buckeye, encouraged the retention of their Hungarian identity. Their clustering into ethnic enclaves was partly a result of prejudice against them, but also a voluntary seeking out of friends and neighbors. Letters home drew many fellow villagers, friends, and relatives to join the Cleveland community. When a degree of concentration was reached, small businesses catering to the Hungarian workers were begun, which led to a thriving community of Hungarian butcher shops, confectionaries, bakeries, taverns, hardware, clothing stores, pharmacies, and the like. There, too, could be found the Roman and Catholic, the Lutheran and Reformed Churches, and the Jewish synagogue all serving them.

They concentrated in the factories and heavy industries with unskilled labor jobs, such as the nation's steel, iron, and rubber works. They also employed a padrone system, particularly to get them work in gangs of stone cutters in the quarries or as laborers in the South. Conditions were often bad. In the 1920's they worked an average 60 hour week for $10.50 (Weinberg: 177). They were mistreated by their bosses. Hungarians in the Georgia lumber camps, for example, were often whipped. One particular situation led to the bosses' being charged under anti-peonage laws, with ironic results:

> As the Hungarian peon recalled, a peculiar kind of justice was enacted. "Of all things that mixed my thinking in America," the Hungarian later wrote, "nothing was so strange as to find that the bosses who were indicted for holding us in peonage could go free on bail, while we, the laborers who had been flogged and beaten and robbed, should be kept in jail because we had neither money nor friends." (Dinnerstein and Reimers: 45).

In those areas where they settled in sufficiently large numbers to be visible and to be perceived as a threat, anti-Hungarian feelings developed among the native stock. The perjorative terms of "Hunky" and "Bohunk" resulted. They, too, were involved in the labor agitation of the 1890's, particularly those involved in the mines. A violent incident in Hazelton, Pennsylvania occurred in 1897. There a posse, headed by a sheriff who was a former mine foreman, opened fire on a group of unarmed strikers, most of whom were Hungarian, killing twenty-one and wounding another forty. There was general agreement among other mine foremen that had the strikers not been foreign born there would have been no bloodshed (Parrillo: 131).

The ending of their sojourner pattern also began with the World War I era and the restrictions placed on immigration. Once it became clear to them that their transient status was detrimental to them, they changed their attitudes and sought permanent status, thinking of themselves as "Hungarian-Americans." With the 1920's, those seeking naturalization rose dramatically. They also began to become involved in politics, and to vote regularly, usually for Democratic candidates.

Second and third generations began to move geographically within the settlements, expanding them outward towards better housing sections of the city. They moved up the employment ladder as well, becoming auto repairmen, carpenters, electricians and similar skilled workers. Boys were expected to learn a trade. By moving up the socio-economic ladder, they acculturated more, but still assimilated little. They remain, today, a strong and persistent subculture.

The Poles

Estimates of the number of Polish immigrants vary because the official records were not always counted separately and the area itself varied, at times being a part of Germany, Austria-Hungary, or Russia. Thomas and Znaniecki place the number at about 875,000. Other sources estimate their number at over one million (Dinnerstein and Reimers: 38; Parrillo: 174; Dinnerstein and Jaher: 232). Lopata (:38) puts the maximum at 1,670,000 for the number who emigrated and remained here from 1885 to 1972, and estimates the total Polish-American group (referred to as Polonia), at about 12 million. Other estimates of the "Slavic- Americans" range from 6 to 15 million (Levy and Kramer: 141-142).

Three-fourths of the Polish immigrants were farm laborers, unskilled workers, and domestic servants. Less than seven percent were classified as skilled. A fourth were illiterate, and virtually all came in with less than $50.00 in their possession (Lopata: 3). Polish immigrants were young males, also displaying the sojourner pattern. Their attachment to the homeland was perhaps enhanced by the fact that the ills of life in Poland could be blamed upon foreign occupation. Resentment of the Polish upper class seemed less than was typical among other Slavic groups.

Nearly a third of the Polish immigrants managed to get into farming in the Northeast and Midwest, concentrating in truck farming in Long Island and the Connecticut Valley, and in corn and wheat farming in the north central Midwest and in the Panna Maria settlement in Texas, which was founded in 1854 entirely of Polish immigrant families. Most, however, concentrated in Buffalo, Chicago, Milwaukee, Pittsburgh, Detroit, and New York. Chicago, with over 360,000 Poles, ranks after Warsaw and Lodz as the third largest Polish center in the world.

81

Men and boys shared common labor jobs, such as working in the coal mines of Shenandoah for ten hour days, six days a week, for an average of less than $15.00 per week! It was common for children to complete but two years of high school before working full time. That pattern, perhaps, explains why first and second generation Polish-Americans were slower in upward mobility than many other immigrant groups. It is not until they reach the third and fourth generation that Polish-Americans begin closing that gap. Today, an estimated two-thirds are blue-collar workers, some forty percent of whom are unionized. A recent survey of a Connecticut valley Polish community found that 22 percent were white collar and only 18 percent had attended college (Parrillo: 176; Lopata: 85-94).

The most influential institutional mechanism in the Polish-American community is the church. Numerous scholars have noted it as the unrivaled instrument for the organization and unification of the Polish-American community (see, for instance, Thomas and Znaniecki: 238; Parrillo: 175; Lopata: 48: and Dinnerstein and Reimers: 53). As with the Italians and the other Slavic groups, the Polish immigrants had difficulties adjusting to the Irish-dominated Catholic Church. Protest against that power structure took several forms: 1) parish mutual aid societies joining the Polish Roman Catholic Union (PRCU) which was organized in 1873; 2) the Polish National Alliance, founded in 1880; or 3) the Polish National Catholic Church (PNCC), begun in 1897 and reformed in 1904. Today there are 50 independent Polish parishes unified into the PNCC, plus an unknown number of isolated parishes spit from Rome but which have not yet joined the PNCC. The majority of Polish-Americans, however, remain loyal to the Catholic Church. As of the late 1960´s, some inroads into the hierarchy have been made with seven bishops and one archbishop of Polish descent. Polonia still maintains an estimated 800 Polish-American Catholic parishes (Lopata: 50).

Closely linked to the Church are the parochial schools. In the late 1950´s there were an estimated 250,000 elementary students being taught by Polish-American Catholic nuns and over 100,000 additional students in catechism classes. As of the early 1970´s, there were still more than 600 Polish parochial schools (Ibid: 51-53).

Another important institutional mechanism was the mutual aid society. They were highly instrumental in developing and maintaining an extensive Polish-American press, among which are five prominent dailies. They served as important links between Polonia and the motherland, and the Polish government tried to influence and manipulate Polonia in various ways through them. Polonia, in turn, sought to aid and affect Poland in various ways. It attempted to affect both immigration and emigration laws. It sent money and military forces to Poland, and applied political pressure on the United States government. Polonia, for instance, exerted great pressure on President Wilson to force the European powers to return Poland to the status of an independent nation-state, succeeding in that the thirteenth of Wilson's famous Fourteen Points called for an independent Polish state.

There were, and are, a great number of these mutual aid societies. They were initially formed to help in emergencies--sickness, death, and the loss of a job. Ethnic pride was such that the disgrace of one was considered to be a disgrace to the whole colony. Likewise, pride in the achievement of one reflected in pride to the whole community. Soon mutual aid societies began to organize balls, picnics, lectures, and periodicals out of which emerged the strong Polish-American press. They were also instrumental in founding or maintaining parishes or in supporting them in any conflict with the hierarchy. As of 1970, there were an estimated 10,000 fraternal, social, and athletic clubs based on ties to the old country. The largest, the Polish National Alliance, has more than 300,000 members. These benefit societies were especially active in American Liberty Loan fund drives. The Polish National Department, for example, which was created just before World War I, became the mechanism through which American Poles channeled over twenty-million dollars into all aspects of the Polish cause. That amount was in addition to the 67 million dollars they purchased in American Liberty Bonds during the War. Polonia sent 28,000 volunteers to fight in World War I. Between World War I and 1918, Polish-Americans invested over $18 million in Polish Government Bonds.

During and after World War II the linkage between Polonia and Poland weakened. While Polish-Americans continued to send money and humanitarian help, they sent few men. Polonia did push hard to get the Displaced

Persons Act passed, which granted exceptions to the quota laws and allowed an estimated 162,400 Poles to enter the United States between 1945 and 1969. Polonia also pressured the government against the Yalta agreements and sought to influence U.S. foreign policy to help rid Poland of its communist government. In 1944 the Polish American Congress successfully influenced our foreign policy to financially assist the humanitarian work of caring for displaced persons.

Polonia also banded together to cope with political and social prejudice. That prejudice is perhaps most evident in their being stereotyped as illiterate and mentally deficient.

Slandered, ridiculed and misrepresented in the media as "dumb Polacks," Polish-Americans have, for the most part, remained silent. This silence, with all its implications of ineffectuality, fear and intimidation, is the greatest problem facing the Polish community today. Too many of us are content to cart around for a lifetime the psychological and emotional damage that has been done to us by a continuing barrage of negative images, slurs, and so-called "Polish jokes"...What the Polish-American community needs more than anything else is an effective process of consciousness raising (Lopata: 77).

Initially, Polonia's reaction to that prejudice was to ignore American culture and to turn their attention to Poland. This was followed by mixed feelings of anger, withdrawal and inferiority. Since the 1930's, however, Polish-Americans have reacted by developing an ideology of America as a pluralistic society rather than as a melting pot. They have attempted to counter the prejudice by stressing Polish-American national heroes and contributions to American culture. They stress such heroes as Pulaski and Kosciusko, and spotlight outstanding sports figures, film stars, successful businessmen, artists, and scientists of Polish-American descent. They have also formed the Committee for the Defense of the Polish Name (Anti-Defamation Committee) to counter "Polish jokes."

84

For some time their lack of political pressure reflected their low levels of effectiveness as a voting bloc. In the 1920´s only about 25 percent of the nearly 130,000 Polish immigrants of voting age in Chicago were naturalized citizens. Their impact was further weakened by the splitting of their vote among candidates rather than voting as a cohesive bloc. Since the 1930´s, however, they have become consistently and highly Democratic, reflecting their blue-collar status. Today, of all white ethnics, Poles are most likely to consider themselves Democrats. Nationally, a 1970 survey found 77 percent of them to so identify themselves, and eight of ten did so in the Midwest. From 1958 to 1964, in a study of 57 elections for such offices as U.S. senator, governor, and president, the Democratic percentage of their vote was 65 percent or higher in 54 of those elections, and in one third of those (19 elections), it exceeded 80 percent. At any level of office, the typical Democratic candidate can expect to receive about two-thirds of the Slavic vote. In 1960 John Kennedy received 80 to 85 percent of the Slavic vote, and that dropped off by only two percent for Johnson in 1964. President Nixon succeeded in wooing away about 7 percent more in his 1968 and 1972 elections, but the Slavic vote is still about two-thirds loyal to the Democrats. A few Polish-American politicians have achieved prominence on the national scene, most notably: Senator Edmund Muskie (D. Maine) who sought the Presidential nomination of his party; and the late Congressman Clement Zablocki (D. Wis.) and Congressman Dan Rostenkowski (D. Ill.) (See Levy and Kramer: 142-155).

The most successful Republican candidates with Polish-American voters are moderate to liberal ones such as former Senators Case, and Percy and Senator Mathias. The first, and so far only, Republican to win a clear majority of the Slavic vote in a statewide race was William T. Cahill of New Jersey, who in his successful 1969 gubernatorial race received an estimated 54 to 60 percent of their vote (Ibid: 157-158).

The Russians

The earliest Russian immigration to the United States goes back to the mid-1700´s, mainly to Alaska and California. In 1792 the first Russian Orthodox Church was built in America, and as early as 1812 a sizable settlement was founded in Sonoma, California, which lasted for thirty years before the entire group of several hundred returned to Russia at the request of the Czar. The headquarters of the Russian Church in America was moved to San Francisco in 1872. It was after 1870, however, before a sizable immigration from Russia was reached. The first wave of Russian immigrants in the 1870´s were Mennonites who fled to the Great Plains area of the U.S. and numbered about 40,000. During the 1899 to 1913 period, 51,500 Russian immigrants arrived, about 45 percent of whom were Jews. The peak period was between 1881 and 1914. Most Russian immigrants were peasants seeking better economic opportunity. The 1917 Russian revolution essentially stopped emigration.

The 1910 Census found 57,926 foreign-born Russian immigrants living in the United States, more than half of whom settled in New York and Pennsylvania. Russian immigrants tended to move little once they settled in an area.

They did unskilled work in coal and other mines, worked in the iron and steel mills of Pennsylvania, and the slaughterhouses of Chicago. In New York they worked in the clothing industry and cigar and tobacco manufacturing. As with other Slavic groups, they held unskilled jobs in construction and with the railroads. Except for the United Mine Workers and the I.W.W., they tended to be non-unionized. Their pay was typically low-scale: in 1909 they worked for an average of twelve hours per day for just over $2.00. As late as 1919 Russian immigrants in Chicago earned only $12.00 to $30.00 per week (Davis: 17-37).

A few Russian immigrants reached agricultural settlements, which tended to be small and scattered. Most lived in enclaves in the cities, crammed into substandard housing. This geographic segregation reflected pressures due to "race" prejudice and their "strange customs," language barriers, and their voluntary desire to live among their own. The Carnegie Americanization studies described their housing as follows:

Wretched and unsanitary housing is not the immigrant´s responsibility alone. The native American must bear a large share of the blame. The coal and iron mining regions of the country to which so many Finns and Slavic peoples turned show some of our worst housing conditions. Shacks are built by both individuals and by mining companies close to mine shafts, pits and coke ovens. Tin cans, tar paper, and old boards furnished building materials for crazy shelters. Into one or more small rooms crowd the large families of the workmen. Toilets are either absent, or else miserable privies are erected and neglected. Outdoor pumps furnished water, and the ground served as sewer (Davis: 60-61).

Nor were the conditions for construction gangs much better. Typically, 36 men slept in three-tier bunk houses, precursor's of today's shacks which house the families of migrant workers and share croppers. In the congested Slavic ghettoes in the mining and iron and steel mill towns health problems were severe: tuberculosis was especially rampant. Moreover, the jobs were dangerous as well--in 1903 some 3,000 miners were killed on the job (Prpic: 87-89).

As with the Poles, the Russian immigrants sought refuge through their churches and mutual aid societies. By 1916 the Russian Orthodox Church had nearly 100,000 members in 169 parishes in 27 districts. They taught nearly 7,000 students in 126 church schools with about 150 teachers. As with the Poles, the Russian Orthodox Church in America split off as independent to escape the autocratic control of the Archbishop, who in this case resided in Russia. By 1920 there were such independent churches established in Chicago, Detroit, New York, Boston, Philadelphia, Brooklyn, Baltimore, Bayonne City, New Jersey and Lawrence, Massachusetts.

The Russian Orthodox Society of Mutual Aid, founded in 1895, grew to 188 Brotherhoods of 7,336 members. Similarly, the Russian Brotherhood Society, established in 1900, had 3,000 members by 1917. These groups were founded to provide health insurance, death benefits, and to help secure jobs. After the 1917 Revolution, however, another avowedly political organization was begun--the Society to Help Free Russia. This latter group was anti-Bolshevik.

Several American institutions served as assimilating agencies, most notably the public schools, the Jane Addams Hull House Movement, the Y.M.C.A. which provided English classes, and the Foreign Language Information Service, with its Russian-language press. Boston and New York each had five or six educational societies serving the Russian immigrants (Parrillo: 189).

Russian immigrants dominated several unions: the clockmaker´s, men and women´s garment workers, the Society of Russian Bookmakers, and the Society of Russian Mechanics. More importantly, some 200 Russian socialistic, anarchistic, and radical clubs were started as of 1917, the largest of which was the Union of Russian Workers. These groups inflamed anti-Russian and anti-Bolshevik attitudes among Americans which contributed to a wave of prejudice and discrimination.

In 1919 the American Communist Party was founded, and a splinter group, the American Communist Labor Party, followed in 1920. This led to the xenophobic reaction of the 1920 wholesale arrests known as the "Palmer Raids," which eventually arrested thousands and deported 500 immigrants.

A related reaction was the suppression of the Russian language press. The oldest such paper was the Alaska Herald, published in both Russian and English. In 1889 the periodical Sign began. From 1900 to 1920 a total of 52 Russian-language papers were published, many of which folded in their first year. As 1921, however, five Russian dailies were still being published, the oldest having begun in 1902. The fifth daily, the radical Novi Mir (The New World), was suppressed by the U.S. government in 1921. The suppression led many immigrants to return to Russia and cut off future immigration here. It also slowed the assimilation of those who remained by greatly depressing their participation in American life and politics. The anti-Bolshevik attitude spilled over and affected other Slavic groups, such as the South Slavs, the Ukranians and Ruthenians.

The Ukranians and Ruthenians

The Ukranians and Ruthenians share a common language and culture but differ in their primary religious affiliation. The Ukranians adhere to the Orthodox Church, while the Ruthenians are predominately Roman Catholic. Religion, as with the other Slavic groups, tends to be their strongest bonding force in the United States.

An estimated 700,000 Ukranians and several hundred thousand Ruthenians immigrated to the United States by 1914. The post 1914 period saw their immigration fall off to a mere trickle, except for the post-World War II period when some 60,000 entered under the provisions of the Displaced Persons Act of 1948. During the period of heavy migration they left in such numbers that "American fever" nearly depopulated some villages and regions of their homeland.

Both push and pull factors operated. A lack of land, high taxation, compulsory military conscription, and political oppression of foreign rulers were among the major push factors. Likewise, they were drawn to the United States by the free land homestead policy, the high wages and general economic opportunity, the personal liberty and freedom of movement both geographically and socially, the easier transit provided by the steamship lines, and favorable reports in letters from friends and relatives who had gone before them.

They settled in the areas popular with the other Slavic groups. Likewise, they were mostly unskilled workers, nearly half of whom were illiterate. They replaced the Germans and Irish in the mines, a succession that often led to rioting as strikebreakers clashed with striking Irish miners who saw them as economic threats (Halich:28-29).

Their typical pay was between $10-$14 per week, usually for a fifty to sixty hour week. Those with skills went into carpentry, plumbing and bricklaying. The women worked as dressmakers in the garment industry. Few of them reached the abundant and cheap land for which America was famous. They did found some scattered settlements in upstate New York, New Jersey, and Pennsylvania, and a few in Texas, Oklahoma, Michigan, Wisconsin, and North Dakota.

They suffered during the anti-Bolshevik hysteria. As a result, few became businessmen or professionals. They formed their own self-help organizations, such as the Ukranian National Association founded in 1893, and the Ukranian Workingmen's Association. One such group started out as the typical benevolent association, went on to develop into an athletic organization which began publishing a newspaper, the Seech, and eventually became a political group working for an independent Ukranian state. The Ukranian/Russian press has been mentioned above. Some 79 Ukranian papers existed between 1886 and 1936, most of which lasted less than a year or so. The press was split between a pro-Russian and pro-Ukranian faction.

89

Religion also played a dominant role in their lives. The Catholic and Greek Orthodox Churches experienced an era of building between 1884 and 1933 when hundreds of such churches were erected. About 96 percent of their clergy were trained in Russia. Since World War II, however, there has been a significant decline in church attendance among second and third generation groups. Church schools are found less frequently among them than the other Slavic groups, but there are a few such schools in Chicago, and even a Catholic Ukranian High School in Stamford, Connecticut (Halich: 95-126).

In political activity, they tend to vote Democratic as do the other Slavic groups. The anti-Bolshevik period discouraged many of them from participation in politics, so their turnout had been low. By the mid-1930's they did show some minimal involvement, with several Ukranian-Americans holding seats in state legislatures in Pennsylvania, New York, and Indiana. One, a George Chylak, was elected mayor of Olyphant, Pennsylvania and served from 1925 to 1930. A few have served as judges and on school boards in Indiana and Illinois. Nonetheless, the Ukranian-Americans, along with their fellow Slavs, remain today, in the words of Levy and Kramer, "the least assimilated of all white ethnic groups" (:142).

Eastern European Jews

Data regarding immigration of Eastern European Jews to the United States is even more sketchy than the other SCE European groups. About 40 to 45 percent of all SCE Europeans entering the United States during the 1870 to 1930 period were Jewish. One sources more detailed estimates of their immigration data is presented in Table Three.

Table 3: JEWISH IMMIGRATION TO THE U.S., 1899-1973		
DATES:	NUMBERS:	PERCENT OF TOTAL IMMIGRATION:
1899-1900	98,179	n.a.
1901-1910	976,263	11%
1911-1920	491,165	8
1921-1930	339,954	8
1931-1940	137,525	26
1941-1950	159,518	15
1951-1960	71,847	3
1961-1970	83,177	2.5
1971-1973	17,670	1.5
1899-1973 Totals	2,381,298	8.5%
Source: Dinnerstein and Reimers: 172-174.		

The Eastern European Jews immigrated for many of the same push and pull factors which motivated the other Slavic groups, plus the added push incentive of religious/political oppression which was ultimately the most compelling cause of their emigration.

By the 1860's the serfs or peasant classes were attaining a degree of freedom and slowly began to develop a small middle-class. Many Jews were among that emerging class. By 1860 about five percent of Russia's labor force was Jewish. Of that segment, eleven percent were employed in industry and thirty-six percent in commerce. By law Jews were forbidden to own land, so they became merchants, tailors, administrators, and other commerce-oriented businessmen. Consequently, many Eastern European Jews were urban people.

The Czarist government used the Jews as scapegoats for long-festering social, economic, and political grievances. They openly encouraged ethnic minorities, particularly Jews, to emigrate. The influx of Jewish immigration to the United States can be directly correlated with events in Russia, particularly the period of "pogroms" which swept Russia during the 1880's, 1890's, and up to World War I. In the "Pale of Settlement" area of Russia--the land between the Baltic and the Black Seas--these pogroms were especially violent, involving looting, pillaging, riots, murders, and in some cases, total destruction of the Jewish ghettos. Government troops would either sit idly by or even join in these ventings of frustrations upon the hapless Jews. Such pogroms were often followed by educational restrictions and eventually by expulsion. Since the Jews fled both religious and political persecution, leaving Russia was not as traumatic an experience for the oppressed Jews as for other Russian immigrants. Indeed, to remain in Russia was to risk life and limb, to remain confined within legal limitations on educational and occupation opportunities, and to suffer conscription of their youth at the age of 12 for 31 years of compulsory military service. Thus Jewish immigrants were not sojourners as were many other Slavic groups (5).

Their main ports of entry were New York, Phildelphia and Baltimore, where they often settled in large numbers in the low-rent areas adjacent to the city's business districts. These areas quickly developed into ghetto areas.

The Jewish immigrants differed from the other SCE European groups in several respects. They tended to immigrate in whole family units with every intention of staying here. They also came with better and more suited job skills, and a more urban background which eased their acculturation, especially into American economic life. Sixty-seven percent of Jewish males entering the United States were classified as skilled workers, as compared to the average of 20 percent for all other groups (Dinnerstein and Reimers: 44).

They were quickly active in unionization, particularly of the garment industry. The Amalgamated Clothing Workers and International Ladies Garment Workers Union (ILGWU) were predominately Jewish and Italian. By World War II, over 60 percent of the ILGWU members were Jewish, and the Dressmakers Local 22 of New York City was 75 percent Jewish. About half of the city's Jewish labor force worked in the trade. Other occupations they filled included cigar manufacturing, book-binding, distilling, printing, and skilled carpentry. In unskilled work they tended towards being pushcart peddlers and salesmen. A 1900 census study by the Immigration Service, however, found that the proportion of Jewish immigrants in the professions was the highest of all the non-English speaking immigrants (Leventman: 40. See also, Bayor: 14-15).

They experienced considerable and growing prejudice here, but nothing akin to the pogroms of Europe. In colonial America they were commonly disenfranchised. Such voting restrictions lasted until 1877, when New Hampshire became the last state to end such voting restrictions. Anti-Semitic attitudes were prevalent, however, and were reflected in the popular culture. Stereotyping was common; Jews, for example, were always portrayed as scoundrels on the American stage.

While their numbers were small, such anti-Semitism was easily dealt with by German-Jews. Early Jewish immigrants were mostly from middle-class backgrounds, mainly from Germany. They were at first fearful of the large-scale immigration of Eastern European Jews, and rejected the newcomers as a potential source of more virulent outbreaks of anti-Semitism. They tended to be correct in their assessment of the result of the large-scale influx. Eventually, however, when anti-Semitism did escalate, they closed ranks and helped the newcomers adjust.

In the 1870´s the largely latent anti-Semitism broke out into the open. In 1877 Jews were blackballed from the New York Bar Association, and in 1878 New York College fraternities followed suit. The Saratoga Springs resort began barring them, and soon a host of clubs, resorts, and private schools were doing likewise. The Ku Klux Klan revived in the late nineteenth and early twentieth centuries and became a leading nativist group which was particularly anti-Semitic.

The pogroms, which broke out again in Russia in 1903 and 1906, led to Jewish efforts here to help their brethren. The American Jewish Committee, made up primarily of Americanized German Jews, began to actively help the Eastern European Jews and to raise money for those still suffering in Europe. In 1913 the B´nai B´rith´s Anti-Defamation League (ADL) was formed. By 1909 there were over 2,000 Jewish charities operating in the U.S. which spent over $10 million that year alone. By the 1970´s annual Jewish philanthropy exceeded a billion dollars! These charities organized orphanages, educational institutions, homes for unwed mothers and for delinquent children. They established hospitals and a wide variety of recreational facilities. They supported the Jewish Theological Seminary, which trained rabbis, and the Yiddish language newspapers. Between 1885 and 1915, they started 150 such papers, including the highly influential Jewish Daily Forward (Howe: 518-551).

In both their religious institutions and their strongly cohesive family life, Jewish immigrants stressed education. Advanced learning was particularly emphasized for males. Professional jobs were held up as the ideal, highly valued for their secure incomes and their social prestige not only within the Jewish community but in the broader culture as well.

By 1915, Jews comprised 85 percent of the student body of New York's free but renowned City College, one fifth of those attending New York University and one sixth of the students at Columbia (Dinnerstein and Reimers: 53).

Education became the entry for the future as Jewish immigrants used their occupations as economic routes to achieve security in middle-class status and as a means of acculturation and assimilation.

Politics was little used at first. Indeed, of all the avenues of American life available to them, the party politics of the old style urban machine was the one which they were the slowest to enter. They brought with them little political experience, and they were uncomfortable with the big city machine politicians with their strange skills, codes, vulgarities, and the resultant corruption (Howe: 360).

The story of their eventual involvement in American politics—a success story to be sure—and their use of politics to influence public policy, both to assure their security here and to aid Israel through U.S. foreign policy, will be left for the next chapter.

Endnotes

1. See Leonard Dinnerstein and David Reimers, Ethnic Americans (New York: Harper and Row, 1975): 10-35; Marcus Hansen, The Atlantic Migration, 1607-1860 (New York: Harper Torchbooks, 1961); and Stanley Lieberson, A Piece of the Pie (Berkeley: University of California Press, 1980).

2. See, for example, Joseph Schafer, "Who Elected Lincoln," in Lawrence Fuchs (ed.), American Ethnic Politics (New York: Harper, 1968): 32-49.

3. These claims are cited in Parillo: 133; see also Louis Adamic, Nation of Nations, (New York: Harper, 1945): 181. They are disputed by the research of Schafer, Op. Cit. Not all German immigrants were enthusiastic supporters of the war. Rippley discusses several rural counties in Wisconsin where the Germans remained loyal to the Democratic Party. He cites the anti-draft riots among Germans in Milwaukee, and in Ozaukee and Washington counties nearby.

4. Parrillo: 137. Dinnerstein and Reimers cite the fact that by 1860 some two-thirds of the domestics in Boston were Irish: 26.

5. See Samuel Joseph, Jewish Immigration to the United States, 1881-1910, (New York: Arno Press, 1969): 5; and Dinnerstein and Reimers: 37-38.

Additional Readings

Babcock, Kendrick C. The Scandinavian Element in the United States. Urbana: University of Illinois 1914.
Burgess, Thomas. Greeks in America. Boston: Sherman, French and Company, 1913.
Davis, Jerome. The Russian Immigrant. New York: Arno Press, 1969.
Dinnerstein, Leonard and David Reimers. Ethnic Americans. New York: Harper and Row, 1975.
Federal Writers Project. The Italians of New York. New York: Arno Press, 1969.
Friis, Erik J. (Ed.) The Scandinavian Presence in North America. New York: Harper and Row, 1976.
Fuchs, Lawrence (Ed.) American Ethnic Politics. New York: Harper, 1968.
Harlich, Wasyl. Ukranians in the United States. Chicago: University of Chicago Press, 1933.
Herberg, William. Protestant, Catholic, Jew. Garden City, N.J.: Doubleday, 1955.
Howe, Irving. World of Our Fathers. New York: Simon and Schuster, 1976.
Iorizzo, Luciano and Salvatore Mondello. The Italian-Americans. New York: Twayne, 1971.
Levy, Mark and Michael Kramer. The Ethnic Factor. New York: Simon and Schuster, 1973.
Lieberson, Stanley. A Piece of the Pie. Berkeley: University of California Press, 1980.
Litt, Edgar. Ethnic Politics in America. Glenview, Illinois: Scott, Foresman, 1970.

Lopata, Helena Znaniecki. Polish Americans. Englewood
Cliffs, N. J.: Prentice-Hall, 1976.
Moskos, Charles. Greek Americans. Englewood Cliffs,
N.J.: Prentice-Hall, 1980.
Nelli, Humbert C. Italians in Chicago: 1830-1930. New
York: Oxford University Press, 1970.
O'Connor, Thomas H. The German-Americans. Boston:
Little, Brown, 1968.
Parrillo, Vincent. Strangers to These Shores. Boston:
Houghton, Mifflin, 1980.
Pierce, Richard L. The Polish in America. Chicago:
Claretian, 1972.
Prpic, George. South Slavic Immigration in America.
Boston: Twayne, 1978.
Rippley, LeVern J. The German Americans. Chicago:
Claretian, 1973.
Soloutos, Theodore. The Greeks in the United States.
Cambridge, Mass.: Harvard University Press, 1964.
Stephenson, George M. The Religious Aspects of Swedish
Immigration. New York: Arno Press, 1969.
Weinberg, Daniel. "Ethnic Identity in Industrial
Cleveland: 1900-1920," Ohio History, 86, 13,
Summer, 1977.

CHAPTER THREE: RELIGIOUS-BASED MINORITY GROUPS

Introduction

Chapter Two focused on the tens of millions of immigrants who flooded into the "Golden America" of the 1820 to 1920 period. A massive portion of those millions, and especially the twenty-three million who arrived during the 1880 to 1920 era, had a second characteristic upon which minority status was based-- their religious affiliation. The xenophobic reaction of the native stock as exemplified by the Know Nothings and the Ku Klux Klan was certainly heightened by anti-Catholic and anti-Semitic sentiments. This chapter will focus on groups whose minority status is based on their religious affiliation.

After examining some general points regarding the relations of church and state in American politics and how and why religion has been used as a basis of minority status, the chapter will discuss how religious minorities within our political system have influenced its political behavior. We will focus on their impact on both domestic and foreign policy, as well as their role in the development of the American two-party system. The major attention will be on three religious-based minorities as case studies of the impact of religious minorities on politics and policy. The Catholic, Jewish, and Mormon groups all share some common experience based on their minority status. More importantly, they exhibit some striking differences in the manner in which they interacted with the majority society's political system.

The chapter closes with a brief overview of how other religious minorities have had similar or different experiences with the American political system. Generalizations about the impact of religious minorities on political behavior and about the modifications of religious tenets resulting from political interaction will be developed throughout this chapter. The linkage between religious and ethnic status will be underscored from the perspective of how that linkage is shaped by and in turn influences the behavior of the American political system.

Church-State Relations

Religious minorities affect political behavior in a number of ways. They shape the structure of American politics by providing an organizational base for ethnic politics. They influence the political attitudes of their members. These attitudes, in turn, affect the political participation of those members both in degree and manner. Religious minorities influence the views of their members with respect to both domestic and foreign policy. Their participation has had a significant impact on both domestic and foreign policy actually enacted by various administrations.

Edgar Litt stressed the organizational base provided by religious minorities in our political system (Litt: 42-43). Religious organizations affect politics in many ways: by providing the pool from which the leadership of ethnic groups is drawn, by helping shape identification of their members over long periods of time, by influencing political attitudes on specific policy questions, by raising certain issues to the point of creating a public policy question regarding those issues, by serving as a screen to disguise the social and political objectives of some members, and so on.

There are various ways in which the church and state interrelate. There are those activities of the two which do not overlap one another, for example, those where the state allows the religious group freedom to preach, or where the state acts as a sort of referee over conflict between competing church groups. A second type of activity involves one in which the state attempts to use the church, for instance, the Kennedy Administration's use of church groups to recruit volunteers for the Peace Corps. A third type of relation concerns the church's using the government. Examples of this would be a church gaining exemptions from gambling laws to run lotteries, or the Women's Christian Temperance Union's pushing of Prohibition, or local Sunday closing laws. A fourth type of relations concerns their mutual cooperation to achieve compatible ends, as when the federal government and the Church World Service cooperated in relief programs for the Cuban and Indonesian "boat people." Then there are cases where the church defies government. We might mention the Mormon conflict leading to their flight to Utah, or the Jehovah Witnesses' long battles over their refusal to salute the flag.

Morgan maintains that conflict between church and state is inevitable because of a number of underlying tensions that exists between the two (Morgan: 19-48). There are, for example, numerous instances of ideological tensions. Differences in religious ideology produce very different civic attitudes about the proper relationship between religious institutions and public authority. Numerous tensions flow from the ideological principle of the separation of church and state. The rejection of "establishment" of any religion is upheld by the ideologies of Protestantism, Jews, and secularists. This view, however, contradicts the accommodationist predisposition of the Catholic Church, which favors cooperative arrangements between church and state.

Several psychological tensions might also be noted. Relations among minorities and between minorities and the state are often affected by unreasoning fears and emotional antagonisms which contribute to conflicts between church and state. Fears such as the Catholics´ almost visceral hostility toward the Protestant free-church tradition have emerged out of the former´s long experience as a minority faith. Anti-Catholicism and anti-Semitism exhibit a pattern which is almost a cycle, seeming to break out into periods of heightened tension every twenty years or so. These outbreaks seem related to economic and social trends. As Professor Truman notes, one of the most basic factors affecting a group´s access to public policy makers in society is the position of the group and/or its spokesman in the social structure (Truman: 265). Thus, when factions in the majority society experience dramatic alterations in their relative social position, they exhibit rapidly rising levels of anxiety marked by heightened antipathy towards social outgroups. Religious minorities are the frequent scapegoats for such anxiety. The 1928 Presidential campaign of Al Smith, for example, led to such tension that a specialized agency dedicated to containing hostility was established--the National Conference of Christians and Jews.

Structural tensions also give rise to church/state conflict. Differing institutions have vested interests which may conflict with one another and are variously affected by public policy. The massive parochial school system of the Catholic Church, for instance, is the basis for many church/state related problems. Jewish private hospitals are structures which shape Jewish views of public health policies which are in sharp contrast to the views of Jehovah´s Witnesses who have a pervasive suspicion of medicine. Proposals to tax church-owned properties will affect the major denominations with extensive property holdings far more than such policy would effect small sects with little or no property holdings.

These underlying tensions related to ideological differences, emotional antipathies, and structural disparities among the various minority religious groups set the stage for conflict among those groups and between them and the state. Such conflict breaks out when an issue arises in which public officials will allocate public resources or power in a manner which will adversely affect them. Morgan refers to such policy proposals as "trigger issues" (:36-48). Church/state questions are raised, for example, whenever a government passes welfare legislation since many religious groups have elaborate welfare bureaucracies of their own operating numerous welfare-type services: hospitals, orphanages, food distribution centers, schools, homes for the aged, and the like. When government passes legislation such as the Hill-Burton hospital program, the surplus food program, the War on Poverty, medicare and medicaid, or state and local programs affecting church-run child-care centers, these programs invariably engender conflict between groups variously aided or hurt by such programs.

Another major trigger issue is education. Aid to the parochial school system is a perennial issue. Tax support through various tax loopholes is yet another on-going issue. Donations to churches are tax deductible, and church income and real property are largely untaxed--property that nationally amounts to many billions of dollars which would, if taxed, produce tens of millions of dollars annually. Many groups favoring the taxing of such property have sprung up. Religious groups who are against the tax advantages of other religious groups, for example, are the Protestant Americans United or the American Jewish Congress. Others are secularist groups opposed to religion in general or against any aid to religion. The Free Thought Society of America challenged the state of Maryland in a case involving the controversial Mrs. Madalyn Murray O´Hair. The Maryland Court of Appeals (that state´s Supreme Court) upheld the church exemptions as constitutional.

Civil rights represent another trigger issue. Many people fear that tax breaks and other types of aid to some church schools will lead, inadvertently or intentionally, to public support of de facto racial segregation. With the recent upsurge in Christian schools founded by fundamentalist and conservative Protestant church groups adding to the already massive parochial school system, such fears take on an added measure.

Foreign policy occasionally acts as a trigger issue, as when the Jewish lobby is activated to support Israel, or when church groups criticize our nation's support of dictatorial governments which may be persecuting certain religious groups, or over fundamental policy such as the nuclear arms freeze, the SALT Treaty and similar questions.

Most such conflict involves domestic policy, however, which tends to be more pervasive in its impact on the religious group(s). As one scholar puts it:

> Despite occasional evidence of cooperation among the faiths at the middle and lower organizational levels, the general public impression of Protestant and Catholic relations has been that of frigidity, if not downright hostility. Nowhere has this impression received greater support than from the newspaper accounts of wrangling by religious leaders over legislative issues. It ordinarily seems safe to predict that if the National Catholic Welfare Conference favors a measure the National Council of Churches will try to rally the opposition. Or, at the local level, it appears that if a state council of churches takes one position the local Catholic prelate can almost surely be counted on to take an opposing one (Stedman: 104).

We can also distinguish the arenas of conflict: the constitutional arena, the national-level legislative arena, and the state/local arena (Morgan: 69-84).

The constitutional arena involves two amendments: the First, the "establishment clause," and the Fourteenth, passed in 1868, which extends the First to the various states. Conflict over issues involving

101

constitutional questions on the separation of church and state has a long tradition. The final vestiges of a link between state governments and particular religious denominations did not end until 1831, when Congregationalism finally lost its hold on the state of Massachusetts. Indeed, conflicts within the constitutional arena have increased over the years. Whereas cases over the First Amendment clause numbered only six or seven before 1940, it has been reviewed forty times since then. Between 1951 and 1957, eleven church/state cases were heard; between 1958 and 1964 twenty-two cases were decided; and the period of 1965 to 1970 witnessed thirty-four decisions, as did the period 1971 to 1974 (Wilson: 193). Those cases concerned a number of issues: state aid to parochial schools, grants to attend religious colleges, aid to construct buildings at religious colleges, busing to parochial schools, and shared-time programs. The central issue is what constitutes "aid." Restrictions against government assistance usually hinge on the "individual-benefit" theory in which "aid" is held to be given to the individual rather than the school or religious group (see, for instance, Sorauf: 261-360, or Morgan: 70-80).

Church-school cases have been numerous, important, and long-standing. The right of parochial schools to operate "in competition" with public schools was upheld in Pierce v. Society of Sisters, in 1925. Since then such questions as "released time," which concerned the Court in several cases during the 1950´s, and "prayers in public schools," forbidden in the Engle v. Vitale case of 1962 and challenged in various ways since then and as recently as the 1983 attempt to amend the constitution to allow such prayer, have been raised before the Supreme Court.

In addition to the "establishment clause," the "free exercise" portion of the First Amendment has been the subject of many Supreme Court cases. While the government clearly cannot forbid a religious belief, it can and does regulate certain "practices." The Mormons, for example, were forced to give up their practice of polygamy. Certain Indian tribes have been allowed the use of drugs in their religious ceremonies, while other self-proclaimed "religions" which used other drugs were held to be not a religion. Religious minority groups are limited in their participation in the constitutional arena by what is known as "judicial standing." In order to pursue a case through the court system, the religious

102

minority must become involved in a "test" case, whereby they back some member who deliberately "breaks a law" in order to test its constitutionality; or they file a "taxpayers suit" arguing some governmental program adversely affects them as taxpayers, thus demonstrating their "standing" before the court. In addition, religious groups attempt to influence court cases by filing "amicus curiae" (friend of the court) briefs.

The national legislative arena involves religious groups in lobbying activities. Professionals who represent the various religious organizations battle one another in their attempts to influence public policy. Various religious groups fought on the pro and con sides, for example, of passing the Elementary and Secondary Education Act of 1964 (see, for instance, Wilson: 84-94). Administrative policy conflict is illustrated in the recent controversy over President Reagan's appointment of an ambassador to the Vatican.

The state and local arena more typically involves amateurs who are only occasionally aroused, but frequently ferociously so. The manner in which state and local school boards have administered the E.S.E.A., for instance, has often sparked heated controversy between various religious groups. Occasionally various minorities ban together for a united front approach to local government--the Committee of Non-Public School Officials, for example, involves representatives of the Hebrew, Lutheran, and Greek Orthodox "Day" Schools. They often take positions in direct conflict with those of the representatives of the Catholic parochial schools.

There are numerous lobbying groups who consistently uphold a separation position (see, for instance, the discussion in Morgan: 49-60, or Stedman: 83-96). They advocate a strict "wall of separation" between church and state. The groups are numerous and varied, including a variety of Protestant and Jewish groups, educational groups, and non-religious groups.

Accommodationist groups represent the competing perspective. They generally advocate a policy which allows some state aid to religious groups. The primary accommodationist organization is the Catholic hierarchy and its various ancillary groups, such as the National Catholic Education Association, and the Knights of Columbus, which backed the Pierce case in 1925. Non-

Catholic accommodationist groups include the Citizens for Educational Freedom, founded in 1959, the journal Christianity and Crisis, and its related informal groups, and the Orthodox Jewish organization, the National Jewish Commission on Law and Public Affairs. These various forms of mutual assistance illustrate the use of "alliances," as described by Professor Truman in his classic, The Governmental Process. They involve the development of a common strategy among groups in pursuit of a policy which bears substantive relation to the interests of each (Truman: 363).

In large measure, the ability of a religious group to influence public policy and/or to compete with other groups depends on their social status in terms of being viewed as a "denomination" versus a "sect." Religious sects tend to be linked more strongly to political radicalism than have the major denominations. A basic tenet of American pluralistic society is that organized religions should confine themselves to general levels of moral discourse and avoid explicit political discussions from the pulpit.

Herberg (1960) argues that out of the cultural clash between immigrants and majority society there emerged three dominant religious communities: Protestant, Catholic, and Jew. Each of these achieved legitimacy and considerable political influence. The "ethnic church," he argues persuasively, was an innovation, an adaptation by the immigrants to their experiences in America, which gave them a sense of security and continuity with their old life within a bewildering new environment. Their religion was the one thing they did not change, nor were they expected to do so, as a result of their migration. Religion was a legitimate element to differentiate themselves as a group. He also posits a three-generational hypothesis in which the first generation immigrant holds on to religion as the one element of continuity between the old life and the new. The second generation, in their attempts to assimilate, weakened their linkage with the church. The third generation, however, typically renews and strengthens that linkage. While subsequent studies have modified his thesis, suggesting that revisions are in order depending on such factors as the person's age, sex, national origin, and even marriage and friendship patterns (see Winter: 197-229), nonetheless Herberg's pioneering work provides an excellent basis for understanding the organizational importance of the

104

church in ethnic politics. Frequently an ethno-political consciousness emerged out of the immigrant's church-related associational ties (Litt: 44-45).

We will turn our attention first to a discussion of the Catholic minority and its linkage with the urban machine and the development of the American political party system. That discussion will be followed by an examination of the comparable, although different, role played by the Jewish religious groups in shaping Jewish-American political participation.

Catholics

Today it is somewhat surprising to many that Catholics would be referred to as a minority group. With the Catholic population in excess of 46 million and comprising some 25 percent of the total population, Catholics have become the largest single denomination in the United States, and in Herberg's analysis, constitute one of America's three major religious communities. Anti-Catholic prejudice and discrimination have largely disappeared. But such has not always been the case. Waves of prejudice and discrimination have arisen and subsided in nearly cyclical fashion throughout much of our nation's history. More intense outbreaks of anti-Catholicism have been noted during the following decades: the 1760's, 1830's, 1850's, 1870's, 1890's, 1920's, and, most recently, the 1940's(1).

Pattern of Discrimination

During the colonial and post-Revolutionary War period anti-Catholicism was not as intense as later since Catholics were but a small portion of the population, and while unpopular, were not viewed as a particular threat. Hatred of Catholics was based on the English heritage of colonial society. Virtually every colonial government passed some version of a "non-popery" law. These laws were stiffened during the 1690's when fears heightened with the French and Spanish Wars. By 1700 anti-Catholic sentiment was so pervasive that Catholics enjoyed full civil and religious rights only in Rhode Island. The sentiment was reflected in a popular ditty of the day:

> If Gallic Papist have a right
> To worship their own way
> Then farewell to the Liberties
> Of poor America(Billington: 17).

105

Although tensions eased a bit when the French became an ally during the Revolutionary War, legal restrictions remained common. Seven states specified officeholders must be Protestant: Massachusetts, New Hampshire, New Jersey, Connecticut, North Carolina, South Carolina, and Georgia. Other states inflicted additional liabilities on Catholics in their constitutions.

Most such laws were dropped after the 1790's, reflecting the greater tolerance inscribed into the Constitution. Vermont, in 1786, and South Carolina, in 1790, dropped their specifically anti-Catholic laws. New Hampshire tried but failed to do so in 1792. New York dropped all of its restrictive laws in 1833.

With the waves of immigrants from the 1820's onward, however, a sense of threat began to grow and intensified into occasional outbreaks of violent anti-Catholicism. A number of anti-Catholic newspapers began publication in the 1820's: the Boston Recorder, the Christian Watchman, and the New York Observer. These were followed by similar magazines and papers in the 1830's: The Protestant, Protestant Magazine, Priestcraft Unmasked, and Priestcraft Exposed. The 1830's also saw publication of several notorious books which set the stage for the intense phase of the Know Nothing movement. Rebecca Reed's Six Months in a Convent (1834), and Maria Monk's Awful Disclosures of the Hotel Dieu Nunnery of Montreal (1836) were anti-Catholic polemics which stirred prejudice and aroused discrimination. They sold hundreds of thousands of copies and were called the "Uncle Tom's Cabin" of Know Nothingism. They were linked to riots in which convents and schools were attacked and burned down (Billington: 53, 70-75). They were followed by a number of imitations which further fanned the fires of hatred, depicting convents and monasteries as dens of iniquity: Master Key to Popery, Female Convents, Secrets of Nunneries Disclosed, Jesuit Juggling, and Forty Popish Frauds Detected and Disclosed. The violence became so common for a time that Catholic Churches had to post armed guards to protect their property and insurance companies refused to insure those not constructed of inflammable materials.

106

Clashes between Protestants and Catholics over the use of the bible in public schools heated local elections. The 1841 election of New York´s City Council turned on that question--an all Protestant slate was elected--as did that year´s city delegation to the state legislature. Even in losing, however, the Catholic bloc demonstrated its clout, running an independent slate, while the Whigs and the Democrats ran all Protestant slates:

> The Whigs swept the polls, going into office with a majority of 290 votes over their opponents, but if the 2,200 voters who supported the Catholic ticket had given their votes to the Democrats, that party would have won easy victory. [Archbishop] Hughes had demonstrated beyond reasonable doubt that the Democrats could not afford to cast off their Catholic supporters if they wanted success (Billington: 152).

The early 1840´s witnessed a new outburst of nativism and anti-Catholicism. Presbyterians, Episcopalians, Congregationists and Methodists united behind several violently anti-Catholic organizations: the Protestant Reformation Society, the Protestant Beneficial Association, and the American Protestant Association. Rioting erupted anew in several northeastern cities in 1835, 1839, 1840, and 1842. These were associated with several organizational manifestations of anti-Catholicism and nativism. The Temperance Movement began during this period. Several cities had formed a Native American Association. The American Republican Party was started in New York and Pennsylvania in 1844. The American Protestant Association led a controversy over church schools and bible reading in public schools. School board elections became tense battlegrounds which spilled over into rioting. The Irish sections of Philadelphia were rocked by three days of rioting, for example, which resulted in some thirty homes being burned down, thirteen people killed, and another fifty wounded.

Revulsion over the riots and bloodshed led to a brief period of decline in overt discrimination between 1845 and 1850. The Protestant Reformation Society sought to "convert" Catholics rather than to suppress them. The Catholic Church, however, reacted with a series of tactical blunders. Arrogant statements by the hierarchy, particularly Archbishop Hughes of New York, characterized the 1850 to 1854 period, during which time rioting again broke out along the east coast. A virtual "war" against the immigrant, with intense political agitation to restrict them was evident during this period, culminating in the rise of the Know Nothing Party. Begun in 1849 in New York as the Order of the Star Spangled Banner, in 1850 it became the American Party, more commonly known as the Know Nothing Party. Its main planks were anti-foreign and anti-Catholic. Despite its gloss and fine phrases, it was essentially a "no-popery" party advocating institutionalized discrimination.

Though short-lived, it enjoyed considerable electoral success. By 1854 it had successfully elected eight of the sixty-two Senators in the United States Senate, and 104 of the 234 Representatives in the House. They also captured nine governorships. Massachusetts was the state in which the Party had the greatest electoral victories--there the governor and all state officers were Know Nothings, as was the entire state Senate, and the State House had but one Whig, one Free-Soiler, and 376 Know-Nothings (Wilson: 313-314).

In part its success depended upon its being a compromise party. The state of Connecticut, for example, had twenty-three parties on the 1854 ballot. Between 1852 and 1860 there were a dozen parties nationally: Democratic, Know-Nothing, Anti-Nebraska, People's, Free-Soil, Fusion, Hard Democrats, Soft Democrats, Temperance, Rum-Democratic, Anti-Main Law Democrats, Union Main Law, Whig, Adopted Citizen, Republican, and even the Know Something Party.

Occasionally the Know-Nothing Party resorted to violence. The party hired thugs, called the "Plug-Uglies," to "plug" unfriendly voters. They terrorized the city of Baltimore in the 1850's. The party split over the slave question, however, and rapidly declined after 1860. The intense discrimination against Catholics subsided for a decade.

Job discrimination heightened in the 1870's when the economy was often troubled with recession or depression. This discrimination was directly related to, and directed against, the enormous number of Catholic immigrants entering the country from various national backgrounds.

In 1887 the American Protective Association was founded. It led the anti-Catholic movement of the 1890´s and was manifested most clearly in the Temperance Movement. The Anti-Saloon League, begun in 1896, directed a campaign in which "Rum, Romanism and Rebellion were pitted against Prohibition, Protestantism and Patriotism (Wilson: 314)." They failed to get the highly restrictive immigration policy adopted before the millions of immigrants from SCE Europe arrived. The intense prejudice of the period was mostly manifested in social and occupational discrimination rather than explicit legislation.

The 1920´s were another period of revived and intense anti-Catholicism. The leading anti-Catholic movement of this era was the Ku Klux Klan. Reborn in 1915 when the film The Birth of a Nation exalted the old Klansmen of the pre-Civil War era, the Klan spread racism and exploited xenophobia far beyond the South. Race riots wracked twenty-six cities in 1919. By 1922 the Klan had chapters in all states and an estimated membership of 5 million. It reached its zenith of power and numbers in 1925 when its membership was estimated at 8 million (Wilson: 315). The Klan pushed for restrictive immigration legislation at the national level and used social discrimination and terrorism at the local level. The Klan´s use of violence, including riots and lynchings of Catholics as well as Blacks, ultimately led to its decline.

Anti-Catholicism waned during the Great Depression when the politics of the country centered on its economic troubles. It arose again during the 1940´s and 1950´s when cold war isolationism and xenophobia increased dramatically. This period saw such anti-Catholicism manifested less violently and more subtly. The American Council of Christian Churches and the Americans and Other Protestants United for the Separation of Church and State became the leading proponents of the anti-parochial school movement.

Currently anti-Catholicism survives among some fundamentalist Protestants who tend to be less educated, relatively poor, and living in small towns, particularly in the South. It is an element within the "Moral Majority" movement of the 1980´s (Wilson: 316; Raab and Lipset: 44).

Although anti-Catholicism has virtually disappeared now, and with President Kennedy's election may have been laid to rest as a substantial factor in voting behavior, the long period of discrimination had significant political impact. As Litt notes:

> The result of these discriminatory experiences was a tenacious clinging to available opportunities in social and political life and, more recently, in the American corporate structure. It was this tenacity, coupled with the resultant problems in adapting to the noneconomic dimensions of liberalism within the modern state, that determined the major characteristics of Irish Catholic political behavior...The two most important facets of this behavior have been sustained Democratic partisanship and strong opposition to many noneconomic "liberal" policies (: 127-128).

We shall turn our attention, then, to the effect minority status had upon Catholic political participation, party development, and public policy stands.

Political Participation

The initial effect of minority status on political participation among Catholics was to suppress the degree of such participation. The Catholic immigrant, due to cultural background factors associated with their immigrant status, was typically a lower-class individual. That status depressed political participation. When a person is struggling merely to survive, political participation is often viewed as a luxury one cannot afford. From the 1830's through the 1850's Catholics participated less actively than Protestants in the political life of the nation. Today, unorganized Catholic groups, such as the Mexican migrant workers, still exhibit this pattern of low participation. Blue-collar workers generally participate less often and in a more limited manner than do middle to upper class, white-collar workers. And Catholics still tend to be disproportionately blue-collar in their employment.

110

Once they began to participate, however, their Catholic heritage shaped and channeled the nature of that participation. Church related groups became the organizational base for their politics. They often voted as a group--bloc voting--rather than as individuals. Politics, moreover, became one of the few avenues open to them for socio-economic advancement. The discrimination which closed off or limited access to the private job market forced Catholics--especially the Irish who led the way--into politics as an occupational endeavor and a means toward climbing the socio-economic ladder.

Once they began to participate, the parish-based political ethnic organizations had value in the eyes of native politicians because they provided a means by which voting behavior could be manipulated and delivered in large blocs. These organizations also supplied the means for distributing political rewards. Ethnic consciousness became an integral part of party identification and party loyalty. Although the party linkage was never absolute, the tendency was strong and long lasting. By the end of the Revolutionary War, Catholics--with Methodists and Baptists--were exhibiting strong Jeffersonian Democratic voting allegiance in contrast to the "high Protestant" groups (the Episcopalians, Presbyterians, and Congregationalists), who generally favored the Federalists or Whigs. By the time of the Civil War the lines were even more strongly drawn; old stock Protestants were Republican, Catholics supported the Democrats.

Political Party Development

Religious minorities figured prominently in the development of the strong two-party system. Political parties which refused to reach out to the minorities and build coalitions of voting blocs died off. The Republican and Democratic parties did develop such coalitions and machine-style organizations, and they survived and prospered. This process of two party domination did not develop instantaneously; it took many years to develop fully.

This two-party domination was not always true in the United States. The inability of third parties to elect members of the Congress in recent years contrasts strikingly with the situation in the nineteenth century. Between 1840 and 1860, some 165 third-party candidates were elected to the House of Representatives. Their success was neither a fluke of the early years of the "second American party system" nor a product of the divisions related to slavery. From 1870 to 1902, another 159 Congresspersons were elected under labels other than Republican or Democratic. After that, the number of third-party Congresspersons began to decline rapidly until they simply disappeared (Crotty: 104).

The Democrats ultimately captured the loyalty of Jews, who became proportionately their strongest voting bloc supporters. Catholic party members, among whom the Irish and the Slavic groups were the most loyal, were followed by those Protestants who generally were Baptists and neo-Fundamentalists, especially in the South. Republicans had the main support of Episcopalians, Presbyterians, the Mormons, and to a lesser degree but still the majority share of the Lutherans and Methodists.

This linkage has been sustained for long periods. Moreover, with both parties it increases as church attendance rises; that is, Catholics who regularly attend church are more likely to vote Democrat than Catholics who do not; and Episcopalians and Presbyterians who frequently attend church services are more likely to vote Republican than their co-religionists who infrequently attend services. Several studies conducted over the 1960 to 1972 period showed that religion is a more powerful influence on party preference than is class status. Indeed, "The influence of religion on political conflict has been to obscure class polarities (Lipset, 1968: 61)." That cross-class-status effect has survived the test of time. In a 1952 to 1972 study of religion and party identification involving voter analysis of Protestants (white and black), Catholics (Irish/Polish and others), and Jews, Joan Fee observes:

112

How does one make sense of these choices by religious groupings? One theory that seems to shed light on these choices is that "outgroups" or "minorities" are attracted to the Democrats. This theory offers a reason why three such diverse groups as white Catholics, Jews, and blacks might find shelter under the same political umbrella. Each group at a certain time in U.S. history has been discriminated against by the establishment-oriented Republican Party. Our findings seem to support the historical "outgroup" theories of Democratic Party identification...[they] tend to refute the spurious correlate theory that religion is merely a reflection of other demographic characteristics and that as old ethnic groups suburbanize the Catholic Democratic ties will diminish (in Crotty: 271-272).

When religion becomes an especially relevant issue, as it did in the 1928 Al Smith campaign and again in the 1960 Kennedy campaign, it can cut both ways. Many Catholics voted for these candidates because of their religious affiliation. But Smith lost many votes, if not the election itself, because of his Catholicism. Kennedy, too, was probably slightly hurt by it. While he gained Catholic support, he lost some expected votes among Protestants for that same reason.

The really intense linkage between Catholics and the Democratic Party was forged in the New Deal. That linkage, firmly set by 1940, has remained remarkably persistent. Their minority status, based on religion, affected more than their participation and party loyalty; it affected the public policy perspectives of Catholics as well.

Public Policy Impact

One of the most profound impacts of Catholicism on its members was a strong trend toward political conservatism. The experience of immigration shared by so many American Catholics produced a set of clerical and communal norms that opposed the general drift of American liberalism after the early period of the New Deal. Catholic Democrats opposed party reforms and much of urban renewal. They took conservative positions regarding the dissemination of birth control information and reformed divorce laws.

113

The Church, noted for its tendency towards dogmatism, stressed the acceptance of authority. Doctrinal orthodoxy and strong hierarchical control in traditional Catholic structures slowed the learning of political heterodoxy. Doctrinal orthodoxy was linked to a life-view manifested in conservatism on civil liberty matters as well. The Irish immigrant family shared a heritage that stressed the values of security and affection, with decidedly less stress on independence or personal achievement. Thus, white Protestants are typically more upwardly mobile than Catholics whose traditional family values stressed nationalism and religiousity. Catholics tended to be isolated from the reform movements of the late nineteenth century.

Such isolationism was, of course, by no means uniform throughout American Catholicism. One reform involvement which exhibited a heavy impact of American Catholicism was the labor movement. The Church hierarchy, awakened to labor problems by the strikes of the 1870's, 1880's and the atrocities of the Molly Maguires, strongly defended the Knights of Labor. Catholics had been prominent in labor leadership from the days of Terrance Powderly to the present.

In the first two decades of this century Catholics strongly opposed child-labor reform laws, even though child labor problems were severe. A 1900 census counted nearly two million children between the ages of 10 and 15 employed full-time. They worked above the streets in sweltering sweatshops and below the ground in the mines; working long hours for low wages. "Breaker boys" of 8 and 9 years of age worked from 7:00 a.m. to dark picking slate from the chutes of dusty, tumbling coal for wages of $1 to $3 per week (We Americans: 251). Despite such conditions, however, immigrant families often depended on those wages, and the Church stood in opposition to reform legislation, even when backed by labor.

Overwhelmingly pro-New Deal in the beginning, many Catholics changed their stance later. Among the most famous Catholic clergy, the "radio priest," Father Coughlin, changed from strong support to vocal opposition of the New Deal. He backed a third party campaign in the 1936 election, supporting Al Smith and his conservative "Liberty League." In turn, this faction was attacked by Fathers Ryan and McGowan and the Catholic Worker Movement, a strong liberal movement during the New Deal years.

114

The 1950´s saw a resurgence of Catholic conservatism, particularly in its support of anti-communism in foreign policy and its backing of McCarthyism in domestic affairs. Many Catholics voted Democratic on economic issues, supporting the Party in state, local, and even Congressional elections, but bolted to vote for Eisenhower in the Presidential elections of 1952 and 1956.

Kennedy´s election in 1960 returned many Catholics to their Democratic loyalties. The civil rights movement of the 1960´s, however, raised a concern over religiously-based social policies which once more led to a split between the Church´s leaders and many of its rank-and-file followers. The Catholic hierarchy was strongly and effectively pro-civil rights. Many ordinary Catholic laity were decidedly conservative and even anti-black on those issues.

Following its traditional concerns over moral issues raised by liberalized divorce and abortion laws, and programs supporting birth control, the Church in the 1980´s has emerged as a leading force in the "right-to-life" or anti-abortion movement. The conservative landslide of the 1980 elections swept a number of anti-abortion Catholics into office. As a recent Congressional Quarterly study noted:

> Once the most under-represented religious group in Congress, Roman Catholics are continuing to increase their numbers beyond their representation in the population as a whole. While Catholics currently number only 23 percent of the entire U.S. population, they make up more than a quarter of the 97th Congress...[following] a trend that began in the early 1960´s (Inside Congress, 1981: 148).

The Catholic percentage of Congressional membership rose from 19 percent in 1961 to 25 percent in 1981, up two percent from the previous Congress alone. Their strong showing reflects a decline in anti-Catholic sentiment, their dispersal throughout the country and especially into the suburbs, and the effects of policy issues such as abortion. Catholic Republicans, moreover, were on the increase. While Catholic Democratic members in Congress declined by about ten percent, from 102 in the 96th Congress to 90 in the 97th, the Republican Roman Catholics nearly doubled, from only 4 G.O.P. Senators and twenty-three House members in 1979 to a total of 46 in 1981 (Ibid: 199).

115

Jews

It is not surprising to most readers that Jews would be seen as a minority. This is, in part, a common recognition of the fact that nationally they comprise a small portion of the total population--about 3 percent. Discrimination against Jews, however, was manifested differently than that against Catholics. Perhaps the relative smallness of their group has contributed to their being perceived as less of a threat to the majority. It may be a reflection of their seemingly greater desire to assimilate. They have acculturated at one of the most rapid rates of any minority in American society.

Jewish immigration prior to 1880 was small. Prior to that time most Jews came from Germany, among whom were the prominent "forty-eighters." The first big wave, as we have seen, came with the Eastern European Jews when about two million immigrated during the 1880 to 1920 period. Unlike so many of their non-Jewish compatriots, they were decidedly not sojourners. While about a third of all immigrants coming here between 1900 and 1914 left, only 7 percent of Jewish immigrants did so; and between 1915 and 1943 the Jewish proportion of departures fell to under 2 percent, while it rose to an average of just over 42 percent for all other immigrants (Marden and Meyer: 397). Immigrating with no intention of returning to Europe was especially characteristic of the Jewish immigrants who, fleeing Nazism and the turmoil of Europe after World War I, came at an estimated annual rate of 10,000 beginning in the early 1930´s.

Jews can be divided by religious affiliation into three subgroups: Orthodox, Reformed, and Conservative. Orthodox Jews sometimes contain distinct "sects," such as the Hassidim, who are highly visible because of their distinctive dress, hair styles, and the character of their worship. They exhibit a strong Spanish/Portugese influence. The Reformed Jews, centered around Cincinnati and reflecting a German heritage, are more noticeably acculturated. They reflect a conscious Americanization in which they emulate the religious style of the Protestant majority. Reformed Jews are the dominant type among Midwestern and Southern Jews. The Conservative Jews are a compromise between the other two.

116

They all evidence a sense of "peoplehood," as the "chosen people," a dogma which operates as a self-segregating force and a divisive factor between gentile and Jew. It figures in the discrimination they have experienced and in their manner of coping with it. This "in-group" sense is also reflected in their strongly cohesive family structure, their cultural opposition to marriage to gentiles, and their high proportion of self-employed persons who concentrate in wholesale and retail sales. It also contributes to their being stereotyped as "excessively clannish" (Marden and Meyer: 400-402)

Patterns of Discrimination

The problem of being negatively stereotyped is among the more prominent manifestations of anti-Jewish discrimination in the United States. Gordon Allport (1958), in his classic The Nature of Prejudice, lists the most common stereotypical images commonly ascribed to Jews in the United States: shrewd, mercenary, industrious, grasping, intelligent, ambitious, sly, loyal to family ties, persistent, talkative, aggressive, and very religious. A 1950 study found Jews often viewed as: clannish, in control of everything, underhanded in business, overbearing, dirty, sloppy or filthy, energetic and smart, and loud and noisy (Allport: 188-189).

To understand discrimination of Jews in America it is important to place such discrimination within the context of anti-Semitism. For centuries the Jew has been a psychological minority—a scapegoat going back to the fall of Judea in 586 B.C. and the Jewish dispersal. Anti-Semitism was heightened in the 4th Century when Jews became typed as "Christ-killers." Law and social custom in Europe restricted Jews severely. They were often legally prohibited from owning land, forced to live in ghettoes, and legally limited to certain occupations. That occupational restriction led to cultural patterns which transferred to new lands when Jews migrated.

Anti-Semitism ebbed and flowed with social conditions which increased or decreased levels of fear among non-Jews. Chronic fear led to anxiety. Anxiety caused prejudice to rise, which was manifested in increased discrimination against Jews.

We are now in a position to understand the anti-Semite. He is a man who is afraid. Not of Jews, to be sure, but of himself, of his own consciousness, of his liberty, of his instincts, of his responsibilities, of solitariness, of change, of society, and of the world—everything except the Jews (Sarte, in Allport: 243).

Any strong emotions can trigger anti-Semitism. Greed led to the desire to grab what belonged to others, which led to anti-Semitism as a means to justify the grabbing. If a group's self-esteem fell, it could be bolstered by making them seem better than the Jews. Even sexual insecurity could increase anti-Semitism. In Europe, Jews are often sexually stereotyped in a manner one seldom hears in the United States—probably because here the Black-American is the preferred target of our sexual complexes.

Anti-Semitism can increase a sense of guilt, resulting in even greater anti-Semitism. Allport notes
... a gentile businessman was guilty of unethical practices that forced a Jewish competitor into bankruptcy. He, too, consoled himself by saying: "Well, they are always trying to run Christians out of business, and so I had to get him first." (:355).

Anti-Semitism in the United States can be divided into several phases. Prior to 1880 discrimination against Jews was not very prevalent, although during colonial times they did impose many of the same religious-legal restrictions as the mother country. Most Jews, for example, could not vote. Those restrictions fell, along with the anti-Catholic laws, after the new Constitution was adopted. Prior to 1880 there was little overt discrimination against Jews, except in a few places where German immigrants settled in large concentrations and brought their anti-Semitism with them.

The beginnings of real anti-Semitism can be traced to the post-Civil War periods of economic displacement. The 1870's were an economically troubled period in which many of the old upper class families were being replaced by a new industrial elite. By the 1880's, when such displacement was a considerable force, the influx of Eastern European Jews provided a convenient scapegoat for a society undergoing the pangs of industrialization.

It was after World War I that rather strong and open anti-Semitism became apparent. Such feelings were probably at their height in the 1920's and 1930's, when World War I and then the Great Depression upset so many social-economic positions. Much of the agitation leading up to the passage of the temporary Immigration Act of 1921 and the Reed-Johnson Act of 1924 [the Quota Act] was clearly anti-Semitic in character.

The only lynching of an American Jew--Leo Frank, a manager of an Atlanta pencil factory--took place in 1915 (2). Although the lynching was attributed to Tom Watson, a Georgia Populist, the more intense anti-Semitism of the 1920's was a product of the revived Ku Klux Klan. The Klan's Searchlight and Fiery Cross linked communism to Jewishness. This same era linked anti-Semitism with the anti-Bolshevik and anti-German attitudes of the World War I era. The infamous Protocols of the Elders of Zion, a fabrication of Czarist Russia, were widely distributed by the Fellowship Forum. Henry Ford contributed to this anti-Semitic campaign through publication of the Dearborn Independent, described as "...the most consistent and widespread anti-Semitic agitation that America has yet known. It touched off other movements and gave aid and comfort to lesser demagogues (Janowsky: 190)."

Social anti-Semitism began in the 1870's. In 1877 the prominent New York banker, and President Grant's nominee for Secretary of the Treasury, Joseph Seligman, was refused accommodation at the Grand Union Hotel in Saratoga Springs. By the 1920's such discrimination in social clubs, hotels, resorts, and the like was common place. A popular ditty sung by members of college fraternities around the turn of the century reflects this type of social anti-Semitism:
Oh, Harvard's run by millionaires,
And Yale is run by booze,
Cornell is run by farmer's sons,
Columbia's run by Jews.
So give a cheer for Baxter Street
Another one for Pell,
And when the little sheenies die,
Their souls will go to hell(Janowsky: 276).

Colleges and universities began to establish informal "quotas" regarding the number of Jews admitted. In 1921, a speech by President Lowell of Harvard stirred up a hornet's nest of controversy by publically

119

suggesting such a quota for Harvard. Although his
suggestion was turned down, the practice became fairly
common (3). Such social discrimination is hard to
document, but its pervasiveness undoubtedly worked as a
form of indirect economic discrimination. It persisted
for decades. A 1948 study by the Anti-Defamation League
noted evidence of educational discrimination:

> A 1948 American Council on Education survey
> reveals that an application for admission to
> college filed by a Protestant has a 77% chance
> of being accepted; by a Catholic, a 67%
> chance; and by a Jew, a 56% chance. Jewish
> students who live in the Northeast, who are in
> the first fifth of their class, and whose
> fathers are college graduates, have only a 60%
> chance of having their applications accepted,
> while Protestants have a 74% chance...A New
> York State Department of Education survey
> reveals that Jewish students who are in the
> top fourth of their class have only a 45%
> chance of being accepted by upstate New York
> colleges, while their non-Jewish classmates
> can count on an 87% acceptance rate
> (Weintraub: 9-11).

Similarly, Wilson cites a 1961 survey by Rights magazine
which found that 67 percent of social clubs practiced
some form of discrimination against Jews, mostly in
covert and hard-to-oppose ways (Wilson: 517).

Another area, somewhat more documented, of
discrimination against Jews has been in employment.
Marden and Meyer report on a study of want ads which
showed that ads requesting "Christians only" or "Gentile
only" appeared at a rate of .3 per 1,000 in 1911, rose
to 4 percent in 1921, to 8.8 percent in 1923, and to
13.3 percent in 1926. Such ads averaged 11 percent per
1,000 from 1927 to 1931, dropped to 4.8 percent in 1931,
but rose back up to 9.4 percent in 1937. And a study of
job discrimination in the 1950's sampled employment
agencies in which restrictions were stipulated in job
orders. That study found the following:

Restrictions in Job Orders:	1956-1957	1957-1958
Total Number of Job Orders Placed	218	303
Total Number of Firms Placing Orders	302	258
Number Restricting vs. Jews	142	83

(Marden and Meyer: 79, 409).

In the 1960's and 1970's, when the Federal Fair Employment Commission was established and began documenting discrimination in employment, Jews were second only to blacks in the number of complaints registered with the Commission.

All types of discrimination against Jews rose in frequency during the 1930's when the Great Depression hit. In 1936 a nativist third party movement surfaced blaming the Depression on "Jewish bankers" and on the "New Deal Jewish radicals." Father Charles Coughlin turned on Roosevelt and the New Deal and exhibited strident anti-Semitism in his Christian Front. William Pelley, in part financed by Nazi funds, established the Silver Shirts and distributed literally tons of anti-Semitic propaganda through the mails. This crescendo of anti-Jewish propaganda correlated with the increasing strength of Nazi movement in Europe. The Fascist group, Friends of New Germany, channeled Nazi funds to Pelley and to Robert Edmondson in the 193o's. By 1940 there were 121 organizations whose stock in trade was anti-Semitism. Among the more prominent of such were the American Aryan Fold Association, the American Gentile Protective Association, the White Shirts, the World Alliance Against Jewish Aggression, the Pro-Christian American Society, the Silver Shirts, the German-American Front, the National Union for Social Justice, the Edmondson Economic Service, the American Vigilant Intelligence Service, and the America First Movement. The foreign-language press, especially the German and Polish press, was often stridently anti-Semitic during this period (Janowsky: 193-195).

As with social discrimination, evidence of housing discrimination against Jews is mostly indirect. Some "restrictive covenants" were used against Jews until that practice--aimed primarily against blacks--was made illegal (see Vose, 1959). The informal practice of realtors to refrain from showing certain homes to Jews, known as racial steering, was allegedly a common practice.

Vandalism against Jewish properties is an ongoing and somewhat cyclically re-occurring example of anti-Jewish discrimination. Cemeteries are popular targets. Another practice is the defacing of Jewish synagogues and other buildings with the Swastica. Such acts seem more prevalent in some areas than in others. For some reason, Arizona exhibits a higher number of such cases relative to its proportion of Jewish population (Marden and Meyer: 412).

121

Another area which many Jews feel constitutes legal discrimination against them, while imposing an economic hardship as well, is that of the Sunday closing or "blue" laws. In 1967 laws prohibiting sales on Sunday existed in 37 of the 50 states. In 1961 the U.S. Supreme Court, hearing four cases, upheld the constitutionality of the blue laws. Chief Justice Warren, speaking for the majority, reasoned as follows:

> Hence, although avowedly recognizing the "religious origin" of Sunday laws, the Chief Justice in his four opinions, hit hard upon the general theme that, in effect, their religious purposes were no longer present; that in the present day the purpose of the legislature in enacting such laws was to set aside a day not for religious observance but for "rest, relaxation, and family togetherness," with the motivation thus being "secular rather than religious;" that--with an eye toward the Orthodox Jewish merchant-- although the freedom to hold religious beliefs and opinions is absolute, what was involved in the cases at issue was not freedom to hold religious beliefs and opinions but freedom to act; and that such freedom, even when motivated by bone fide religious convictions, did not supersede laws duly enacted under the state police powers (Abraham: 203).

Justice Douglas, in dissent, observed the inherent economic penalty of the blue laws. In contrast, he argued:

> If the Sunday laws are constitutional, Kosher markets are on a five-day week. Thus those laws put an economic penalty on those who observe Saturday rather than Sunday as the Sabbath. For the economic pressures on these minorities, created by the fact that our communities are predominately Sunday-minded, there is no recourse. When, however, the State uses its coercive powers--here the criminal law--to compel minorities to observe a second Sabbath, not their own, the state undertakes to aid and "prefer one religion over another"--contrary to the command of the Constitution (Ibid: 203-204).

Discrimination against Jews in the United States, then, has been pervasive and persistent. While undoubtedly more moderate than in Europe, American anti-Semitism has sometimes been intense, although clearly less violent than American anti-Catholicism. No violent mob actions of burning down synagogues, attacking rabbis, or lynching Jews has broken out in the United States even during periods of more intense anti-Semitism. Here it has been more subtle, if none-the-less pervasive.

Political Participation

American Jews, as was the case with Catholics, found that politics became a necessary activity for coping with minority status. The Jewish minority was initially not very active in politics. Their first few decades were spent consolidating their economic positions in urban America. The split what little voting participation they had among the various political parties available. The older Jewish immigrants from Germany and Austria tended to be more politically active and showed a slight trend to support Republicans. The newer immigrants from Eastern Europe were initially very inactive, and the few who did involve themselves in politics tended to support the Democratic urban machines or were found among urban radical groups such as the Socialist or Communist parties.

Jewish organizations had to develop before effective political participation could be manifested. In New York City, for example, as late as 1923 only six of the thirty-six district leaderships were Jewish, despite that city's very Jewish concentration. It was not until 1973 that the first Jewish mayor of New York was elected.

What finally brought Jewish voters into an active and cohesive bloc was the highly motivating emotion of fear (see Mathias: 991). That fear, which another analyst considers to be the greatest single factor accounting for the high level of Jewish political activity which recently has been marked above the national average, also influences the higher levels of financial contributions. "Jews are paying to put in power the kind of men who will neither confiscate Jews' assets, wall them into ghettos, nor annihilate them " (Issacs: 15).

123

Jewish voters are highly cohesive, have higher than average turnout rates, and bloc vote in a manner which crosses class lines.

Normally some part of voting behavior is due to race or religion or ethnicity, but most is due to class. With Jews, less of their voting is due to class. This could mean that in politics, Jews ignore self-interest. But is self-interest necessarily the same as class interest? It was not because Jews were businessmen or workers, lawyers or clerks, that Hitler murdered them. In the United States, it is not that the class interest of Jews has not counted at all--the 10 percent who voted for Goldwater in 1964 were surely richer, on the average, than the 90 percent who voted against him--only that it has counted for relatively little (Himmelfarb: 302).

Their cross-class voting is often motivated by their rejection of a candidate as much as it is by their voting for a liberal candidate. In 1964 President Johnson--to Jewish voters hardly a hero on a par with Franklin Roosevelt--still received as high a proportion of their vote as did hero Roosevelt. Many of the 90 percent who voted for Johnson were undoubtedly voting against Goldwater. Although "Mr. Conservative" was hardly an anti-Semite nor an enemy of Israel, the day before the election a leading rabbi could cry out: "A Jewish vote for Goldwater is a vote for Jewish suicide," and 90 percent seemed to agree (Ibid: 300).

As a group Jews have not only shown a high turnout and financial support for politics, but also a strong allegiance to the Democratic Party. It is to that commitment we next turn our attention.

Political Party Development

Initially the Jewish vote was neither high in turnout nor cohesive in affiliation. Prior to the Civil War the lack of anti-Semitism allowed Jews who wished to do so to participate in whichever political organization their interests inclined them to support. They voted for Whigs, Republicans, and Democrats depending mostly on the section of the country within which they lived and in a manner roughly comparable to native-stock voters.

124

Between the 1870's and the 1930's the more active Jews were those from Germany or their descendents. They tended to be more Republican than Democratic, at least in national-level elections, but not overwhelmingly so. In state and local politics they presented an even greater mix of party affiliations. While many of the Eastern European Jews supported the Democrats, relations with the growing machines, such as Tammany Hall, were neither close nor sustained. When Tammany offered the mayoral nomination to a prominent New York Jew, Nathan Strauss, in 1884, he rejected the offer as "tainted." During this period other Jewish voters were "Mugwumps," intensely issue-oriented. Rather than supporting parties, they supported candidates who took stands on issues which they favored. Some Jewish reformers were associated with the Progressive Movement [e.g. Wise, Seligman, Nathan and Brandeis]. Jewish leaders within the Citizen's Union, begun in 1897, and the Jewish Worker's Alliance, supported Teddy Roosevelt. Jewish immigrants from Eastern Europe were the backbone of the minor Anarchist and Socialist movements from 1880 to 1920. Jewish voters were often pushed by the dominant Irish leadership of the Democratic Party as they were attracted to the Republicans, but they would support a candidate from any party given the right issue. Thus, Woodrow Wilson received strong Jewish support in 1914. James Curley, in his 1913 bid for mayor of Boston, won an estimated 85 percent of that city's Jewish vote. The Socialist Eugene Debs was popular among New York's Jewish voters. Yet at the state level, of eleven Jews elected to the New York Senate in 1914, two were Republicans and nine were Democrats, and in the House, five were Republicans and two were Socialists (4).

This mixed pattern remained during the interwar years, although a slight shift towards the Democratic Party was seen even then. In New York City the Republican Party, under La Guardia, first put Jews into "cabinet-level" positions. But the Tammany Hall machine also worked hard to attract Jewish support. The Tammany Hall Law Committee became a virtual "Jewish preserve," and Jews began to enter the bureaucracy and party positions. Wilson's popularity was further enhanced with Jewish voters when he appointed Louis Brandeis to the Supreme Court in 1916. That shift was further established by Al Smith's candidacy in 1928. His selection of several Jewish advisors, such as Belle Moskowitz, attracted many second generation Jewish intellectuals to the party and foreshadowed the New Deal coalition of the 1930's (see Howe: 383-391).

The growing anti-Semitism of the 1920's, which led to social ostracism by an upper-class which was overwhelmingly Republican, drove many Jews of all classes into Democratic ranks. Roosevelt also attracted them with his liberal policies and his Jewish "kitchen-cabinet" advisors. The American Labor Party, which in 1936 was dominated by Jewish leadership, endorsed Roosevelt. By 1944 that party had evolved into the Liberal Party which consistently supported Roosevelt. As Greeley notes, the New Deal coalition was built in large measure by new voters entering politics for the first time, moving in overwhelming percentages to the Democratic column:

> The Roosevelt realignment was essentially the result of the New Deal winning to the Democratic Party the hitherto unaffiliated sons and daughters of the urban working class--particularly its recent immigrant Jewish and Catholic components (Greeley: 277).

Father Charles Coughlin and the isolationist movement of the late 1930's and early 1940's further cemented the Jewish/Democratic bond. The anti-Semitic campaign here, plus the events in Europe, created a level of fear which served to bond Jewish voters to the New Deal with a strength that withstood the strains of time better than any other group except perhaps the black voting bloc, which while it may have been as cohesive, was seldom as high in proportionate turnout. Indeed, Jewish support for President Kennedy in 1960 was proportionately higher than his support among Irish-Catholic Americans! (See Feingold: 274-275).

Table Four illustrates the high and continuous Jewish voter support for Democratic Presidential candidates from 1940 to 1984. Although that support began to weaken and erode throughout the 1970's and into the 1980's, it is still a major bloc upon which the party relies. And as we shall see more fully below, the liberal public policy impact of the Jewish minority has been as consistent and persistent as has been their Democratic Party allegiance during this century.

Table 4:   JEWISH PRESIDENTIAL VOTE: PERCENT DEMOCRATIC,
1940-1980

ELECTION YEAR: PERCENT DEMOCRATIC,   JEWISH VOTERS

1940	84%
1944	91
1948	72
1952	72
1956	71
1960	85
1964	90
1968	82
1972	63
1976	68
1980	45
1984	65

Source: Data for 1940-1960, Ladd: 115;   for 1964-
1968, Feingold: 274-275;   for 1972-1976,
Pomper,   1976: 61; for 1980, Pomper, 1981:
71;   and for 1984, Time, November 19,
1984: 45.

Public Policy Impact

Two key features mark the Jewish impact on United
States public policy: 1) a marked liberal stance on
domestic social and economic policy, and 2) a strong
internationalist emphasis in foreign policy with a
zealous support for the creation and continued well-
being of the State of Israel.

Their liberalism in domestic policy, along with
their long-term attachment to the Democratic Party, are
the distinguishing features of Jewish political
behavior.   They are committed to a view which favors the
use of the powers and programs of the federal government
to ameliorate social ills.   Their high level of
participation in voluntary organizations and in the
opinion forming networks of American public life have
pushed that view consistently.   They strongly support
racial integration, and the use of governmental power to
promote the educational, social, and psychological well-
being of the individual.

Litt argues that there are two critical elements to
Jewish liberalism: 1) from their culture, a high
motivation to succeed coupled with a concern for the
oppressed;   and 2) an emphasis on group success, from

127

family to various voluntary organizations. Litt stresses the fact that of all ethnic groups in America, the Jews developed the broadest and most specialized organizational structures—for welfare, trade unions, political clubs, professional and fraternal associations (Litt: 119).

Himmelfarb, however, argues persuasively that Jewish liberalism is in large measure due to the fact that traditionally their enemies—even in Czarist Russia, and in Poland—have been on the political right. And in America:

> For most of the past hundred years nativism has been strong in America; it has been against the Jews, and it has usually been of the right...the Ku Klux Klan was of the right. Quotas against Jews in colleges and professional schools were the work of a conservative elite. So were discrimination in the professions and business, and exclusion from clubs and fraternities. Nativist isolationism was anti-anti-Nazi, and mostly conservative (Himmelfarb: 299-300).

Organizationally, Jewish defensive groups such as the Anti-Defamation League of B´nai B´rith, the American Jewish Congress, and the American Jewish Committee were all begun to counteract anti-Semitism, but all have developed into liberal research and clearinghouse organizations for minority groups in general—becoming active in minority issues beyond those specifically related to the Jewish minority.

Indeed, at times their liberal policy concerns override the appeal of more narrowly perceived ethnic appeals. In 1964, for example, many Jews—particularly the younger and more affluent, voted for liberal Republican John Lindsay over the machine candidate and fellow Jew but conservative Abraham Beame. Party label and religious affiliation counted for less with these Jewish voters than did the candidate´s liberalism (Feingold: 319).

With respect to education policy, Jews support public education, and have been leading proponents of the "absolute wall of separation" view of church and state relations with respect to federal aid to parochial schools. They have also been very strong proponents of

128

welfare programs, which they seem to view as an extension of Jewish cultural values in that government power is used to heal society's ills and to expand—to other powerless minorities—the distribution of power and equality of opportunity.

In foreign policy, American Jews have a strong tradition of involvement and an abiding emphasis upon internationalism. Since the 1840's, with the Damascus case, and with the Moratara Kidnapping incident in 1858, American Jews have attempted to influence U.S. foreign policy towards international involvement. They sought to use national power to defend or aid Jews throughout the world. In 1855 they created the Board of Delegates of American Israelites. This group, operating until 1887, sought to force U.S. foreign policy to restrict or contain the harshly anti-Semitic policy of Czarist Russia.

The bloody Kishineff pogrom of 1903 re-aroused Jewish efforts to influence American foreign policy. Throughout the 1900 to 1920 period they attempted to influence Presidents Taft, Roosevelt, and Wilson to support the creation of a Jewish home state or to provide relief to Jewish refugees from oppression in Europe. The Zionist Movement in the United States agitated for a Jewish homeland in Palestine. In Britain the Balfour Declaration of 1917 was the culmination of British Zionist efforts. The American Zionist movement pushed to have America support the Declaration. In 1918 the American Jewish Congress was particularly successful with the Wilson Administration in that the 13th of his famous Fourteen Points called for the creation of a Jewish state.

This policy concern continues today. In 1981, for instance, the Jewish lobby attempted to stop the AWACS sale to Saudi Arabia. More will be said of the Jewish foreign policy impact in Chapter Nine. Suffice it say here that their influence has been both strong and abiding, clearly among the most active and influential in Washington, D.C. and the overwhelming U.S. support of Israel is in no small measure a reflection of the effectiveness of that lobby.

As with Catholics, American Jews have recently picked up seats in the current Congress and now have greater representation in Congress that their proportional share of the total population. In the 97th

129

Congress, they comprise 6 percent, while their share of the total population, according to the 1980 census data, is only 3 percent. There are 27 Jewish members in the House, 21 Democrats and 6 Republicans (Inside Congress: 198-199).

In this period of increasing conservatism in American politics and with the old coalition of the New Deal having fragmented, the continued link between Jewish affiliation and their liberal stance and the effectiveness of the Jewish lobby is open to question. The U.S. foreign policy shift towards the Arab states and the sale of the AWACS to Saudi Arabia despite intense Jewish lobby efforts to block the sale, indicate a weakening of influence. In domestic policy, moreover, the traditional Jewish pro-welfare stance has clearly been moderated. Black/Jewish conflict which has marked the 1970's and 1980's, exacerbated most recently with the Reverend Jesse Jackson's campaign for the Democratic Party's presidential nomination, also portends a decline in Jewish interest in the liberal cause.

The Mormons

The Church of Jesus Christ of the Latter-Day Saints undoubtedly experienced the most severe repression, at least if measured by the violence against them, legal restrictions imposed upon them, and their ultimately being forced to change an important tenet of their faith because of majority societal pressure. The case of the Mormons, moreover, presents a much clearer example of religious discrimination since, initially at least, it was a native-born minority faith and therefore involved no "anti-foreign" prejudice against it.

Its founder, Joseph Smith, was born in Vermont in 1805. His family moved to Palmyra, New York, in 1816. It was near there that Smith claimed he first received his revelations from God, through the visit of an angel, Moroni, which began in 1823. In 1827 Smith supposedly "discovered the tablets" which he published in July of 1829, known as The Book of Mormon. On April 6, 1830, Smith and six of his followers formally established the Church of Jesus Christ of the Latter-Day Saints.

Moving from New York to Ohio and then to Missouri, because of persecution, Smith was killed by a mob storming the jail in which he was being held in Carthage, Missouri, on June 28, 1844.

130

It is not surprising that the first, and until the assassination of Malcolm X in 1965 the only, American religious leader to be murdered was a Mormon, for the Saints have always inflamed passions (Hirshon: 50).

Patterns of Discrimination

Discrimination against the Mormons developed early involved the reactions of expulsion through the use of violence, as well as applying the force of law to pressure the minority to change its tenets to be more acceptable to the views of the majority society.

The principle of their faith which caused the Mormons so much trouble was polygamy, or the plural marriage principle. Other aspects of their religion also contributed to the majority's antipathy. Early Mormons stressed "speaking-in-tongues," and faith healing. Its Catholic Church-like dogmatism also aroused much animosity, although that aspect of the faith also attracted many of its early converts who came from the lower classes and seem to respond to its dogmatism which provided a sense of security in the pre-Civil War period which was so wracked with disorder. Also like Catholics, the Mormons revered a "priesthood." Every adult male loyally adhering to the faith was considered a priest. The Mormons quickly developed a group of Melchizedek priests, the Council of Seventies, which was every bit a militant as the Jesuits. Mormonism was more than a church, it was a total way of life. The Saints created a society--in every sense "a people." They migrated in large groups, demonstrating that a new society following some model could even be moved physically from one part of the world to another (see Hirshon: 18-19).

Since the plural marriage tenet was initially a well-kept secret, it was probably those other aspects which caused the initial hostility to the sect while in New York. There skeptics frequently broke up their meetings with jeering and by throwing stones at the faithful. It was in New York, however, that Brigham Young was converted in 1832.

They Church, and Young, moved to Kirtland, Ohio, where many Mormons were assembling in 1832-1833. The plural marriage tenet, supposedly revealed to Smith in 1831, was being secretly practiced among the elite of

131

the Church by the 1840's. The Mormons built their first
temple at Kirtland in 1833, but abandoned it almost upon
completion. Hit by the panic of 1837, they fled Ohio
because of financial difficulties, a rather shaky
financial venture, some degree of persecution, and a
desire to aid the Mormon community beginning to develop
in Missouri.

It was in Missouri that the most violent conflict
between the Mormons and the majority society--called
Gentiles by the Mormons--broke out. Smith had announced
the Church's intention to start a new Zion in the
Carthage/Panock/Nauvoo triangle of Mormon settlements in
Missouri/Illinois. In 1833 Nauvoo was a malaria-ridden
dot of a town of a mere 240 settlers. By 1842 it had
grown to more than seven thousand people. The initial
conflict broke out in Jackson County, Missouri. The
area around Independence, Missouri witnessed a virtual
state of war between Mormons and Gentiles. Some 1,200
Mormons were engaged in pitched battles. Gentiles
burned down Mormon homes, destroyed a Mormon paper, and
tarred and feathered several Saints. The Governor
called for their expulsion. Mormons responded by
creating a militant "Legion of Nauvoo." Several battles
ended with the killing of Mormon women and children.

In 1840, Brigham Young was sent with several others
to serve as missionaries in England. In their first
year they converted some eight to nine thousand, many of
whom migrated to the New Zion when Young returned in
July of 1841.

"Celestial Marriage" was increasingly being
practiced by the upper elite of the Saints. Polygamy
was looked upon with horror by majority society, and
increasing conflict led to Smith's arrest and death in
1844. His martyrdom led to the last great migration of
the Mormons, to Utah. The polygamy issue was frequently
raised because "apostates" revealed the practice after
leaving the church.

In 1845 some 150 Mormon homes were burned down in
Missouri. The conflict, however, was not one-sided.
Mormons committed violent acts against their neighbors
as well: they stole, robbed and plundered from their
neighbors (see Hirshon: 63).

132

In 1846 the temple at Nauvoo was finished. There Brigham Young married thirty-four of the thirty-five brides he took in Nauvoo after Smith's death. Young ultimately had seventy wives and fathered 56 children. This practice, more than any other, made him a symbol of evil even in death.

In February, 1846 Young left Nauvoo with some 4,000 people to establish "winter quarters" near what is now Omaha, Nebraska. In April of 1847 he led a party of 148 Saints in 73 wagons, heading for the far frontier. On July 21, 1847 they saw the Salt Lake Valley, stopping on July 23rd at the site which became Salt Lake City. Another group of 500 soon joined them. John Nelson, a gentile frontiersman who first guided them to the Salt Lake area and who was to join the Church for a while, described the original caravan.

> The class of people who made up these Mormon caravans were generally poor and ignorant. Some, however, amongst them belonged to a better class, and I always fancied these had joined to save their necks from the gallows of the district from which they migrated...The secret of polygamy amongst the Mormons was this. They thought that if each man had ten wives, and each wife had from three to five children, in twenty years time they would be strong enough to protect themselves from the gentiles (Nelson: 118).

Life on the frontier was harsh for the early Mormon settlers. Certainly their polygamous life-style, which Young extended from the elite to the rank-and-file members of the faith, seemed strange and threatening to the majority society. Although only the leaders had a great number of wives, about twenty percent of the Saints were polygamous. The practice was formally made public by the Church in 1852. It was legally banned by the United States government in 1890.

The pressure of public law applied against the Mormons was upheld in three Supreme Court cases. The first case, in 1879, upheld the validity of an act by Congress proscribing the practice or the advocating of polygamy against the Mormon claim of freedom of religious practice. In this case, Chief Justice Waite, writing for a unanimous Court, first expounded the "wall of separation" doctrine with regard to church/state relations. The case ruled that religious beliefs did not justify polygamy as a practice. The final case, rendered in 1890, upheld the validity of an 1887 Congressional Act which annulled the charter of the Mormon Church and declared all of its property forfeited save for a small portion used exclusively for worship (Abraham: 194).

The Mormon settlement in Utah grew rapidly. In 1848 there were only about 5,000 Mormons in the territory, virtually all of whom were in Salt Lake City. By 1850 there were over 11,000 and by 1852 they numbered 32,000. By 1855 there were some 60,000 Mormons in the territory, over 15,000 of whom resided in Salt Lake City alone (Hirshon: 98,140).

Flight to the frontier did not end Mormon conflict with majority society. In December of 1848 the Council of Elders of the Church created a territorial government with Young at it head. He began colonizing beyond Salt Lake City. The colonization process led to conflict with gentile settlers in the territory. Likened to the Czar of Russia, Young ruled with absolute power. During the 1856-1858 period of "Reformation," violence erupted frequently. In September of 1857 a party of 120 gentiles was massacred by Mormons disguised as Indians. Mormons became enough of a national issue that a federal force was dispatched toward Utah to stamp out a supposed rebellion. More atrocities followed: the Aiken party massacre and the Yates murder in 1858 (Furniss, 1980. See also, Hirshon: 140-176; and Nelson: 117-131).

John Nelson, who had earlier joined the Church and led them to Salt Lake City, served as a guide for the Union expedition. He described the Mormon behavior leading up to the use of military force against them.

> Brigham Young and his Saints had outgrown their discretion, and suddenly took to murdering immigrants who did not belong to their denomination, to robbing trains, and to killing people who were bound for California (Nelson: 117).

As the Union forces advanced upon them, the Mormons abandoned and burned down many of their settlements, fleeing to the stronghold of the Wasatch at Provo. The Union force and the Mormon military reached a virtual standoff without blood being shed. After weeks of

134

tension, a compromise was reached by which a garrison of troops was stationed at Salt Lake City, showing the federal presence in the Mormon region. Young was pardoned and he returned to Salt Lake City in July of 1859. John D. Lee, a leading Mormon in its military forces, was ultimately executed for the Mt. Meadow massacre murders (Nelson: 131). Young died in August, 1877, and the extensive practice of polygamy began to die with him (see Hirshon: 324).

Political Participation

Mormons were active in politics almost from their inception. Members of the early church were mostly native-born and could participate in politics without restrictions. They were active in Ohio politics to the point that their activities led to their having to flee. Smith was able to deliver the votes of his members as a bloc. They were a small but sizable minority in local politics and aroused fear in Ohio, especially during the Panic of 1837.

When they fled to Illinois and Missouri, Smith again entered politics. His flock voted en masse for the Democrats. After the move to the west, the Church split into factions. By 1870 there were three main factions whose phenomenal growth made them a force to be reckoned with. In 1850 Mormons had over 10,000 members in 16 branches. By 1870 they had 171 branches with over 87,800 members. The leaders of each of the three factions could and did deliver his members´ votes as blocs.

The largest faction, led by Young, established the "State of Deseret" in January of 1862. It set up its own government and for eight years petitioned Congress for admission into the Union. Congress ignored the petitioners. Young became obsessed with establishing the "Kingdom of God" with its principles of violence, unquestioning obedience, and holy war against the Gentile.

Once statehood was achieved, the Mormons tended to dominate Utah politics. Currently, no overwhelming party linkage is evident, although they more often favor Republicans. In the House of Representatives, the 97th Congress shows two Democrats and five Republicans who are Mormons. In the Senate, however, there is one Republican and three Democrats who are Mormons. Their public policy stance presents a similarly mixed picture (Inside Congress; 198). 135

During the frontier era the Mormon´s primary policy concern was defensive in nature. They were attempting to achieve statehood without relinquishing their practice of polygamy. The practice of "celestial marriage" was the chief tenet over which policy conflict evolved. Their clinging to this tenet was not only theological. A practical aspect was noted by several observers of Mormonism. "For practical reasons Mormon leaders urged men to marry often. A polygamist rarely apostatized, noted Horace Greeley during a Utah stay, for he had no place to go" (Hirshon: 123). As we have seen, Nelson noted that the practice was viewed as a means of massively and rapidly exapanding the church.

As governor of the territory Young used public policy to do whatever he desired. He used it to accumulate personal wealth as well as to build the property of the Mormon Church, and to rid himself of rivals (Hirson: 104). Young and the church leaders often fought with Presidential appointees who were gentiles assigned to the territorial government, such as Indian affairs and the territorial judiciary. They also tried to develop the region agriculturally, industrially, and through control over railroad development.

Anti-Semitic and anti-black attitudes among many Mormons led them to a very conservative position on civil rights and welfare policy. Their view of women has made them active opponents of the ERA. Today Mormon conservatism reflects the defensive posture of a minority faith. They support policy which they feel will benefit them as a group and oppose any policy which threatens them as a group. Hirshon´s description of their policy orientation of 1890 is still appropriate:

Considering themselves outcasts in the land of the free and home of the brave, the Mormons, while calling a portion of the United States their Zion and praising the federal Constitution as divine, retaliated by rejecting many things dear to America; its marriage system, its appointed and elected officials, its reverence for free enterprise and an unplanned economy, its stress on the worth of the individual, its democratic

traditions. Quite naturally, the Saints
distrusted those people who had laughed at
them and supported their enemies. They
remembered that in Ohio, Missouri, and
Illinois lawmen had fore-closed their
mortgages and shot and jailed them, but had
watched as mobs killed their prophet, burned
their homes, and forced them to flee.
Equating Gentile laws and Gentile government
with oppression, the Mormons substituted for
something Gentile something Mormon (Hirshon:
247-248).

"OTHER" RELIGIOUS MINORITIES

Patterns of Discrimination

Various other religious minorities have experienced
a rocky road in their dealings with majority society
which have involved numerous questions of church/state
relations. Some, like the Jehovah´s Witnesses,
Christian Scientists, and the Salvation Army have been
embroiled in legal controversies bringing them before
the U.S. Supreme Court. Scientology has been legally
declared not to be a religion despite its claims to that
status, while Transcendental Meditation was declared to
be a religion, even though it did not claim to be so.
The Unification Church, more commonly known as the
"Moonies," was declared to be a political group by the
New York Supreme Court in 1977. Perhaps so many
religious minority rights questions have come before the
courts because, as Professor Truman noted, the courts
have been the segment of governmental institutions most
looked upon as the "guardians" of minority rights
(Truman: 486).

This section will briefly review some problems of
particular religious groups, and how those have required
resolution in the Courts because, since our colonial
days, religious freedom has been deemed to belong to the
individual rather than to any group to which that
individual might belong. Hence, the religious practices
of a group may come into conflict with the majority
culture´s norms, and their protection under the freedom
of religion clause is not always a foregone conclusion.

Courts at all levels have upheld local ordinances
prohibiting, for example, the handling of poisonous
snakes in a religious ceremony [e.g. State v. Burns, 366
U.S. 942, 1949]. Draft exemption has been granted to

137

some but denied to others on the basis of religious "conscientious objection" to military service. While the Quakers were granted C.O. status, the Black Muslims were denied it in 1968; but the Supreme Court eventually over-ruled that, in 1971. Jehovah´s Witnesses and Christian Scientists have clashed with local health officials over vaccination and blood transfusions. Sunday closing laws have been upheld as constitutional despite their adverse effects on Jews and Seventh-Day Adventists. The courts have allowed Catholic parochial schools to use public school buses on the grounds of public safety for children while tax support of expenses in traveling to parochial schools has been denied. A Mormon has been arrested for polygamy as recently as 1946. Leaders of the "I Am" sect have been jailed for fraud in connection with their claims of religious healing powers. While Scientology and Timothy Leary´s League for Spiritual Discovery have been denied the use of certain drugs on religious grounds, the Navahoes have been allowed the use of peyote in their religious ceremonies. The Hasidic Jews and the Old Order Amish have had long-standing battles with local authorities over compulsory school attendance.

The Jehovah´s Witnesses provide a study of court embroiled controversy over several church/state issues for many years. Their refusal to salute the flag, for example, has engendered fierce prejudice and legal conflict since 1928. David Manwaring, in his study of the Witnesses´ conflict with majority society, Render Unto Caesar, states that: "The wave of anti-Witness persecution which swept the country after the Gobitis decision is legendary (:163)."

From 1941 through 1951 the Jehovah´s Witnesses were involved in six Supreme Court cases which ended in rulings in which local ordinances were upheld and the individual was denied free exercise of the prohibited behavior on the grounds of freedom of religion (5). Similarly, the question of C.O. status has been another long and controversial issue embroiling religious dissenters in court conflicts. During war periods emotions run high, and the refusal to serve, on any grounds, usually precipitates some discrimination. During World War I some 4,000 C.O.s from various religious minorities, primarily the Mennonites, Jehovah´s Witnesses, Dunkers, Seventh-Day Adventists, Adventists, and Quakers experienced harsh treatment. Such incidents were far fewer during World War II, and

138

even more infrequent during the Korean and Vietnam Wars, because the churches were more divided among hawks and doves. More recent cases, such as the Seeger case (1965) and the Yoder case (1973), have shown increasing court support for the C.O. status, although in several 1971 cases the Court rejected the argument based on simple objection to a "particular war" (6).

The Supreme Court has upheld the individual's right to certain religious beliefs or practices against a state or local government's ordinance or law which the Court ruled as an unconstitutional abridgment of the individual's freedom of religion or as breaching the wall of separation between church and state (7).

Public Policy Impact

Minority religious groups affect public policy in a variety of ways. They affect the political behavior and attitudes of their members through religious education. In passing moral judgement on social issues, they often raise societal problems to the level of public policy questions. They are able to keep certain problems off the agenda of government or to force some questions to be considered by public policy makers.

The state often solicits the support of "religion-in-general" for its policy by mixing public service with religions. Clergy can solemnize marriages. Chaplains are provided for the military service. Churches are granted tax exempt status on their property, assets, and businesses. Individuals are allowed tax deductions on gifts, inheritances, and general contributions to religious institutions. The state does so because these institutions are agents of society in the process of socializing persons to support and obey the law and to follow the direction of public authorities.

Sometimes the majority churches use the power of the state against minority churches. In the late 1880's the American Protestant Alliance pressured the government to adopt restrictive immigration policies. They also opposed the legal establishment or recognition of parochial schools. Various nativist Protestant groups proposed constitutional amendments that would have denied citizenship to anyone acknowledging allegiance to the Pope. They have used state, local, and even federal laws and policies to harass or constrain the behavior and religious practices of Jews, Mormons, Jehovah's Witnesses, Black Muslims, "Jesus People," and the "Moonies." In the 1780s they tried to evoke sedition laws against the Shakers. The Ku Klux Klan often successfully employed local ordinances and law officials against Jewish rabbis and Catholic priests. At the national level the Klan attacked the Catholic Church and priests as conspirators under the direction of a foreign power. Nativist groups were the driving force which led to the passage of the quota system for immigration. The Prohibition effort was a Protestant-dominated attempt to use public policy to restrict "Rum and Romanism." The Religious Liberty Association lobbied for federal, state, and local laws which maintained separation of church and state at an absolute degree.

Churches often consciously attempt to influence the political views of their membership, although such attempts can lead to a split between church leadership and their followers or can split a church regionally. In the 1950's and 1960's, for example, the Catholic hierarchy was ahead of the laity in support for civil rights policy. Often a more long-term influence of the religious institution itself promotes new political opinion among its faithful, for instance, the growing Republicanism among Conservative Jews. Some social or public policy questions produce conflicts within religious groups which influence their general public behavior and their participation in politics. The factional splits among the Methodists into various regions, for example, resulted from dissension regarding integration. In such cases, organizational goals of the religious group usually have primacy over their social goals. This reflects the fact that the clergy recognize that it often has difficulty enforcing its social policy positions. Religious groups, like all other groups, face a problem of internal control. The have recognized that inducements or persuasion are often the best methods of of handling such a problem (see Gamson: 57). On thorny social issues (which generally involve public policy questions), churches tend to follow; they rarely lead.

Another way churches influence public policy is in forming coalitions with non-religious groups, employing "alliance" and "logrolling" tactics (Truman: 363). For example, the Christian Scientists joined forces with the American Medical Association in the late 1950's and early 1960's to fight medicare legislation, and the

140

Catholic Church has joined with various groups to fight governmental programs easing birth control and divorce legislation. They have often joined with different groups to uphold local Sunday-closing laws.

Religious groups have traditionally played supporting roles in public policy involving military and foreign policy. In wars, "God is always on the side of a given nation-state's government."

Religion has been associated with prejudice in a complex way. Studies indicate that a person who is most devout, more personally absorbed in his or her religion, is less likely to be prejudiced than others. But persons of religious affiliation who evidence an "institutional type of attachment," more external and political in nature, turn out to be more highly associated with prejudice. "The chief reason why religion becomes the focus of prejudice is that it usually stands for more than faith--it is the pivot of the cultural tradition of a group (Allport: 445)."

The growing secularization of American society since the 1950's led to a relative decline of religious influence on public affairs. This decline has probably served as a major catalyst in provoking the political behavior by religious groups so recently evident in the "Moral Majority" movement. Religious PACS (political action committees) are increasingly well organized, vocal, and well-financed in their efforts to shape policy at all levels of government, largely through electoral politics. Candidates for public office have to stand the test of the moral scrutiny of the "Moral Majority." Though this movement is mainly conservative Protestant, their current tactics and involvement harken back to the old-time, religious/ethnic politics. In the words of Litt (1970):

> ...ethnic and religious organizations have perpetuated ethnic politics by providing identification, political styles, and core values for their members. However, the political impact of religious institutions is tempered by circumstances of organizational strength and position. Organizational resources are most readily mobilized for defensive politics, that is, when a basic tenet of the ethnic group (ultimately its survival) is threatened. Religious organizations are least likely to enjoy political impact when divisive social policies are at issue (:59).

Endnotes

1. See Morgan: 26. For perhaps the most comprehensive and authoritative discussion of anti-Catholicism up to 1860, see Ray Allen Billington, The Protestant Crusade, 1800-1860, (Chicago:Quadrangle Books, 1964).

2. See Milton Himmelfarb, "The Case of Jewish Liberalism," in Lipset (ed.), Emerging Coalitions,: 300. See also, Feingold, Zion in America, (New York: Twayne, 1974): 266.

3. See, for example: Janowsky: 193; Feingold: 268-269; or Marden and Meyer: 406.

4. See Feingold: 229-235; Howe: 361-370; or Marden and Meyer: 401-402.

5. Minersville v. Gobitis, 310 U.S. 586, 1940; Cox v. New Hampshire, 315 U.S. 569, 1941; Chaplinsky v. New Hampshire, 315 U.S. 568, 1942; Jones v. Opelika, 316 U.S. 584, 1942; Prince v. Massachusetts, 321 U.S. 158, 1944; and Beard v. City of Alexandria, 341 U.S. 622, 1951. For a brief discussion of the cases, see Abraham: 194-196.

6. See, for instance: Winter: 264; Wilson: 200. Cases are: United States v. Schwimmer, 279 U.S. 644, 1929; U.S. v. Macintosh, 283 U.S. 605, 1931; Hamilton v. Regents of the University of California, 293 U.S. 245, 1934; and In re Summers, 325 U.S. 561, 1945.

7. Abraham lists and briefly discusses seventeen cases, spanning the years 1892 through 1965, in which the Court upheld the individual in "Free Exercise" cases. He also discusses six cases, rendered from 1815 through 1963, in which the Court found a constitutional violation in a "Separation of Church and State" case. See Abraham: 194-200.

Additional Readings;

Abraham, Henry J. Freedom and the Court. New York: Oxford University Press, 1967.

Allport, Gordon. The Nature of Prejudice. New York: Doubleday, 1958.

Billington, Ray Allen. The Origins of Nativism in the United States, 1800-1844. New York: Arno Press, 1974.

Cramer, Carl. The Farm Boy and the Angel. New York: Doubleday, 1970.

Feingold, Henry. Zion in America. New York: Twayne, 1974.

Furniss, N.F. The Mormon Conflict, 1850-1859. New Haven: Yale University Press, 1960.

Herberg, William. Protestant, Catholic, Jew. New York: Doubleday, 1960.

Hirshon, Stanley. The Lion of the Lord. New York: Knopf, 1969.

Janowsky, Oscar. The American Jew. New York: Harper and Brothers, 1942.

Lenski, Gerhard. The Religious Factor. New York: Doubleday, 1961.

Ladd, Everett C. and Charles Hadley. Transformation of the American Party System. New York: W. W. Norton, 1975.

Litt, Edgar. Ethnic Politics in America. Glenview, Illinois: Scott, Foresman, 1970.

Manwaring, David R. Render Unto Caesar. Chicago: University of Chicago Press, 1961.

Mathias, Charles McC. Jr.,"Ethnic Groups and Foreign Policy," Foreign Affairs, July 17, 1981: 975-998.

Meinig, D. W. "The Mormon Cultural Region: Strategies and Patterns in the Geography of the American West, 1847-1964," The Annals of the Association of American Geographers, 55, 2(June, 1965): 217-218.

Morgan, Richard. The Politics of Religious Conflict. New York: Pegasus, 1968.

Stedman, Murray. Religion and Politics in America. New York: Harcourt, Brace and World, 1964.

CHAPTER FOUR; MIXED BASES GROUPS--HISPANIC AMERICANS

Introduction

Hispanic Americans are a logical group to discuss here, in a chapter which links our discussion in previous chapters of minority status based on national origin and religion with our next chapter dealing with race, because they have variously been ascribed minority status on all such grounds. In the Southwest, many Hispanics--who can trace their ancestry back to generations before Anglo-Americans ever set foot into the area--are none-the-less treated as "Mexicans." Virtually all Hispanics are popularly viewed, and thereby often discriminated against, as Catholics--even those who are Protestants or non-practicing Catholics. Many Americans treat all Hispanics as "racially" different from Caucasians, even though the majority are not so.

Since the mid 1950´s immigration to the U.S. has shifted from European countries to those of North, Central, and South America and Asia. From 1956 to 1976, for example, while immigration from European countries declined by over 27 percent, Asian immigration rose by a spectacular 369 percent, and South American by 27 percent. By the late 1970´s, legal immigrants to the United States were 34 percent Asian, 44 percent Latin American, and only 15 percent European (McClellan: 28).

Another troublesome aspect for the various Hispanic groups is the Anglo tendency to treat them all alike, when in fact there are very considerable and important differences among the various Hispanic groups. According to recent census data, the Hispanics are comprised as follows: Mexicans, 59 percent; Puerto Ricans, 15 percent; Cubans, 6 percent; Central/South Americans, 7 percent; and all other Spanish-speaking, 13 percent. In 1980 nearly 90 percent of Hispanics resided in metropolitan areas--more than one-fourth of whom (3.5 million) lived in the Los Angeles and New York areas alone. The "top-ten" metropolitan areas with the most Hispanics in 1980 were: 1) Los Angeles, 2,065,727; 2) New York, 1,493,081; 3) Miami, 581,030; Chicago, 580,592; 5) San Antonio, 481,411; 6) Houston, 424,901; 7) San Francisco, 351,915; 8) El Paso, 297,001; 9) Riverside/Ontario, 289,791; and 10) Anaheim, 286,331.

A new study released by the Population Reference Bureau estimates the Hispanic population will reach 47 million by the year 2020, displacing blacks as the largest minority in the country. A recent Census Bureau study shows that Hispanics averaged 97.9 births per 1,000 women in 1981, compared to 68.1 for every 1,000 anglo women and 83.6 per 1,000 for black women (Parade, September 4, 1983). These birth rate data are graphically portrayed in Figure Two , which compares the growth-rates of Hispanics with white and black non-Hispanics.

FIG. 2. HISPANIC-AMERICANS

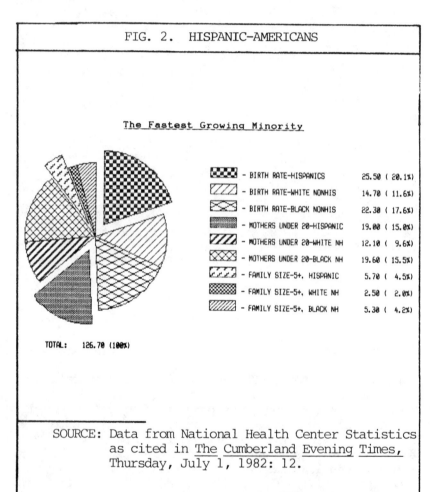

The Fastest Growing Minority

	BIRTH RATE-HISPANICS	25.50 (20.1%)
	BIRTH RATE-WHITE NONHIS	14.70 (11.6%)
	BIRTH RATE-BLACK NONHIS	22.30 (17.6%)
	MOTHERS UNDER 20-HISPANIC	19.00 (15.0%)
	MOTHERS UNDER 20-WHITE NH	12.10 (9.6%)
	MOTHERS UNDER 20-BLACK NH	19.60 (15.5%)
	FAMILY SIZE-5+, HISPANIC	5.70 (4.5%)
	FAMILY SIZE-5+, WHITE NH	2.50 (2.0%)
	FAMILY SIZE-5+, BLACK NH	5.30 (4.2%)

TOTAL: 126.70 (100%)

SOURCE: Data from National Health Center Statistics as cited in The Cumberland Evening Times, Thursday, July 1, 1982: 12.

One observer recently noted some effects of this rapid growth rate:

Since 1970, the number of Cuban, Mexicans, Puerto Ricans and other Spanish-speaking people--called "Hispanics" by government census-takers--have risen from 9 million to more than 15 million, a 61 percent increase, the largest gain of any group in the nation. In Los Angeles, Miami, and San Antonio, Hispanics are so numerous that they have tipped the political scales to dominate the local governments and schools. In the Chicago school system, the Hispanic student population has grown to the point where it equals the number of non-Hispanic whites. It is clear that these numbers will continue to grow. Hispanics´ "natural increase"--the excess of births over deaths--is more than a quarter of a million people a years. And their steady immigration--both legal and illegal--is estimated to be a million a year. At that rate, by the 1990 census, the Hispanic population will have nearly doubled again, to 27.3 million (Ehrlichman: 4).

Their increasing numbers have led to a greater political electoral strength. A number of Latino politicians are becoming mayors of their cities--Maurice Ferre of Miami, Henry Cisneros of San Antonio, also interviewed as a possible Vice-Presidential candidate for 1984, Frederico Pena of Denver, Robert Martinez of Tampa, and Louis Montano of Santa Fe. There are currently eleven Hispanic members in Congress (A Guide to Hispanic Organizations, 1983).

Such political success, however, is a very recent phenomenon. Throughout their history in the U.S. most Hispanics have been subjected to prejudice and discrimination--in jobs, housing, voting, civil rights, and social activities. They have traditionally ranked close to the bottom in studies of social distance. Their lack of political potency is related to their higher proportions of lower class members, a sojourner attitude, a prominent feeling of political apathy, ineffectiveness, a pattern of discrimination and violation of their civil rights, small dispersed populations except for a few locales, inter-nacine quarrels, and a general distrust of government. As a result, until recently, few Spanish-speaking people achieved, or even sought, positions of political leadership.

Even in the 1980 election, their percentage of eligible voters who actually turned out was among the lowest of identifiable groups. A census bureau report on turnout in that election indicated the following: among registered voters, 90 percent; among whites, 63 percent; among blacks, 52 percent; among all groups, 59.2 percent; but among Hispanics, 44 percent (Cumberland Evening Times, Tuesday, July 20, 1982: 16).

Their relative lack of political power is not only due to the fact that they tend to have a lower level of turnout. When they do vote, they are so overwhelmingly Democratic in their voting affiliation that they constitute a virtual "captive voting bloc." Although they have begun to organize more effectively since 1960, Hispanics are still a highly fragmented group in terms of both nationality backgrounds and philosophical approach to their relations with majority society. Even though the majority society tends to see all Hispanics as alike, the Cubans, Puerto Ricans, Mexicans, and the various South and Central American groups all see themselves as different. They often conflict with one another. Thus, "Pan-Hispanic" unity has been largely illusionary—despite "LaRaza Unida." A recently published guide to Hispanic organizations lists a total of 113 such groups: 74 "Hispanic," 20 "Chicano," 10 "Puerto Rican," and 7 "Cuban" (A Guide to Hispanic Organizations, 1983. See also, Burma: 267-324).

Various Hispanic organizations have employed, over time, several major tactical approaches to their relations with majority society. Stoddard (1973) distinguishes three tactics used by Mexican-Americans . After W.W.II., Mexican American veterans returning home found they were still barred from social clubs, veterans´ and fraternal organizations on the basis of their racial and ethnic characteristics. They adopted a policy of separatism and attempted to created a plural society in which the Mexican-American and Spanish cultures would share a position of pride equal to that of the middle-class Anglo-American culture. In the mid-1960´s, as part of the larger civil rights and radical movements, Mexican-Americans fought for ethnic autonomy—a course based on self-determination. Using radical tactics modeled partially on Black Power methods, they employed threats of violence, defiance of legal statutes, public confrontations, and the like to make their demands heard. In 1970, however, factors beyond their control, such as backlash and economic

148

slump, as well as internal dissension, caused their demands to be met with political, military, and public resistance. Strategic penetration then came to the fore. It involved a more adroit and subtle strategy--the penetration of existing social organizations, public agencies at all levels, and professional organizations. Presently, this trend appears to be the most promising long-range thrust towards realigning the larger societal structures in a way that will enable Mexican-Americans to have more equal access to educational and occupational rewards in America (:242-243).

Different tactics often reflect differences among the groups as to status and opportunities available to them. The Cubans, many of whom entered under a protected status of "refugees," tend to be better educated, organized, and equipped to acculturate into the American job market structure. The majority society has been more willing to accept them, and--as we shall see more fully below--the government has aided them with special legislation, resettlement programs, and assistance through local sponsors. All of this has eased considerably their transition into American society. Their assimilation, both politically and economically, has been more rapid than other Hispanic groups and even the immigrant groups who came in under the quota system.

By contrast, many Mexicans who have entered the U.S. illegally remain totally unorganized and at the mercy of an economic system that exploits them. They remain at the lowest level of society economically, living in a social and cultural world apart from the majority society, lacking any real political voice because of their illegal status. The majority society rejects them as persons who, at best, will lower wages and depress working conditions and, at worst, will swell the ranks of criminals and the violent.

Although success stories are to be found, the majority of Hispanics suffer from the low status they occupy with the associated problems of crime, educational deprivation, ethnic discrimination and economic exploitation. Hispanics in rural areas (about ten percent of those in the United States) typically live in run-down shacks provided migrant workers. Those in the nation's cities can usually only afford housing in slums and housing projects. A quarter of all Hispanic families live below the poverty level. Among

149

Puerto Ricans, 16 percent earn less than $4,000.
annually. More than one million Puerto Ricans live in
substandard housing in New York City alone. In many
Hispanic neighborhoods street gangs terrorize the
population. East Los Angeles, for example,claims 30
such gangs alone. In the past two years there police
have classified more than 600 murders as gang-related.
Among Cubans, many fear the "Marielitos." Among the
125,000 Cuban refugees who fled here since 1980, some
1,800 were identified as having come directly from Cuban
jails. Miami police estimate their actual numbers as
being far higher, and they are held to account for about
half of all the crimes committed in Miami this past year
(Ehrlichman: 4).

Hispanic poverty is related to their low
occupational backgrounds. They continue to have among
the highest levels of unemployment among minority groups
in the United States. A recent report on unemployment,
for instance, indicated that whereas the total
percentage of the labor force that was unemployed stood
at 10.8 percent, the white rate was 9.7 percent, but the
Hispanic rate was 15.3 percent. This pattern, moreover,
was consistent across age and sex factors, as shown in
Table Five.

Table 5: HISPANIC UNEMPLOYMENT AS OF DECEMBER, 1982			
CATEGORY:	TOTAL %:	WHITE %:	HISPANIC %:
Female (20 yrs.+)	9.2	8.1	14.1
Males (20 yrs. +)	10.1	9.2	13.6
Teenage (16-19 yrs.)	24.5	21.6	29.6
Teenage Male	25.8	22.8	34.6
Teenage Female	23.0	20.4	23.1
Source: U.S. Department of Labor, Bureau of Labor Statistics, December, 1982.			

Of those Hispanics employed, a substantial majority are
in low-status, low-paying blue collar jobs. Except for
the American-Indian, the Spanish-speaking rank lower
than any other single minority group in such areas as
education, housing, and employment.

Their low status is likewise reflected in their lower levels of formal educational achievement. While 67 percent of all whites and 46 percent of all blacks complete high school, only 40 percent of Hispanics graduate from high school. In New York City, twenty-four percent of the high school population are Puerto Rican youth, yet only 15 percent of them will graduate. In California, while 14 percent of high school students are Chicanos, only one-half of one-percent of the state's college students are Chicanos (Steiner: 215; Kuenster: 21). In California, the average Mexican-American drops out of school by the seventh grade. One study found an illiteracy rate among Chicanos of 24 percent, in contrast to the 4 percent rate among Anglos (Moore and Packon: 143).

Indeed, California provides a sort of microcosm of the nation's explosive rate of growth among Hispanics, and other minority populations, and their attendant problems. Los Angeles has emerged as the Ellis Island of the 1980's, becoming America's new mixing pot if not melting pot. Approximately 2,500 Mexicans, Salvadorans, and Guatemalens enter L.A. each month, with an estimated fifty times that number of illegal aliens slipping across the border. A Rand study found that since 1970 two million immigrants have settled in L.A., some 90,000 of whom came in 1982 alone. In 1960 one in nine of L.A. County's residents were Hispanic, and one in 100 was Asian. Today, nearly one third are Hispanic, and one in ten is Asian. Anglos now comprise a numerical minority of the entire L.A. County population (3.8 million out of 7.9 million). A remarkable two-thirds of L.A. kindergartners are Hispanic. Among the county's half-million school children, 117,000 speak one of 104 languages other than English as a native tongue. The explosive nature of the county's ethnic population is illustrated in Table Six. It is estimated that by the year 2,000 Hispanics will comprise 40 percent of its total population, by then outnumbering the anglo population which is expected to be only 31 percent of the total.

Table 6: ETHNIC EXPLOSION IN L.A.		
ETHNIC GROUP:	1970 POPULATION:	1983 POPULATION:
Mexican	822,300	2,100,000
Iranians	20,000	200,000
Salvadorans	*	200,000
Japanese	104,000	175,000
Armenians	75,000	175,000
Chinese	41,000	153,000
Koreans	8,900	150,000
Filipinos	33,500	150,000
Arab-Americans	45,000	130,000
Israelis	10,000	90,000
Samoans	22,000	60,000
Guatemalans	*	50,000
Vietnamese	*	40,000

*fewer than 2,000

Source: Adapted from Time, June 13, 1983:18.

The nation's only Hispanic Governor, Anthony Anaya of New Mexico, headed Hispanic Force '84, an effort to mobilize the nation's approximately six million voting-age Hispanics into an influential force in the Democratic presidential campaign for 1984. Their main goal was to register one million new Hispanic voters. This would have raised the total registered Hispanic voters to over 4 million, and comprise nearly 5 percent of the '84 voter rolls. The Southwest Voter Education Project was headquartered in San Antonio. Hispanic potential electoral clout is considerable. Hispanics are concentrated in six states: California, Florida, Illinois, New Jersey, New York, and Texas. These states account for 173 electoral votes, or three-fifths of the 270 needed to elect a president. The group aims to make Hispanics the crucial swing vote in those states. In California, which alone casts 47 votes, Hispanics are now nearly twenty percent of the population.

Their raw numbers, however, overstate their likely actual political strength. About one-third of Hispanics of voting age are resident aliens who are ineligible to vote. And of those eligible, less than one-half are registered to vote. Perhaps even more telling, of those registered, the turnout rate is typically about 30 percent, a full 23 percentage points below the national average.

Nonetheless, their growing numbers and concentration in key states makes them an attractive potential bloc that the Republican Party is also vigorously wooing. President Reagan received about thirty percent of the Hispanic vote in 1980, and exit data indicates he received thirty-one percent of their vote in 1984. President Reagan declared a National Hispanic Heritage Week, and the G. O. P. launched its own Viva '84 campaign aimed at registering one-half million new Republican Hispanic voters.

Having briefly reviewed the Hispanic minority overall, this chapter will now examine the three largest subgroups of the Hispanic minority: the Mexican Americans or Chicanos, the Puerto Ricans, and the Cubans. Each group will be discussed as to patterns of discrimination against them and what actions, political or otherwise, they are taking to cope with their minority status.

The Chicanos

The Chicano population is estimated at about ten million and is concentrated in California, Texas, New Mexico, Arizona, and Colorado. About 90 percent of the Chicano population resides in those five states. Although Chicanos are the largest Hispanic group, even they might more accurately be discussed as two subgroups: the Spanish-Americans, who trace their ancestry back to the settlers of the area now comprising northern New Mexico; and immigrants from Mexico, who have come, in large measure, since 1900.

The heritage of the Spanish-American subgroup is different from the Mexican immigrant's. The ancestors of most Spanish Americans arrived in the Southwest of the U.S. while Mexico was still a Spanish colony. They mixed in varying degrees with the Pueblo Indians of the area. They lived for generations as farmers, cattle ranchers, and sheep herders—isolated from both more modern Mexican or Anglo cultural influence. They thought of themselves more as Spanish than as Mexican and have preferred to be called Spanish-American. To most Anglos, however, these people were "Mexicans" and have been treated as such and discriminated against as such in inter-group relations. Their problems and prospects, moreover, are alike and intertwined with the Chicanos.

153

The Spanish-Americans of northern New Mexico have a distinctly higher formal educational pattern than the rest of the Spanish-surnamed persons in the Southwest, although they do not exhibit greatly higher income or occupational mobility. The New Mexico Chicanos, however, tend to be distributed more evenly throughout the socio-economic strata, unlike the Chicanos in Arizona, Texas and California, who are more concentrated in the lower socio-economic class.

These Chicanos became a minority by absorption. When Texas became independent in 1836 it sought union the United States. Events led to the Mexican-American War in 1846. Many Spanish-Americans now living in northern New Mexico have forbearers who lived in the area for nearly a century and-a-half prior to its annexation by the U.S. in 1848. The Mexican-American War ended with the Treaty of Guadalupe-Hidalgo in 1848, with Mexico losing about 45 percent of her land. The treaty guaranteed that the Mexicans who remained in the conquered territories would retain their "civil, political, and religious rights," among which were specified equal protection and treatment under the U.S. Constitution and the freedom to maintain their culture, language, and property. With the exception of religion, little was done to honor those rights (Kuenster: 8-9).

The Gold Rush in 1849 induced a great migration of Anglos into the region. In 1850 New Mexico, Utah, and California were designated territories by the United States. Anglos soon achieved economic domination. In Sante Fe a ring of notorious land grabbers operated with "abuses so flagrant that they invoked the wrath of President Grover Cleveland" (Stoddard: 12).

Moore characterizes the Spanish-American system in New Mexico as "traditional colonialism," by which she means the transfer, in fact, of an entire social system from central Mexico, complete with both Spanish-surnamed elites and lower classes. This pattern is also evident in Arizona, which was dominated by New Mexico as a territory. She characterizes the situation in California as "economic colonialism," and in Texas as "conquest colonialism." These early differences in attitude towards Mexican-Americans are borne out later in the respective treatment of the minority in those states. Acuna also characterizes the Chicano as a "colonized people in the U.S.," noting parallels between their experiences and those of other Third World peoples:

154

1) The land of one people is invaded by people from another country, who later use military force to gain and maintain control.
2) The original inhabitants become subjects of the majority involuntarily.
3) The conquered have an alien culture and system imposed on them.
4) The conquered become the victims of racism and cultural genocide and are relegated to a submerged status.
5) The conquered are rendered politically and economically powerless.
6) The conquerors feel they have a "mission" in occupying the area in question and believe that they have undeniable privileges by virtue of their conquest (:3).

The label of "Spanish American" did not come into common usage in New Mexico until the mass exodus from Mexico after its revolution in 1909 when the Spanish-speaking residents wanted to distinguish themselves from the incoming "Mexicans." Anglos, however, considered and treated all the Hispanics as "Mexicans." It is to that latter group we will next turn out attention.

Large-scale immigration to the United States from Mexico is a phenomenon of this century, during which time about one-and-a-half million legal immigrants entered the country. Until the 1960´s there were no real restrictions placed on immigration from Mexico. The first significant flows came into the country during the gold rush era of the 1840´s, but no massive movement north took place until after the Mexican Revolution. After 1910, however, the trickle of immigration became a steady flow. Ultimately, eight to ten percent of Mexico´s population immigrated north to the United States. In fact, many were pushed north by the violence and turmoil associated with the revolution. Then, too, the tremendous growth rate of Mexico´s population--among the highest in the world--provided a significant push factor. Mostly, however, the movement north was induced by a pull factor--the economic growth rate in the U.S. and the resulting need for cheap labor.

155

In the first decade of this century Mexican immigration was used to fill the void created by the increasing restrictions placed on Asian immigration. The Chinese restriction acts of the 1880´s and 1890´s and the Gentlemen´s Agreement of 1907 which restricted the Japanese created a void that Mexican laborers soon filled. By 1909 98 percent of the crews employed by the Atchison, Topeka, and Sante Fe Railways west of Albuquerque were Mexicans, and the Southern Pacific Railroad employed a similar percentage (Acuna: 132).

Although the Immigration Act of 1917 placed a head tax on Mexican immigrants and applied the literacy provisions of the act to them, these were seldom enforced and had little impact on the steady flow of Mexicans induced by the post-World War I economy and the need for "temporary farm workers." During the 1920´s Mexican immigration reached a peak of one-half million immigrants entering the country during the decade. Opposition to unrestricted Mexican immigration crystallized during the 1920´s. Restrictionists first attempted to have them covered by the 1921 and 1924 Immigration Acts, but in both cases Mexicans were excluded from the quotas. In 1926 they launched another effort, the Box bill, which attempted to apply the quota system to the whole of the western hemisphere. Again they failed. In 1928 the fight loomed once more. Congressional hearings were held, but the proposals all died in committee. The restrictionists were bigots, but the anti-restrictionists were more powerful economic opportunists. The growers of the Southwest forced the Departments of State, Agriculture, and Interior to form a united front to overwhelm the restrictionists.

The anti-restrictionists were aided by the tapering off of Mexican migration that coincided with the Great Depression during which the influx slowed to a virtual half. The 1940´s and 1950´s witnessed another surge in response to the war-generated boom which continued until 1964. The "bracero" program legally brought in tens of thousands annually.

Starting with just over 4,000 workers entering the U.S. under contract in the braceros program in 1942, the annual total rose steadily until its peak year of 1956 when 445,197 entered. During the period of 1953 to 1960 the average annual influx was about 300,000. The program coincided with a new wave of illegal migrants known as "wetbacks." "Operation Wetback" in the 1960´s

156

entailed a concerted effort to deport the illegal immigrants. Over a five year period some 3.8 million illegals were captured and returned to Mexico.

This new wave of immigration from Mexico resurrected the opposition of the restrictionists who finally succeeded with the passage of the 1965 Immigration Act. This law imposed a regional quota system which allowed only 170,000 immigrants to be admitted annually from the entire Western Hemisphere. This effort in large measure passed because of the support of Anglo-organized labor which feared the impact of cheap labor from Mexico. American-organized labor ignored, and mostly excluded, Mexican-Americans from their ranks during this period.

The discrimination Mexican-Americans faced was both intense and pervasive. Next to the American Indian, the Chicano ranks lower than any other single group in American society in such areas as education, housing, and economic conditions. They were referred to by a variety of derogatory slang terms: "cholo," "spik," "Mex," "beaner," "pachuco," and "greaser." They faced discrimination in jury selection, voting rights, and school enrollment. Until as recently as 1970 Houston had a plan to "integrate" blacks and Mexican-Americans into their schools and have whites attend their own. They are still highly segregated in their housing, evidence low inter-marriage rates, and manifest highly ethnically-related friendship patterns. Their degree of assimilation more nearly resembles a mixing bowl than it does a melting pot.

> Both in rate and degree of acculturation and assimilation Mexican Americans are among the least "Americanized" of all the ethnic groups in the United States (Burma: 20).

Burma stresses three factors which he feels retard their assimilation: 1) their continued pride in their Mexican culture, heritage, and language; 2) their poor education; and 3) the racial bias they face since some 40 percent are full-blooded Indians and approximately ninety-five percent have at least some Indian blood. Their close proximity to Mexico, moreover, has meant their culture has survived more intact than it has for most other minority groups. Mexican-Americans are classically "marginal men;" they partake partly of two cultures and wholly of neither (1).

157

These various factors--conquest, racism, nativism, and the continued dependence of Mexico´s economy on the Unites States--have all played a role of keeping them ascribed to the status of servants. Chicanos make up a "secondary labor force;" they are concentrated in un-skilled jobs such as laundry workers, packers, taxi drivers, or in the semi-skilled crafts such as masons, painters, plasterers and bakers. Over sixty-two percent of Chicanos are unskilled or semi-skilled blue-collar workers (Lopez y Rivas: 43-44). The Chicano male is even more under-represented in white collar jobs than is the female. Only recently, as Chicanos moved into urban areas, have they begun to improve their economic opportunities. Even then, the opportunity is rarely open to the first-generation immigrant.

Their low status and occupational levels are related to their poor levels of formal education. Measured by the average school year completed, Chicanos have a lower level of education than virtually any other minority group. In large measure this low level in formal educational achievement can be attributed to their very high attrition rates in school. Table Seven, for instance, compares the attrition rates of Anglos, Blacks, and Chicanos at various levels in schools in the Southwest as of 1970.

Table 7: COMPARATIVE EDUCATION ATTRITION RATES (BY RACE) AT SELECTED LEVELS IN THE SOUTHWEST UNITED STATES			
EDUCATIONAL LEVEL:	ANGLOO(%)	BLACK(%)	MEXICAN-AMERICAN(%)
Grade 1	100.0	100.0	100.0
Grade 8	100.0	98.6	91.1
Grade 12	85.0	66.6	60.3
Enter College	49.3	28.8	22.5
Complete College	23.8	8.3	5.4
Source: Adapted from Stoddard: 131.			

In California, where 14 percent of the public school children are Chicanos, less than one-half of one percent of college students are Chicano (Steiner: 215). Illiteracy rates among them are 28 percent, compared to 4 percent among anglos (Moore and Pachon: 143). One out of ten who starts school will complete it at the high school level.

158

Much of this attrition rate is due to language problems. In the past Chicano children were cajoled, enticed, threatened, and sometimes even beaten to stop them from using Spanish, not just in the classroom, but even for speaking it in the halls or while playing on the playground. One Chicano leader, Reies Tijerina, expressed the feelings of many Chicanos when he observed: "If you cut out our Spanish, you have cut out our heart" (in Steiner: 220).

Numerous problems resulted from the campaign to force Chicanos to speak English. Many educators feel that a portion of Chicano children are now essentially "alingual," or biculturally illiterate, not truly speaking either Spanish or English. In 1970 the Civil Rights Commission found extensive assignment of Chicano students to classes for the mentally retarded solely as a result of their inablty to perform in English dominant classes (2).

In 1968 Congress attempted to alleviate this educational problem by passing the Bilingual Education Act. In 1969 some 25,000 children were covered by the program. By 1980 about one-half million children were covered, at an annual cost of $700 million dollars. Yet the program has been criticized as a failure. In California, for instance:

> The state requires that a school form a
> bilingual class when 20 or more students in
> any grade speak a specified foreign tongue as
> their first language. Now dozens of schools
> in the mammoth Los Angeles district have two,
> three, or four qualifying minorities in
> everything from Tongan to Farsi; in all, the
> district needs 2,000 more bilingual teachers
> and can´t find them all. So, in many classes,
> the frustrated simply go on trying to teach
> the baffled (McClellan: 107).

Congressional action was followed by Court and bureaucratic action. In 1974, in the case Law v. Nichols, the Supreme Court ruled that an education taught only in English was a violation of the rights of children who can´t speak it. In effect, the ruling says that school systems are required to offer some type of bilingual program for Chicano students. In that same year, H.E.W. issued a directive requiring that all public school districts with enrollments of five percent

159

or more of their children being of a language minority had to offer some time of bilingual program for those children or face losing their H.E.W. funding (U.S. Commission on Civil Rights, 1975: 176).

Related to the language problem is the alienation of the young, many of whom turn to drugs and violence. Gangs of these youth terrorize the barrios of Chicano America. Some 300 Chicano youth gangs are identified in the Los Angeles area alone. Many of them are violent drug-users. The L.A. police estimate there were approximately 260 gang-related homicides in 1982 alone (Time, June 13, 1983: 18-27). The impact of these gangs on the entire Chicano community is heightened by the segregation in housing which traps so many in the barrios. One study found that 30 percent of the housing units occupied by Spanish-surnamed people in the Southwest were dilapidated or deteriorated as opposed to only seven and-a-half percent of the units occupied by Anglos.

The trend toward assimilation does seem to be stronger among the younger Chicano. One good indicator of this effect is a 1963 study of exogamy (marrying outside the group). That study found that forty percent of the marriages involving Mexican-Americans were exogamous. That means that twenty-five percent of as Chicano individuals married non-Chicano. The rate was higher for women than for men--27 percent to 24 percent. Both men and women were more likely to marry Anglos if they married outside their group, and the third generation were the most exogamous (Burma: 239).

Another indication of the trend toward assimilation has been their growing political involvement. Stoddard (1973) categorizes five distinct periods of Mexican-American organizational development which demonstrate increasing involvement with and assimilation into the broader American society and culture. The first period, which lasted from 1519 to 1909, he labels as The Conquest and Colonial Period. It was characterized by minor organizational development and a virtually totally apolitical stance. This period saw some mutualista (mutual aid societies) develop, a few of which became somewhat involved. The Alianza Hispano Americana founded in Arizona in 1894 advocated political as well as social and economic goals and was an integrationist organization. In 1906 a migrant worker strike (huelga) led by Ricardo Flores Major achieved temporary

160

notoriety. It more or less died with its leader who was arrested and died in jail under suspicious circumstances (Acuna: 157).

The second phase, one of Cultural Accommodation, lasted from 1910 to 1941. This period is characterized by the development of several organizations which advocated and assisted in cultural accommodation with minimal political activity. Some of the more prominent developments in this period would be the La Liga Protectiva Mexicana (The Mexican Protective League), and the Order Hijos de America (Order of the Sons of America), both founded in 1921; the Order of Knights of America and the League of Latin American Citizens who merged in 1929 to form the League of United Latin American Citizens; the Confederation de Uniones Obreras Mexicana (Confederation of Unions of Mexican Workers), and the Union Trabajadores del Valle Imperial (Union of Migrant Workers of Imperial Valley) in 1928; and the Liga Obrera de Habla Espanol (League of Spanish-speaking Workers), founded in 1934, and whose leader, Jesus Pallares, was deported for organizing Chicanos.

This period was highlighted by a number of Chicano-led strikes: a cantalope pickers strike in 1928, celery and berry workers strikes in 1933, and the San Antonio Pecan Shellers strike in 1938. Although these workers received less than $2.00 per week in 1934, their organization was hailed as communist-inspired. The labor-organizing efforts of this period aroused opposition from majority society. From 1931 to 1934 some 300,000 Chicanos, thousands of whom were U.S. citizens, were deported to Mexico under a largely forced "repatriation" program. Although a considerable degree of racism was involved, the program was mostly a depression-related response and seems to have been mostly a "money-saving" device.

The late 1930's saw two other groups emerge: The Mexican-American Movement, and El Congress de Pueblos de Habla Espanola (The Congress of Spanish Speaking Peoples), founded in 1938 and led by the fiery Luisa Moreno.

This period was followed by one Stoddard calls Ethnic Separation, lasting from 1942 to 1962. Prominent developments during this phase indicate increased politicization. In 1943 Los Angeles was the site of the "Pachuco riots," better known as the "Zoot-Suit" riots.

The temper of these times was illustrated by the Sleepy Lagoon Case in which an L.A. sheriff's officer, one Lt. Ayers, stated that "crime is a matter of race." The Chicanos were handy and visible targets for the aggression aroused during this war-torn time of social upheaval. Anti-minority riots, such as the one in Denver in 1943, were aimed at other minorities as well. Chicano youth responded with patriotism, compiling an outstanding war record. Returning Chicano veterans, however, were not about to return to the apathy of the preceding period. In 1947, Arvin California was shaken by the massive DiGiorgio strike marking the new activism. That same year the Community Service Organization was started, inspired by the Sol Alinsky tactics. This group launched a massive voter registration drive and helped elect Edward Roybal to the L.A. City Council in 1949. In 1948 the G.I. Forum was started. By the early 1950's new forums in twenty-three states totaled membership in excess of 20,000 of the returning G.I.s. The early 1950's, however, marked the time when the Chicano movement was largely defensive and, to an extent, even driven underground. 1952 saw the passage of the McCarran-Walter Act, a U.S. Immigration and Nationality Act that marked a resurgence of restrictionism. Lt. General Joseph M. Swing, called by Acuna a "professional, long-time Mexican hater," was placed in command of deporting illegal aliens. The deportation drive inspired the development of the Council of Mexican-American Affairs in 1954 in L.A., the Mexican-American Political Association (M.A.P.A.) founded in California in 1958, the Political Association of Spanish Speaking Organizations (PASO), started in 1959 in Texas, and the American Coordinating Council on Political Education (ACCPE) that same year in Arizona. The 1960 elections inspired the Viva Kennedy Clubs which marked the close of this phase.

The turbulent 1960's were a decade Stoddard calls the period of Ethnic Autonomy and Radicalism. The early 1960's saw them begin the search for their own identity that led to the development and common usage of the term "Chicano" to distinguish Mexican Americans from other Spanish-speaking groups. Chicano veterans returning from Vietnam, where, as in World War II Chicano casualties were disproportionately high, were disposed to be far more radical than their predecessors. This increasingly radical movement pursued a wider range of political activities than in previous periods. It was by the emergence of four major Chicano leaders (Moore: 137-155).

162

The beginning of this phase was the 1963 grape pickers strike that launched Cesar Chevez to national prominence. La Huelga, as it was known, activated the political consciousness of the migrant workers. It showed that a new civil and human rights movement was emerging, based roughly on the tactics of the Black Civil Rights Movement.

In 1965 Chavez formed the National Farm Workers Association, leading a five-year campaign toward the successful recognition of his union as the organization of migrant workers. Chavez came out of the Community Service Organization of the 1950's, but became disenchanted with its increasingly middle-class orientation. He first formed the National Farm Workers Association in 1963, leading the grape strike. In 1966 he led a nationwide boycott. In 1966 the N.F.W.A. merged with the Agricultural Workers Organization Committee of the A.F.L.-C.I.O. to form the United Farm Workers Committee. In 1970 the 26 Delano grape growers, producers of 50 percent of all table grapes, signed a three-year contract with the U.F.W.C.

The second major leader was Reies Lopez Tijerina, known as El Tigre, who started the Alianza Federal de Mercedes (Federal Alliance of Land Grants) in 1963. Claiming some 10,000 members, the Alianza proclaimed, in October of 1966, the Republic of San Joaquin del Rio de Chama and tried to take over the Kit Carson National Forest. In October, 1967 the Alianza forged a "Treaty of Peace, Harmony, and Mutual Assistance" among the Alianza, and S.N.C.C., C.O.R.E., and the Black Panthers. Tierjina also received statements of support from the Crusade for Justice and M.A.P.A. In 1968 he ran for Governor of New Mexico on the independent People's Constitution Party ticket. In 1969 the Alianza group briefly seized the Tierra Amarilla courthouse.

In 1965 a "barrio youth" leader emerged on the national scene, Rodolfo "Corky" Gonzales. He started the Crusade for Justice in 1967, based in Denver, Colorado. Noted for his highly influential poem, "I am Joaquin," Corky Gonzales was also instrumental in establishing the La Raza Unida party in 1970. He ran for several state and local offices.

The goals of the Crusade for Justice include better housing, educational opportunities, jobs and land reform. For Gonzales, the key

163

to attaining these goals is in the laying of an an adequate power base, and he has come to put heavy reliance on nationalism and political separatism among the Chicano (Kuenster: 40-41).

The fourth major Chicano leader emerging during this period was Jose Angel Guitierrez. Like Gonzales, he is primarily a youth leader and helped found the La Raza Unida Party in 1970. The period of 1966-1967 saw the development of a "Brown Power" Movement on campuses across the nation. Guitierrez was a leader from the Mexican American Youth Organization (M.A.Y.O.), started in 1967. Other such groups were: United Mexican American Students (U.M.A.S.), Mexican American Student Association (M.A.S.A.), Movemento Estudiantial Chicano de Aztlain (M.E.C.H.A.), National Organization of Mexican American Students (N.O.M.A.S.), and the Association of Mexican-American Educators (A.M.A.E.).

The late 1960´s also witnessed the emergence of a number of barrio-based groups of more radical Chicano youth. The Latin American Defense Organization (L.A.D.O.) started in Chicago in 1966. The militant Brown Berets started in 1967 in Los Angeles and Chicago. San Antonio was the base for the Mexican American Nationalist Organization. In the spring of 1968 some 15,000 Chicano high school students walked out of East Los Angeles schools. The "1968 school blowout," as it came to be called, started a chain reaction in barrios throughout the Southwest where schools were shaken by student strikes. This phase culminated in the Denver riot of 1969.

The final period characterized by Stoddard is the Strategic Penetration phase, which began in 1970 and continues to the present. This phase is characterized by the La Raza Unida Party, an attempt to develop "pan-Hispanic" political unity. The strategy during this phase is to flex their political muscle and force both the major parties to woo their vote. In the past, the Chicano vote was overwhelmingly Democratic. Democratic candidates for Congress and the presidency received roughly 95 percent of the Chicano vote in the elections of 1956, 1958, 1960, 1962 and 1964 (Kuenster: 11). The first experiment with attempts to exercise more independent political clout were in the mid-1960´s. A "third force" maneuver in 1966 in Texas, Arizona, and New Mexico to give the Chicano vote to one major Republican was designed with the hope that this would demonstrate to the Democrats that they had to be more responsive to the Chicano aspirations or suffer a loss at the polls. In Texas this resulted in the election of Republican Senator John Tower. An estimated one-half million Chicano votes went to Tower and, at the same time, they voted for Democrat John Connally for Governor.

The 1970's saw the development of La Raza Unida and the voter registration drives by Chicanos, such as the previously cited Southwest Voter Education Project. In 1971 President Nixon made a concerted effort to woo the Chicano vote through such appointments as Mrs. Romana Banuelos as Secretary of the Treasury, Phillip Sanchez as head of the Office of Economic Opportunity, and as Director of the Immigration and Naturalization Service. President Reagan appealed to the Chicano vote, capturing about 30 percent of that vote in 1980. His 1984 campaign is likewise making a strong appeal to that bloc.

Despite some rather prominent successes, the Chicano voting strength is still more potential than actual. Only 44 percent of their eligible voters turned out in 1980. Proportionate to their share of the population, there ought to be fifteen representatives in Congress. As of 1980 there were only eight. There numbers in the population ought to enable them to elect ten to twenty percent of the legislators serving in the various Southwest state legislatures; their actual percentages range from zero to one percent. Despite a population in excess of 250,000 Chicanos in Chicago, they have not elected a single alderman or ward committeeman.

Yet they have begun to move a bit in the 1980's. This chapter has previously mentioned their newly prominent mayoral victories. Other prominent Chicano politicians include Governor Anthony Anaya of New Mexico and Democratic Vice-Chairwoman Polly Baca Baragan. Eight Mexican-Americans serve in Congress: E. Kika de la Garza (D., Texas), Henry B. Gonzales (D., Texas), Manuel Lujan (R., New Mexico), Matthew G. Martinez (D., California), Solomon Ortiz (D., Texas), Bill Richardson (D., New Mexico), Edward R. Roybal (D., California), and Esteban Torres (D, California).

Perhaps another indication of their growing political strength was their recent effort to block the passage of the Simpson-Mazzoli immigration bill. Pressure has been building for some time to do something about the problem of illegal immigration: after years of low numbers, the INS began reporting ever rising numbers of apprehended deportable aliens. In 1978, for example, over a million were apprehended, which is just under the all-time high of 1,089,583 apprehended in 1954 (U.S. News and World Report, January, 1979: 38). The estimates of illegals in the country range from 3 to 12 million. Some 800,000 illegals enter the United States annually, 92 percent of whom are from Mexico. The 300 or so border patrolmen who have to patrol the 2,200 miles of the U.S./Mexican border are stretched too thinly to effectively control the problem, even though their rate of seizure is up to 30 to 50 percent over last year. Los Angeles County estimates that its costs of educating the children of the area's illegal aliens runs as high as $415 million, and Texas estimates their cost to be $50 million (Time, June 13, 1983: 18-27). Some organized labor leaders, such as AFL-CIO President Lane Kirkland and Jay Mazus, President of the ILGWU in New York, have advocated amnesty to "legalize" the illegal aliens here so that they will have a less depressing effect on the wage and working conditions of the market (McClellan: 35-38).

In May of 1982 the Immigration and Naturalization Service launched a week-long effort, called "Operation Jobs," to root out illegal aliens from jobs that unemployed Americans might desire. It crystallized the various perspectives on the problem of illegal aliens. In a week's time the raids netted roughly 5,800 illegals who had been earning an average $4.75 an hour. The raids were targeted on Detroit, Denver, Chicago, Houston, Dallas, Newark, San Francisco, and Los Angeles. In those areas citizens and legal aliens began to apply for the jobs that the illegals held, some of which payed as much as $10 an hour.

Critics of the raids argued that the jobs the aliens filled were not being "taken away" from Americans.

One critic was Nickie Becker, office manager of the Petaluma Poultry Co. in Santa Rosa, California, who said she is having trouble finding Americans to replace aliens in jobs

166

paying $5.25 an hour in her chicken-processing plant. She said in a telephone interview that when 30 INS agents raided the company last Monday, "You should have seen the goon squad. It looked like a Gestapo raid. I've never seen anything like it in my life..." Becker said all the workers at Petaluma have shown some sort of identification, such as a Social Security card or official alien documentation. She said most of the workers are foreign because Americans don't like that kind of work. "They have to take live chickens out of the truck and hang them upside down. Their throats are split and they bleed all over the place before they go into the processing room where the guts are taken out. It's not a nice job. It's cold, it's damp. It's not the kind of job a nice, white, middle-class American wants to do," she said. After the raid, Becker said she hired 27 Americans, but by week's end only about a half dozen remained. As they left, she said, many of the Americans told her, "I'd rather be on welfare (<u>The Washington</u> <u>Post,</u> May 2, 1982: A 10).

The A.C.L.U. and some clergy attacked the raids on the basis of their being "discriminatory" because they were aimed solely at Hispanics. Another charge was that the raids were a scapegoating public-relations ploy "to shift blame for the administration's dismal failure in coping with increasing unemployment" (Ibid).

Supporters of the raids and spokesmen for the INS counter that not all the jobs were so undesirable or so low paying. In Chicago, 43 illegals earning $6.50 an hour were picked up at the Claussen Pickle Company. 250 people applied for their jobs. Over 1,000 applied for the 88 jobs illegal aliens held at the Price Feaster Brassworks near Los Angeles. A spokesman for the INS listed other raids that created desirable jobs:
  1) Fifty illegals earning $7 to $9 per hour were arrested at the Robert Bosch Company auto parts business near Chicago.
  2) The INS arrested 34 illegals earning $7.35 an hour at a Denver meat packing plant.
  3) Another 58 making $6 and up an hour were arrested at the Trinity Steel Works in Fort Worth.
  4) Forty illegals making $7 and up were arrested at Bell industries, a San Francisco computer assembler (Ibid).

The Reagan Administration backed the Simpson-Mazzoli bill which, if signed into law, would be the first major re-writing of the government´s tangled immigration policy in 30 years. The bill would give amnesty to most illegal aliens who entered the country before 1980, allowing them to apply for resident status. The federal government estimates that 2.3 million people would be eligible. The bill would punish employers who hire undocumented immigrants with fines up to $2,000 for each worker.

The bill, which had the support of the Administration and such groups as the National Association of Manufacturers and the U.S. Catholic Conference, was passed by the Senate in 1982 and 1983 but killed in the House in December of 1982 and again in October of 1983. A coalition of groups opposing passage of the bill include the American Civil Liberties Union, the American Farm Bureau, the U.S. Chamber of Commerce, and various Hispanic groups such as the League of United Latin American Citizens. Farmers who employ migrant workers also oppose it. Even some black groups who fear loosening of the rules opposed it on the basis that the law would permit easier deportation of Haitian refugees (The Washington Post, Sunday, December 19, 1982: A15). An amended version of the bill was finally passed by the House in June, 1984 and will now have to go to a Conference Committee to work out differences between the earlier passed Senate version and the House version of the law.

Puerto Ricans

The second largest subgroup among Hispanics are the Puerto Ricans. Estimates of the number of Puerto Rican migrants to the mainland and their descendants run as high as 3 million people (DeLeon: 17). Migration to the mainland has been a major factor of island life for the past thirty years. Puerto Ricans are unrestricted in their movement back and forth to the island since they are internal migrants. Between 1940 and 1960 alone, the island lost a million persons due to migration. Movement to the mainland has been primarily a post-World War II trend. In 1910 there were 1,513 Puerto Ricans on the mainland, 500 of whom lived in New York City. By 1920 New York City´s Puerto Rican population reached over 7,000 and by 1940 it exceeded 60,000. In the next thirty years the number of Puerto Ricans in New York City grew by fifteen times, to over one million. By

1970 there were more in the Bronx and Brooklyn than in San Juan. There were nearly 100,000 in Chicago, and 135,000 in New Jersey (DeLeon: 2-3).

Currently, Puerto Ricans live in every state, including Hawaii and Alaska, but they are concentrated in major cities, especially New York, Chicago, Bridgeport, Connecticut, Miami, Newark, Paterson and Jersey City, Boston, New Orleans, Lorain, Ohio, and Philadelphia. Connecticut has over 80,000, California over 50,000 and Florida around 30,000.

The Puerto Rican population on the mainland is overwhelmingly urban--in excess of 90 percent. It is young--the median age is nineteen years old compared to a median of 27.7 for the total American population. It is poor: their median family income is about six-tenths that of the total population's. In New York City about 85 percent of the Puerto Ricans live in low income areas. Puerto Rican families headed by the male in New York City in 1970 earned an average of about $4,000 per year less than the national median figure; those headed by females earned $1,300 less than the national median. That same year, 82 percent of female-headed Puerto Rican families in New York City received some welfare assistance, as did twenty-three percent of the male-headed families (DeLeon: 31-32).

Occupationally, their highly urban background is reflected in the fact that thirty times as many Puerto Ricans work in manufacturing as in agriculture. One in three Puerto Rican families depend on two or more wage earners for its family income. Puerto Rican workers are concentrated in blue-collar factory jobs such as machine operators, garage workers, and laundry workers. They are also concentrated in service jobs in hotels, restaurants and cafeterias. As craftsmen they frequently work as repairmen and cabinet makers

Their educational level, as with other Hispanic groups, tends to be low. Among Puerto Ricans twenty-five years or older, the median school years completed is 8.7 years. Just over 23 percent are high school graduates; they trail both blacks and whites in years of formal education.

Puerto Ricans come from a rich cultural background; a mixture of Indian, African, Spanish, and North American influences. On the island, the white versus

169

nonwhite population is 80 percent to 20 percent. In New York, that ratio is 92 percent white to 20 percent nonwhite (Fitzpatrick: 101-107).

The United States acquired Puerto Rico in the aftermath of the Spanish-American war when a military governor was installed. The island was declared a possession of the U.S. in 1899 through ratification of the Treaty of Paris. Instead of independence, the island merely experienced a change of ownership. Spanish was replaced by English in the schools, American holidays were celebrated instead of Spanish ones, and an American governor was appointed. In 1917 Puerto Rican people were granted U.S. citizenship and served in the American military--which raises the interesting irony that Puerto Ricans living on the mainland cannot vote for the President yet are required to fight in wars having had no choice in electing the president who shapes U.S. foreign policy (DeLeon: 11-12). It was not until 1946 that the first appointed governor was a Puerto Rican. In 1947 they were allowed to elect their own governor. In 1952, Puerto Rico was declared a Commonwealth, or Associated Free State of the United States. Since that time the island has been represented in Congress by a resident Commissioner. The current Commissioner is Baltasar Corrada, a Democrat.

Puerto Ricans began migrating to the mainland in large numbers in the 1960's. They can come and go to and from the island to the mainland at will, that is, without legal restriction, since a Puerto Rican is fully an American citizen. They are not immigrants, but migrants--relocating to seek the better job and life opportunities available on the mainland. During the decade of 1960-1970 over 100,000 a year returned to the island. Like the Chicano, the proximity and ease of transferring back to their native culture has magnified their cultural identity problems. Both blacks and whites at times reject the Puerto Ricans and at times seek them as allies. This was illustrated in New York City during the controversy over the neighborhood school district at Ocean Hill-Brownsville. That confrontation, between the city administration and the Puerto Rican Community Development Project supporters, illustrates the problems facing the Puerto Ricans because they are the last minority to enter New York. The Director of the Puerto Rican Community Development Project, Mrs. Betanzos, expressed the issue as follows:

170

The blacks want us to be blacks and the whites
want us to be white because they both want to
use us. In terms of issues, I would have to
side with the blacks--but I'm a Puerto Rican
and no one has the right to tell me or want me
to be black or white (Burma: 481).

Their primary motive for migration to the mainland
is to seek work. Some also come for social or
psychological reasons--to escape marital or family
problems, troubles with the police, and the like. They
migrate at a young age, most commonly between 15 and 39
years old, but over half of all migrants are less than
21 years of age (Lewis: 112-121).

They suffer from racism here, manifesting itself in
discrimination in hiring and training programs. Their
unemployment rate has generally been between two to
three times the national rate, and Puerto Ricans
typically fare worse than Black Americans in the job
market. They also trail blacks by about 20 percent in
voter registration and turnout, and are generally worse
off in housing and education.

Their family incomes rank the lowest among
minority groups in New York City. Their percentage of
families on welfare has risen more rapidly than any
other group, and they have the highest unemployment rate
of any minority in the city. As one scholar sums it up:

Puerto Ricans are acutely aware that on every
count--housing, education, employment, income,
welfare--the puertorriqueno ranks last in
comparison to other groups comparable or
larger in size in New York City (Burma: 475).

Over 850,000 Puerto Ricans are scattered about New
York City's five boroughs, and their numbers increase
dramatically daily. In fact, New York City's Puerto
Rican population is more than twice that of San Juan's,
the largest city on the island. The net migration
annually for the past several years has exceeded 30,000.
Almost all the Puerto Rican migrants are urbanized.
Chicago is the city with the next largest mainland
Puerto Rican population where they are concentrated in
"el barrio," the Spanish Harlem.

The spatial segregation leads to several negative effects. The social isolation slows their acculturation. Spatial isolation restricts their employment opportunities, decreasing their options for mobility and assimilation. The negative influence of residential segregation is differentially experienced within the Puerot Rican group. Working females are better able than males to get white collar jobs in the central city, as clerks, secretaries, and in operative positions. Residential segregation and mobility patterns have resulted in Puerto Ricans developing along the lines of the black minority rather than like immigrant groups, slowing their development of an independent, self-sufficient ethnic community, since they tend to live in mixed settlement areas, usually with blacks.

Puerto Ricans in the barrios complain of the cold, the feeling of being shut-in, and the impersonality and anonymity of life on the mainland (Lewis: 125-132). The most commonly cited disadvantage of life in New York, however, were exposure to crime, violence, drug addiction, and delinquency. Besides drug addiction, the most commonly cited health problems associated with life in the slums of the mainland were mental illness, high infant mortality rates, and tuberculosis.

Although they experience racial discrimination on the mainland, they tend to view Americans very favorably, except for American Blacks. As Fitzpatrick puts it:

> First, the Puerto Ricans make a clear distinction between an American Negro and a Puerto Rican who is de color. The colored Puerto Rican is identified primarily as Puerto Rican, not as a Negro. Furthermore, relations between Puerto Ricans and American Negros are often characterized by tension (:109. See also, Lewis: 182).

The lack of cohesion among Puerto Ricans is a major aspect of their political relative weakness. Unlike most immigrant groups, the church has not played its typical role of engendering ethnic cohesion among Puerto Ricans. Although over a third of New York City's Catholic population is Spanish-speaking, there are few Puerto Rican priests, and not a single Puerto Rican bishop on the mainland. Most Puerto Rican children

172

attend public rather than parochial schools. Church attendance among Puerto Ricans is low--one study found that 85 percent of Puerto Ricans were non-practicing Catholics. Even on the island, an estimated 80 percent are non-practicing. Spiritualism and "store-front" churches of the Pentacostals, or even no particular denomination, are growing phenomenons among Puerto Rican communities.

Their political action is a limited and rather recent development. Their youth, low S.E.S., and tradition contributed to their low registration and voting turnout patterns. Also, their heavy concentration in New York City was diluted in its potential clout by the fact that, until 1964, Puerto Ricans in New York were required to take a literacy test in English before they were permitted to register. This was ruled out by the 1965 Voting Rights Act which stipulated that completion of the sixth grade of schooling in Puerto Rico, or on the mainland, constituted literacy for voting purposes.

Several organizations comprise the major community development organizations among Puerto Ricans on the mainland. The Puerto Rican Forum was begun in the mid-1950's. Another important national group is the Puerto Rican Family Institute. We have previously cited the Community Development Project. Of all the grass-roots organizations of the Puerto Rican community, Aspira has probably been the most effective. One of the most articulate spokesmen among Puerto Ricans is the Director of the Commonwealth of Puerto Rico office in New York, Joseph Monserrat. Other more recent groups developing within the community are the Puerto Rican Educators Association, the Puerto Rican Legal Defense and Education Fund, the Puerto Rican Institute for Democratic Education, and the National Association for Puerto Rican Civil Rights.

As with other Hispanic groups, they have voted overwhelmingly Democratic, usually in the low 90 percentile range. Indeed, they have voted so solidly Democratic that, in 1968, Hulan Jack, a black Democrat, received 88 percent of the Puerto Rican vote against the 14 percent cast for a Puerto Rican running on the Republican ticket (Fitzpatrick: 66).

173

Since the late 1960's, also as with other Hispanic groups, Puerto Ricans have shown signs of increasing militancy and radicalism. This trend is perhaps best exemplified by the Young Lords, a Puerto Rican version of the Black Panthers or Brown Berets. The tenor of their political militancy is evident in their thirteen-point program:

1. We want self determination for Puerto Ricans--liberation on the island and in the U.S.
2. We want self-determination for all Latinos.
3. We want liberation of all third world people.
4. We are revolutionary nationalists and oppose racism.
5. We want community control of our institutions and land.
6. We want a true education of our creole, culture, and Spanish language.
7. We oppose capitalists and alliances with traitors.
8. We oppose the Amerikkan military.
9. We want freedom for all political prisoners.
10. We want equality for women, machismo must be revolutionary, not oppressive.
11. We fight anti-communism with international unity.
12. We believe armed self-defense and armed struggle are the only means of liberation.
13. We want a socialist society (Freedman and Banks: 84-86).

Since the 1970's, Puerto Ricans have also joined with other Hispanic groups, in the La Raza Unida Party for instance, and have begun to organize for more standard electoral action and success. Various Puerto Rican groups have stressed voter registration drives. The more prominent Puerto Rican politicians include, besides Baltasar Corrado, the Resident Commissioner, Herman Badillo Rivera, Antonio Mendez, former Congressman, Judge John Carro, the first mainland Puerto Rican to become a United States judge, Teodoro Moscoso, head of the Alliance for Progress under President Kennedy, and the only current member of Congress (besides the Resident Commissioner), Robert Garcia, a Democrat from New York who is the first New York-born Puerto Rican to serve in the United States Congress.

The Cubans

With over 900,000 in population, the Cubans in America are the third largest Hispanic group, comprising about 6 percent of the total Hispanic population in the country. Like the Puerto Ricans, their migration here has been a recent phenomenon. Their influx came in two large waves: some 700,000 refugees were accepted, through a variety of legal means, after the fall of the Batista regime in 1959 and prior to the most recent influx in 1980; the remainder of the 900,000 Cubans have come since 1980, including some 123,000 in that year's "Freedom Flotilla." These "refugees"--including the Vietnamese and Haitians--cost the United States government an estimated one billion dollars in direct aid (McClellan: 45-46). The Cuban boat people of the 1980 influx came in at a rate of some 3,000 per month and were a significant part of the estimated one million immigrants who entered the United States in 1980 alone, some 700,000 of whom were illegals (Newsweek, July 7, 1980: 27).

The initial Cuban refugee influx began with a flood that approached chaos. Following Castro's seizure of power in 1959, the first Cubans to flee were typically people of some measure of wealth. Being a select group--government officials, army officers, bankers and the like--they had little trouble blending into the pattern of a culture where money constituted an international language, and where anonymity meant safety.

The next wave followed the agrarian reforms and land confiscations in Cuba in 1960 and 1961. These events sent middle-class doctors, lawyers, architects, and disillusioned white collar workers to seek refuge here. They were soon followed by farmers, peasants, and fishermen until the social strata of the refugees began to become an all-inclusive cross-section of Cuba itself. By air and by boat, both legally and illegally they came to the United States until, by November of 1960, there were 40,000 Cuban refugees in Miami.

At that time President Eisenhower appointed Tracy Voorhees as his special representative to investigate the situation. On December 1, 1960, the President made available one million dollars, under the Mutual Security Act which declared Cuba a communist country, to be used for: 1) resettlement, 2) registration, and 3) aid to unaccompanied children.   175

These funds became the seed money to start the Cuban Refugee Emergency Center, which opened in Miami in December of 1960. Various governmental agencies worked through the center: the Immigration and Naturalization Service, the United States Public Health Service, the United States Employment Service, and the Florida State Welfare Agency. These governmental agencies worked with, and were supplemented financially by a variety of volunteer associations such as the Catholic Relief Services of the National Catholic Welfare Conference, the International Rescue Committee, United HIAS Service, the Children's Service Bureau, the Church World Service Immigration Services, the National Protestant Committee on Cuban Refugees, and the Task Force of the Protestant Latin American Emergency Committee (Stanley: 11).

Their resettlement program really got under way in February of 1961 when President Kennedy began a Cuban Relief Program designed to provide relief, rehabilitation, and resettlement. The resettlement program was based on a cooperative effort between the federal government and four voluntary agencies: 1) Catholic Relief Services of the National Catholic Welfare Conference, 2) United HIAS (Jewish), 3) the International Rescue Committee (nonsectarian), and 4) the Church World Service.

The failure of the Bay of Pigs Invasion in April of 1961 drove home the point that the refugees could not go back to Cuba, at least not for a long time. They were compelled to accept the fact that they would have to make permanent new homes for themselves in the United States. After the failed invasion attempt the rate at which new refugees entered rose to nearly 2,000 per week. By the end of 1961 there were more than 100,000 Cuban refugees here. By the fall of 1962 some 3,000 more entered, adding to the minority population in Miami and bringing severe problems to the city in handling the massive influx.

The center launched a resettlement program to find the refugees homes and jobs elsewhere in the U.S. A series of "Freedom Flights" began in February of 1962. Between then and December of 1963, when the program ended, a total of 69 flights resettled 3,802 persons. The single largest such flight carried 118 persons to be resettled in Kansas City. By March of that year the center had registered 161,941 Cuban refugees. The various voluntary organizations managed to resettle

176

about 60,000 of those. The center also developed programs for the influx of Cuban refugees who came via Jamaica, Mexico, and Spain.

The next large wave of Cuban refugees came in the mid-1960´s. On September 28,1965 Castro offered the opportunity for all Cubans who wanted to leave the island for the United States to do so. A few days later, October 3, 1965, President Johnson, at the signing of the new Immigration Act at the Statue of Liberty, indicated that "those who seek refuge here will find it" (Stanley: 42). These events launched a literal armada of refugees. In less than one months time over 500 boats carrying over 3,000 persons arrived. In November of 1965 another 2,000 arrived in a sea lift. The greatest number came with an airlift organized by the United States which flew between December 1, 1965 and August 5, 1966. It brought in an additional 30,487 Cubans.

The various resettlement centers were being flooded with 4,000 refugees monthly. In January of 1966 nine denominational Cuban Refugee Welfare Centers merged to form a single corporate venture: the Christian Community Service Agency. Working out of two main centers, the Opabecka Center and the Freedom Center, they processed 165 refugees a day. The total number of Cuban refugees resettled from June of 1961 to July of 1966 was 114,416. Stanley (1966) summarized the program as follows:

> For six years the Cuban refugee has been the object of casual interest and deep concern, laws and exceptions to laws. As of June 1966, any Cuban can enter the country who is a spouse, a parent, or a minor child of a Cuban refugee in the U.S., waiving the labor certification requirement. The very special interest he has had for the government has been evinced in the fact that more than $118,000,000 has been spent for his benefit; as many as forty to fifty persons have been involved in the resettlement of a single refugee by an agency such as CWS. In a country that showed a dire need of doctors, Cuba supplied nearly 2,000 from its refugee lists. Dentists, engineers, teachers, accountants--from the top of the professional strata down to the lowest laborer, Cuban refugees have found work in the U.S. (:55).

177

Their reception in other places was not always so welcome. Conflict among minorities, particularly between blacks and Asians, Asians and Hispanics, Chicano versus Puerto Ricans and Cubans sometimes became intense, especially when one minority in an area saw the "refugees" as getting special treatment and as constituting an immediate threat. In Denver, for example, Hispanics reacted violently when 24 Vietnamese families were to be given apartments in a Chicano housing project with a long waiting list of Hispanics. Rock and bottle throwing incidents finally forced the agency to find other housing for the Asians. State officials in Colorado made it clear they wanted no Cuban refugees, as the Chicanos were bitterly complaining about the months they had to wait for space that, prior to the protests, was about to be suddenly given to the Asians (McClellan: 49).

Although the resettlement program did involve a large number of Cuban refugees, the vast majority--some 80 percent--remain in the Miami metropolitan area. To date their political involvement has been restrained. There are no Cuban-American politicians in the Congressional Hispanic Caucus, for example, nor any state-wide officials or mayors who have achieved national notoriety. Cuban Americans have assimilated largely through the route of economic success. Indeed, of the 113 Hispanic organizations cited earlier, only seven are Cuban, several of which reflect a "professional" basis of organization. These are: the Association of Cuban Engineers, the Coalition of Cuban Professionals, the National Association of Cuban American Women and Men of the United States, Inc., the National Association of Cuban American Women U.S.A., Inc., and the Cuban American Legal Defense and Education Fund, the Cuban National Planning Council, and the National League of Cuban American Community-Based Centers (A Guide to Hispanic Organizations,:19, 23, 49, 60).

Their success in this country has been attributed to several factors. They were greatly aided by the government resettlement and related assistance programs. As special "refugees" from a communist-dominated country, they were received by the majority society with far less antipathy than many other immigrant groups, a far higher percentage of them came from middle-class backgrounds than did most of the older immigrant groups entering the United States. Thus, upon their arrival

178

here, although they started on a lower rung of the socio-economic ladder than did many European immigrant groups, within a decade they equaled or exceeded the status of European groups. Today, some 20 percent of Cuban Americans are professional or managerial in their occupation. Their unemployment rate is low: in 1980 when Miami´s overall unemployment rate was 7.7 percent, the Cuban rate was only 6.7 percent (McClellan: 75-79). Their success has caused friction and even occasional violent confrontation with Miami´s black population, such as the riot of May, 1980 which was sparked by black frustration with the Cuban success at what blacks felt was their expense.

John Ehrlichman (1982) has summed up their experience as follows:

> No other group of refugee immigrants in recent history has had greater social and financial success than the Cubans who settled in Florida after fleeing Fidel Castro in the 1960´s. Miami is now the home to prosperous Cuban doctors, lawyers, and financiers, most of whom arrived in Florida as refugees with few if any assets (:5).

Endnotes

1. This assessment is reached by several scholars of the Mexican-American. See, for instance: Acuna: 153; Briggs: 10; Burma: 131; Stoddard: 58-70; and Guzman: 548-554.

2. See "Mex-America," The Washington Post, March 28, 1978; and the U.S. Commission on Civil Rights, "Strangers in One´s Land," Washington, D. C.: U.S. Government Printing Office, May, 1970: 23; and U.S. Commission on Civil Rights, " A Better Chance to Learn; Bilingual-Bicultural Education," Washington, D. C.: U. S. Government Printing Office, 1975: 176.

Additional Readings

Acuna, Rodolf. Occupied America: The Chicano Struggle Toward Liberation. New York: Canfield Press, 1972.
Burma, John. Mexican-Americans in the United States. New York: Canfield Press, 1970.
Castro, Tony. Chicano Power. New York: E. P. Dutton, 1974.

Fitzpatrick, Joseph. _Puerto Rican Americans,_ Englewood
   Cliffs, N.J.: Prentice-Hall, 1971.
McClellan, Grant. _Immigrants, Refugees_ and _U.S. Policy._
   New York: H. W. Wilson, 1981.
Moore, Joan. _Mexican Americans._ Englewood Cliffs,
   N.J.: Prentice-Hall, 1970.
Philip Morris, Inc. _A Guide to Hispanic Organizations._
   New York: Philip Morris U.S.A., 1983.
Rosenberg, Terry. _Residence, Employment and Mobility of
   Puerto Ricans in New York City._ Chicago: University
   of Chicago Press, 1974.
Stanley, Frances. _The New World Refugee--The Cuban
   Exodus._ U.S.A.: Church World Service, 1966.
Steiner, Stan. _La Raza._ New York: Harper and Row,
   1969.

CHAPTER FIVE: RACIALLY-BASED MINORITIES

Of all the bases upon which majority society discriminates against groups, the racial base has been the strongest. It has led to more violence, more legal restrictions and constraints, more pervasive and institutionalized discrimination, than any other factor.

Racism involves attitudes, behavior, and institutionalized structures which together act to subordinate a person or group because of their color. Racism differs from racial prejudice, or hatred in that it involves having the power to carry out systematic discrimination by the various major institutions of society. Thus, in the United States, only the whites can be racists since they control the society's norms, customs, and values. Blacks, Asians, or Indians may be prejudiced against whites but they cannot be racists.

The major institutions of society--our government, businesses, unions, schools, churches, voluntary associations--have significant power to reward and punish. These institutions reward some individuals by providing them with career opportunities or by the way in which social goods and services are distributed. These institutions decide who receives the training and skills, medical care, formal education, political influence, self-respect, moral approval, productive employment, fair treatment by the police and courts, and decent housing. They have the power to punish others by denying them or decreasing their access to those rewards. In Black Power, Carmichael and Hamilton (1967) distinguish between individual and institutional racism as follows:

> Racism is both overt and covert. It takes two, closely related forms: individual whites acting against individual blacks, and acts by the total white community against the black community. We call these individual racism and institutional racism. The first consists of overt acts by individuals, which cause death, injury or the violent destruction of property. The second type is less overt, far more subtle, less identifiable in terms of specific individuals committing the acts. But it is no less destructive of human life. The second type originates in the operation of established and respected forces in society, and thus receives far less public condemnation than the first.

181

When white terrorists bomb a black church and kill five black children, that is an act of individual racism, widely deplored by most segments of society. But when in that same city--Birmingham, Alabama--five hundred black babies die each year because of the lack of proper food, clothing, shelter and proper medical facilities, and thousands more are destroyed or maimed physically, emotionally, and intellectually because of conditions of poverty and discrimination in the black community, that is a function of institutional racism (:4).

Racism in the United States has led to the systematic slaughter of entire groups of people. For a long period of the nation's history, the government had as a policy the annihilation of the Indian. Racism has led to the imprisonment in concentration camps nearly 120,000 Japanese-Americans. Racism has led to a system of social discrimination which has excluded black members of our society from positions of control and leadership, after a long period during which it justified the institution of slavery.

This chapter discusses groups which suffer from racism. It first examines the case of Asian-Americans, concentrating on the Chinese and Japanese. It then studies the patterns of discrimination against Black-Americans, from slavery to social segregation. The chapter briefly previews the various approaches used by Blacks to cope with their status, emphasizing the development of "protest politics," which offers a new model of majority/minority relations that sets the patterns for subsequent groups to follow. This chapter closes with a discussion of the American Indian. It covers the policy shifts from annihilation to their geographic segregation on reservations and their attempt to cope with these policies.

Of all the racially-based minority groups, the most successful in the struggle for influence has been the Asian-Americans. A larger proportion of Asians than any other racial minority group has achieved middle-class status. It is to their success story we first turn our attention.

Asian-Americans

Asian-Americans comprise one of our nation's smallest ethnic minorities. Immigration data establishes their respective influx as, total Asian, 3,272,827, distributed as follows: Chinese, 567,629; Japanese, 415,159; and "Other Asian" (principally the Philippines, Koreans, and Indians), 2,290,039. Despite their relatively small size, Asian-Americans were once feared as the "yellow peril." Table Eight present their immigration data for the decades of 1820 through 1980.

TABLE 8: ASIAN IMMIGRATION TO THE U.S., BY DECADES, 1820-1980			
DECADES:	CHINA:	JAPAN:	OTHER ASIA:
1820-1850	232		15
1850-1860	41,397	---	15
1861-1870	64,301	186	72
1871-1880	123,201	149	243
1881-1890	61,711	2,270	1,910
1891-1900	14,799	25,942	3,628
1901-1910	20,605	129,797	11,059
1911-1920	21,278	83,837	5,973
1921-1930	29,907	33,462	12,980
1931-1940	4,928	1,948	7,644
1941-1950	16,709	1,555	11,537
1951-1960	9,657	46,250	88,707
1961-1970	34,764	39,988	315,688
1971-1980	124,326	49,775	1,414,007
Total	567,629	415,159	2,290,039

Other Asia includes Korea and the Philippines, except for the years 1934-1951, and India. Recent decades includes post-Korean and Vietnam War influx of war brides, refugees, etc.

Source: U.S. Department of Justice, INS, 1978 Statistical Yearbook, (Washington, D.C.: U.S. Government Printing Office, 1978: 35-37; updated by the 1980 Statistical Yearbook: 4).

The Chinese-Americans

The Chinese were the first Asian immigrants to come to the United States in significant numbers. After the discovery of gold in California in 1848, Chinese laborers surged into the state. The largest groups came from the Kwantung and Fukien provinces of Southern China. In part, they were fleeing the economic depression, local rebellions such as the Tai Ping Revolution, floods, famine, and the general social discontent of their homeland. They were also pulled here by the demand for labor in California generated by the gold boom. Railroad and steamship companies were especially heavy recruiters of Chinese immigrants to America.

For the first few years the arrival of Chinese laborers was generally welcomed by the people of California and by state and local government officials. The Chinese were viewed as industrious and thrifty, adaptable to various kinds of tasks, and willing to perform labor unattractive to whites. Indeed, the Chinese quickly became essential to the state's economy. The fact that they had an organization which also made it possible for an employer to secure any number of workers by negotiating with a single contractor placed Chinese labor in a comparatively advantageous position. Once employed the Chinese laborer stayed on the job, agreeing to do the most undesirable tasks. With the lack of unskilled labor and the lack of women, they found work in the mines, building railroads, as ranch hands, farm laborers, and domestic servants. The Central Pacific employed some 9,000 Chinese immigrants a year. By 1860 they comprised about ten percent of California's population and twenty-five percent of the state's work force (Thompson: 71).

The warm welcome was short-lived. By the 1850's hostility broke out. In the mining regions the Chinese were often robbed and beaten, and occasionally murdered. The crimes against them were rarely punished, since, by 1849, a Know Nothing judge of California's Supreme Court ruled that the Chinese were forbidden to testify against white men.

In part, their problems reflected resentment against them because they were perceived as threats to white labor. The Chinese immigrants were overwhelmingly young males who came here as sojourners. The imbalance

184

of the Chinese male to female ratio led to problems concerning prostitution. The Chinese male to female ratio from 1860 to 1900 was literally a couple of thousand to one. The fact that fourteen states had laws against miscegenation, plus the extreme scarcity of Chinese females, left the men with no alternative but to totally abstain or to turn to prostitution. The prostitution, moreover, was usually associated with opium traffic which led to a severe "criminal image" problem for the Chinese immigrant. The difficulty of importing Chinese females contributed to the long-lasting nature of the imbalance. By 1882 immigration was greatly reduced. As of 1890, only 2.7 percent of Chinese were American-born. The ratio began to be redressed during the 1920´s when thirty percent were native-born. But real parity was not achieved until a 1943 law ended the total ban on Chinese immigration and provided for a quota system which allowed Chinese women to enter the United States. By 1960, two-thirds of the Chinese-Americans were native-born, and the male/female ratio was nearly balanced.

The miscegenation laws were but one manifestation of legal constraints imposed upon the Chinese in America. By the 1850´s California laws expelled them from mining work camps, forbade their entry into public schools, denied their right to testify against whites in court, and barred them from obtaining citizenship. By 1865 calls for restrictions on their immigration began. In 1867 the Democratic Party swept the offices in California´s elections by running on an anti-Chinese platform. The Panic of 1873 brought on economic conditions which greatly increased the sense of competition from the Chinese, and calls against the "yellow menace" broadened. In 1887 the Workingmen´s Party, led by Dennis Kearney running a blatantly anti-Chinese campaign, won control of the City of San Francisco. The party called for an end to all Chinese immigration. By the 1870´s such anti-Chinese sentiment was so strong on the West Coast that it was virtual political suicide to take their side. This anti-Chinese legal action culminated in the Chinese Exclusion Act of 1882.

The impact of that law, first passed with a provision imposing a ten-year ban and amended in 1884 to further tighten the ban, was immediate and drastic. In 1881, 11,900 Chinese immigrants entered the country.

Over 39,500 came in 1882. But that figure dropped to a paltry 8,031 in 1883, and by 1885 a mere twenty-three Chinese managed to enter! In 1892 Congress renewed the Exclusion Law for another ten years, and in 1902 the law was extended indefinitely.

Laws were not the only device used by the majority society to restrict the Chinese immigrant's life and work opportunities. Violence and social segregation were prominently employed. Anti-Chinese feelings reached a fever-pitch by the mid-1870's. Many whites felt that the legislation was inadequate as a solution to the "Chinese problem." They turned to violence. In 1871 21 Chinese were killed in Los Angeles. In 1880 there was a severe anti-Chinese riot in Denver. A typical example of the use of such violence was the Trukee Raid of 1876. Whites burned a Chinese home and shot and killed the Chinese as they attempted to escape the flames. The white citizens tried for the crime were acquitted. The Order of Caucasians was formed at this time; it advocated the elimination of Chinese through the use of violence. They raided and burned various sections of Chinatowns. In 1885, at Rock Springs, Wyoming, a mob killed 28 Chinese and drove hundreds of others from their homes. In Tacoma, Seattle, and Oregon City, mobs expelled hundreds of Chinese from town. Unionized labor, particularly the Teamsters, became a major force behind the violently anti-Chinese movement.

The violence subsided after the restriction laws were passed. But the strong prejudice and discrimination remained. Discrimination in jobs and housing was especially common after 1890. Newspapers spread the stereotyped images of Chinese with stories about prostitution, gambling, and opium dens in Chinatown. "Chinks" and "John Chinaman" were names used as racial slurs.

Job discrimination was rampant. Violence was often used to keep the Chinese out of the mine fields, but so too was legislation. In 1855 the Foreign Miners Tax was passed in California. It required foreign miners to pay a four-dollar-per-month tax. In addition, the tax increased each year the miner did not become a citizen. Since the Chinese were legally excluded from naturalization, they were forced to pay the higher rates. This legislation and the violence soon forced them to seek other areas of employment.

186

The general lack of women in the frontier West opened up the area of domestic service to the Chinese as one field in which they would not be viewed as a competitive threat. Laundries, restaurants, and other domestic services required little capital or job skills. The increasing job discrimination and violence encouraged the Chinese tendency to cluster together into urban Chinatowns. Even there, however, they did not escape legislative harassment. The City of San Francisco, for example, passed ordinances between 1876 and 1880 clearly aimed at the Chinese only. They placed a special tax on small, hand laundries which were all operated by the Chinese at the time. They passed a "Cubic Air Act," which jailed the occupants of overcrowded housing, rather than the landlords, if each person did not have 500 feet of living space. The city also enacted a "Queu Tax," that is, a tax on pigtails, which were worn exclusively by the Chinese. An ordinance was passed restricting the shipment of human bones. This was aimed at the Chinese custom of sending a deceased person's bones back to China for burial. Although these laws were nearly impossible to enforce, and were ultimately found to be unconstitutional, they did contribute to the atmosphere and the institutionalization of a rigid social and geographic segregation of the Chinese.

When the Chinese immigrant did enter industry pay discrimination was enforced which furthered segregation. The Chinese virtually took over San Francisco's shoe industry. The cigar industry was soon 91 percent Chinese. They comprised 64 percent of the state's textile industry workers. In these occupations wages almost immediately fell from $25 per week to $9 per week (Kitano: 197).

Chinatowns developed in Los Angeles, San Francisco, New York, Boston, Pittsburgh, and St. Louis. This pattern continues today. Recent census data estimates the Chinese-speaking population in excess of 300,000, and the total Chinese-American population at about one-half million. They are overwhelmingly urban. San Francisco's Chinatown exceeds 66,000 in population, and New York's is estimated at over 50,000.

The Chinese reacted to the discriminatory pressures by forming organizations for self-protection, for social and educational benefit, and for pooling their economic resources. The older organizations, such as the Six

187

Companies of San Francisco, were highly specific, limited in scope and membership, and conservative. These groups offered education and medical services, settled disputes among members, and gave legal aid or money to those involved in lawsuits with whites. During the period of heightened tensions and violence, the Six Companies hired a dozen policemen to guard the property inside Chinatown. They fought legal cases to overturn the anti-Chinese laws passed by local, state, and even the national governments. The Six Companies helped bury their dead and cared for their graves. Before the establishment of official diplomatic and consular offices in America, the Six Companies served as the unofficial voice of the Chinese Imperial Government on behalf of Chinese citizens residing in America (Kung: 71-79).

Newer Chinese organizations reflect American patterns—Chinese golf clubs, Boy Scout organizations, and Chinese Lions Clubs. Organized religion plays a very minor role in their lives. A more confrontational stance has been adopted by the Asian-American Political Alliance—a group comprised of Chinese and Japanese youth who reject the accommodationist posture of their elders. A more middle-of-the-road position was taken by the Chinese-American Citizens League. Founded in 1895, this organization promotes mutual interests among Americans of Chinese ancestry.

A major factor in easing the situation of the Chinese American was the basic attitude shift of the majority society during the 1930's and 1940's—when China became our ally against the Japanese. A significant pro-Chinese shift took place in American society. Our society and culture suddenly began to stress their peace-loving nature. We stressed how they had fought valiantly against the "sly, tricky Jap." We emphasized how different they were from their aggressive neighbor: that they were honest, hard-working, gentle and compliant (Kitano: 200).

The alliance between China and the United States in the war with Japan was the main factor in leading to repeal of the Chinese Exclusion Act. Madame Chiang Kai-shek visited the United States in 1943. A citizen's committee was formed to advocate for repeal. That law was passed on December 13, 1943. Quotas were established. The McCarran-Walter Act of 1952 further codified the many immigration and naturalization laws into one statute. It changed all references of exclusion to a systematic restriction by nationality. Increased Chinese immigration was allowed by a refugees law enacted under President Kennedy in 1962. Finally, in 1965, President Johnson signed into law an act which abolished the national origins system and pooled all unused nationality quotas into one group.

Even in California the attitude against the Chinese changed dramatically during and after World War II. Majority society there began to praise the high ethical standards of the Chinese in faithfully meeting their contractual and other obligations. The commercial ability of the Chinese was praised. The personal word of a Chinese merchant was accepted by American bankers, businessmen, lawyers and even customs officials. The Chinese had a reputation for promptly paying their bills, taxes, rents, and other debts.

The war period also opened up other avenues for more rapid acculturation. Because of the manpower shortage during the war Chinese-Americans were allowed to enter skilled as well as unskilled positions in industry. They proved to be hard-working employees. They soon began to compete in most occupational fields with much less discrimination, although Parrillo notes that even today there is evidence of subtle discrimination in employment in that they are under-represented in executive, managerial, academic, sales and personnel positions, and in the more highly-paid crafts such as ironworkers, operating engineers, plumbers and electricians (:283).

The cohesive and extended family structure of the Chinese American heritage also contributed to a more rapid acculturation. Their heritage emphasizes education very much. The third-generation Chinese-Americans were able to get good educations because of the post-World War II economic gains made by the first and second generations. With a good education, Chinese-Americans were able to enter the professional job market. They have done exceedingly well in the education system and now rank as one of the highest educated of the minority groups. The third-generation has completely acculturated in their style of clothing, observance of American holidays of Christmas, Thanksgiving, Easter, and the Fourth of July—although they still celebrate the Chinese New Year. The typical Chinese-American eats with knife and fork, not with

189

chopsticks, and more often than not he eats traditional American dishes.

Of course, the Chinese laundry and restaurants are still highly popular forms of business. Quantitatively speaking, the laundry business surpasses all others, but the amount of revenue received is less than that of the Chinese restaurants. The hand laundry still predominates, but laundries which perform specific functions such as shirt-processing are more mechanized. The Chinese restaurant has grown into an American favorite and produces good profits for its owners. Most such restaurants are either run and owned by a partnership or a single owner; few are incorporated. Chinese food has become popular in our diet and is now sold canned or frozen in most American supermarkets. Other popular Chinese businesses are the Chinese grocery and the import/export gift shops.

The very image of Chinatown has also changed. While once despised as dirty, crime-ridden denizens of iniquity, Chinatowns are now viewed positively, as a bit of quaint old China set down in our streets, providing the tourist with a unique and pleasure-filled cross-cultural experience.

By the 1960's, Chinese-Americans were well-acculturated. As a group they are largely middle-class. Being native-born they speak English as a native tongue. With few exceptions they are Americanized in virtually all cultural aspects. Structural assimilation, however, remains to be achieved. Their income levels are still a bit below the white average. Chinese-Americans exhibit a higher than average rate of mental illness. Tuberculosis remains a nagging health problem. In housing, they remain clustered in the Chinatowns of Hawaii, San Francisco, Los Angeles, and New York. Delinquency and gang behavior are serious problems, and gang behavior serves as an alternative means of filling status and identity needs among many Chinese-American youth (Parrillo: 283; Kitano: 205-210). The rate of inter-marriage, another good indicator of assimilation, remains low. Social contacts between whites and Chinese-Americans still reflect a degree of racial prejudice. While they are no longer feared in the job-market place, there is still concern about this level of assimilation. While increasingly common, intermarriage is still frowned upon on the mainland, as opposed to Hawaii, by members of both races. Curiously, that is less a problem with the Japanese, who we will view next.

190

Japanese-Americans

Japanese immigration to the United States began in 1868 when 148 contract workers came to Hawaii as plantation workers, but the majority came between 1890 and 1924. It was not until the Meiji Restoration in 1868 that Japanese were allowed to emigrate. Initially, they were encouraged to do so and were well received in Hawaii. They first came expecting to stay temporarily. They worked under a three-year contract which had been arranged by the Hawaian government. They were viewed as a source of cheap labor and an alternative to the Chinese "coolie" labor force.

After the initial three-year period, some immigrated to the mainland, concentrating along the West Coast, and especially in California. In 1870 there were only 56 Japanese immigrants on the U. S. mainland. By 1890 they exceeded 24,000, were just over 72,000 by the 1910 census, and by 1920 they exceeded 110,000, at which level they stabilized because the Immigration Law of 1924 specifically barred them until it was rescinded in 1952. By 1941, when the Japanese attacked Pearl Harbor, there were only 127,000 Japanese aliens or Japanese-Americans in the United States, some 94,000 of whom lived in California, and among whom 63 percent were native-born.

They adapted well to working conditions in the United States. The majority were young males (the ratio of male to female was about 4 to 1) from the farming class. In Japan that placed them in middle-class status. They were highly literate: nearly 99 percent were able to read, distinguishing them from their western and eastern European counterparts. In Hawaii, most Japanese immigrants worked in farming, usually in all-male work gangs under the supervision of an agent. Those who went to the mainland established a more diversified occupational pattern. The most typical job was working on the western railroad, but they were also employed in canneries, in the mines, as domestic servants, cooks, waiters, and in groceries and dry goods. Their low wage scale troubled them as they evidenced strong desire for upward mobility. They soon turned to agriculture, particularly truck farming, and became strong economic competitors. Prior to World War I, although the Japanese immigrant farmed less than one percent of the agricultural land in California and that often the most marginal land, they produced ten percent of the state´s total crop (1).

191

The Japanese faced immediate hostility and violence upon entering the mainland. The anti-Chinese feelings were extended to the Japanese. The shoemaker´s union attacked Japanese cobblers in 1890. Similar attacks by cooks and waiters´ union members followed in 1892. Fears of the Japanese "Yellow Peril" grew markedly with the success of Japan in the Russo-Japanese War of 1905. In May of that year the Japanese and Korean Exclusion League was formed. It was soon renamed the Asiatic Exclusion League. Labor and the San Francisco Chronicle led another large protest movement in 1905.

Legal action against them soon followed. In 1906 San Francisco passed an ordinance segregating Japanese children into Chinese schools. In 1907 President Theodore Roosevelt issued an order which lasted until 1948 barring Japanese entry into the United States from a bordering country or U.S. territory (that is, Canada, Mexico, and Hawaii, respectively). Opposition to their immigration and calls for legal restrictions came from the full spectrum of political opinion. In 1907, for instance, even the American Socialist Party unanimously agreed to oppose immigration from Asiatics. In 1908 the Roosevelt Administration used diplomatic and economic pressure to force Japan to accept the Gentlemen´s Agreement to voluntarily restrict emigration. The importing of Japanese wives was excluded from that restriction, so the peak years of Japanese immigration were 1907-1908, after which it sharply declined except for the "picture-bride marriage" system which brought wives here. From 1911-1920, 87,000 Japanese were admitted, but 70,000 returned to Japan, for a net gain of a mere 17,000 for the decade. Legal action against them continued. In 1913 the Webb-Henry bill, known as the California Alien Land Act, was passed. This law restricted Japanese aliens from owning land, limited them to leasing land for three years, and forbade land already owned or leased from being bequeathed. California Attorney General Webb frankly described the law he authored as follows:

The fundamental basis of all legislation...has been and is, race undesirability. It seeks to limit their presence by curtailing their privileges which they may enjoy here, for they will not come in large numbers and long abide with us if they may not acquire land. And it seeks to limit the numbers who will come by limiting the opportunities for their activities here when they arrive (Kitano: 17).

The Japanese got around the law by placing the land ownership in the names of their native-born (Nisei) children who held citizenship or in the names of their caucasian friends, the racist nature of the law signaled the troubles to come. In 1921 the Supreme Court ruled, in Ozawa vs. the United States, that the Japanese were not caucasoid and were therefore subject to the restrictive laws. In 1923 California attempted to plug the loopholes of its Alien Land Act by prohibiting aliens from being guardians of a minor´s property. When the U.S. Supreme Court upheld the constitutionality of that law, similar laws were quickly passed by New Mexico, Arizona, Louisiana, Montana, Idaho, and Oregon (Parrillo: 284-285).

The Immigration Act of 1924 was the final legal restriction aimed at totally blocking Asian immigration. Restrictions on their acquiring citizenship further complicated the acculturation process. The Japanese government was especially upset by this latest manifestation of racism. Not only did the government feel the law was a "slap in the face" to the Japanese people--for whom "face" or honor is all-important--but they considered it a direct violation of the Gentlemen´s Agreement which had specified that the United States would not adopt any discriminatory legislation against Japan (Kitano, 1969: 28).

The effect of this legislation was to develop an unusually pronounced generation gap among the Japanese-Americans. They can be categorized by age/generation, split by the pre-war and post-war generations. The "Issei" were born in Japan and immigrated here. They were prevented from becoming naturalized citizens until 1954, were unable to vote or to own land, and were subject to miscegenation laws. The "Nisei" are the generation born between 1910 and 1940. They are native-born Americans who were citizens and could vote, own land, and the like. They have been characterized as the quiet generation who are now in their middle-ages. The "Sansei" were born after World War II and are today finishing college and entering the work force. A final group, the "Kibei," were Nisei children born in the United States but sent to Japan to be raised in the traditional culture. By the time the war broke out, many of the kibei were desperately trying to get transportation back to the United States (see Kitano, 1974:214-216; and Hosokawa: 207).

193

During the 1930´s, as Japan expanded its "Co-Prosperity Sphere," tension between the U.S. and Japan increased. On the West Coast, hostility towards Japanese-Americans continued to rise alarmingly. That tension culminated in racial hysteria with the Japanese attack on Pearl Harbor on December 7, 1941.

That attack began a virtual nightmare experience for the Japanese-Americans living on the mainland. Nearly 120,000 Japanese-Americans, some 70,000 of whom were native-born citizens, were sent to "relocation camps" in the interior because of what was termed "military necessity." The relocation camps were, in fact, concentration camps. Conditions, especially in the beginning, were grim. Surrounded by fifteen foot high barbed-wire fences, the camps were guarded by tommy-gun armed troops stationed around the perimeter and on spotlight towers. Residents lived in crude barracks in which stalls a mere 18 X 21 feet housed families of six or seven. They were partitioned off with seven-foot high partitions, with four-foot openings--affording virtually no privacy. Residents had to use outside latrines. They were locked in by nine o´clock and had a ten p.m. lights-out curfew. The camps were located in seven states shown in the following table. They were governed by the War Relocation Authority and the War Relocation Work Corps. McLemore describes the early conditions at Poston in Arizona, whose peak population reached 17,867 by August of 1942. The barracks were flimsily constructed. Sometimes as many as eight people lived in one room. Mattresses were made by stuffing cloth bags with straw. There was hardly any furniture. The heat was intense in the summer, and the minimum temperature during the winter occasionally fell below the freezing mark. And then there were the barbed wire and the guards. It is little wonder that some people felt betrayed at having been sent to such a place and either actively resisted or failed to cooperate fully with the administration´s plans (: 179).

Only racial prejudice can adequately explain the interment policy. Indeed, the chief author of the plan, General DeWitt, provided a blatantly racist rationale for it:

194

In the war in which we are engaged racial affinities are not severed by migration. The *Japanese race is an enemy race* and while second and third generation Japanese born on the United States soil and possessed of United States citizenship have become "Americanized," *the racial strains are undiluted*...[Italics mine] (2).

```
┌─────────────────────────────────────────────────────┐
│        TABLE 9: THE CAMPS AND THEIR CAPACITIES        │
├─────────────────────────────────────────────────────┤
│ STATE:          CAMP:               CAPACITY:        │
│                                                      │
│ Arizona         Gila                  15,000         │
│                 Poston                20,000         │
│ Arkansas        Jerome                10,000         │
│                 Rohwer                10,000         │
│ California      Manzanar              10,000         │
│                 Tule Lake             16,000         │
│ Colorado        Granada (Amache)       8,000         │
│ Idaho           Minidoka              10,000         │
│ Utah            Topaz                 10,000         │
│ Wyoming         Heart Mountain        12,000         │
├─────────────────────────────────────────────────────┤
│ Source: Data from The Washington Post,               │
│         Sunday, December 5, 1982: A 14.              │
└─────────────────────────────────────────────────────┘
```

In addition to the emotional trauma, these American citizens suffered a huge financial loss--estimated at about $400,000,000 in 1942 dollars! They were eventually to recover about $38,000,000 in evacuation claims, less than ten cents for every dollar lost. And since the claims were made on the basis of 1942 prices and payments were made during the inflated post-war period, in terms of real purchasing power, only a nickel for every dollar lost was actually paid to the evacuees. No price, however, can be placed on the broken hearts or sorrows of separated Japanese-American families. The overall cost to the American taxpayer was about $250,000,000 for a program which history has clearly demonstrated was simply not justified by military necessity. In the succinct words of McClemore (1981): "One hundred thousand persons were sent to concentration camps on a record which wouldn't support a conviction for stealing a dog (:184).

One might well wonder why President Roosevelt signed Executive Order 9066 on February 17,1942 authorizing the evacuation of the Japanese on the west coast because of "military necessity." When he did so, Congress passed a bill supporting the order, and only one Senator--Taft--voiced strong opposition to the theory of evacuation. Paradoxically, the territory of Hawaii, in a much more vulnerable position, never even attempted a mass evacuation of its 120,552 Japanese-American citizens. The war passed without a single proven act of espionage or sabotage by a Japanese-American either on Hawaii or on the mainland. The army announced that "the shipping situation and the labor shortage make it a matter of military necessity to keep the people of Japanese blood on the Island." Yet the army used the words "military necessity" to justify the west coast evacuation plan (Hosokawa: 457-467).

That the Japanese-Americans in Hawaii were not evacuated en masse had nothing to do with loyalty or lack of it. It was a matter on manpower and logistics. Their skills and energies were needed in Hawaii. The government did not have the ships necessary to move 100,000 Japanese-Americans, plus 20,000 military dependents to the mainland and bring back an equal number of workers to take their place. Given an opportunity to do so, the Japanese-Americans in Hawaii demonstrated that nothing needed to be done to restrict them. On the mainland, however, they were never given that opportunity, even though the danger of attack was more remote.

On the west coast, anti-Japanese activity was particularly widespread and intense. Newspaper headlines, editorials, political speeches, as well as mob actions and nativist organizations,reflected the prejudice against Japanese-Americans. Politicians struck out at them, exploiting the tensions of the average voter and avoiding reference to more critical issues. Even before World War II, many politicians made use of that prejudice to help win elections. There was a strong correlation between waves of anti-Japanese agitations and election years. The Japanese group was small, economically and politically weak, and an ideal scapegoat. Politicians running for office could attack them without fear of reprisal. And there were economic as well as political motives for the anti-Japanese activities. Trade unions and small landowners took part in the agitation, but most organized opposition stemmed from the owners of huge estates. The large landowners diverted attention from their own control by attacking the Japanese farmer as the cause of everyone's problems.

The racial homogeneity of the Japanese-American made them easily visible targets of stereotyping. Whereas Germany had Hitler and Italy had Mussolini, both of whom were easy to hate and caricature without any linkage to German- or Italian-Americans, there were no such handy targets in Japan. Tojo and Hirohito were virtually unknown to the American public. The old stereotype of the Japanese as a "buck-toothed, bespectled, monkey-face sneak" was easily applicable to the Issei and Nisei. Their physical characteristics made it easy to segregate them. A Nisei instantly became a "Jap," no matter how removed his family, interests, and culture were from Japan. Japanese-Americans were caricatured as the schoolboy, the vegetable farmer, the gardener, and the corner grocer in a Japanese military uniform. But the German- and Italian-American had become more or less indistinguishable. They had different heights, different shades of white skin, and hair coloring ranging from blonde to brunette. Whereas the "German-Nazi" and the "Italian-Fascist" were verbally distinguished from the German-American and the Italian-American, the term "Jap" was applied to all Japanese-Americans, whether they were long-term resident aliens, native-born citizens, friends or enemies.

In the West, anti-Asian racism was never really questioned. It was comparable to the South's feelings against blacks. There were many whites in California who actually felt that violence against Japanese-Americans such as throwing a brick through one of their store windows was helping to win the war. Their mentality was akin to the sheeted and hooded riders of the deep South. In the hysterical weeks immediately after Pearl Harbor, someone chopped down four Japanese cherry trees along the Tidal Basin in Washington, D. C. (Time, August, 1961: 15).

In short, the climate of opinion which had been built up by those who saw economic and political gain in anti-Japanese agitation was the important factor in the evacuation. Those few alien Japanese who truly were a "military danger" were already known to the FBI and were taken into custody within a few days. That all the rest, including some 70,000 American citizens, should be

197

treated as a military threat was an act of official racism. There was never a single act of convicted sabotage or any type of criminal activity connected with the war by a Japanese-American. By contrast, although there were efforts of sabotage by some German- and Italian-Americans, they were never even considered for evacuation.

Direct responsibility for the program lies with several parties: the general public, particularly in the West, who clamored for something to be done against them; Secretary of War Stimson, who ignored the professional opinion of top Army and Navy commanders that, by February, there was almost no possibility of invasion; California Attorney General Earl Warren and U.S. Attorney General Francis Biddle, who legally justified it; President Roosevelt and his staff who concurred in the decision; Congress which reinforced the process with legislation; and finally, the Supreme Court which gave the relocation order a dubious constitutional sanction. Behind the fear and error stood racial prejudice, distorting their ability to deal with the situation rationally.

Top military commanders were not the only people who felt that the evacuation was not really a military necessity. FBI Chief J. Edgar Hoover said:

The necessity for mass evacuation is based primarily upon public and political pressure than on actual factual data. Public hysteria and in some instances, the comments of the press and radio announcers, have resulted in a tremendous amount of pressure being brought to bear on Governor Olson and Earl Warren, attorney general of the state (Hosokawa: 276).

Some of those involved in the program tried to justify it by contending that the Nisei could demonstrate their patriotism by accepting the evacuation. Others said the evacuation and relocation were necessary to protect the Japanese-Americans from hysterical Americans. The former contention is absurd. No one suggested the German- and Italian-Americans should do so. The latter contention simply is not supported by the evidence. From December 1941 to the end of the following March, there were only seven killings and 29 other incidents of violence against Japanese-Americans, with one-third of those incidents occurring during the Christmas and New Year's holidays immediately after the Pearl Harbor attack. That violence hardly indicates that the entire Japanese-American population was in danger of being massacred. Thirty-six cases of illegal violence hardly justifies the "protective evacuation" of nearly 120,000 persons. The danger to them was more in the minds of those demanding evacuation than in the facts as such.

The Japanese-Americans accepted the evacuation and internment surprisingly peacefully. There was one strike at Poston and a riot at Manzanar during the early period when conditions were especially bad. But once the immediate period of hysteria passed, Japanese-American evacuees of proven loyalty were allowed to leave the camps and join the United States army. Some 20,000 did so, 6,000 of whom served in the Pacific, but most of whom were in the famed 100th Battalion, 442nd Regimental Combat Team which went on to become the most highly decorated unit in the European theater (Hosokawa: 366).

In Hirabayashi v. the United States, in 1943, and in Korematsu v. the United States, in 1944, the Supreme Court upheld the constitutionality of the evacuation program. In the latter decision, approved by a 6-3 vote, the dissenting justices rendered sharp dissents. Justice Francis Murphy labeled the evacuation as "the legalization of racism." Justice Robert Jackson wrote:

> Once a judicial opinion rationalizes an order to show it conforms to the Constitution, or rather rationalizes the Constitution to show that the Constitution sanctions such an order, the Court for all time has validated the principle of racial discrimination in criminal procedure, and of transplanting American citizens. The principle then lies about like a loaded weapon ready for the hand of any authority that can bring forward a plausible claim of an urgent need. Every repetition imbeds that principle more deeply in our law and thinking and expands it to new purposes (in Parrillo: 291).

Fortunately, the principle did not lie about for long. In Endo v. the United States, in 1944, the Supreme Court revoked the West Coast Exclusion Orders. Effective January 2, 1945, the Japanese-Americans were no longer under forcible detention. By June of 1946 all camps were closed (Kitano, 1974: 218).

199

Ironically, the forced geographic segregation in the interment camps ultimately contributed to a more rapid acculturation of the Japanese-American and advanced their level of assimilation. The camp experience proved to be a catalyst in their assimilation process in several ways.

The wartime relocation forced them out of their ghettos; it broke up the "Little Tokyos" of San Francisco and Los Angeles. It also ended the nearly feudalistic control that the Japanese father held over his children and it emancipated the women of the Japanese-American families. Power within the Japanese-American community shifted from the Issei to the Nisei. Propelled into the mainstream of American life, the Nisei entered new occupations, improved their economic status, and helped pull down the legalized racial barriers against them (see, for example, "Disguised Blessing," Newsweek, December 29, 1958: 23; and Kitano, 1974: 227).

Educational barriers particularly began to fall. By May of 1942, the National Student Relocation Council was organized. That fall, hundreds of Nisei were enrolled in interior schools. In 1942-1943, 928 students from the relocation centers were enrolled in colleges and universities--in addition to 650 Japanese-American students who were not evacuees. Over 280 colleges and universities in 38 states accepted them. About 20 percent of them were able to finance their own educations, and the colleges, universities, church boards and foundations aided the other 80 percent. They did well: reports from the receiving institutions were highly commendatory. The Nisei demonstrated an encouraging assimmilability once freed from the strictures of the West Coast.

Another early spur to their dispersal was the increasing need for manpower. Sugar beet producers and processors created an insistent cry for evacuees to be released as laborers in the beet fields of the western states outside the restricted military zones. Seasonal work permits were granted to approximately 1,700 evacuees, most of them young men, during the spring and summer months. There were effective workers, and, during the fall harvest when the demand was even greater, nearly 10,000 evacuees went out on seasonal work permits. (Survey Midmonthly, August, 1943: 210-211).

200

By the fall of 1942, work permits granting indefinite leave were given to those who were found not to be "security risks." As manpower needs grew desperate, mid-west employers began to call for more Nisei help. Many Nisei urged others in the camps to move out. This completely altered their pre-war employment patterns. On the coast they were farmers, produce merchants, fishermen, gardners, and domestic helpers. In Chicago and other cities, they worked in factories and in such occupations as social work, teaching, chemistry, engineering, dental and lab technicians, draftsmen, and mechanics. Soon they were earning two to ten times as much as they had received in pre-war times. Some Nisei reported they were supervising persons of other races, a situation unheard of on the coast. Less than ten percent were employed domestically. Many soon had their own businesses. Japanese-American women were hired as stenographers, at first reluctantly, then enthusiastically as their good qualities became known. They rarely had a chance at good secretarial jobs in California. Many of the women found well-paying jobs in the clothing industry operating sewing machines. Their reputations as good workers soon spread.

In Chicago, the Japanese-American owned stores were interspersed with others and they had to cater to the general public in contrast to Los Angeles where Nisei had to look to their own community for employment. In the midwest, instead of setting up their own churches, they attended more than 100 of Chicago's established churches and found themselves welcomed. This new atmosphere, in part due to the regional shift, was also made possible by the work of the Relocation Authority. The support of the community or at least the approval of responsible citizens was necessary for the success of relocating evacuees. Usually a WRA officer would spend two or three weeks conferring with local government officials, heads of leading civic organizations, union leaders, and ministers before authorizing any resettlement office in a community (Survey Midmonthly: 212).

The Japanese-American Citizens League (JACL), founded in 1930, began during the war to lobby quietly but effectively against the prejudice and discrimination facing their community. The JACL worked with the WRA, the American Civil Liberties Union, the Common Council for American Unity, Norman Thomas of the Post-War

201

Council, the American Baptist Home Mission Council, the YWCA, and the Friends Service Committee to help evacuees find jobs and housing to adapt to life outside the camps.

The JACL held the Nisei together and kept them in touch with one another through its paper, The Pacific Citizen. It gave Nisei a strong, clear editorial voice when most newspapers were either against or simply ignoring them. It was through this paper that they expressed their goal as an organization for Japanese-Americans: the emancipation of all Japanese-Americans from the stigma of limited citizenship and the cloak of questioned loyalty through their total assimilation into the general culture and their complete acceptance as co-Americans by their fellows.

The war-time related dispersal was fairly widespread. Nearly 43,000 had resettled in nine states: Illinois, 15,000; Colorado, 6,000; Utah, 5,000; Ohio, 3,900; Idaho, 3,500; Michigan, 2,800; New York, 2,500; New Jersey, 2,200; and Minnesota, 1,700 (3). Nisei liked their new homes as they had job challenges and opportunities unknown to them in California.

After the war the JACL continued to work against legal discrimination. They led the fight towards the naturalization of the Issei, recognizing that only as citizens would the Issei have equal protection under the law. The JACL also sought to revise the discriminatory features of the immigration laws.

Congress moved slowly. An amendment to the Soldiers Brides Bill was passed which allowed the Japanese spouse and children of American servicemen to enter the United States without regard to the Oriental Exclusion Act. Individual Congressmen sponsored more than 200 private bills benefiting Issei and Nisei. Tenure, which had been cancelled as a result of the evacuation, was restored to Nisei under the federal civil service. The JACL found strong friends in Congressman Francis E. Walter of Pennsylvania and Senator Pat McCarran of Nevada. The Walter-McCarran Immigration and Naturalization Act of 1952 provided for repeal of the Oriental Exclusion Act of 1924, extending to Japan and other Asian countries a token immigration quota. It also eliminated race as a bar to citizenship. Truman vetoed the bill for reasons not linked to the Japanese-Americans. The JACL made a determined effort to override the veto. Nisei sought editorial support in local newspapers. Nisei veterans got in touch with men they had known while in uniform. Support for the measure poured into Congress, which passed it over the veto by a vote of 278-113 in the House, and 57-26 in the Senate (Hosokawa: 454).

The Walter-McCarran Act was a big step for the Issei. Hundreds of them enrolled in citizenship courses sponsored by churches, the JACL chapters, and other organizations.   Further JACL legal success came with the new immigration law passed in 1965, which ended the quota system based on national origins.   Since the 1970's, Japanese immigration has averaged about 4,000 annually.   In 1976, Mrs. D"Aquino, a kibei better known as "Tokyo Rose," was finally legally cleared (Parrillo: 291-292).

During the late 1950's and throughout the 1960's, the nation became deeply preoccupied with the problems of all minority groups, most visible of which were the Black-Americans.   In the South, the Japanese-Americans were often regarded as white by the whites and as colored by the blacks.   Whites insisted that Japanese-Americans sit in the front of the bus, drink from the white man's fountains, and use the white man's restrooms. By contrast, blacks urged, "Us colored folks has got to stick together." There was no middle ground in the South.   In the rest of the nation, Nisei were yellow-skinned (Hosokawa: 473).

Since the 1960's, the Japanese-Americans, and more especially the Sansei, have achieved remarkable success. By nearly any criterion one could use, they have become the most successful of all minority groups. Speaking of that success, Kitano (1974) wrote: "Perhaps the model choice for handling the problem of visibility has been 'psychological passing:' identifying and acquiring the American culture at such a rapid rate that they have been termed as America's model minority (:200)."

The Nisei and Sansei have a higher average formal education than any other group in the United States, including whites.   They have been decidedly upwardly mobile. In occupations, they have concentrated in the professions, particularly architecture, medicine, dentistry, engineering, teaching and pharmacy.   They have moved into highly technical fields.   Their average income exceeds all other non-whites and are comparable in amount and distribution to whites.   As a group, and in contrast to the Chinese-American, they exhibit low rates of juvenile delinquency, divorce, and mental illness. They overwhelmingly live in middle-class housing.

Current estimates place the number of Japanese-Americans at about 600,000, or less than three-tenths of one percent of the total population. Of these, 250,000 reside in Hawaii and 350,000 are mainlanders of whom an estimated 225,000 now live in California. More than fifteen percent hold professional jobs, far higher than any other minority and, in fact, on a par with whites. In Los Angeles County, where the largest concentration on the mainland is located, school authorities report that children of Japanese ancestry outstrip all others in I.Q. test results. A Japanese-American child can expect to live six to seven years longer than a white child, and ten to eleven years longer than a black.

Crime figures are even more telling. While arrests rates for white, black, and American Indian adults have soared during the last three decades, the rate of Japanese-American adults, which never was high, actually decreased sharply. Despite their overall favorable employment record, however, few Japanese-Americans occupy the highest levels of business and professional life.

They exhibit considerable evidence of secondary and even primary cultural assimilation. Their record in business, the professions, housing, joining voluntary associations, and dating are remarkable. Even their level of out-marriage demonstrates an assimilation rate higher than that of any other racial minority. One study found their outmarriage rate changing from 11 percent in 1949 to 20 percent in 1959. Another found the change from Nisei to Sansei outmarriages to rise from 8 percent to 33 percent. Finally, a 1973 study found that <u>fifty percent</u> of Japanese-Americans married outside their race (McLemore: 186-190; see also Kitano, 1974: 229).

Two theories have been advanced to account for this rather remarkable record of successful assimilation. The "value-compatibility theory" stresses the fact that traditional Japanese values are highly compatible with white middle-class values, and also stress upward social mobility. Traditional Japanese values emphasize politeness, respect for authority, attention to parental wishes, and duty to the community. They stress hard work, cleanliness, neatness, honesty and the importance of education, occupational success, and good reputations. In short, many of the traditional Japanese values are the same as many traditional values of the Anglo-Americans. The "community cohesion theory" attempts to account for the reasons why these values are so effectively socialized among the Nisei and even the Sansei generations by adding a new and important emphasis. This perspective stresses that the success of the Japanese-American has depended upon the way these values have been transmitted. The entire ethnic group has been involved in this transmission process (see McLemore: 195).

Despite their rather impressive record, there are still some gaps. While the third and fourth generations are rapidly entering such status fields as the professional ones cited above, their major quantitative contribution thus far has been in agriculture. Gardening, for example, is still dominated by Japanese-Americans in California. In business, they have not yet achieved the highest corporate levels. They are largely unrepresented in the arts and entertainment fields. Outside of Hawaii, where they comprise about 37 percent of the population, they have achieved relatively little political power. Their impact on national-level electoral politics has been minor. Former Senator Hayakawa of California and Mayor Mineta of San Jose, California are the most prominent mainland elected officials of Japanese-American descent.

Since the late 1960´s a few confrontationist-type groups have formed, with such names as the Asian-American Political Alliance, the Council of Oriental Organizations, the Yellow Brotherhood, the Third-World Liberation Front, and the Red Guards (see Kitano, 1974: 228-229). They are concerned about racism and discrimination, and have shifted away from the accommodationist stance and towards ethnic identity and cultural autonomy. Gidra, a newspaper published by Sansei, challenged local Japanese and other Asian establishment groups, advocating radical stands and promoting "yellow power." Pan-Asian coalitions are a new phenomenon, since in the past national identities have prevented an overall Asian identity. It is difficult to ascertain the number, representation, and power of these Pan-Asian groups, but their emergence has greatly disturbed the older generations of Japanese,

Chinese, Koreans, and Filipinos. Perhaps achieving total assimilation is no longer their ultimate goal. If that drive has modified, previous patterns of accommodation, ritualism, and retreat will have to change as well. Increased confrontation and more radical political participation will surely result. The confrontational approach is even more characteristic of the black political movement. It is to that racial minority we now turn our attention.

Black-Americans

Of all the minority groups in American society, only Black Americans experienced the problem and status of slavery. Most Black Africans who immigrated to the United States prior to 1808, when the slave trade was officially ended, were forced to come here as slaves. In recent years, voluntary immigration by blacks--both Black Africans and West Indians--has been significant, about 65,000 annually. Blacks in the U.S., at over 26 total population. Black Americans, suffering more than two-hundred years of master/slave relations, are somewhat unique in that their slave status slowed their assimilation and set the norms and attitudes between the two races.

In the South, the existence of slavery meant that society developed an elaborate caste system which clearly and strongly delineated norms and interactions between members of both races. The repression, prejudice, and discrimination against blacks was exceptionally strong. Even the free blacks of the South, of whom there were nearly one-quarter million prior to the Civil War, faced more rigid discrimination because of the caste system. Except for three states, Tennessee, North Carolina, and parts of Louisiana, they could not vote. In the 1830´s even Tennessee and North Carolina disenfranchised them. The white South restricted them by law and customs. By the time of the Civil War, "free blacks" were barred from public school, serving in the militia, most public places, and from various types of employment. They were subject to curfews and a registration system somewhat akin to blacks in South Africa today. They suffered both physical and verbal abuse. While they were able to make contracts, be married, sued, and hold property, they were barred from testifying against whites or serving on juries. And they faced severe penalties if convicted of crimes (Dinnerstein, Nichols, and Reimers: 45).

For the millions of slaves who lived in the South by 1860, conditions were far worse. The Northwest Ordinance of 1787 had outlawed slavery in the North in what became the states of Ohio, Indiana, Illinois, Michigan and Wisconsin. The Constitution of 1787, however, prevented the banning of the slave trade for 20 years--until 1808. Even after that date, slaves were illegally brought into the South for decades. The natural increase in the slave population, however, accounted for the significant rise in the black population.

The interstate slave trade among the Southern states was among slavery's most inhumane aspects. Prior to the Civil War there were nearly four million slaves in the United States. This practice not only degraded the individual but also had a profound impact upon the black population for years by greatly influencing their acculturation. It destroyed existing links with their Afro-culture and groupings, frequently destroyed slave family units, and dispersed the slave population throughout the South.

The hardness of life under the slave status was an important ingredient in subsequent Black-American development. Slaves were highly limited in their occupational training and education. Moreover, the degradation of slave status contributed to the development of a sense of racial superiority among whites. The antebellum slave codes were severely repressive and designed to cause fear of the white man among the slaves.

Slaves were both legally and culturally considered as property. They were, by definition, subhuman. They could be bought and sold, given away, or eliminated. Slave women could be sexually used by their masters or for breeding purposes. Discipline was strictly maintained as slaves had to be taught to be subservient, but productive. Slaves were made fearful of and dependent upon the whites in order to insure their submission and loyalty. Family life was unstable or non-existent. Morbidity and mortality rates among slaves were very high. Illness, filth, and disorder were common aspects of the slaves' everyday lives. Since they were owned and maintained solely for labor, equal social interaction with whites was non-existent.

Slave status depressed the need for achievement among blacks. It also developed a matri-focal (mother-centered) family live tradition which contributed not only to higher rates of female-headed households among blacks but also to a weakening of the male role. It has been argued that this pattern frequently led the young black male toward violent anti-social behavior.

But the effects of the slave system were not limited to the black population. Whites were equally, if differently, affected by the slave system. As Thomas Dye (1971) notes:

Slavery also had a lasting impact upon Southern whites. DeTocqueville characterized the typical slaveholder as a "haughty and hasty man--irascible, violent, ardent in his desires, impacient with obstacles but easily discouraged if he cannot succeed upon his first attempt." Southern whites were not oblivious to the evils of slavery, and they soon developed a profound defensiveness about Southern culture and a suspicion of outsiders incapable of "understanding" their peculiar problem. Moreover, Southern whites felt obliged to protect themselves against the ever-present possibility of slave revolt. The specter of Nat Turner and his sixty black followers killing fifty-seven whites in two days in 1831 haunted Southern society. This fear conditioned otherwise compassionate Southern gentlemen to overlook excessive brutality practiced against blacks. But more importantly the fear of black revolt provided all white men with a common bond, a sense of mutual concern that became the basis of white unity within the South. Fear of the Negro obliged whites to set aside many of their differences in the interest of maintaining white supremacy, for they realized that petty factionalism might enable the blacks to gain an advantage over a divided white community. The basis for one-party politics and Southern unity in national affairs has its roots deeply within the slave period (:9. See also, Moynihan, 1965).

The 1850's brought increasing despair to the black population as the slave issue began to divide the nation. The Compromise of 1850 and the Kansas-Nebraska Act of 1854 failed to settle the growing conflict over the issue. The infamous Dred Scott case of 1857 gave a constitutional defense to the fact that blacks were not citizens nor were they entitled to the constitutional safeguards enjoyed by white Americans. Nor did the great abolitionist, William Lloyd Garrison, have to travel to the deep south to be in danger--he was almost lynched in Boston.

The abolitionist movement continued to grow and open conflict was clearly developing. "Uncle Tom's Cabin" was written in 1852 and sold more than 300,000 copies. John Brown's raids raised hopes among blacks and fears among whites that slavery might be ended by force. The election of Lincoln on an anti-slavery platform increased those hopes and fears. His election precipitated the attempted secession of the eleven Southern states from the Union. When the Civil War broke out, blacks were not allowed to enter the Union's armed forces. Only when a severe shortage of troops plagued the Union Army, late in 1862, were the segregated units of "United States Colored Troops" finally formed. While a total of 186,000 blacks served, they did not receive the same pay as white soldiers until 1864 (National Advisory Commission on Civil Disorders; 211-212).

Even in the North, racial tensions were high during the War period. Violent rioting, mostly between blacks and Irish workers, occurred in Cincinnati, Newark, Buffalo, and Troy in 1862. The most violent rioting took place in the "New York City Draft Riots" of 1863. A three-day rampage broke out during which a mob of some 700 ransacked and set afire the office of the provost-marshall in charge of conscription. An entire city block was gutted. The mob then attacked the black section of the city. Thousands of blacks were forced to flee, and many were slain. Likewise, at the end of the war a riot in New Orleans left 34 blacks and four whites dead and over 200 people injured. General Sheridan described it as a massacre perpetrated by the police without the shadow of necessity (see Dye, 1971: 213).

The promise of peace and equality afforded by the Reconstruction Period was short-lived, lasting but a decade or so. The radical Republicans gained control of Congress in 1867. The Southern states, under military rule, adopted new constitutions which assured blacks the vote and other civil liberties. Blacks were elected to the U.S. Congress and to the various state legislatures. Between 1870 and 1901, twenty-two blacks served in Congress—twenty in the House and two in the Senate. All were elected as Republicans. Thirteen of the twenty-two were former slaves. A prominent black politician was Governor of Louisiana for forty days. The Reconstruction Congress passed the Thirteenth, Fourteenth and Fifteenth Amendments and the Civil Rights Act of 1875. The Civil Rights Act declared that all persons were entitled to the full and equal enjoyment of all public accommodations—such as inns, public conveniences, and places of public amusement. It specifically forbade the denial of such accommodations unless the reasons for the denial were applicable to citizens of every race. It held violators liable to a civil suit for damages or to prosecution for a misdemeanor. In short, Congress established as national policy nondiscrimination in all aspects of public life. From 1865 to the 1870´s, the Reconstruction period saw considerable success with the civil rights movement: the prevalence of black voting throughout the South, the election of many blacks to federal and state-level offices, and the nearly equal treatment of blacks in theatres, restaurants, hotels, and public transportation facilities. These gains, however, began to recede by 1877.

The "Compromise of 1877" ended the military occupation of the South. More importantly, a series of Supreme Court cases spelled the collapse of the Reconstruction experiment. The Slaughterhouse Cases of 1873 nullified the privileges and immunities clause of the Fourteenth Amendment. The Civil Rights Cases of 1883 declared the Civil Rights Act of 1875 unconstitutional. In 1884, the Hurtado v. California ruling severely restricted the due process clause of the Fourteenth Amendment. Finally, in Plessy v. Ferguson, in 1896, the Court approved the segregation of society through the application of the "separate-but-equal" doctrine which essentially nullified the equal protection clause of the Fourteenth Amendment (Dye: 11-12).

Even during the Reconstruction Period Southern whites used campaigns of violence and intimidation. The Ku Klux Klan led the movement to suppress the emergence into society of the new black citizens. Major riots occurred in Memphis, where 46 blacks were killed and 75 wounded, and in the Louisiana centers of Colfax and Coushatta, where more than 100 blacks and white Republicans were massacred (Commission on Civil Disorder: 213).

Southern opposition to blacks serving in state and local government was open and bitter. The press, and white politicians campaigning against them, described the black candidates as ignorant and depraved, making no distinction between blacks who had graduated from Dartmouth and those who had graduated from the cotton fields. Blacks who voted or held office were refused jobs or visited in the night by a hooded delegation of Klan members. A group of Mississippi Klansmen boasted of having killed 116 blacks and throwing their bodies into the Tallahatchie River. In a single county of South Carolina, the first six months of 1870 saw six blacks murdered and more than 300 whipped (Ibid: 213-214).

Segregation in its full-blown Jim Crow form took shape gradually, being closely associated with the rise of Populism in the South. Southern blacks voted well into the 1880's and 1890's. Blacks held office, served on juries, local government councils, state legislatures, and the U.S. Congress. Blacks and whites rode the railroads in the same cars, ate in the same restaurants, and sat in the same theatres and waiting rooms. Reconstruction legislation remained on the books in Southern states for some years after 1877.

As Southern whites began to regain control over government, however, a program of relegating the black to a subordinate place in society was accelerated. Beginning in Virginia as early as 1869 and spreading throughout the South, the use of Jim Crow laws and Klan intimidation characterized the "new South's" approach to the end of Reconstruction.

Disenfranchisement was the initial step taken. Blacks who defied Klan pressure and tried to vote were met with an array of deceptions and obstacles. Polling places were changed at the last minute without notice to blacks. Severe time limits were imposed on blacks completing long and complex ballots. Votes cast incorrectly in a maze of ballots were "nullified." State constitutions were rewritten disenfranchising blacks who could not read, understand, or "correctly interpret" complex and obscure sections of the constitution. Yet state constitutions permitted those who failed the test to vote "...if their ancestors had been eligible to vote on January 1, 1860, when no Negro could vote anywhere in the South" (Advisory Commission Report: 214).

In 1896 blacks registered to vote in Louisiana totalled 130,344. In 1900, after the state rewrote its suffrage provisions, only 5,320 blacks remained on the registration books. With the 1883 Supreme Court decision declaring the 1875 Civil Rights Act void and the 1896 Plessy case's promulgation of the "separate-but-equal" doctrine, the door was open to legal segregation reinforcing that of social custom. Soon blacks and whites were segregated, by law, on public transit and in all places of public accommodation--even hospitals and churches. Blacks and whites swore their oaths on separate bibles in Southern courthouses. They were even buried in segregated cemeteries. And segregation meant discrimination, for the facilities, school conditions, and salaries were invariably worse for blacks. They were always separate, but never equal.

Conditions in the North were not much better. There blacks were crowded by local ordinances into one section of the city where housing and public services were invariably sub-standard. Discrimination in employment was the general practice. Blacks were largely limited to menial jobs. Labor unions excluded them from membership, or granted them membership only in separate and mostly powerless Jim Crow locals. Yet if blacks took jobs during strikes, they were castigated for undermining the principles of trade unionism.

Northern whites also resorted to violence. Anti-black riots occurred in New York in 1900; in Springfield, Ohio, in 1904; in Greensburg, Indiana, in 1906; and in Springfield, Illinois, in 1908. The latter riot, a three-day rampage initiated by a white woman's charge of being raped by a black, left six persons dead. Property damage was extensive. Many blacks fled the city permanently; most of them migrated to Chicago. Throughout the nation about 100 lynchings occurred every year in the 1880's and 1890's. One hundred sixty-one blacks were lynched in 1892 alone.   A pioneering study by the NAACP appropriately entitled "Thirty Years of Lynchings   in   the United States,   1889-1918" lists   the names of 3,224 lynch victims (see Dye, 1971: 18-19).

Those blacks who fled from Springfield to Chicago found they had left the frypan for the fire.   In 1919 the nation was embroiled in the "Red Summer" race riots, the worst of which shook Chicago--which had experienced the in-migration of 60,000 blacks from the South in the 1910 to 1919 decade.   The riot began when an 18 year old black drifted across the imaginary line segregating black and white swimmers at the 29th Street beach. White rock throwers caused him to drown.   Soon after, blacks mobbed a policeman who refused to arrest the whites responsible.   Shortly after, a crowd of Italian-Americans killed the first black they saw, touching off a riot which left 38 more dead, 1,000 homeless, and 537 injured (Levy and Kramer: 27).

As more blacks migrated north, race riots became almost commonplace.   Northern whites increasingly began to accept the white South's views on race relations. Social customs followed public policy in the North. Soon little signs reading "white only," or "colored" were everywhere.   Although these lacked the sanction of law, black children were taught in their segregated schools that they were to obey those signs.   Segregation replaced slavery as society's method of keeping blacks "in their place." The vast majority of blacks remained mired at the bottom of the country's social and economic system.   Segregation was supported by state laws, and by various social practices and institutions.   Blacks were segregated throughout their lives--from birth in a segregated hospital, to attendance at segregated schools, to living in segregated neighborhoods, to employment in a segregated job, to burial in a segregated cemetery.

Black response to these conditions, as with all minority groups, can be categorized into three basic strategies: accommodation, separatism, and radicalism. They will be briefly discussed here to help understand the black response and the case of the American Indian, but will be covered more fully in Chapter Seven.   All three approaches were employed by blacks, each favored by a different faction, leader, or period (see Litt, 1970, Chapters 4-6).

The accommodation strategy was a commonly used approach following the example of the nationality-based minorities such as the Irish. The best known black advocate of accommodation was Booker T. Washington. Widely known and respected by both blacks and whites, he served as an informal advisor to Presidents Roosevelt and Taft, and was the founder and President of Tuskegee Institute. His philosophic approach to race relations exemplifies the accommodation strategy. He advocated that blacks should basically accept a subordinate position in society, but quietly and slowly begin to improve their position and status by an economic route by finding and filling a niche that whites would accept as non-threatening. He stressed training in vocations such as farming, preaching, and blacksmithing. He felt blacks should remain in the South, acquire land and build their own homes, and educate themselves to the point where they could eliminate the ignorance and poverty which plagued them and be accepted by white society. Among Tuskegee´s most outstanding faculty members was George Washington Carver whose research and various inventions and innovations in crop practices and farming devices earned him a national reputation. Several other black colleges and universities, for example Fisk and Howard, developed out of the Tuskegee Institute model.

> Self-help and self-respect appeared a practical and sure, if gradual, way of ultimately achieving racial equality. Washington´s doctrines also gained support because they appealed to race pride--if Negroes believed in themselves, stood together, and supported each other, they would be able to shape their destinies (Advisory Commission Report: 216).

While publically advocating a policy of accommodation, conciliation and gradualism, Booker T. Washington also secretly funneled thousands of dollars to groups fighting disenfranchisement and segregation laws.

Several black groups espoused the strategy of separatism. In one sense, when blacks fled the South and moved north, they were attempting to separate themselves from the more open and blatant discrimination experienced in the South. In a manner reminiscent of the refugees fleeing the repression of the communist regimes of post-World War II Europe, we could describe them as having "voted with their feet." A more conscious espousal of the separatist approach was that of Marcus Garvey and the "Back to Africa" Movement. In 1914 he founded the Universal Negro Improvement Association (UNIA) which sought to liberate both Africans and Black Americans from white oppression by the wholesale migration of American blacks to Africa. Garvey argued that white racism would never be overcome. He denounced integration and stressed racial pride and history, arguing that the Black American had to develop "...a distinct racial type of civilization of his own and...work out his salvation in his motherland (Ibid: 221)." In the meantime, he urged the development of black-owned businesses and, through UNIA, organized a chain of groceries, restaurants, laundries, a hotel, printing plant, and steamship line. Irregularities in the operation of the steamship line led to his arrest and eventual deportation for mail fraud, and his movement quickly died. The Garvey movement exemplified, however, the bitterness and alienation of many Northern black slum dwellers who had migrated expecting to find escape the repression of white society only to find overcrowded and deteriorated housing, massive unemployment, and the violence of race riots.

The "Nation of Islam," more commonly known as Black Muslims, provide an excellent example of an even more significant and permanent separatist movement. It exemplifies a type of "psychological separatism" in which the members are provided with a sort of psychological shell to separate them and protect them from the discrimination and ego-damages of the racist society. They will be discussed further in Chapter Seven.

The third major strategy has been called radicalism. Various proponents of this approach have used different tactics to pursue their goal of black resistance and protest designed to drastically change the public policy of the nation.

One of the earliest leaders of this strategy was the brilliant W.E.B. DuBois, an historian and sociologist at Atlanta University. In 1905 he and a small group of black intellectuals met in Niagra Falls, Canada. The "Niagra Movement" rejected moderation and compromise. It called for a radical change ending black inferior status, loss of voting rights, Jim Crow laws, segregated schools, inhumane conditions in Southern prisons, denial of equal job opportunities, and segregation of blacks in the federal armed forces. Out of this meeting came the establishment, on February 12, 1909, the one-hundredth anniversary of Lincoln's birth, of the National Association for the Advancement of Colored Peoples (NAACP). Over the years, the NAACP led the campaign of establishing black rights through legal action. In 1915 it achieved its first major victory in one of the hundreds of cases they pursued at all levels of government. The Supreme Court declared unconstitutional the grandfather clause of the Oklahoma Constitution. In 1954 the NAACP won an even greater victory in **Brown** v. **Board** of **Education** of **Topeka,** which finally overturned the "separate-but-equal" principle of the **Plessy** decision of 1896.

In 1941 A. Philip Randolph led the March on Washington protest resulting in President Roosevelt's establishing a federal Fair Employment Practices Commission. The Congress on Racial Equality (CORE), founded in 1942-1943, grew out of the pacifist organization the Fellowship of Reconciliation. It combined the nonviolent direct-action techniques of Ghandi with the sit-down strikes of the 1930's and developed the "sit-in." CORE concentrated on attacking discrimination in public accommodations.

The direct-action approach was ignited into a truly massive national movement with the 1955-1956 bus boycott in Montgomery, Alabama. The Reverend Dr. Martin Luther King, Jr. emerged out of this action, establishing the Southern Christian Leadership Conference (SCLC) in 1957.

Non-violent direct-action protest became a very popular tactic to fight segregation across the nation. The 1960's saw new groups and leaders emerge. In April of 1960, the Student Nonviolent Coordinating Committee (SNCC) was organized at Raleigh, North Carolina. CORE began "Freedom Rides" into Alabama and Mississippi. Its development, as the Civil Right's Movement generally, went through various stages.

SNCC's development can be traced through three stages. In the first stage civil rights activists came together in SNCC to form a community within a social struggle. SNCC sought to create a rationale for activism by eclectically adopting ideas from the Ghandian independence movement and from American

216

traditions of pacifism and Christian idealism
as formulated by the Congress of Racial
Equality (CORE), Fellowship of Reconciliation
(FOR), and Southern Christian Leadership
Conference (SCLC). SNCC, however, was
typically less willing than other civil rights
groups to impose its ideas on local black
leaders or to restrain southern black
militancy. Viewed as the "shock troops" of
the civil rights movement, SNCC activists
established projects in areas such as rural
Mississippi considered too dangerous by other
organizations...
The second stage of SNCC´s development began
after the defeat of an attempt by the
Mississippi Freedom Democratic Party (MFDP) to
unseat the regular all-white delegation to the
Democratic National Convention in August
1964...The third phase of SNCC´s development
involved the members´ efforts to resolve their
differences by addressing the need for black
power and black consciousness, by separating
themselves from the white people, and by
building black-controlled institutions. After
his election as Chairman of SNCC in May 1966,
Stokely Carmichael popularized the
organization´s new separatist orientation, but
he and other workers were unable to formulate
a set of ideas that could unify black people
(Carson: 2-3).

The National Urban League, led by Whitney Young, Jr.
even became more outspoken and firm with businessmen who
had previously been treated with the greatest of tact
and caution.

Substantial gains were made during the mid-1960´s.
The Civil Rights Act of 1964 was the most far-reaching
legislation against racial discrimination ever passed by
Congress. That law´s provisions were tightened still
further by the 1965 Voting Rights Act. The dramatic
closing of the voter turnout gap by blacks of both sexes
is clearly the result of the 1964 and 1965 voting laws
(see Flanigan and Zingale: 28). Those laws, strongly
supported by a Democratic Administration and Democratic-
controlled Congress, resulted in continued strong
electoral support for the Democrats among black voters.
The next table shows black support for the Democratic
Presidential candidates remained strong throughout the
1960´s and 1970´s, even as that party´s white coalitions
weakened and fell.   217

		Table 10:	BLACK-WHITE VOTING PATTERNS, BY PARTY, 1952-1980		
YEAR:	RACE:	% DEMOCRATIC:	% REPUBLICAN:	% OTHER:	
1952	Black	80	20	--	
	White	40	60	--	
1956	Black	64	36	--	
	White	39	61	--	
1960	Black	71	29	--	
	White	48	52	--	
1964	Black	100*	--	--	
	White	65	35	--	
1968	Black	97	3	--	
	White	36	52	12	
1972	Black	87	13	--	
	White	30	70	--	
1976	Black	83	17	--	
	White	48	52	--	
1980	Black	82	14	3	
	White	36	55	8	

* 100% result probably due to small size of sample

Source: 1952 to 1972 data from Survey Research Center, University of Michigan as cited in Barker and McCorey: 248. Updated for the 1976 and 1980 elections from Pomper, The Election of 1980: 71.

Initial indications from the 1984 election results show an even more dramatic split. While "WASP's" split their vote 70 percent for Reagan to 30 percent for Mondale, the black voter was about the only traditional Democratic voting bloc to remain solidly behind the Party's ticket, registering 92 percent support for Mondale and only 8 percent for Reagan (L.A. Times Syndicate, November 9, 1984).

Black voting loyalty has often been significant (President Carter owed his election to their margin). The percent of eligible blacks who could and did vote increased markedly after the 1964 and 1965 voting rights laws. Figure Three shows that rise for Presidential elections from 1952 to 1980. Those voting rights improvements were reflected in actual electoral success. By 1980 there was a total of 4,890 black elected officials in the United States at all levels of government (U.S. Statistical Abstract, 1981: 495).

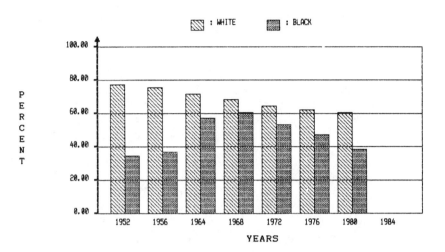

However, social and economic gains did not keep
pace with the political change. "De facto" segregation
in schools, continued occupational discrimination, and
much slower change in the social norms gave rise to
frustration and increasingly radical tactics.

As the various black protest groups and tactics
increased, the advances they were able to make fell
short of the expectations of "Freedom Now." As
frustrations grew, the ideology and rhetoric of the
civil rights movement became angrier. Radical protest
leaders like H. Rap Brown decried the non-violent
tactics. The Black Muslim's Malcolm X perhaps best
embodied the belief that racism was so deeply ingrained
in white America that appeals to conscience would bring
about no fundamental change.

From this mood the rhetoric of "Black Power" emerged in the summer of 1966. That term expressed the feelings of disillusionment and alienation from white America and a pride in black independence and self-respect or "black consciousness." Phrases like "Black Power," "Black is Beautiful," and "Black Consciousness" were soon expressed by the full range of black organizations. The more extreme form of the Black Power ideology became associated with the fringe groups from SNCC and CORE. The Black Panther Party exemplifies this trend.

The late 1960´s witnessed an increase in violent behavior as well as rhetoric. From 1963 through 1968 283 riots rocked the cities of America. This is in sharp contrast to the previous fifty-year period when there were only seventy-six major racial disorders (Henry: 361).

The riots of the mid to late 1960´s were far more intense and destructive. The Watts Riot of 1965 left a scorched area in excess of forty-five square miles, with 34 dead, of whom 31 were black. Six hundred buildings were destroyed. The Newark riot of 1967 required 4,000 officers to quell it. Twenty-three persons, of whom 21 were black, perished in that riot. Detroit erupted in 1967. This five-day riot was the worst of all. Of the 43 dead, 39 were black. A total of 15,000 police officers were needed to restore order. Some 1,300 buildings were levelled. Over 2,700 business were looted. In 1967 alone, there were 139 riots in 114 cities, resulting in the deaths of 95 people, injuring 1,700 more and resulting in 12,000 arrests. The army or National Guard was called into 15 cities. The property damage in 8 cities in that year alone totaled in excess of $250 million. In July of 1967 President Johnson established the National Advisory Commission on Civil Disorders. He charged them to study the riots, to determine what happened, why it happened, and what could be done to prevent them from happening in the future.

The results achieved by the riots were a mixed bag. Some income improvements could be noted, but by no means was steady improvement the results. Poverty rates fell between 1959 and 1975, for example, indicating some improvement. In the 1959 case, total population below the poverty line was 14.1 percent, at which time the black population below the line was 55.1 percent. By

220

1969 the black portion below the poverty line had fallen to 32.2 percent compared to a white percentage of 9.5 and a total population figure of 12.1 percent. By 1975 the black percentage had dropped slightly more, to 31.3 percent. This compared to a white percentage of 9.7 and a total population figure of 12.3 percent. That same period saw a slight proportionally greater increase by non-white than by whites in the technical, professional, and management jobs (Parrillo: 379-384).

Yet black incomes did not indicate comparable gains. Although the gap between blacks and whites has narrowed slightly in percentage terms, it has widened in terms of real income. The median family income of blacks in 1964, for instance, was $3,724 compared to a white family's income of $6,858. That year the black income as a percent of white income was 54.3, with an income gap of $3,134. By 1974 the median family income for whites had risen to $13,356, but for blacks it was only $8,265. Thus, while in 1974 black income as a percent of white income was 61.9, the actual income gap had increased to $5,091 (Parrillo: 377). By 1980, the median family income was $20,502 for whites, but only $11,644 for blacks. White per capita income was $7,234 compared to $3,981 for blacks (U.S. Statistical Abstract, 1981: 439).

Black unemployment has been consistently well above that experienced by whites. As of December, 1982 while the white unemployment rate was at 9.7 percent, black unemployment was more than double that figure, at 20.8 percent. This held across age and sex lines. While white female unemployment was 8.1 percent, black female unemployment was 16.5 percent. Whereas white teenage unemployment was at 21.6 percent, the black teenage unemployment was 49.5 percent (U.S. Department of Labor, Bureau of Labor Statistics Report, December, 1982).

Black Americans made more uniformally encouraging gains in education since the Brown decision signaled the beginning of the civil rights movement. In 1950 the median school years completed for black males was 6.4 compared to 9.3 for white males. For black females the 1950 figure was 7.1 compared to 10.0 for white females. By 1980 the gap was clearly closing. In that year, the black male median school years completed had risen to 12.0, in comparison with a white male figure of 12.6. Similarly, the black female median had increased to 12.0 in comparison to a white female figure of 12.5 (U.S. Statistical Abstract, 1981: 142).

The year 1983 witnessed some symbolically important gains for blacks. While they may not rank with voting rights legislation, or a break-through court ruling on affirmative action, they do validate the opening of doors. Guion Bluford, a jet pilot, became the first black astronaut in space. Less than a month later, Venessa Williams, Miss New York, became the first black woman to hold the title of Miss America, although she later had to resign her title over an issue not related to her race.

Perhaps the most important strides have been in politics. Since the 1970´s the civil rights movement has turned from radical protest to more standard accommodationist-style politics. In part, the cooling off of black urban violence can be attributed to the Vietnam War which became "the issue" of national protest politics. Another factor was the change in black leadership. Some of the 1960´s black leaders were assassinated--King, Medgar Evans, and Malcolm X. Others were imprisoned, such as Carmichael, Newton, and Seale, or went into exile like Cleaver. The new leadership (Andrew Young, Jesse Jackson, Ralph Abernathy) had new political resources with which to work. Electoral gains in the 1970´s proved that standard politics had a chance of producing results not possible in earlier decades.

As of 1980 the total number of black elected officials rose to 4,890. Of these, 326 were in Congress and the various state legislatures; 2,832 held city and county offices; 526 served in law enforcement, and 1,206 were in education. Some really significant gains have been made among the mayoralities of American cities, which have been a recent focus of the black power movement. As late as 1966, no big city was run by a black. Now 17 cities with populations in excess of 100,000 have black mayors, and there are 245 black mayors in cities of all sizes.

In the 1984 election the Reverend Jesse Jackson ran impressively if unsuccessfully for the nomination of the Democratic Party for President. His campaign highlights that push. An April, 1983 public opinion poll by the Gallop, Harriss, and Washington Post-ABC polls all show that 77 percent of the public said that they would vote for a well qualified black candidate for president, which is a higher percentage than those who, in 1960, said they would vote for a Catholic (The Washington Post, Weekly Edition, November 21, 1983: 42).

The Jackson candidacy augmented an impressive trend in black registration and voting turnout. The Voter Education Project, based in Atlanta, has been leading a voter registration drive for several years, with considerable success. The 1982-1983 elections for mayoral and state legislative races in various parts of the nation showed that the black vote could be decisive, and in some cases the black turnout for the first time ever exceeded that of white voters. In the 1980 election, black turnout at the polls increased by 18 percent, ending a sixteen year decline, while white voter turnout remained the same. In 1982, black turnout rose by 5.8 percent over the previous off-year election, which was more than double the increase in the white voter turnout. The gap between white and black voter turnout was only 6.9 percent, the lowest of any national election in American history. The Jackson effort added a substantial number of new black voters to the registration lists.

The American Indian

The 1980 census recorded 1.4 million Indians, about half of whom lived off the reservation in the nation´s cities. Despite some $3 billion a year spent in federal support for Indians, they have the lowest incomes and education levels and the worst housing and health conditions of any minority group in the nation. They are truly the poorest of the poor. They "top" the nation only in their unemployment and birth rates. The American Indian children are the most poorly prepared students in the nation. They have the highest dropout rates, the lowest test scores, and the worst alcoholism and suicide rates of any student group (The Washington Post, December 27, 1981: A-1).

Like Black Americans, they represent a racial case with some unique aspects. Despite their being the only true native population of the nation, they were not legally declared as citizens with the right to vote until 1924. They are the only minority group legally segregated into specific geographic areas. They are the only minority to have suffered from an avowed policy of annihilation. No other minority in the nation´s history has the unfortunate distinction of having experienced actual genocide.

National policy towards the Indian has taken many approaches over the years. Those policy shifts have ranged from avowed friendship recognizing independence for the Indian to expulsion and genocide, forced geographic segregation, forced acculturation through termination, and recent attempts to allow cultural pluralism. In the process, hundreds of treaties were made and broken. Indian affairs have been shifted and parceled out among various agencies housed in several departments of the federal government.

The decimation of the Indian population by contact with whites, whether intentional or not, is well established. At the time of the first European settlement of the North American continent, the number of Indians residing in that territory has been estimated at one to ten million. Those residing in what is now the United States probably numbered around one and a-half million. By 1800 their population had fallen to around 600,000. By 1850, the ravages of malnutrition and disease, coupled with the policies of expulsion and genocide, had reduced the American Indians to around 250,000! Their population has climbed upward from that low point of 1850, reaching approximately 1.4 million with the 1980 census.

The Indians were treated as sovereign nations during the colonial period. Despite some violent clashes between white colonists and Indian tribes, official government policy was peaceful. Indian tribes had favorable treaty relations with Spain, France, and England. British policy, expressed in a 1763 proclamation of King George III was to officially protect the Indian (Hagan: 29).

When the American Revolutionary War broke out, both sides attempted to win the friendship and alliance of the Indian tribes through treaties. After the war, the new national government followed the British tradition and continued an avowed policy of "friendship" based upon treaties with independent nations. But just as the British could not stop the colonies from developing their own relations with the Indians, the new federal government was largely unable to control the states from making their own treaties with the Indians, despite the fact that the national government was supposed to have sole jurisdiction over trade and treaty relations with the Indian tribes. In any event, although supposedly friendly, most of the treaties resulted in the taking of

Indian lands by white settlers. From 1778, when the first Indian treaty was signed, until 1871 when the United States officially stopped recognizing the Indian tribes as independent nations, 389 treaties were ratified. In a sense, all were broken. The Northwest Ordinance, passed in 1787, promised the Indians that their lands could not be taken without consent, except in case a war was declared by Congress. Since no war was ever really declared, the numerous conflicts with Indians which resulted in the whites´ seizing their lands were illegal. The policy of "friendship" continued under the administrations of Presidents Washington and Adams.

Henry Knox, Washington´s Secretary of War, was the first government official to speak of assimilating the Indian. Knox felt the best way to do this was to introduce the Indian to the concept and custom of private property. President Washington spoke to a delegation of Indians about learning the white man´s ways of farming and raising stock. Thus, even when the official policy considered the Indians as independent nations, the idea of assimilation and acculturation-- whether benign or forced--was begun. The friendly policy, however, did not last long.

> The tribesmen presented the federal government with a cruel dilemma. On the one hand, responsible officials wanted to maintain peace; on the other hand, they wanted to satisfy the host of westward-moving land seekers. Unfortunately, any policy likely to satisfy the Indians outraged the pioneers. As a result the government seemed to follow conflicting and contradictory practices, but in reality the policy changed little (Dinnerstein, Reimers, and Nichols: 36).

By the early 1800´s, problems with the Indians had become acute, especially in the South. While technically the Indian could choose to either take a portion of land and farm as did the whites, or move west, in reality few were given any choice as greedy miners, lumbermen, and farmers pushed them aside. Federal officials soon began to demand that they migrate.

Policy seemed to vacillate for a time. Under Presidents Jefferson and Madison a policy of removal was begun. In 1804 a provision was included in the Louisiana Territory Act for the exchange of lands; Indians were to be moved west of the Mississippi River. In 1809, 100 million acres were "appropriated" through some fifteen treaties by which William Harris, then Governor of the Indiana Territory, received the lands purchased from the Indians at one cent per acre. The Indians agreed to these treaties under the threat of forced (Hagan: 55-56).

In 1819 Congress established an Indian Civilization Fund for which it set aside $10,000 a year. This was to be used to educate the Indian. Between 1783 and 1815, some tribesmen responded by learning English, farming, and white-style business. The Cherokee tribe of North Carolina, for example, became bicultural for several generations. They were literate, articulate, land fully bilingual. By the mid-1820´s they owned 22,000 cattle, 1,300 slaves, 31 grist mills, 10 saw mills, and 8 cotton gins. They ran 18 schools and published the Cherokee Phoenix, a bilingual newspaper. Most Indians, however, retained their allegiance to family and clan and refused to acculturate (Dinnerstein, Reimers, and Nichols: 37-38).

After the War of 1812 relations with the Indians began to deteriorate. As the threat of British intervention faded, the national government felt less of a need to conciliate the Indian tribes. White settlers kept pushing westward and desired Indian lands. The government was forced to oblige them. A "removal" policy was formally adopted, although between 1816 and 1848 the pretense of the "Independent Nations" was continued. An Indian removal policy was first officially adopted by President James Monroe in 1825. Federal officials envisioned Indian territories and states in the far West. Apparently no one at the time anticipated the spectacular speed with which white Americans pushed west beyond the Mississippi. The rapidly advancing frontier prevented any chance of the removal policy actually succeeding.

President Andrew Jackson, nonetheless, wholeheartedly approved of the policy of removal; although he felt it "absurd" to continue to deal with the Indians as independent nations. In 1830 Jackson pushed the passage of the Indian Removal Act, which provided $300,000 for "...an exchange of lands, compensation for improvements, and aid in the removal and initial adjustment to their new homes." Most often, force was used (Hagan: 66-72).

Even those who went "voluntarily" suffered greatly in the migration. White officials oversaw the transportation and resettlement of the Indians in their new lands west of the Mississippi. Exploitation was common. Contractors supplying transportation and food, for example, bought condemned meat and spoiled flour to feed their charges. For transportation they rented cheap and untrustworthy boats to get the Indians across major rivers, sometimes with fatal results. One steamboat crossing the Mississippi River sank and 311 Indians drowned. Nearly 4,000 of the 15,000 Cherokee who started west at gunpoint died on what the Indians called the "Trail of Tears" or during the first few months in what is now Oklahoma (Dinnerstein, Reimers, and Nichols: 39-40).

The Cherokee, being the most acculturated of the tribes, sought legal redress. They appealed to the United States Supreme Court. In Cherokee Nation v. Georgia (1831) and Worcester v. Georgia (1832), the Court ruled in the Indian's favor. President Jackson simply ignored the ruling, allegedly remarking, "John Marshall has made his decision. Now let him enforce it (Ibid: 40)." In the Worcester case the Court referred to the Indians as "Wards of Washington," which later became the basis for the approach of the Bureau of Indian Affairs. The refusal by President Jackson to comply with the Court's ruling dashed the hopes of the Indians for a peaceful and legal resolution of the conflict.

> In spite of the Supreme Court, in spite of
> solemn treaties, in spite of the Constitution,
> and in spite of professed belief in the right
> of self-government of all peoples, the native
> groups east of the Mississippi were
> relentlessly driven westward (Forbes: 105).

Twelve treaties in 1854 alone took almost 18,000,000 acres of Indian land, leaving them about 1,500,000 acres of what they originally owned.

The Seminole tribe in Florida refused removal and, in 1835, started a guerrilla war that cost thousands of casualties and at least $50 million. The fighting dragged on until the mid-1840's when the army captured Indian leaders by treachery. While the immigrants and slaves helped build the American economy with their labor, the Indians contributed their property. Modernization received a tremendous boost from this involuntary Indian contribution. In the process, the Indian tribal civilization was nearly destroyed, and some tribes were totally destroyed.

Northern tribes fared little better. In 1836 the Potawatomi were forced to leave Illinois and migrate to Missouri. Many of them died during the mid-winter forced march. The Sac and Fox tribes fought removal but were forced to move to Missouri in 1831. In 1832 they attempted to return to their lands, led by an aged warrior called Black Hawk. Some 1,000 men, women, and children returned to Illinois. They were met by Illinois militia who, despite a white parley flag, attacked. In the "Battle of Bad Axe," the militia killed all but 150 of the 1,000 Indians (Dinnerstein, Reimers, and Nichols: 63-64).

During the period of 1832-1843 the federal government conducted the removal of the Iroquois to new western territories. This term referred to the League of Five Nations involving the tribes of the Seneca, Onondaga, Cayuga, Oneida, and the Mohawk. Later a sixth tribe, the Tuscaroras from North Carolina, joined them. These tribes were literally decimated during the removal, with most of the survivors fleeing to Canada.

Federal control of Indian affairs was transferred from the Department of War to the Department of the Interior in 1849. In 1851 the Commissioner of Indian Affairs proposed an idea that soon became quite popular. Indians were to be segregated on reservations and then "civilized." Acculturation was to be forced. Although acculturation and assimilation were goals of previous administrations, this was the first time that force was mentioned in conjunction with "civilizing" them. Although not immediately accepted, the need for more land increased as more settlers pushed westward and so did support for the policy.

In 1857 yet another Commissioner of Indian Affairs that reservations should have just enough land to live on and farm. Reservation property was to be privately owned, and the Indian must live on the land. He maintained that these conditions would not only segregate the Indian, but also civilize them (Forbes: 108).

Most of the reservations were established after the Civil War and before 1880. During this period conflict with the plains Indians, sometimes referred to as the "horse nomadic tribes," was especially intense. The Blackfoot, the Arapaho, Cheyenne, Commanche, Apache, and the Crow Tetons (one of the tribes of the Sioux) were under constant pressure of the white movement west. The white and Indian's concepts on the use of land were were so incompatible that both could not survive together, and the introduction of the rapid-fire revolver and cattle into the west spelled the doom of the horse nomadic tribes. With the coming of barbed wire, the Homestead Act, cattle ranches, and the railroads, the plains Indians increasingly were viewed as menaces that had to be removed. A series of battles and treaties were needed to subjugate them. The 1874 discovery of gold in the sacred Black Hills sealed their doom. Not even the 1876 defeat of Custer at the Little Big Horn could forestall the inevitable end.

In Nevada a major newspaper called for "...the total extermination of every redskin from the Canadian to the Mexican frontier (Dinnerstein, Nichols, and Reimers: 227)." Yet another western editor recommended welcoming the Indians when they asked for peace and then slaughtering them "...as though they were so many nests of rattlesnakes (Ibid: 228)."

In California the Indians were suppressed by both Anglos and Mexicans. In the late eighteenth century the total Indian population in what is now California had been estimated at 135,000 to 250,000. After two decades of American occupation of the area, the Indian population had fallen to an estimated 21,000--only 3,000 of whom were under the "protection" of U.S. reservations. Most of the population decline was due to the "peaceful attrition" caused by the ravages of European diseases. But many were killed in random murders and by army or civilian massacres. By 1900 the state's Indian population was down to 10,000. For some tribes, such as the Yahi, the entire tribe was wiped out.   Ishi,   the last of the Yahi tribe,   died in 1916, the final victim of a truly successful policy of genocide (Kitano: 142-146).

Some tribes resisted the extinction.   In 1887 the Yaquis Tribe began a guerrilla warfare campaign which lasted until 1926 in Mexico.   Some of the remainder of that tribe moved to Arizona, settling near Tucson.   "The Yaquis have resisted their encounters with different ´white´ cultures;   they maintain a pluralistic style and insist on group solidarity (Ibid: 143)."   In California the surviving Indians lived unbelievably poor, landless, and nomadic lives.   They had virtually no civil rights, were prohibited by law from testifying against white men,   and were often arrested for vagrancy, taken to jail,   then farmed out to the highest bidder for up to four month´s labor.   They existed in a state close to slavery.

> Perhaps the symbolic end to overt Indian resistance was the massacre at Wounded Knee, South Dakota, in 1890.   The "battle" was the culmination of the army´s attempt to disarm and herd the Indians under Chief Big Foot into a cavalry camp.   By the end of the massacre, an estimated 300 (out of 350) Indian men, women, and children had been gunned down (Kitano: 150).

That massacre ended the fighting.   From the 1830´s to the 1930´s federal policy shifted to forced acculturation.   Between 1890 and the 1930´s, tens of thousands of Indian children were legally kidnapped and forced to attend schools hundreds of miles from home. The school curriculum was designed and applied with the idea of eradicating all signs of their native culture. The schools were run like virtual prisons.   The children were fed at a cost of about twelve cents a day per student when the army was spending fifty-two cents per day on each soldier´s food.   This resulted in widespread malnutrition and disease.   The slightest infraction of the school´s elaborate rules resulted in beatings.   As one group of scholars assessed the state of the Indians at this time:

> By the early decades of the twentieth century the position of Indians seemed hopeless. Using almost any standard of measure--family income,   infant mortality,   life expectancy,

unemployment, alcoholism, or suicide--American Indians stood firmly mired at the bottom of the social and economic ladder. Whether by accident or design, most Indian tribes had ceased to function or had been reduced to ineffectiveness.(4)

Assimilation was the avowed rationale of the Dawes Severalty Act of 1887 (also known as the General Allotment Act), but it really just continued the taking of Indian land. This act authorized the President to divide Indian lands into parcels of 40,80, or 160 acres to be used for farming and raising stock. The Indian family or individual had to work the land for twenty-five years or longer while the federal government held the title. Afterwards, the Indian could continue to use the land or to sell it. As long as the individual stayed away from his tribe and held title, he could become a citizen. "The rationale behind the Dawes Act was that an Indian who possessed land would automatically become a farmer and that a farming Indian would become ´civilized´ and self-supporting (Levitan and Hetrick: 16)." But because the Indian culture rejected farming or the private ownership of land, they usually lost it. The Indians lost 85 million acres of land by 1934, when allotment finally stopped.

During the 1920´s conditions began to improve slightly for the Indians. The Indian Rights Association and the American Indian Defense Association were formed. They initiated the public protest over the treatment of Indians. The Bureau of Indian Affairs was faulted for its inefficiency and exploitation. A "Committee of One Hundred" was appointed. In 1924 Congress passed the Indian Citizens Act, which finally awarded the native-American the status of citizenship and the right to vote.

In part, this law was passed in recognition of the American Indians´ contribution in World War I. Many Indians had volunteered and had distinguished themselves in battle. Few American Indians were impressed with this gesture, however, and regarded it as further proof of the nation´s disregard for the real needs of the Indian people. The right to vote was a more symbolic reward which did little to alleviate their situation since their collective rights were still almost entirely subject to the Bureau of Indian Affairs whose powers were defined by Congress. And Congress did not always pass legislation that was in the Indians´ best interests, especially when the conflicting demands of whites were considered. Thus, while they were now officially citizens, they continued to be treated as a conquered people whose rights could be expanded, contracted, or otherwise modified as the conquerors saw fit.

Yet reform sentiment was building. In 1928 the Institute of Government Research published the Meriam Report, which documented the wretched conditions of the BIA schools. The Hoover Administration made several attempts to improve the situation for Indians. Improvements were made in the field of education--the number of boarding schools was reduced and more day schools begun. Indians were encouraged to attend public schools, and funding was increased. The loss of Indian lands was slowed down. Even the Board of Indian Commissioners publically announced the failure of the allotment program (Hagan: 154).

Under the Roosevelt Administration, John Collier, Commissioner of Indian Affairs, announced his policies for dealing with Indians. For the times, his ideas were revolutionary. Indian lands under the allotment program were to be given back to the tribes. Boarding schools were to be eased out, while day schools were to be used more efficiently, aimed at adults as well as children. Indians were to be given more jobs in the Indian service and more self-government which would be recognized by the federal government. Freedom of religion was restored. These policies embodied in the Indian Reorganization Act of 1934 were also known as the Wheeler-Howard Act. An important feature of the act was that Indians were to be given a choice whether they wanted to accept the changes or not. The act also insured the Indians´ right to purchase land and to establish businesses. Pluralism was accepted, although the idea of Indian assimilation was not completely abandoned.

The immediate response by the Indians to this policy reversal was incredulity. As the reality sunk in, however, they began forming their own governments-- an aroused people after so long a period of apathy. The policy was more enlightened, sensitive to the appraisal of Indian needs--one which provided a better solution of all parties concerned. By building up their own economic resources, the Indians could contribute to majority society while retaining their traditional culture which was so important to their identity as a group and as individuals. By trying to force assimilation, the government left the Indian with little choice but to become increasingly isolated from majority society in order to preserve as much as possible of the traditional culture which whites were constantly attempting to eradicate.

Another impact of the policy changes during the Roosevelt Administration was noted by the former Executive Director of the National Congress of American Indians, Vine Deloria, Jr.

> Strangely enough, the Depression was good for Indian reservations, particularly for the people at Pine Ridge...The Civilian Conservation Corps set up a camp on the reservation and many Indians were hired under the program...While the rest of America suffered from the temporary deprivation of its luxuries, Indian people had a period of prosperity, as it were. Paychecks were regular. Small cattle herds were started, cars were purchased, new clothes and necessities became available. To a people who had struggled along on $50 cash income per year, the C. C. C. was the greatest program ever to come along. The Sioux had climbed from absolute deprivation to mere poverty, and this was the best time the reservation ever had. World War II ended this temporary prosperity. The C. C. C. camps were closed; reservation programs were cut to the bone and social services became virtually nonexistent (Josephy: 239-240).

By 1940 there was disenchantment with the Indian Reorganization Act, and Congress even considered repealing the act and abolishing the Bureau of Indian Affairs. In 1946, however, the Congress created the Indian Claims Commission allowing Indians to file suit against the government. In 1949 the Hoover Commission proposed the idea of termination, ending federal support for the Indians. It endorsed the transfer of Indian social programs to state and local governments and the policy of getting the Indians off the reservation and into the "mainstream of American life (Hagan: 161)."

When Dillon Myer became Commissioner of Indian Affairs in 1950 he supported completely the policy of termination. State and local governments were given control of most Indian health and education programs by the Johnson O'Malley Act. The first measure toward termination was Public Law 2890 which authorized any state "...to impose on any and all tribes its own civil and criminal codes and enforcement machinery and thus to annihilate the tribal codes and tribal authorities of self-protection (Forbes: 120)." Congress passed a resolution in support of termination. The resolution was a policy statement which asked the Secretary of the Interior to offer legislation to stop federal aid to several tribes. During the next session, six more termination bills were passed. One result of termination was that the Menominee and Klamath tribes lost large amounts of land.

By the mid-1950's support for termination began to decline. Indian protest was sufficiently vocal to all but officially end the termination program during the Kennedy-Johnson years. The war on poverty programs brought some reforms by giving the tribes some decision-making power over what Indian programs should be on the reservations and how they should be run.

Nixon appointed Louis Bruce, a Sioux-Mohawk, Commissioner of the Bureau of Indian Affairs in 1969. He realigned the top management, appointing a majority of Indians to those positions for the first time in history. Funds for the BIA and other federal allocations for Indian programs were increased significantly. President Nixon's special message to Congress on July 8, 1970, called for Indian self-determination. He said, "The time has come to break decisively with the past and to create the conditions for a new era in which the Indian future is determined by Indian Acts and Indian decisions (Marx: 74)."

In 1975 Congress passed the Indian Self-Determination and Education Assistance Act. It gave them the right to handle federal services themselves and tried to make them equal partners with the federal government. Its stated aim was to respond to the strong expression of the Indian for self-determination by assuring maximum Indian participation in running education and other federal services. The BIA, however, still had the final say over many of these services.

Various Indian groups have adopted a militant stance. Several have conspicuously copied the "direct-action protest" tactics of the Black Civil Rights Movement. These groups tended to be led by urbanized Indians, a younger and better educated leadership segment than are the more traditional tribal leaders on the reservations. In 1961 the National Indian Youth Council was established. By 1964 they were sponsoring "fish-ins" in Washington State, advocating "Red Power," and wearing lapel buttons proclaiming, "Custer Died for Your Sins"(Dinnerstein, Nichols and Reimers: 304). Indian protest songs by Johnny Cash, a Cherokee, Floyd Westerman, a Sioux, and Buffy Saint-Marie, a Cree, inspired them. The "Red Power" writings and speeches of such leaders as Vine Deloria, Jr., Clyde Warrior, Wallace "Mad Bear" Anderson, Hank Adams, Lehman Brightman, Tillie Walker, and Alvin Josephy activated them as well.

College students of Indian descent formed clubs, conducted seminars, and held conferences on Indian problems. They advocated the introduction of Indian Studies. They and urban Indian groups formed activist organizations modeled on the Black Civil Rights Movement. The American Indian Movement (AIM), led by Clyde Bellecourt and Dennis Banks, and the United Native Americans, Inc. led by Lehman Brightman, joined others to form a nationwide federation called American Indians United, whose first head was Jess Six Killer, an Indian who was an officer of the Chicago Police Department.

Protest action grew. Protests over the loss of fishing rights in Washington waters by the Paiutes of Pyramid Lake, the Taos Pueblos´ rights to their sacred Blue Lake, the Puget Sound Indians´ right to fish, and the Alaskan natives´ right to their land culminated in the November 1969 occupation of Alcatraz by a party of 78 Indians calling themselves the Indians of All Tribes. This protest action was hailed by some as the beginning of a new era of Pan-Indian awareness and activity. It certainly indicated a period of increased militancy and a willingness to employ direct-action, confrontation style politics. In 1971 the federal government forced them to leave. In 1972 AIM occupied the offices of the BIA in Washington, D.C. They claimed to have seized documents showing BIA corruption or complicity in the exploitation of the Indian.

Perhaps the most dramatic confrontation was the 1973 occupation of Wounded Knee, South Dakota. The action was inspired by the best selling book by Dee Brown, <u>Bury</u> <u>My</u> <u>Heart</u> at <u>Wounded</u> <u>Knee.</u> AIM leaders Dennis Banks and Russell Means led a group which seized the town on the anniversary of the massacre. Although the organization failed to achieve its stated goal of overthrowing the elected tribal leaders at the Pine Ridge, South Dakota reservation or obtaining recognition for the tribes as independent nations within the general society, they did demonstrate the discontent among many Indians in America over their position in society. The seizure also demonstrated the extent of rift between the young and radical militants and the older tribal leadership. In the words of Josephy:

As they protest and demonstrate with the only method they have to call attention to their plight, the method hardens the attitudes of the white law-enforcement agencies toward them in a manner which recalls the nineteenth century use of troops against their forefathers, and further, divides the Indians between the fearful ones, the venal ones, and the determined patriots (5).

A wave of resurgent ethnicity which marked the 1970's is evident among almost all minority groups as they awaken to group consciousness and strive for group goals. For Indians, this feeling of nationalism has been voiced in the call for recognition, from Indians as well as whites, of the equality, and in some respects even the superiority, of the Indian ways to those of other Americans. "This new tribalism has meant the revitalization of reservation culture, the revival of traditional religion, and demands for a revisionist Indian/white history (Feaver: 24)." While Indians are not yet as united as they need to be in order to overcome the obstacles they face, their blossoming pride in their cultural heritage is an important step towards the group consciousness necessary to bring about such a change. Reform will no doubt follow such unity. But achieving such unity will not be easy, and the problems which must be faced are staggering. There are 315 tribal groupings in the United States. They range in size from the mammoth Navajo Tribe of 132,000 with sixteen million acres of land to the tiny Mission Creek of California, a mere fifteen people surviving on a tiny parcel of land. They now reside in every part of the country, as can be seen in Table Eleven which shows their 1980 population data by region, division, and state.

Table 11: AMERICAN INDIAN, ESKIMO AND ALEUT POPULATION, 1980, BY REGION, AND STATE	
United States Total	1,420,400
New England	21,597
Maine	4,087
New Hampshire	1,352
Vermont	984
Massachusetts	7,743
Rhode Island	2,898
Connecticut	4,533
Middle Atlantic	57,441
New York	39,582
New Jersey	8,394
Pennsylvania	9,465
North Central	248,393
Ohio	12,239
Indiana	7,836
Illinois	16,283
Michigan	40,050
Wisconsin	29,499
Minnesota	35,016
Iowa	5,455
Missouri	12,321
North Dakota	20,158
South Dakota	9,195
Kansas	15,373
South	372,230
Delaware	1,328
Maryland	8,021
District of Columbia	1,031
Virginia	9,454
West Virginia	1,610
North Carolina	64,652
South Carolina	5,757
Georgia	7,616
Florida	19,257
Kentucky	3,610
Tennessee	5,104
Alabama	7,583
Mississippi	6,180
Arkansas	9,428
Louisiana	12,065
Oklahoma	169,459
Texas	40,075

West	720,739
Montana	37,270
Idaho	10,521
Wyoming	7,094
Colorado	16,068
New Mexico	106,119
Arizona	152,745
Utah	19,256
Nevada	13,308
Washington	60,804
Oregon	27,314
California	201,369
Alaska	64,103
Hawaii	2,768

Source: Adapted from State and Metropolitan Area Data Book, 1982.

The depths from which they must extricate themselves would cause even the most optimistic person to falter. Their suicide rate is 100 times that of whites; their unemployment rate is ten times the national average. The average Indian life-span is a third of that of the national average. Their deplorable housing conditions are often worse than those found in Appalachia or among the nation's urban slums, with 50,000 Indian families living in grossly substandard units, many without running water, electricity, or adequate sanitary facilities. Infant mortality among them is three times the national average. Fifty to sixty percent of Indian school children drop out before completing high school--more than double the national average.

Alcoholism and drug dependency are especially severe problems for them. Moreover, they lead to related crime problems. In South Dakota, where the Indian population is 5 percent of the state's total, they make up 33 percent of the state's prison population. Related, too, is the staggering problem of poverty. The Indian is the poorest of the poor, with an average annual family income 75 percent less than the national average, and over $1,000 below that of the average black family (Josephy: 3).

In terms of overcoming these problems, perhaps equally problematic to their abject poverty is the rift between the urban and reservation Indians. About half the Indian population now resides in the nation's cities. That split fragments what little political power they might muster in electoral politics.

The value system of the Indian culture is often incompatible with that of the white majority society's. The urban Indian is severely strained in attempting to adjust to those value differences--often resulting in widespread drinking and high suicide rates.

> Everywhere that Indians live, the whites speak of them as lazy, living off the federal government...It is essentially the same view of the Indian that prevailed in the 17th century--as long as the Indian does not live according to Locke's conception of labor and land, so long will the aspirant gods have failed to make him their brother, and so long will his captors withhold human justice (Viewpoints; 116).

While some of the younger and more militant urbanized Indians have achieved success, thereby demonstrating that it is possible to succeed in white society without totally abandoning their Indian heritage, they are few. But Indians, especially the urbanized among them, are on the warpath against second class status. They want decent homes, jobs, and schooling. They want to share more fully in American life, but they also want to remain Indians. The old policies of assimilation are seen as irrelevant and bankrupt. They want to control their own destinies--on or off the reservations. Finally, they want the government to live up to its commitments, to make good on the solemn promises and treaties so often broken in the past.

As with most other minority groups, the greatest hope for their achieving a stake in the future lies in gains made in education. Recent years have shown some significant progress, although that progress is being slowed by the severe budget cuts of the Reagan Administration. Among the signs of hope have been a greater willingness by Congress, during the past decade, to turn over more control of the Indian schools to the tribes, while increasing its funding of special programs. In 1981, for instance, the Lebre School graduated 52 seniors. Ted Rowland, who did not even start college until age 30, is now president of Dull Knife Memorial College, a school that did not even exist until 1979. The number of Indians attending college jumped from a few to 40,000. The number of Indian lawyers climbed from about 20 in 1970 to 200 by 1980. The Haskell Indian Junior College in Lawrence, Kansas, and the Rough Rock Demonstration School on the Navajo Reservation in Arizona stress bilingual education and bicultural development. Basil Brave Heart, a Lakota Sioux who is principle of the Busby High School on the Northern Cheyenne reservation, remembers when he was going to school teachers who caught him speaking Sioux made him hold a rubber band in his teeth and then snapped his lips with it five times. Today, the Busby system has a $154,000 bilingual education program. But its general funds dropped from $1.2 million to $432,000 the last three years because of changes in the funding formula enacted by the Reagan Administration.

Educators have noted that with Head Start and similar programs, Indian children seem to do well until the fourth or fifth grades, then their progress drops off markedly. By the high school years drop out rates and drug and alcohol abuse rise alarmingly. One high school counselor observed:

> Its as if they lose the innocence of childhood... when these kids reach adolescence a lot of them feel there are no jobs out there on the reservation. They get a sense of hopelessness from the poverty around them (The Washington Post, December 27, 1981: A-2).

The federal government spends about $500 million annually to educate some 400,000 Indian children, about 80 percent of whom are in public schools. The enrollments in schools run by the BIA was cut by 42,000 in 1981 and has been steadily declining. The Reagan Administration made deep cuts in federal Indian services in 1982 and 1983. The budget battle has reopened the old split among Indian leaders over whether or not they should try to wean their people away from government dependency.

One school suffering budget cuts is Dull Knife, named for the Cheyenne Chief who led his people on the long march from Oklahoma to eastern Montana in 1878. It stands to lose nearly one-half million dollars in vocational training funds, which represents a large portion of the schools total budget. The public schools at Lodge Grass, on the neighboring Crow reservation, will lose much of the "impact aid" money the federal government allots to pay for the schooling of Indian children. The elementary school there, where most of the young students arrive speaking Crow rather than English, counts on that aid for a full 75 percent of its budget.

Ted Rowland, at Dull Knife, believes that colleges such as that one, are the answer to the survivability of reservation Indians. His school stresses vocational training for more than 100 Northern Cheyenne who work at the nearby Montana Power plants. Despite deep cuts, he remains optimistic about the school's future:

> We're going to be a four year college. We realize President Reagan wants people to get off their butts and go out and do something. And we will. Higher education is the key that's been missing from the Indian people historically. Naturally, we will need government help. But we want to be more and more independent (Ibid: 2).

In terms of political participation, as measured by voting behavior, the Indians are the least active of minority groups. Their lowest of voting records is reflected in the few elected or appointed officials of Indian origin. As of the 1970's, there was but one congressman of Indian background, and fifteen state legislators. Neither major political party shows any leadership from this group. As one scholar assessed their status:

> The causes of these conditions appear to lie with the confused status of the Indian, his delayed entry into full citizenship status (in Maine he did not gain the right to vote until 1953, and in Arizona and New Mexico, with large Indian populations, not until 1948), lack of trust in the white man's word (the result of many years of treaties being broken by the federal and state government), lack of experience with the democratic process, inaccessibility of polling places, and related procedural barriers... The result of these factors is that a very low percentage of

241

Indians eligible to vote exercise their
franchise. (In Minneapolis, Minnesota, a very
recent survey showed that 44 percent had never
voted in a public election.) (Herzog: 199-
200).

Lately the Indian has been achieving better results
through the legal process. The failures of the Cherokee
Nation and the Worcester cases have been mitigated by
more recent judicial actions. Since those two cases
there have been in excess of 2,000 federal court
decisions. Since the 1950´s, Indians have been winning
cases more frequently and with better effect. The
Indian Commission, set up by Congress in 1946 to hear
Indian suits, was to operate for ten years, five of
which were given to the Indians to enter claims. There
were 852 claims, mostly concerning broken treaties and
the value of Indian lands seized. Since only 75 cases
had been ruled on by 1956, the Commission was extended
until 1962. Through 1959, a sum of $17,650,000 was
awarded to Indians out of $123,800,000 requested (Hagan:
167). In later years they have had more luck with the
courts. The Court of Claims granted the Colorado Ute
tribe $31,200,000 in compensation for lands taken from
them. Other tribes which have sued and won sizable
suits are the Passamaquoddy and Penobscot tribes
(Parrillo: 255).

A recent AP newsfeature noted the contrast between
the Wounded Knee seizure and an April, 1981 claim for
the Black Hills National Forest. The Black Hills are
sacred lands to the Sioux and have been in dispute
between the red and white man for more than a century.
The recent peaceful takeover at the National Forest was
starkly different from the Wounded Knee incident. The
latter lasted 71 days and ended in two deaths and more
than 300 being arrested. The Black Hills takeover,
which the Indians named Yellow Thunder Camp, involved
unarmed Indians pledged to nonviolence. They formally
petitioned the government for 800 acres under an 1868
Fort Laramie treaty, which first gave them that land,
and an 1897 law which allows schools and churches to be
built on U.S. Forest Service land.

Indian tactics, reflecting the broader culture´s
political trend, has grown more conservative. Disputes
that led to violent confrontations in the early 1970´s
now are being argued in courtrooms, governor´s offices,
state legislatures, and even the board rooms of energy

242

companies. In part, the change in tactics is due to the governments finding validity to the Indian's arguments. The Supreme Court awarded the Sioux $105 million for the seizure of the Black Hills; Congress settled a land dispute claim by granting two Maine tribes $82 million. Land claims involving millions of acres from Florida to New York to Arizona and Washington state are now before the courts, with the South Dakota and Maine cases now standing as precedents.

Perhaps most symbolic of the change in atmosphere and tactics was the June, 1980 presentation in Washington, D.C. of the Jefferson Medal to Hank Adams, an Assiniboise Sioux. Adams had been arrested eight years earlier during the Indian takeover of the Bureau of Indian Affairs office in the capital. In 1980 he was cited for "leadership in seeking equal opportunities for Indians" and received the honor along with Walter Cronkite, David Stockman, and Warren Christopher of the State Department.

The reason for the change is as old as free enterprise--supply and demand. The combined tribes control an estimated 40 percent of the nation's uranium deposits; a third of its low sulfur coal and large deposits of coal, oil, natural gas, shale rock, and geothermal energy. It gives them bargaining power with both the government and the energy companies (AP Newsfeature, September 24, 1981: 16).

This chapter closes with a table which presents a summarization of the milestone events in federal/Indian relations over the past two-hundred years.

Table 12: MILESTONES IN FEDERAL/INDIAN RELATIONS	
1763	King George III's proclamation setting aside "reserved lands for Indians.
1778	First U.S./Indian treaty signed.
1794	First Indian treaty providing for the education of Indians signed.
1824	Bureau of Indian Affairs created, under Secretary of War.
1830	Passage of Indian Removal Act by Congress.
1832-43	Federal Government conducts removal of the "Five Civilized Nations" Tribes.
1849	Bureau of Indian Affairs moved to Department of Interior.
1867-68	Indian Peace Commission negotiates final treaties with the Indians, the last of 389 treaties with the Nez Perce, passed on August 13, 1868.
1871	Act abolishing all Indian treaty-making passed by Congress.
1870-76	Federal Indian policy, backed by military support, places remaining Indians on reservations. Practice of giving Indians food and clothing rations begun.
1887	Dawes Severalty Act establishes land allotment policy.
1902-10	Start of Federal/Indian reclamation, forestry and conservation programs.
1906	Burke Act, amending Dawes, describing Indian "competency."
1924	Act giving Indian citizenship and right to vote in national elections).
1928	Meriam Report published advocating new Indian-policy reforms.
1934	Several new policies enacted; allotment ended, tribal self-government; Johnson-O'Malley Act dispersed Federal Indian Administration into several agencies.
1946	Indian Claims Commission created, allows Indians to file suits against U.S. government.
1953	House Concurrent Resolution 108 calling for termination of Federal Trusteeship over Indian affairs and property.
1954	First of several acts on termination of federal trust status over Indian lands.
1964	Economic Opportunity Act programs provide Indians opportunity to participate and control their own programs.

| 1968 | Civil Rights Act passed, including so-called "Indian Bill of Rights." Executive Order creating National Council of Indian Opportunity upholding Indian involvement in policy-making regarding Indian policies. |
| 1975 | Indian Self-Determination and Education Assistance Act passed. |

Chapter Endnotes

1. See, for instance, Harry Kitano, 1969: 16; Peterson: 28; Parrillo: 284; and McLemore: 168-169.

2. See, for example: Eugene Rostow, "Our Worst Wartime Mistake," Harper's Magazine, (September, 1945): 193-201; and Ken Ringle, "What Did You Do Before the War, Dad?" The Washington Post Magazine (December 6, 1981): 54-62; and McLemore: 174. This assessment also reached by other scholars: Hosokawa: 275; Simpson and Yinger: 94; Kitano, 1969:217.

3. See, "Disguised Blessing," Newsweek, December 29, 1958, 23; Kitano, 1974: 227; Hosokawa: 436; and "Success Story: Outwhiting the Whites,' Newsweek, June 21, 1971: 24-25; Parrillo: 291-292; McLemore: 155-157.

4. Dinnerstein, Nichols, and Reimers: 231. See also: Hagan: 121; Forbes: 113; Viewpoints: Red, Yellow, and Brown: 30.

5. Josephy, 1977: 286-287. See also, Dinnerstein, Nichols and Reimers: 305; Feaver, "Wounded Knee and the New Tribalism," Encounter, March, 1975: 22-33.

Additional Readings

Barker, Lucius J. and Jesse J. McCorry, Jr. Black Americans and the Political System, Cambridge, Mass.: Winthrop, 1976.
Carmichael, Stokely and Charles Hamilton. Black Power, New York: Vintage Books, 1967.
Daniels, Roger. The Politics of Prejudice. New York: Atheneum 1969.
_____ and Harry Kitano. American Racism. Englewood Cliffs, N.J.: Prentice-Hall, 1970.
Dinnerstein, Leonard, Roger Nichols, and David Reimers. Natives and Strangers. New York: Oxford University Press, 1979.

Dye, Thomas R. The Politics of Equality. Indiannapolis: The Bobbs-Merrill Company, 1971.

Forbes, Jack (ed.). The Indian in America's Past. Englewood Cliffs, N.J.: Prentice-Hall, 1964.

Fuchs, Lawrence H. (ed.). American Ethnic Politics. New Harper and Row, 1968.

Glazer, Nathan. Affirmative Discrimination: Ethnic Inequality and Public Policy. New York: Basic Books, 1975.

Hagan, William. American Indians. Chicago: University of Chicago Press, 1949.

Hosokawa, William. Nisei: The Quiet Americans. New York: William and Morrow, 1969.

Kitano, Harry. Japanese Americans: The Evolution of a Subculture. Englewood Cliffs, N.J.: Prentice-Hall, 1969.

_____. Race Relations. Englewood Cliffs, N.J.: Prentice-Hall, 1974.

Levy, Mark R. and Kramer, Michael S. The Ethnic Factor. New York: Simon and Schuster, 1973.

McLemore, Dale S. Racial and Ethnic Relations in America. Boston: Allyn and Bacon, 1980.

Parrillo, Vincent. Strangers to These Shores. Boston: Houghton Mifflin, 1980.

Parsons, Talcott and Kenneth B. Clark (ed.). The Negro Americans. Boston: Beacon Press, 1968.

Peterson, William. Japanese Americans: Oppression and Success. New York: Random House, 1971.

United States National Advisory Commission on Civil Disorders. Report of the Commission. New York: Bantam Books, 1968.

Introduction

As we have seen, minority status in the United
States has been based on national origin, religion,
race, gender, age, and sexual preference. Groups
ascribed such status in American society have varied
considerably in the rate and degree to which they have
assimilated. Some groups, such as the Scandinavians and
the Germans, moved up in society rather quickly. Other
nationality groups, such as the Italians, Greeks, and
Slavic groups, faced stiffer resistance and moved more
slowly. Religious groups sometimes faced violent
persecution. The Mormons, for instance, were forced to
give up a basic tenet of their faith before they were
able to assimilate into the broader culture. Racial
groups experienced the greatest prejudice and
discrimination and have generally moved the slowest of
all. Even among the racially-based minorities there is
considerable variation over the means and rate of their
assimilation. The question of variations in the rate of
assimilation is by no means a simple one. Many
alternative perspectives have been employed by scholars
of racial and ethnic relations to deal with the question
of how and why different subcultures merge into the
majority culture at different rates and through varied
routes of access.

In his brilliant and highly sophisticated analysis
of the causes and nature of the gap between
South/Central/Eastern European groups and Black
Americans, Stanley Lieberson (1980) explicitly presents
the assimilation/rate question with respect to those
groups. That question could be asked equally well of
the variations among all minority groups in American
society. His study dealt with the question of why the
"new" immigrant groups, that is, those who began to
migrate in sizable numbers from South, Central, and
Europe after 1880, fared so much better in the United
than did Black-Americans. The usual response has been
to argue that the handicaps faced by blacks were more
severe than those encountered by the new Europeans. The
immigrants, notwithstanding their foreign tongues, and
broken English, their clothing, alien ways, non-
Protestant religions and the like, nonetheless, were
white. Therefore, it was possible for their descendents

to shed as many of those distinguishing characteristics as was necessary. Blacks, however, were blacks no matter how anglicized their surnames, the lack of ties to distant homelands, their language, clothing, or their Protestantism. Another common reason given for the differences in their rates of assimilation was that the new Europeans arrived in the Northern cities in sizable numbers first, before the demand for unskilled labor declined. Blacks, arriving in the North a few decades later, faced entrenched and hostile unions and all sorts of discrimination in the North as well as the South to a degree never experienced by the Europeans. While he found such answers satisfactory for classroom purposes, he nonetheless had a nagging dissatisfaction with the answer. If these comments were true, were they all of the truth? He concluded he did not know the answer, nor did his colleagues. "There was a reluctant suspicion held by many that some unknown part of the gap between the new Europeans in America and blacks was a reflection of something else (Lieberson: xi).

This chapter will attempt to elucidate that "something else." After a brief survey of the major single-focus explanations of the variations in assimilation, it will discuss a systems dynamic framework for analyzing rates of change. The advantage of the systems perspective is its focus on the multiplicity of variables which affect the object of one's analysis. The model presented here is the first and admittedly rather tentative application of the systems approach to the question of the rate of assimilation. The model graphically portrays the major interrelationships among the variables useful in accounting for how a minority subculture gradually merges into the majority. These relationships have all been illustrated in the cases of the various minorities we have reviewed in the previous five chapters. This chapter closes with some suggestions as to the type of data needed to operationalize such a model; that is, what type of data will be needed to empirically measure variations in the rate of assimilation.

Some of the differences among the theoretical perspectives on rates of assimilation may be the result of their varying perceptions of the basic concepts involved. Assimilation is best viewed as a gradual process of transformation either within the individual or within a group as more and more of its members begin to individually change. This transformation involves persons typical of the subculture becoming more and more like individuals typical of the majority culture.

248

Acculturation, or cultural assimilation, is the process by which minority members gradually absorb the cultural ways, values, and life-style of the majority society, or that portion of majority society which operates within the regional and class confines of the minority member.

Assimilation is a complex process in which an individual from a minority subculture gradually merges into another culture, manifesting itself in a number of dimensions or subprocesses: cultural, structural, marital, identificational, attitude receptional, behavioral receptional, and civic (Gordon, 1964: 71). The continued absorption into the majority culture depends on both the minority members seeking assimilation and the majority's acceptance of their doing so. The pace of assimilation may vary from person to person and from group to group. It is possible for individuals, and thus for groups, to progress to the cultural and even on to the structural stage and then to remain there for some time. Indeed, a group may even regress for a period if majority hostility is suddenly increased (e.g. against the German-Americans during World War I). Once the stage of marital assimilation occurs the pace is likely to increase rapidly, and Milton Gordon maintains that once structural assimilation has been achieved the other stages will inevitably follow.

Joseph Fichter adds another perspective which we may usefully recollect here. He identifies four categories of individuals in terms of their degree of group-relatedness: nuclear, modal, marginal, and dormant. A nuclear member of a group is one whose self-identity is totally involved in the group. A modal member is one who accepts most of the norms and values of the group and who manifests nearly all of the physical and/or cultural traits that are characteristic of the group. A marginal member is one who manifests only a few traits or internalizes only some of the norms and values of the group. Finally, a dormant member is one who exhibits few, if any, of the physical traits of the group and has internalized in a latent manner only a few of the norms and values of the group (Fichter, 1954: 29-79). A dormant person is well on his/her way towards total assimilation; one who has reached at least the identificational stage in Gordon's typology. As a particular subcultural group develops more and more marginal members its rate of assimilation speeds up.

Fig. 4: THE ACCULTURATION/ASSIMILATION CONTINUUM

Subcultural Group → Majority Culture

The Group as a Whole

Cultural	Begins to shed some cultural norms (food, clothing style) typical of the subculture and adopts those of the majority.
Structural	Begins to enter job market, voluntary associations of working class and lower-middle class levels.
Marital	Outgroup marriage becomes common (50% or more).
Identificational	Most of group members begin to think of themselves as hyphenated-Americans or Americans of "n-descent".
Attitude Receptional	Majority shows no more prejudice against group.
Behavioral Receptional	Absence of Discrimination
Civic	Full participation in civic life of majority—no value, power conflict.

An Individual of the Subcultural Group

Cultural	Name-change (anglicized); acquires some norms typical of new culture: voluntary food, clothes, language; and begins to shed those of the subculture.
Structural	Gets job in working class of his/her own group or higher, begins to join into the majority associations of group. e.g. labor unions, Lions Clubs, etc.
Marital	Marries out of his/her own group.
Identificational	Person thinks of him or herself as belonging to the majority, but still recognizes the subcultural heritage.
Attitude Receptional	Person experiences no prejudice due to subcultural background
Behavioral Receptional / Civic	Person no longer experiences discrimination. Begins to participate fully in the civic life of the majority.

NULCEAR MODAL MARGINAL DORMANT

250

These points are summarized in the preceding figure, which presents the acculturation/assimilation process as a continuum. Gordon's seven types are presented as stages along the continuum, representing the gradual absorption by either the individual or the entire group as many of its members individually progress along the continuum and move the entire group towards civic assimilation. Once total absorption has taken place, the former minority subculture would cease to be an identifiable subculture. All of its members would have become so assimilated that neither its former members nor the majority society could realistically distinguish the group as existing any longer as a separate subgroup. For our purposes here, that degree of total assimilation need not be reached. Civic assimilation is the end stage of the process for the purposes of the model herein presented.

CURRENT PERSPECTIVES

The Psychological Approach

A variety of perspectives or explanations of assimilation stress a single variable as the one which best accounts for differing rates of assimilation. A scholar employing the psychological perspective, for instance, might emphasize the minority group and its members' capabilities to cope with the stresses of minority status. Another might account for such variations by emphasizing the minority group members' motivation to succeed, or lack of such motivation. Dale McLemore (1983), for example, offers a psychological explanation to account for variations between Italian and Jewish immigrant groups with respect to their speed of acculturation. He notes that while they both were exploited at every turn by the majority by their countrymen who "knew the ropes," were forced to work at unfamiliar jobs, at low wages, and with no job security, and were left with no choice but to move into the tenement slums with their crowding, noise, filth, lack of sanitation, and crime, the Jews were somewhat more insulated than the Italians. Despite the bad conditions, the Jews found in America a degree of freedom from persecution unimagined in eastern Europe. Thus, Jews were extremely eager to make use of this new freedom and, consequently, embraced the opportunities that existed in public education and politics much more rapidly than did the Italians. The Jews came over in families and had quickly erected a "cultural tent" which gave them added protection against the psychological insults and deprivations that were so common in the urban slums of the new world.

An even more explicit and developed application of this perspective would be represented by the various achievement motivation studies, illustrated by the work of Bernard Rosen (1969). Rosen stresses the individual´s psychological and cultural orientation towards achievement: the individual´s need to excel; his/her desire to enter the competitive race for social status; his/her initial willingness or not to adopt the high valuation placed upon personal success. Rosen believes racial and ethnic groups differ in their orientation towards achievement, especially as expressed in the drive for upward social mobility, and that those differences in orientation have been a singularly important factor contributing to the dissimilarities in their social mobility rates (:47-48). He describes what he calls the achievement syndrome, which is comprised of three components. The purely psychological factor is achievement motivation which imparts in the individual the internal impetus to excel. The other two components are cultural ones. Value orientations, determined by the groups subculture, implement achievement-motivated behavior. Culture also influences the educational/vocational aspirations of a subculture. This view sees these three factors as variously affecting one´s status achievement by moving the individual to excel and organizing and directing his/her behavior towards high status goals.

A similar emphasis on the psychological dimension underlies those studies which account for prejudice and discrimination within the majority society members by focusing on personality types. The "frustration/aggression" personality studies exemplify this approach (e.g. Dollard and Miller). Childhood patterns are viewed as contributing to the development of a pathological personality type. Early childhood restrictions and later adult limitations can create an inordinate need for power and prestige. When an individual fails to achieve perceived needs, the person may become highly frustrated. Sustained frustration can lead to the development of the authoritarian personality type which compels the person to aggression and scapegoating against a highly visible and readily accessible minority. The individual uses the minority as a means of displacing the frustrations. In a similar manner, certain minority members may develop psychological disorders. Social blindness, self-hatred, and identification dilemmas lead to high frustration levels. This may lead some minority members into an aggressive response. Their very powerlessness enables the majority's power elite to exploit or control them. Their sense of being controlled or exploited leads to further frustrations, and the cycle goes on (Kinloch, 1974: 64).

The Social-Psychological Approach

Another closely related approach is the social psychological one. This perspective includes the psychological factor, but stresses the social milieu within which that factor operates. Prejudice is seen as a function of the individual's position in the social structure, which is to say that it is determined by a person's degree of socio-economic security. It is further influenced by the racial socialization to which one is exposed: it is subject to family, peer, and regional pressures. This view sees racial prejudice as a function of the extent and quality of inter-racial contact to which a person has been exposed (Kinloch, 1974: 77). This perspective emphasizes that several factors effect the "speed of inclusion," (that is, the rate of assimilation): 1) whether people have migrated voluntarily or not, 2) whether or not they desire to integrate, 3) the racial identification of the individual or group, and 4) the extent to which the majority is willing or not to accept the minority for inclusion (McLemore, 1983: 6-8).

Richard Schermerhorn admirably exemplifies this approach in his discussion of congruent and incongruent orientations towards centripetal or centrifugal directional movement by subordinate and superordinate groups (Schermerhorn: 207).

The mixture of social structural elements with psychological orientations is important in Milton Gordon's theoretical work. He discusses the variables we need to study in order to account for the type and degree of assimilation, and the degree of intergroup conflict. He argues persuasively that a general theory of ethnic relations must integrate all variables. Biosocial variables would include a measure of the sense of self and the tendency towards protection of self. These variables would recognize that "...a man defending the honor or welfare of his ethnic group is a man defending himself." Likewise, there are variables Gordon calls interaction process ones, dealing with stereotyping, frustration/aggression mechanisms, felt-dissatisfactions, goal attainments, and conflict reducing mechanisms. A measure of the level of felt-dissatisfaction is necessary for understanding the prevailing ideologies and value systems of both the majority and the minority. Perceived sanctions determine how the minority assesses its chances for success. The tendency for conflict to escalate leads to the need for the majority to develop conflict-reducing mechanisms. The third type of variable Gordon discusses is societal variables: the absolute and relative sizes of the majority and minority, their comparative rates of natural increase, their territorial dispersion, and the consensus or lack thereof among both the majority and the minority.

For societal variables Gordon would focus on the nature of ideologies of race, religion, and ethnic groups; on the distribution of relative power resources; on the degree of access, by the minority, to societal rewards; and upon the political nature of the majority society along a democratic/totalitarian scale (in Glazer and Moynihan, 1975: 91-107).

Nathan Glazer concentrates on social/psychological aspects of the minority group as the more important factors which affect the rate of assimilation. He emphasizes whether the minority is isolated or concentrated (that is, rural versus urban settlement patterns), and whether the group is coming from "nations struggling to become states" (such as the Poles, Lithuanians, or Slovaks) or from "states struggling to become nations" (such as Italy, Turkey and Greece) (in Kurokawa: 74-86).

The social psychological perspective underlies those studies which focus on the minority´s orientation toward majority society coupled with a structural assessment of the group´s reaction to its minority status: whether the group is assimmilationist or pluralist in orientation. Irwin Rinder, for example, discusses three types of minority orientations which blend the psychological element with social-structural ones. His three types of pluralism are: accommodated pluralism, in which moderately deprived minorities like the Chinese and Jews meet with moderate barriers with a

254

subordinate group identity which possesses important centripetal strengths, such as high morale, continuity, and economic versatility; <u>segregated pluralism,</u> in which severely disadvantaged minorities, stigmatized as either culturally primitive, racially different, or both, are able to sustain their members´ identity by maintaining a strong traditional social order isolated from the majority society´s; and <u>exotic pluralism,</u> in which minorities are neither severely disadvantaged nor moderately deprived, but rather are temporarily advantaged by their distinctiveness from the dominant group--for example, immigrants from the British Isles. Their differences seem to be rewarded rather than penalized because they create no obstacles at the same time that they afford a marginal differentiation which is considered to be exotic without being unsettling so (also in Kurokawa: 43-54).

Stanley Freed´s (1957) discussion of separatist societies exemplifies a similar focus. In discussing the Old Order Amish of Pennsylvania, the <u>shtetl</u> (the Jewish small towns of Eastern Europe), and the "controlled acculturation" of the Hutterites, he notes the similarities of such separatist groups: 1) a readiness for change in some aspects of culture (especially economic) outside of the central core of the culture, 2) patterns of mutual aid which are manipulated so as to shield the focal aspects of the culture, 3) strong means to control deviants, 4) strong opposition to secular education, 5) endogamy, and 6) possession of a distinctive language (:55-67).

The Sociological Approach

The sociological perspective is historically the oldest one employed in the analysis of assimilation owing to the fact that sociologists were among the first to become concerned with explaining the process. Robert Park, for instance, posits the idea of a race relations cycle. He argues that when different racial/cultural groups come into contact, they cannot avoid falling into competition. Park argues that the race relations cycle of contact, competition, accommodation, and eventual assimilation is progressive and irreversible. Its rate may vary, but its direction cannot be reversed (Park, 1950: 150). Several other sociologists--Bogardus, Brown, Glick, and Rose to name a few prominent examples--have followed Park´s lead in constructing variations of "cycles" they believe are sociologically

255

determined.(1) This perspective forms the basis of the entire ethnic stratification literature which focuses on the socially-structured nature of intergroup relations. Donald Noel (1968) states that:

> Ethnic   stratification   will   emerge   when
> distinct   ethnic   groups   are   brought   into
> sustained contact only if the groups are
> characterized   by   a   high   degree   of
> ethnocentrism, competition, and differential
> power.   Competition provides the motivation
> for stratification; ethnocentrism channels the
> competition along ethnic lines; and the power
> differential determines whether either group
> will be able to subordinate the other (: 157-
> 172. His italics).

The sociological perspective is implicit in Ralph Dahrendorf´s (1959) discussion of class conflict in industrial   societies.   In that work he stresses the point that the greater the deprivation of a group in its economic, social status, and social power resources the more probable it is that the weaker group will resort to intense and violent conflict to achieve gains in any of those areas.   As the social-class position of the subordinate group increases, intergroup conflict will become less intense and less violent (:215-218).

Lloyd   Warner and Leo Srole´s (1945)   similar perspective of the rate of assimilation maintains that when similarities between the minority group and the majority group exist, the probability is greater that the relationship between the two will be relatively harmonious and that assimilation will eventually occur; whereas the greater and more visible the cultural differences   between   the groups,   the greater   the likelihood that conflict will occur (:285-286).   This perspective is also evident in Hubert Blalock´s (1967) discussion of   competitive and pressure   resources available to minority groups determining the rate and degree of assimilation (:119).

Pluralist theorists would disagree with Park´s "inevitable and irreversible cycle" notion.   Pluralism recognizes   that   minorities   can   maintain   their distinctiveness and simultaneously interact with the larger society (e.g.   Parsons and Clark: 709-754). Although arriving at far different conclusions, they share Park´s basic sociological perspective on the question of how one explains differences among groups and their rate of assimilation.

The Economic Approach

The economic perspective is an equally venerable and important approach to the question of assimilation. Marxian theory employs the economic perspective to explain all inter-group relations. Numerous scholars have employed various forms of economic analyses to explain acculturation and assimilation. Vincent Parrillo (1980) notes that sometimes economic and technological conditions facilitate minority integration. When the economic conditions are healthy and jobs are plentiful, newcomers find it easier to work their way up the socioeconomic ladder. In this view occupation mobility--the ability to improve one's job position--becomes the key to rapid assimilation. This view notes that downward social mobility increases the ethnic hostility among that portion of the majority suffering the greatest economic decline. Numerous studies have noted that upwardly mobile persons are generally more tolerant than nonmobile or downwardly mobile individuals (:90).

Some scholars focus on the occupational rank and skill-levels of groups to explain variations in their rates of assimilation; maintaining, for example, that the higher the immigrant's former occupational status and the more transferable his/her skill the greater the rate of acculturation; and that the less positive value placed upon ethnic identity by members of the host society and the more equal the prestige of the occupational fields of the two societies, the greater the rate of acculturation (Kurokawa: 24-27; Weinstock: 144-149).

A persuasive critique of Marxian theory which nonetheless employs an economic perspective to explain rates of assimilation is the split-labor analysis of Edna Bonacich (1976). She argues that dominant group workers realize economic gains by "keeping down" minority group workers. The antagonism which white workers feel towards blacks and other minorities stems from the fact that the price of labor in the two groups differs initially and that the capitalist class does not create but rather is faced with a "split labor market." Such a market is characterized by conflict among the three groups: the capitalists (those doing the hiring), higher-paid labor, and cheap labor. The economic interests of the two labor groups are fundamentally different. Higher paid labor is genuinely threatened by

257

cheap labor groups which undercut the dominant higher paid labor group by doing the same work for lower wages. Since the business class gains by substituting cheap labor for higher paid ones, the attempt by the latter to improve their wages and working conditions by organizing and striking can be broken by the "reserve army" of cheap laborers (:40).

Implicit in each of these perspectives is a different theory of discrimination. The psychological and social-psychological perspectives imply a cultural transmission theory of discrimination; the economic perspective reflects a group-gains theory of discrimination; and the sociological view reflects a situational-pressures theory of discrimination. Each of these perspectives is valuable in that it focuses our attention upon a necessary variable to explain or even to discuss the assimilation/rate question, although none provides a sufficient variable. While each adds a bit of truth in explaining varying rates of assimilation, none adequately accounts for all variations nor is equally applicable to all minority groups (2). The advantage of the systems perspective is that in attempting to develop a systems model we are forced to consider all of these perspectives. It is to that approach we now turn our attention.

The Systems Dynamic Perspective

The concept of a system emerged as a major focus in the social sciences after World War II (3). The concept of a system reflects the understanding that many things, from a car or a typewriter to a whole universe, are more than a collection of parts. The car is more than a bunch of steel, plastic, rubber, wires and glass parts. These parts are assembled in such a way as to interact such that people can be moved from place to place. The typewriter is more than some keys, springs, and carbon-coated ribbon assembled in a plastic cabinet. The typewriter is a system which facilitates communication between or among individuals.

More importantly, one system can be viewed as being related to other higher-order systems. The car, for example, is part of a transportation system, but may also be viewed as part of or affecting the ecosystem through air pollution. Similarly, the typewriter affects our business system, our governmental system, our educational system, and our mass media system.

Everyone of those systems will be markedly affected by a change from the typewriter to the word processor as the technological system impacts upon them all.   In   short, every system may be viewed as being part of a larger system [a subsystem] or an encompassing system [a supra-system].

A Systems Dynamic Model of Assimilation

While each single variable perspective reviewed above is valuable and contributes to our understanding of the factors that influence the highly complex process of assimilation, they are necessarily limited in their focus.   Taken individually, none of them adequately accounts for all the variation in rates nor applies equally well to all the relevant groups found in American society.

The psychological perspective, for example, in focusing on achievement motivation, emphasizes the minority´s contribution to its rate of assimilation. But such a focus ignores or may underplay the importance of the majority´s interaction with the minority.   A minority group might have a high desire to assimilate, but be rejected by the majority.   Over time, such rejection might adversely affect the minority´s desire to assimilate.   The economic perspective usefully focuses our attention on the level of the economy and the willingness, or not, of the majority to accept an in-coming group.   If many unskilled jobs are available during a period of economic boom, the majority will be more willing to accept the minority, especially if they have some needed job skills highly desired by a segment of the majority society.   But such an analysis would fail to account for a group, such as the Amish, who reject the basic value system of the majority and do not desire to assimilate, even though they may be economically capable of doing so.

The systems perspective has the advantage of attempting to interrelate: it focuses our attention on many--ideally upon all--of the factors which might influence the rate of assimilation.   One must recognize the fact that assimilation is necessarily and inherently a process which is reciprocal; that is, simultaneously involving the actions of both the majority and the minority.   It reflects the interaction--the feedback effect--among the various factors or variables which influence the process.   The following figure offers a rudimentary systems dynamic model of assimilation.

The model graphically portrays the following relationships. The rate of assimilation [3] will vary (that is, increase or decrease) depending upon the level of acculturation (the type and degree of acculturation in Gordon's terms) that a particular minority has achieved at a given point in time. In turn, that level is determined by two factors: the majority's willingness to accept acculturation rate [1]; and the minority's ability to acculturate rate [2]. Each of these latter two rates is determined by three functions.

The majority's fear function [A] represents the degree to which the majority perceives the minority as a threat. That threat may be viewed as an economic one, a religious-values one, a cultural one, and so on. The model simply states that the greater the degree of fear within the majority, the less willing it is to accept the minority. This is exemplified in the earlier chapters, for instance, by the case of the Mormons.

Closely linked is the influence of the size of minority function [B]. This variable must be understood in a relative sense. That is, the size of the minority in relation to the majority is the key aspect of how that size function influences the majority's willingness, or lack of such, to allow the minority to acculturate. Moreover, since we are dealing with the majority's willingness, it must be understood that this function refers to the majority's perception of the size of the minority. The visibility of the minority to the majority, because of highly visible physical features, geographic concentration versus dispersal, and so on) influences the latter's sense of size of the former. The perception of threat implicit in the size function also means that if the majority feels the potential size of the minority is a source of threat it will adversely affect the majority's willingness to accept the minority's acculturation. Thus, a religious minority that is small but growing rapidly through intense proselytism will be perceived by the majority as a larger and more threatening group than one which is relatively small and is not aggressively seeking new converts. Likewise, a minority which is small but which is exhibiting a very high birth rate relative to the majority's birth rate will be perceived as a larger threat. A group which is still experiencing a rapid rate of influx, due to immigration or internal migration, will be viewed as being larger or potentially more threatening as well, as we saw with the cases of the Irish and eastern European immigrant groups, for example, in contrast with that of the Scandinavians.

Finally, the model states that the majority's willingness to accept the minority's acculturation is also a function of the time of entry [C] of the minority subculture into the majority culture. As with size, this function is one dependent upon the majority's perception of the minority. If the group is entering during a time of economic recession or depression, or during a period of social upheaval and instability, the majority is less willing to allow a new minority to acculturate than if the minority "enters" during a time of economic expansion or "boom." Immigrant groups entering during the decade of the 1870's and 1880's, when there were several recessions and depressions such as the "Panic of 1873," were much less well received than those groups which came prior to the Civil War era. "Entry" means the beginning of initial and sustained contact between the two cultures. It may be the time when an immigrant group enters a country or when a new religious minority emerges. It may be the result of internal migration from one region to another within the majority culture's geographic area. How sustained is the influx of the new group will also influence the majority's perception and determine the willingness or not to accept the acculturation process by the minority.

The second major element determining the level of acculturation of the minority is the minority's ability to acculturate rate [2]. That rate is determined by three functions which cause it to change over time. The first is called the minority's ability to organize function [D]. Groups cannot adequately cope with the prejudice and discrimination, nor develop new norms or values among their membership, unless they are well organized. The more organized a group, given its desire to acculturate, the faster will be its rate of doing so. The less organized a group, the slower will be its rate of acculturation. The Jewish and Greek immigrant groups, as we have seen, organized and thereby acculturated more rapidly than did the Italian immigrants.

The second major function determining the minority's ability to acculturate rate is its marginal membership function [E]. The greater the number of marginal members a group has the faster its rate of acculturation. The more nuclear or modal the membership of a group, the slower its rate of acculturation. The more rapid intermarriage rates among the Japanese-Americans than among the Chinese-Americans, for instance, illustrates this function.

Finally, the minority's ability to acculturate rate is determined by the <u>similarity</u> <u>of</u> <u>cultures</u> <u>function</u> [F]. The closer in basic norms and values the two culture are the easier it is for the minority to acquire the new culture. If an incoming group, for instance, uses a language which is vastly different than English, it will acquire the norms and values of American society more slowly than will an English-speaking immigrant group. If the foreign language is linguistically close to English, the group will learn more readily. This function also concerns such cultural aspects as urban living patterns, clothing styles, child-rearing practices, physical features, religious beliefs and practices, and the other norms, values and customs that make up a culture. The Scotch Irish and Welsh, for instance, assimilated more rapidly than did the Greeks or Slavic groups.

The model specifies that the level of acculturation is <u>simultaneously</u> <u>influenced</u> by these two major variables or rate elements. The model also includes an informational feedback process. The feedback flow indicates that as a group acculturates it becomes easier and more desirable for its members to do so. Likewise, the majority becomes more willing to accept the group and to allow further acculturation. Acculturation is a sharing process, a two-way street. The majority may begin to accept as an aspect of its own culture some influence from the minority subculture. Thus, even without changing the minority becomes more like the majority and hence more acceptable to it. Italian and Chinese food, for example, may become "Americanized." Then too, a majority culture may drastically change its perceptions of some aspect of the minority subculture. Norms and customs may suddenly become more acceptable without changing. After World War II, for instance, many Chinese norms and customs became to be viewed as charming, quaint, or desirably exotic. In any event, the feedback influence increases the willingness of the majority to accept the minority's acculturation, which, in turn, reinforces the minority's desire and capability to do so, thus raising the level of acculturation and speeding up the rate of assimilation.

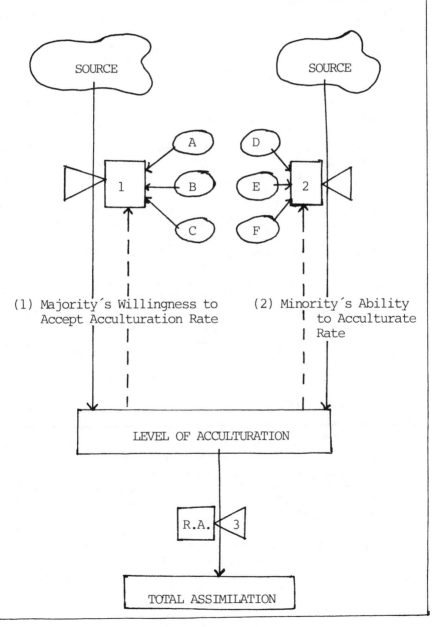

Fig 5: A SYSTEMS DYNAMIC MODEL OF ASSIMILATION

A=Majority´s Fear Function
B=Size of Minority Function
C=Time of Entry Function

D=Minority´s Ability to
  Organize Function
E=Minority´s Marginal
  Membership Function
F=Similarity of
  Cultures Function

SOURCE

SOURCE

A

B

C

D

E

F

1

2

(1) Majority´s Willingness to
    Accept Acculturation Rate

(2) Minority´s Ability
    to Acculturate
    Rate

LEVEL OF ACCULTURATION

R.A.   3

TOTAL ASSIMILATION

While this model of assimilation is useful to focus on the multiplicity of variables, and while the model stresses the dynamic nature of those interrelationships, its primary usefulness will come only after the model has been "operationalized," when empirical indicators or measures for each of the rates and functions have been specified. Only then can the model be tested for its explanatory or predictive value. While the development and testing of this model is beyond the scope of this chapter, some suggestions as to likely operational measures will be discussed briefly here. This discussion will hopefully clarify further for the reader how the functions of the model operate to increase or decrease the level of acculturation.

Our ability to develop such measures is frequently hampered by a lack of data. Some of the groups to which we might wish to apply the model began their acculturation/assimilation process long before such data were kept or whose reliability is seriously questioned. Sometimes the data is unavailable because we do not how to measure something or we do not yet have an agreement among scholars as to whether or not some set of data accurately reflects a given variable. The "closeness of culture" from one culture to another, for example, depends upon one's judgement about the compatibility or lack thereof concerning certain cultural norms, values or practices. Therefore, we may often have to rely upon surrogate measures for certain functions specified in the model. The following, then, should be viewed as rather tentative suggestions regarding the nature or type of empirical data needed to operationalize the model's various rates, levels, and functions.

Operational Indicators of the Model

Since the rate of assimilation is the dependent variable we will commence our discussion of operational measures with that concept. What we need to measure this element of the model are some readily accessible data which indicates civic assimilation. An index, comprised of three or four indicators, might be the most fruitful manner in which to approach this variable. Since we are attempting to measure the assimilation rate achieved by a group in a civic sense, election data will be used to comprise such an index. The degree to which a group bloc votes would be one such indicator. The closer the group votes, as measured by percent split in votes between the competing parties in the election, to that of the split by the majority, the more assimilated the group. To the contrary, the more the group cohesively bloc votes, the less assimilated is the group. Equally important, the index would need to have a component that measured the turnout rate; that is, the percent of the group actually voting from among those eligible to do so. Again, the closer the group's turnout rate is relative to the majority's average turnout the more assimilated the group is, and vice-versa. The index might also employ a negative indicator, such as the willingness of the group to cross ethnic lines and vote against one of its "own" for some other electoral reason. The willingness of the Scandinavian-Americans to vote, let us say, for an Italian-American over a Scandinavian-American because the former is on the Republican ticket while the latter is on the Democratic ticket would be one such indicator. An illustration of this effect would be Jewish voters in New York voting for John Lindsay, a _liberal_ Republican, rather than a conservative Jewish Democrat, Beam, because of their liberalness. Such _cross-group_ voting, for whatever the reason, indicates a degree of civic assimilation. Finally, such an index may include the number of members from the minority group to have been elected to national-level office (for example, to the Congress, or nominated or elected President). Since to get such a candidate successfully elected to that level of office would necessitate a fair degree of acceptance of that minority member by voters of the majority, it seems logical to include such data in an assimilation index.

The _majority's_ _fear_ function could be measured indirectly. The "fear" of a group is difficult to measure directly at any time and would be impossible for the majority members of the historical past—we can no longer "opinion poll" persons from the 1880's. Several surrogate indicators are possible, however and could be used to develop an index of the majority's fear. Presuming that unemployment threat is a major cause of fear among the majority, the percent unemployed at a given time might be used. Likewise, the sociological literature suggests several methods of measuring segregation (both residential and social) of a given group. A "degree of segregation" measure could be a possible indicator of the majority's fear of the minority. The use of "ethnophaulisms" (a racial or ethnic group's derogatory nickname for another) might also be a component of a fear-function index. A high degree of association between the amount of prejudice against an outgroup and the number of ethnophaulisms for a group has been shown on a limited basis (Palmore: 205-210). Similarly, the number and types of racial stereotypes have been shown to correlate highly with levels of prejudice (Katz and Braly: 67-73). Another surrogate measure which might prove useful would be some index of ethnic violence--perhaps measured by the number of riots, lynchings and so on. So too, the size and strength of organized opposition groups measured, for example, by estimated membership in groups such as the Ku Klux Klan, or percent vote for nativist political parties such as the Know Nothing Party, the American Party, and the like might be employed. For earlier periods of U.S. history, the availability of "cheap" land open to the majority might be used as a negative indicator of the fear factor, assuming that Turner´s "frontier safety-valve" concept has merit. For more recent periods, perhaps an index of white flight to the suburbs might be usefully employed.

The size of minority function might be measured by the relative percent of the minority population. However, since this variable concerns the majority´s willingness to accept the minority´s acculturation, the perception by the majority of the size of the minority is the key aspect. Thus, relative birth rates might be used to indicate this function, since a rapidly growing minority would be perceived as a larger threat than would one whose birth rate was comparable to or lower than the majority society´s birth rate. In the case of a religious minority group, a "conversion rate" indicating the growth due to proselytism would have to be added to the natural birth rate data for the group.

Likewise, the time of entry function would have to include not only a peak decade for the relevant group´s emergence within the dominant culture, but also the length of the in-migration or emergence period. Lieberson (1980) very effectively notes the importance of the flow of migrants concept in his analysis of the differences between the South/Central/Eastern European groups and blacks (:376-381). A continuous influx of a group over long periods of time adversely affects its occupational queuing and its ability to employ a special niche in the occupational structure. Sizable continuous numbers of newcomers raises and maintains a level of ethnic and/or racial consciousness between and among members of both the majority and minority groups. The long-term influx of a group may also cause a shift in ethnic and racial group boundaries. If, for instance, the large and continuous migration of blacks to the north takes place while the previous discriminated against white immigration flow basically stops, then the negative dispositions towards the white immigrants would be muffled and modified as they come to be viewed as relatively more desirable neighbors, co-workers, political candidates, and so on than were blacks. As Professor Lieberson puts it:

> Ethnic ties and allegiances float and shift in acceptance with the threats and alternatives that exist. The presence of blacks made it harder to discriminate against the new Europeans because the alternative was viewed even less favorably (:381).

Certainly this effect seems relevant to account for the differences in rates of assimilation between Asians and blacks. Although both are racial minorities, the rate and patterns of their assimilation are far different. The fact that the Asian immigration influx was comparatively small and of brief duration may be exceedingly important a difference to account for their widely divergent rates of assimilation--at least in so far as we can discern a difference in the racial attitudes of the majority against the two groups.

With respect to measuring the minority's willingness to acculturate rate, each of the three functions would be measured by an index composed of several indicators. The minority's marginal membership function might be measured by the percent of "outgroup" marriage.(4) Another indicator might be the number and relative size of clearly identifiable ethnic associations for a given group.

The minority's ability to organize function might be tapped by several likely indicators that could serve as surrogate measures of this function. The size of the ethnic press, indicated by the number and circulation of newspapers catering to a specific group might be one component of this function's index. The number and relative size of ethnic associations for a given group is a possible measure. The relative wealth at the time of entry is data of possible use with respect to immigrant groups. Similarly, the formal educational

267

levels and percent literacy for a group are possible surrogate indicators of a group´s ability to organize. Job skills at the time of entry might also serve, since the immigration service has some fairly good data on occupational status at time of entry for most groups since 1900. Lieberson suggests using the measure of "life expectancy" as a surrogate measure of the relative social status of a group at the time of entry. Presuming the higher the status of a group´s members the greater the ability to organize themselves, such data might serve as a component of this index.

The similarities of cultures function might be measured by an index comprised of several indicators (see, for instance, Babics study of Yugoslav assimilation). Agreement in settlement patterns might be one component. A rural to rural or an urban to urban settlement pattern would be a positive indicator, whereas an urban to rural or rural to urban settlement pattern would be a negative indicator. The linguistic closeness of the language of a group to English would also be an indicator of cultural closeness. Protestant faith (measured by percent of a group who adhere to a Protestant denomination) would be an important component of any cultural closeness index. The group members being of the caucasian race or not would also be included. A "skin-color" weighting of closeness or distance from "white" would be suggested by an extensive body of sociological literature. Some sort of measure of the "compatibility" of cultural norms associated with food, clothing style, child-rearing practices, and so on might possibly be developed.

Such empirical measures, if they were developed, would be sufficiently operationalize the model that it could then be tested. Using statistical tools such as regression analysis, the applicability of the model to explain past group´s assimilation could be measured. Perhaps the model could ultimately be refined enough to "predict" future assimilation rates. The important point here is that the very attempt to measure these functions exemplifies the value of such modeling. The process of developing the model forces us to think about the assimilation rate problem in a manner which lends itself to developing specific empirical measures of what is occurring in the very complex "real-world" process. It may suggest the future collection of data not currently available which could more accurately or directly serve as an indicator of the process and interrelationships suggested by the model. Just as the development of a consensus about the concept of GNP contributed significantly to the expansion of economic theory, perhaps a comparable effect might be achieved within the social sciences with respect to our developing a general theory of ethnic and race relations.

James VanderZanden (1983), in his review of the literature on American minority relations, has identified a number of factors which he found to be somewhat "research substantiated :282-284)." Although the wording is somewhat different from that used here, all ten of his propositions parallel the expectations of the model described in this chapter. We close the chapter, then, with a list of his ten factors influencing the rate of assimilation, noting references to the previous studies from which the propositions are drawn and the manner in which they relate to the model presented here.

1) The greater the difference between the host and the immigrant cultures, the greater will be the subordination, the greater the strength of the ethnic social system, and the longer the period necessary for the assimilation of the ethnic group (Warner and Srole, 1945). [Similarity of Cultures Function]

2) The larger the ratio of the incoming group to the resident population, the slower the rate of assimilation (Williams, 1947). [Size of Minority Function]

3) The more rapid the influx of the incoming group, the slower the rate of assimilation (Williams, 1947). [Time of Entry Function]

4) The greater the dispersion of the immigrant group, especially in the same territorial pattern as the dominant group, the more rapid the immigrant´s assimilation (Schermerhorn, 1949). [Similarity of Cultures Function]

5) The higher the educational, income, and occupational levels of the incoming groups, the more rapid its assimilation (Weinstock, 1964). [Minority´s Ability to Organize Function]

6)   The greater the predisposition of the incoming group to change, the more rapid the rate of assimilation (Borrie, 1959). [Minority's Marginal Membership Function]

7) The greater the predisposition of the receiving community to recognize differences (as legitimate), the more rapid the rate of assimilation (VanderZanden, 1983). [This is a negative way of expressing the Majority's Fear Function]

8) The greater the degree of economic competition between the native and immigrant groups, the slower the rate of assimilation (VanderZanden, 1983. See also, Lieberson, 1980). [Majority's Fear Function]

9) The greater the proximity and access to the homeland, the slower the rate of assimilation (VanderZanden, 1983. See also, Fitzpatrick, 1971; and Burman, 1970). [A negative way of expressing the Minority's Willingness to Acculturate Rate and/or the Marginal Membership Function]

10)   In situations of continuous intergroup contact, subordinate migrants (newcomers who are politically and economically dominated by an established indigenous population) tend to be more rapidly assimilated than subordinate indigenous populations (native groups who are subjected to political and economic domination by a migrant group). (Schermerhorn, 1949; VanderZanden, 1983; Blauner, 1969 and 1972; Acuna, 1972; and Burma, 1970). [Relevant to both the Minority's Willingness to Acculturate Function and to the Majority's Willingness to Accept Acculturation Rate]

Chapter Endnotes

1. E.S. Bogardus suggests the following stages in acculturation: (1) curiosity, (2) economic welcome, (3) industrial and social antagonism, (4) legislative antagonism, (5) fair play tendencies, (6) quiescence, and (7) second generation difficulties. See his "Race Relations Cycle," American Journal of Sociology, 35 (January, 1930): 613. W. O. Brown states that race relations have a "natural history" of: (1) initial contact, (2) emergence of conflict, (3) temporary accommodation, (4) struggle for status, (5) mobilization, and (6) solution. See his "Cultural Contact and Race Conflicts, in E. B. Reuter (ed.), Race and Cultural Contacts (New York: McGraw-Hill, 1934: 34-

37). E. C. Glick posits a sequence of phases: (1) precontact, (2) contact and predomination, (3) domination, and (4) accommodation. See his "Social Roles and Types in Race Relations," in A. W. Lind (ed.), Race Relations in World Perspective (Honolulu: University of Hawaii Press, 1955: 239-241). As we cited, Peter Rose maintains that all minorities will respond in one of four ways to discrimination: submission, withdrawal, avoidance, or integration.

2. Not all scholars discuss assimilation as inevitable or even likely. Barth and Noel, for instance, argue that in addition to assimilation there are at least four other possible stable outcomes of intergroup contact: exclusion (including both expulsion and annihilation), symbiosis, stratification, and pluralism. See their "Conceptual Frameworks for the Analysis of Race Relations: An Evaluation," Social Forces, 50: 333-347.

3. This entire section of the systems model draws heavily from William Davisson and John Uhran, Jr. "Modeling and Simulation: A Systems Science Approach," (Unpublished manuscript, Notre Dame: University of Notre Dame Mimeograph, 1976). See also, David Easton. A Framework for Political Analysis. (Englewood Cliffs, N.J.: Prentice-Hall, 1965).

4. Rates of intergroup marriage have been shown to be important in numerous studies. See, for instance, Bugelski, B. R. "Assimilation Through Intermarriage," Social Forces, 40 (1961): 148-153; Fitzpatrick, D. P. "Intermarriage of Puerto Ricans in New York City," American Journal of Sociology, 71 (1966): 395-406; Mittelbach, Frank G. and Joan W. Moore, "Ethnic Endogamy--the Case of Mexican Americans," American Journal of Sociology, 71 (1968): 395-406; Peach, C. "Which Triple Melting Pot?, A Re-examination of Ethnic Intermarriage in New Haven, 1900-1950," Ethnic and Racial Studies, 3 (1980): 1-16; and Wessel, B.B. An Ethnic Survey of Woonsocket, Rhode Island (Chicago: University of Chicago Press, 1931).

Additional Readings

Bahr, Howard M., Bruce Chadwick, and Joseph Strauss, American Ethnicity, Lexington, Mass.: D. C. Heath, 1979.

Blalock, Hubert W. Towards a Theory of Minority Group Relations. New York: Wiley, 1967.

Easton, David. A Framework for Political Analysis, Englewood Cliffs, N.J.: Prentice-Hall, 1965.

Fichter, Joseph, S. J. Social Relations in the Urban Parish, Chicago: University of Chicago Press, 1954.

Glazar, Nathan and Daniel Moynihan. Ethnicity, Cambridge, Mass.: Harvard University Press, 1975.

Gordon, Milton. Assimilation in American Life, New York: Oxford University Press, 1964.

Kinloch, Graham. The Dynamics of Race Relations, New York: McGraw-Hill, 1974.

Kurokawa, Minako (ed.) Minority Responses, New York: Random House, 1970.

Lieberson, Stanley. A Piece of the Pie Berkeley: University of California Press, 1980.

McLemore, S. Dale. Racial and Ethnic Relations in America, Boston: Allyn and Bacon, 1983.

Park, Robert E. Race and Culture, Glencoe, Illinois: The Free Press, 1950.

Parsons, Talcott. Societies: Comparative and Evolutionary Perspectives, Englewood Cliffs, N.J.: Prentice-Hall, 1966.

Parrillo, Vincent. Strangers to These Shores, Boston: Houghton-Mifflin, 1980.

Schermerhorn, Richard A. Comparative Ethnic Relations, New York: Random House, 1970.

VanderZanden, James W. American Minority Relations, New York: Alfred A. Knopf, 1983.

CHAPTER SEVEN: STRATEGIES OF MINORITY GROUPS

Any group which finds itself a subculture ascribed to minority status must react to that fact. Be it quickly or slowly acculturating, whether it is subject to discrimination and prejudice because of national origin, religious beliefs, race, gender, sexual preference, age or whatever, a minority simply cannot ignore the fact that the majority society is subjecting its members to discrimination. Various scholars have suggested different typologies for minority group reaction to the dominant group's treatment. Murako Kurokawa (1970), for example, lists the following minority responses: assimilation, accommodation, submission, contention, and revitalization. As she puts it:

> Again, all of these reactions are contingent on the views of the dominant group members. If the dominant group is willing to accept minority members as equals and to comply with their desires, minority orientations of assimilation and accommodation are feasible. In assimilation the minority group wants to be absorbed or merged into the dominant group, thereby losing its original identity. Accommodation occurs when the minority seeks separation and equality. Incongruence between the dominant and minority views will result in minority responses of submission, contention, or revitalization. If the dominant group ascribes inferior and segregated status to the minority members, the latter may passively accept it or fight it. In a contention response the minority members demand equality and integration within the existing social system. In contrast, a revitalization movement attempts to overthrow the existing society in order to build its own system, which will be superior to the present one (:4).

Hubert Blalock (1982) distinguishes four broad classes of alternatives open to minority groups. His four strategies are: 1) to disappear as a distinct group by "passing" as members of the majority, 2) to isolate or insulate itself from the majority, 3) to find coalition partners by pooling resources with other similar such groups in order to gain power in relation to the majority, or 4) for the minority, itself, to engage in a power struggle with the majority without

benefit of coalition partners (:105-116).   With respect
to a minority engaging in a power   struggle, Professor
Gamson   discusses what he terms "challenging" groups who
seek   acceptance.   He defines   such acceptance   as
involving a change on the part of the majority with
respect to the challenging group from hostility or
indifference to a more positive relationship.   Such
positive relationship is indicated by: 1)consultation,
2) negotiation, 3) formal recognition, and 4) inclusion
(Gamson: 31-32). His study found that groups which used
violence had a higher-than-average success rate (:79).

      Harry   Kitano   (1974)   likewise   discusses   four
minority reactions: 1) conflict, 2) acceptance, 3)
aggression, and 4) avoidance. He goes on to distinguish
forms   of   acceptance: ritualistic   behavior,
superpatriotism, and the internalization of stress. He
suggest four kinds of aggression: direct, such as
insurrection,   strikes,   boycotts,   and race rioting;
indirect, such as use of the arts, ethnic humor or
passive resistance; displaced aggression, scapegoating;
and change of goals, avoidance, withdrawal manifested as
drug or alcohol addiction, schizophrenia, or suicide
(:100-114).

      Roberta Ash, in her discussion of social movements
in America, distinguishes a series of choices that all
such movements must make: 1) between single issue
demands and multiple demands; 2) between radical demands
and ones which do not directly attack the legitimacy of
the present distribution of wealth and power; and 3)
between influencing elites (or even incorporating their
members into the elite), and attempting to replace such
elites (:230).

      Vincent Parrillo (1980) elaborates seven reactions
to discrimination: 1) avoidance, 2) deviance, 3)
defiance, 4) acceptance, 5) negative self-image, 6) the
vicious cycle, and 7) marginality (:41-51).   And Jack
Van de Slik (1980), in his discussion of black racial
conflict with white America, specifies four categories
of reactions: 1) competition, 2) cooptation, 3)
confrontation, and 4) combat (:63-283).   These various
typologies all provide useful perspectives on the
reactions of minorities to their status situation.

This chapter presents a similar typology which is our adaptation of Edgar Litt´s (1970) analysis of American ethnic politics. He describes the politics of accommodation, separatism, and radicalism (:60-109). We will herein treat each type of politics as a separate strategy. For each strategy we further distinguish two basic tactical approaches. The strategy of accommodation may be pursued primarily via an economic or a political route. The strategy of separatism may rely upon physical or psychological methods of separation from the majority culture. Finally, the strategy of radicalism may be either an old-style or a new-style of radicalism. Each of these strategies and their associated tactics will be discussed, employing the various minority groups which have been dealt with in the previous chapters to illustrate key points.

The Strategy of Accommodation

In pursuing the strategy of accommodation, the minority group must be one whose members basically accept the value system of majority society. They want "their fair share" of what majority society has to offer. They want to be accepted by the dominant group, eventually to become virtually indistinguishable from the dominant group. The question facing them is how to best approach that goal. Two basic tactics or approaches are most often employed to overcome their minority status and achieve acceptance by the majority: an economic route or a political route. Which approach is adopted by a particular group depends on several factors.

The most likely group to pursue an economic route to accommodation are those who are voluntary migrants to the area of the dominant culture. Groups who immigrate into the majority society are more likely to desire to assimilate and are therefore more likely to accept the majority society´s values. If they have some desired economic skills or arrive with sufficient means to be able to use an economic approach, this strategy is especially attractive to them.

Timing is a critically important ingredient in the choice of economic accommodation. An incoming group which arrives during a period of an expanding economy is more likely to find available points of access. During such periods, moreover, the majority´s fear of the foreign or the minority is likely to be at a reduced level.   This means that the majority is more likely to accept the minority´s first attempts at acculturating, thus reinforcing the desire of the minority to do so.

Groups whose members possess desirable job skills will not only be welcomed, they will possess a means for beginning to climb the socio-economic ladder.   If they have the ability to get to rural areas they can acquire land and be more socially acceptable in the frontier regions where their labor is a more needed commodity. Some groups have sufficient capital, or quickly acquire it, to start their own businesses and establish a special economic "niche" for themselves.   These often involve occupational areas viewed by the majority as non-competitive or non-threatening.   Such groups are sometimes labeled as "middle-man minorities."

The   Scandinavian and German immigrant groups exemplify this strategy.   They entered the United States at a time when the frontier was still open and available.   They often arrived with sufficient resources and job skills to reach the interior farmland or to gain desirable jobs in the early stages of our industrialization process.   Improved economic status led to their gradually improved social status as well. Political involvement generally followed their socio-economic acculturation.

The Greeks, Eastern-European Jews, Chinese, and Japanese also illustrate a pattern of economic accommodation.   Each used an approach based on "special niches" or "occupational queuing."   Simply put, occupational queuing involves the concept that jobs may be ranked in desirability for a given group.   Members of the majority, by definition enjoying a favorable position among employers, will tend to fill as much as they can of that society´s more desired jobs, leaving the least attractive ones for the minority population (Lieberson: 296-297).   One may proceed on down the ranking of jobs until all groups have attained their positions.   If there are more potential workers than total jobs available in that society, those minority groups at the bottom of the pecking order will experience the highest rates of unemployment or underemployment.   In short, the dominant group will tend to perpetuate its continued dominance.   Since the majority members are more likely to be employers, key co-workers, union officials, and so on, they and their offspring will be in the best position to get the most desirable jobs. Although the system is not entirely rigid, such occupational queuing obviously pertains to many occupations in our economy.

A group at the bottom of the ethnic/racial hierarchy will tend to find the least desirable positions available in rough proportion to its percentage of the total population. If that minority is rather large it will find some opportunities higher on the occupational hierarchy since the majority would not be pushing as far down. If the minority is a small percentage of the population, there will be room for them only at the very bottom because the majority will tend to compete successfully for the other jobs. This queuing effect makes the shifts in unemployment the most radical for the lowest-ranked minorities. When the economy is sluggish or in a recession, the minority groups at the bottom are pushed out of jobs as the majority members are forced to "push downward." On the other hand, when the economy is booming, a labor shortage is created. In such a case, the minority finds new job opportunities open because the majority members cannot fill all of their traditional employment opportunities. In short, the lowest-ranked minorities are "the last hired and the first fired."

The following two tables illustrate such occupational queuing. Table Thirteen specifies the percent of non-farm male labor force employed in a variety of crafts as of 1960 for five groups: native whites born of native parents (NWNP), second-generation ethnics from north-western European backgrounds, second-generation born of parents from south-central-eastern European nations, blacks, and second-generation born of Mexican parents. Table Fourteen details the relative employment of men in craft and semi-skilled occupations as of 1960 with the immigrant groups specified by national origin. The latter table compares the percent of a group employed as draftsmen, foremen, and similar positions in non-farm trades and presents the ratio of craftsmen to semi-skilled workers. A clear pattern of queuing is reflected in these two tables.

Table 13:	NON-FARM MALE LABOR FORCE EMPLOYED IN SPECIFIED CRAFTS, 1960 PERCENT EMPLOYED				
OCCUPATIONS:	NWNP:	NW-E:	S/C/E-E:	BLACK:	MEXICAN:
Carpenters	3.10%	2.98%	1.63%	1.35%	1.88%
Construction/ Machine Operators	.69	.50	.64	.36	.52
Electricians	1.78	1.89	1.24	.19	.73
Foremen *	2.35	2.88	2.12	.33	.86
Machinists	1.41	1.82	1.77	.28	.34
Mechanics/ Auto Repair	2.19	1.67	1.54	1.28	1.90
Painters/ Paperhangers/ Glaziers	1.31	1.51	.84	.85	1.09
Plumbers	.86	1.03	.73	.33	.61
Tool/Diemakers & Setters	.35	.67	.76	.02	.15

Source: Adapted from Lieberson: 345.
* Not Elsewhere Classified

Lieberson (1980) explains the concept of "special niches."

> As for special niches, it is clear that most racial and ethnic groups tend to develop concentrations in certain jobs which either reflect some distinctive cultural character- istic, special skills initially held by some members, or the opportunity structure at the time of their arrival. In 1950 among foreign- born men of different origins there were many such examples: 3.9 percent of Italians in the civilian labor force were barbers, eight times the level for all white men; 2.5 percent of the Irish were policemen or firemen, three times the rate for all white men; more than two percent of the Scottish immigrants were accountants, about two and one-half times the level for whites; 9.4 percent of Swedish immigrants were carpenters, nearly four times the national level; 14.8 percent of Greek immigrant men ran eating and drinking establishments, 29 times the national level; and 3.3 percent of Russian immigrant men were tailors or furriers, 17 times the rate for all white men (:379).

Table 14: RELATIVE EMPLOYMENT OF MEN IN CRAFT AND
SEMI-SKILLED OCCUPATIONS, 1960

Group:	Percent Non-farm Foremen & Crafts:	Ratio of Craftsmen to to Semi-skilled:
NWNP	23.0%	.97%
2nd-Generation, White NW Europe:	25.3	1.39
Denmark	27.8	1.58
England/Wales	24.0	1.32
France	24.4	1.30
Germany	27.2	1.38
Ireland	20.0	1.16
Netherlands	27.0	1.17
Norway	25.7	1.54
Scotland	23.2	1.33
Sweden	26.6	1.60
Switzerland	27.0	1.52
2nd-Generation S/C/E Europe:	20.6	.80
Austria	21.1	.85
Czechoslovakia	26.5	.88
Finland	25.4	.89
Greece	13.3	.64
Hungary	23.5	.85
Italy	21.5	.74
Lithuania	21.9	.77
Poland	22.9	.70
Romania	13.3	.89
Russia	11.9	.86
Yugoslavia	25.2	.76
Mexico	16.3	.55
Blacks	10.1	.38

Source: Adapted from Lieberson: 343.

The minority group members concentrate in certain occupations first open to them either because of a special skill or interest or because the majority society considers that job to be undesirable or a non-threatening position. These minorities develop a network of ethnic contacts and experiences which attract still more of their compatriots to those occupational opportunities.

When the in-migration of a minority rapidly accelerates, however, the ability of that group to exploit such special niches is reduced markedly. Such specialties can absorb only a relatively small portion of the group's total work force when that group is experiencing rapid growth or becoming a more substantial proportion of the total population. Not all Chinese men can open a restaurant or laundry in a city where they are a sizable fraction of the total population. Not all Jews can own their own stores or garment businesses in New York. Not all Greeks can be confectioners or restaurant propriaters in Baltimore. In cities where a given minority is a sizable one, it is more difficult for such special occupational niches to provide adequate opportunity for many of the group's members.

But for those groups who can develop such niches, especially if their migration ceases or tapers off, they can then exploit those jobs to climb the socio-economic ladder. The job stability associated with such niches enables the group members to plan ahead, to save more of their resources, and to enable their children to avail themselves of more formal education. As the children achieve more formal education, they begin to attain even higher-status jobs, and the entire group, after a generation or two, rises up the status ladder of that society.

The availability and development of such niches is an important element in making the economic-accommodation strategy more attractive to a group. The majority society views the minority as being less threatening to its favored job-status position. The minority sees that approach as being more probably successful and thus a more desirable alternative strategy for them to pursue.

For some groups, even though they desire assimilation, such economic opportunity is not sufficiently open to them to make the economic route the more attractive tactical approach. They may enter the majority society at the wrong time, when such expanding job opportunities are not there, or they may lack the needed job skills or resources. It takes capital to open one's own restaurant, retail store, garment business, or import/export firm. It takes farming skill and the capital necessary to get to where farm land is abundantly available and thus cheap in order to own one's own farm and to thrive economically and socially on that fact.

When a group desires assimilation but finds its
economic route generally blocked, the tactic of
political action becomes an attractive one for coping
with minority status. As with economic accommodation,
political accommodation is favored by a group as its
overall strategy only when certain conditions pertain.
Generally, the political path will be all the more
attractive when a group's economic route is blocked by
relatively strong occupational discrimination. "No
Irish Need Apply" signs preceded the development of the
Irish urban machine.

For the political accommodation strategy to work a
minority must have the organizational skills and
experience necessary to develop the base to deliver
cohesive bloc voting. It needs the political
organization to direct its activity towards a specific
group goal. The group must possess the vote; that is,
the majority society must allow the group a degree of
entrance into the political life of the society.

Another important ingredient is the need that the
majority segment of society be split into several
factions. One or another of such factions will then be
desirous of forming a coalition with the minority to
consistently win in its electoral struggles with the
other dominant society faction(s). If the minority can
demonstrate its capability to move in organized voting
blocs it becomes a desirable coalition partner. For
the majority faction to acquire the sustained loyalty of
the minority bloc it has to grant some rewards to the
minority, enabling them to gradually use politics as a
means to climb the socio-economic ladder.

Fuchs (1968) points out the importance of these
characteristics for ethnic politics to develop and
elaborates on the importance of politics to ethnic
groups. As he states it:

Two historical facts have made ethnicity in
American politics extremely significant. The
first is that nineteenth-century immigrant
groups--particularly the non-Protestants--were
not assimilated through friendships and
intermarriage into American society. In large
measure, they confined their primary
relationships to members of their own groups
(even through the second and third
generations) throughout all stages of the life

cycle. The second factor that has made ethnicity in politics so important is that the newer immigrants and their children found the political culture of the United States, different as it was from that in the old country, congenial to their needs. By the 1840's American politics, compared with the politics in Europe or Asia, was characterized by: 1) widespread participation, 2) a widespread diffusion of power with many points of access, 3) competition for power among interest groups (whether ethnic, economic or others), 4) ideological unity with respect to the classic European political issues (class warfare, separation of church and state, republicanism vs. monarchism), and 5) a moralistic, legalistic, and egalitarian (anti-elitist) political style (:3-4).

In order for the political tactic of accommodation to be the most attractive alternative for a minority the group must be one which has a psychological need for the rewards which political recognition can bring. If there is an economy expanding sufficiently to provide for many unskilled jobs which can be dispensed by a political elite the dominant faction can easily reward its minority coalition partners. The political strategy must rely on a political organization capable of distributing those rewards for political loyalty (an urban political machine). The three main methods of political accommodation are: 1) divisible political rewards to the few, combined with recognition of the ethnic group, 2) collective welfare benefits which use public resources to satisfy broad-scale group needs, and 3) the awarding of political preferments and secondary gains in which long-term social, economic, and political patterns of distributing benefits are based on prior attainments of ethnic groups in electoral politics. Each successive method requires increasingly greater demands on the political system (see Litt: 60-61).

The Irish provide the classic illustration of the use of this tactical approach to accommodation. The Slavic and Italian groups also emphasize this approach, although with less massive reliance upon it and with less success than their Irish predecessors.

Native politicians soon realized the value of appealing to ethnic groups to attract their votes in massive and easily manipulated blocs. They saw that individuals closely attached to a given ethnic group were most likely to vote for a co-ethnic. These native-born politicians responded by offering an ethnically-balanced slate. Including an Irish immigrant as a council member, a Jew as city auditor, a Greek as city clerk, and so on assured the party of the loyal support of these groups. Erecting a statue to Columbus in an Italian ward or naming a new high school in a Polish area after General Pulaski were easy ways to appeal to these groups for their vote. Litt refers to this as recognition politics. It is an inexpensive way for the dominant group to operate since it confers mass psychic rewards rather than mass power and involves specific offices rather than general policies. The specific ethnic politician gets a reward, the mass of co-ethnics only the appearance of inclusion in the existing political organization.

Fred Greenstein (1970) has identified five factors as the basis upon which the classic urban machine developed and operated (:44-51). First was the explosive rate of growth of the nation's cities. Prior to the flood of immigration, only one city in the nation, Philadelphia, exceeded 250,000 in population. By 1890, eleven cities attained that size, three of which were more than one million. In four decades the urban population had increased six-fold, while the rural population had only doubled. Chicago, in 1850, was under 10,000 in population. By 1900, it had reached 1,690,000! This explosive growth rate meant an increase in demand for the basic public services essential for survival. Large cities needed highly developed transportation networks to supply food and other resources. Cities needed extensive streets, lighting, bridges, and mass-transit systems. Massive sewer systems had to be installed, and tons of garbage had to be hauled away. Extensive police and fire departments had to be created and manned. Building codes and inspection programs had to be put in place. Hospitals, health services, and schools led to nearly overwhelming demands on city governments. All of those needs meant there was a substantial market for relatively unskilled labor to fill those jobs. And those jobs could be awarded by the politicians who ran the cities to those persons who loyally supported them at the polls.

A related factor was the disorganized municipal government structure. City governments were ill-prepared to face the challenges created by the explosive urban growth rate. Hundreds of offices were individually elected, sometimes annually, and had little built-in incentives to work together. Power was fragmented still more by the large and unwieldly city councils and a host of boards and commissions. The machine developed, in part, as an informal and extra-legal method to unify what was structurally so fragmented.

A third factor was the influx into the cities of millions of immigrants who formed a highly dependent population. The machine politicians soon learned the value of catering to the needs of this dependent population via their ethnic-based organizations in return for their loyal electoral support.

A fourth factor was the needs of the businessmen. Business which varied in size from the very large to very small, both legal and illegal, had needs to which the politicians could cater. Some needed governmental services, such as street maintenance or sewer or water system expansion. Some needed government permission to build or expand. Some sought relief from governmental restrictions on plant operations, safety conditions, disposal of industrial waste, and so on. For many their prime need was to operate without governmental interference. Still others had the opposite need--they did business with government itself: contractors, utility producers, mass-transit operators, and the like were all engaged in the profitable pursuit of serving the very massive process of rapid urban growth. Such businessmen often provided the machine politicians with graft in return for favored treatment. The politicians, in turn, used the graft not only to enrich themselves, but also to provide the material incentives and welfare-type services they dispensed among the needy immigrant population in exchange for the latter s loyal electoral support. These private businessmen often agreed to hire persons referred to them by the politicians. This system enabled the machine to dispense private sector jobs to many of their loyal supporters. The patronage system of public and private-sector jobs became the oil which greased the machine's smooth operation.

The final factor was relatively unrestricted suffrage. Since even the lowliest citizen was entitled to vote, the machine politicians catered to those groups who could provide bloc voting. Indeed, the party apparatus performed the valuable service to the immigrants of initiating them into citizenship and the value of participating in and using the political system. Despite the machine's raw, and at times corrupt and inefficient policy process, it did accept and welcome the immigrants and provided them with an invaluable commodity--the vote. Machine workers often met the disembarking immigrants and shepherded them into naturalization and voter-registration ceremonies. Although corrupt, the machine politicians did much to reduce the hopelessness of the immigrant's condition. In return, the immigrant responded with loyal and easily manipulated electoral support of the machine's endorsed candidates. Greenstein summarized the process as follows:

> The party organization served as brokers, or middlemen, responding to the conditions of urban life and--for a broker's commission-- meeting at least some of the needs of various groups of citizens. A key determinant of organization effectiveness was the capacity of partisanship to unite what law and tradition had separated. By confining nominations for public office to party politicians--each of them beholden to the organization, rather than to his own private constituency--parties were able to pull all the diverse threads of urban government into a reasonably unified command structure. City governments, once unified, could decide on and carry out policies design- ed to meet the problems of urban growth and, at the same time, confer benefits on business groups, both those who wanted to deal with government and those who wanted freedom from public harassment (:48).

The parties ability to deliver was based on their meeting the needs of the large mass of urban citizenry. Their votes were won by means of a 24-hours-a-day, 365 days-a-year social-service operation. The typical immigrant had little conception of the value of his vote. The politicians did, however, and were disposed to do whatever was needed to get that vote. Jobs, welfare activities, and symbolic recognition were especially important.

Patronage was crucial to the machine's development because the immigrants were desperate for steady jobs. There were no governmental programs to provide for employment or pay out unemployment insurance benefits. The machine's provision of jobs was greatly needed and appreciated. The explosively expanding cities provided many job opportunities to be filled by loyal party workers: jobs in police, fire, sanitation, street construction and maintenance. Private jobs in many businesses and industries indebted to machine politicians also became a significant part of the patronage system of the urban machine.

The machine supplied the immigrant voters with a host of welfare services. Tammany Hall Boss George Washington Plunkitt, commonly known as the philosopher-king of the old-style urban machine politics frankly described that aspect of machine politics as follows.

> What holds your grip on your district is to go right among the poor families and help them in different ways they need help. I've got a regular system for this. If there's a fire in Ninth, Tenth, or Eleventh Avenue, for example, any hour of the day or night, I'm usually there with some of my district captains as soon as the fire engines. If the family is burned out I don't ask whether they are Republicans or Democrats, and I don't refer them to the Charity Organization Society, which would investigate their case about a month or two and decide they were worthy of help about the time they are dead from starvation. I just get them quarters, buy clothes for them if their clothes were burned up, and fix them up til they get things runnin' again. It's philanthropy, but its politics too--mighty good politics. Who can tell how many votes one of these fires brings me? The poor are the most grateful people in the world, and let me tell you, they have more friends in their neighbor-hoods than the rich have in theirs (cited in Greenstein: 49).

The boss or party official helped immigrants with all aspects of their dealings with government. He personified government for the newcomer who desperately needed that service. The party was their friend and intermediary in dealing with the courts, police, and the local bureaucracy--indeed, the broader society. The machine gave them much needed psychological support simply by recognizing the group and the value of its subculture. The politicians appealed to their sense of group loyalty and bound that loyalty to the party apparatus. Whether it was running an entire slate of officials representing a wide variety of ethnic groups found in that city, or erecting a statue or naming a school, park, or other public building after some ethnic hero, or simply attending such group gatherings as weddings, funerals, dances or similar social gatherings, the machine politicians appealed to the group's members because such actions were signs to them that the machine cared and was concerned about the group. It made minority group members feel valued. And the immigrants responded with loyal bloc voting.

After a generation or so, such recognition politics were no longer sufficient. The ethnic group members began pressing for more. They sought and could extract from the machine and the political system a number of collective welfare benefits. The tendency to try to "get more benefits" over time Litt refers to as the "rule of expansion" (:67). It was applied to politicians sensitive to increased ethnic demands. The old machine strategy involved the ward boss acting as a political broker seeking to hold together a diverse and often uneasy coalition of many ethnic groups, some of whom had been bitter opponents of one another in the old country or who carried ethnic enmities from Europe with them when they migrated here. After a while this changed. Groups had sufficient clout within the party to seek group-wide benefits instead of divisible rewards dished out to the loyal few, or psychological rewards instead of real material incentives. Instead of a few individuals going to the ward boss for help in finding housing, the group demanded public housing projects distributed broadly to all group member--whether or not those individuals in the housing projects were politically active. The groups demanded a change from getting specific rewards for specific elections to altering the allocation of public benefits by governmental bureaucracies and their political allies.

The final phase of successfully employed political accommodation is what Litt labels preferment politics. In this stage the minority group has achieved sufficient access and power within the political machinery that the group is able to influence the fundamentals of the

287

system which in large measure determines the allocation of political claims made within its framework. A group like the Irish-Americans can not only succeed in getting a few divisible rewards allocated to them (for example, getting the native politicians help in finding a job or housing), such a group can even go beyond demanding a collective-welfare benefit such as a public housing program. In this final stage, the group, by capturing the political party machinery, can actually take over the bureaucracy and determine the rules by which it will distribute a general welfare service such as public housing. Such power to influence public policy is not likely to be shared without a struggle.

> This sticky phase of ethnic political claims may be handled by party leaders in several ways. A major factor in stable accommodation is the extent to which heretofore dominant groups have secured preferments outside of their political positions. If the dominant group is secure enough to yield the social and economic benefits of party preferments to assertive ethnic claimants, accommodation is facilitated; the most difficult problems are likely to arise when relative newcomers must displace others who have not yet to securely reap the social and economic benefits of political preferments (Litt:72).

The Irish-Americans used their ability to capture many urban machines to get ahead. They nudged aside the native politicians whom they no longer needed. Once gaining control, they used that controlling position to achieve broader social and economic status. An Irish immigrant eventually became Mayor of Boston. The son of an Irish immigrant went on to become Governor of Massachusetts. The Ivy League schools and prestigious business enterprises, and soon even the more elitist social clubs, accepted the Governor s son. And even, in the case of John F. Kennedy, the grandson of an immigrant went on to become President of the United States. The Boston Brahman--having a wide variety of social and economic opportunity open to them--were more willing to step aside when the uprising Irish politicians applied pressure to move up the ladder.

These same Irish politicians, however, were less likely to step aside for the aspiring Italian politicians who followed. The Irish-Americans were simply too new, too psychologically insecure in their place on the ladder, to easily move aside for the next group pushing up. More often than not, they forced the later arriving ethnic politicians, such as the Italian Volpe, to seek access to upward social mobility by means of the Republican Party (see, for example, Levy and Kramer: 159-190: Dahl: 216-217).

The Strategy of Separatism

Sometimes the minority group rejects the value system of the majority society. In such a case, the minority seeks to be left alone rather than to assimilate into the majority. It does not seek to impose its values on the majority, but it likewise wants the majority to respect its differing values and allow it to hold such values, norms, and customs without suffering discrimination because of those values. Often such groups are ones which have come into sustained contact with the majority culture in some largely involuntary manner. Forced migration--the importing of slaves, for instance--can bring two such cultures together. In such a case, the minority culture rejects its status and position in the new society. Often internally developed subcultures--such as a new religious minority--come to reject the value system of the majority. The Mormons provide a classic example of this type. Sometimes the minority culture finds itself in such status due to boundary absorption--as in the case of Hispanic Americans and the various Indian tribes.

When a subculture, for whatever reason, wants to pursue a strategy of separatism, it may attempt to do so in one of two ways: 1) physical separation or isolation, or 2) the psychological separation of its members from the norms, customs and values of the rejected majority society.

The choice of the physical separation route, obviously, is dependent upon the group's being able to physically isolate itself from the majority. This may be done by seeking out frontier or rural areas with low enough density of settlement that the minority group members can largely fill in the area as the numerically superior group. The Amish and Mennonite groups, clustering in rural enclaves, provide such an example. They thereby reduce their contact with members of the majority culture to a bare minimum. The rejection of the majority society media reinforces the isolating effects of their rural settlement patterns. The initial fleeing of the Mormons to ever-more isolated frontier regions in response to majority society persecution is another classic example of this route, as is Marcus Garvey's "Back to Africa" Movement, representing a small scale attempt of this approach by a faction of the Black minority.

A critical ingredient in the successful use of such physical separatism is that the group maintains an economic system capable of supporting its members in such isolation. Generally it is the necessary economic interaction with the majority society that hastens the decline of the group attempting such separatism, by sometimes bringing subtle changes in their values which gradually introduces a degree of acculturation.

Sometimes the physical separatism is not really a matter of choice—it is to varying degrees forced upon the group by their being rejected by the majority in a manner which somewhat physically isolates them. The Chicanos in the Southwest are often forced, through informal economic or social pressure, to remain isolated in rural areas as migrants or in the urban ghettos called "barriers." While the Chicano often rejects the "Gringo" culture and voluntarily lives with other Chicanos, the slum-like conditions of the ghetto areas are forced upon them. Chinatowns are a similar case of combined forced/choice separatism. The Mormons fled to Utah in large measure because the majority society violently expelled them for their polygamy. The military forced the American Indian tribal survivors of an earlier policy of annihilation on to ever-decreasing areas of "reservation." The use of physical separatism is typically restricted to minority groups which are small in size, making the isolation a more realistic tactic.

The use of psychological separatism is usually an option of a millenial movement whose strong ideology provides a means by which a sort of psychological shell can be developed around the individual, thus isolating him or her from the influence of the majority society even though the minority member may be living in the midst of that broader culture. An excellent example of this approach is afforded by the Black Muslim movement (see Litt: 75-91).

As in all separatist politics, the Black Muslims exhibit distinct organizational and cultural norms specifically designed to compensate for the effects of discrimination by the dominant society. The group withdraws from the ongoing polity. Black Muslims are given a myth which accounts for their past in a way which overcomes the psychological damages of racial discrimination, and which provides a glorious image of the future.

Whether the prophet by Troitschke, Doestoevsky, Hitler, Moses, Mazzini, Mussolini, or Elijah Muhammad, the myth of the past and the illusion of the future remain a remarkably consistent, nationalistic, mass movement formula. To convince an alienated people of their worth and unity, one must remind them of their sacred origin. To explain the disheartening realities of their present plight, one must convince them of their natural superiority and ferret out corruptors and devils. To gird them for the trials ahead, one must reveal a glorious destiny ordained since the beginnings of time. Past, present, and future must intermingle in one expression of Divine Intent (Litt: 78).

The rehabilitative effects of the movement on many members of the sect have been remarkable. From the nation's prisons and slums, the Muslims have recruited drug addicts and pushers, prostitutes and pimps, alcoholics, criminals and the despairing ghetto residents alienated from society. These men and women have been transformed by the Muslims into employees of value in honest jobs, who conscientiously marry and raise a family. They obey the laws, save money, and tithe to their faith. They no longer drink, use drugs or tobacco, gamble, engage in sexual promiscuity, dance, take long vacations, steal, lie, nor exhibit idleness or laziness. Their women are models of domesticity: thrifty, keeping fastidiously clean homes, devoted to their mates and children. Instead of buying expensive clothes or cars, they pool their resources to help each other. Muslim families, even in the midst of the nation's worst slums, exhibit a healthy living standard. "The movement has, in its own strange way, repaired some ´irreparable´ damages and saved some of the damned (Litt: 79)."

The movement achieves this success by demanding total commitment to Islam. In return, it provides its converts with an elaborate organization with a variety of institutional supports which radically change the member's life-style. The members are totally immersed in the new Muslim culture. The movement provides the temple, a well-disciplined elitist security force, a daily publication filled with inspirational messages and Muslim ideology. Women's auxiliaries teach homemaking skills, child care, and the woman's "proper role." Children attend Muslim grade schools and summer camps. Teenagers are provided with Muslim community centers. The movement provides employment training, and it runs a variety of retail and service businesses. They have even created their own University of Islam. The Muslims strengthen the search for collective identity by symbols which furnish deified objects for mass loyalty and expressions of aspirations. All such nationalistic movements have flags or gods around which the faithful may rally. For the Black Muslims there are Allah, the star and crescent, their version of the Koran, and the Islamic tongue (Litt: 80).

Perhaps even more important for understanding the separatist success in building a psychological shell around its members are the various symbols and norms utilized for the benefit of individual members. Black Muslim men reject their "slave" names and accept a Muslim name or the letter "X". They dress in dark conservative suits, white shirts, and ties. Their women wear a nun-like garb--full headress and habit covering arms and legs. These changes in clothing style serve several identification functions. They reject the stereotypical "flamboyant" appearance of the lower-class black. The sober neatness expresses strength and a new sense of dignity. The nun-like garb of the women again rejects the "flashy and wild colors" which is the stereotypical image of the black female. Their new dress stresses the protected, sequestered and obedient role she plays in the Muslim life and family. The uniformity of both men and women, as in the military, both heightens a sense of group cohesion and affords a readily detectable commonality that sets them aside from non-Muslims. Brothers and sisters are differentiated from all others.

Racial pride is stressed. Black features are upheld as the highest human representation of Allah. "Black is beautiful" becomes the prevailing esthetic. Self-composure and control are maintained at all times. Loud and boisterous behavior is forbidden. Displays of emotion are discouraged. A Muslim is told to listen to music quietly, without swaying or crooning--again rejecting the stereotypical behavior of blacks.

There are numerous prescribed foods. A Muslim is forbidden to eat pork, sea food, or scavenger creatures. "Soul food" is held to be reminiscent of the slave past, and so corn bread, black-eyed peas, collard greens, 'possum, and the like are also prohibited. These dietary norms bolster the new identity while helping to eradicate the old. The result is a new sense of the black man's self-worth. Muslims are taught that feeling inferior results in acting inferior--accepting the white man's view of the black. Rejecting the stereotypes is their way of liberating the individual from the "slave mentality." As Muhammad teaches, "Love yourself and you will not need the white man's love (Ibid: 83)."

In short, the movement is distinguished from most other civil rights groups by its stress on the changes in individuals. It holds that the major responsibility for the betterment of the individual rests with the black man, not with white society.

But Black Muslims also show a typical softening of their separatism over time, as they changed from a revolutionary to an institutional force. It followed a path typical of millenial movements which are too weak to achieve their dreams of paradise, but too strong and too structured to simply wither away. By attaining structural stability and longevity, the movement began the process of transformation from separatism to accommodationism. The very success of the movement in turning its members into "haves" rather than "have-nots," and the organizational structures which tend over time to undercut the charismatic leadership of the movement, work to take the edge off the movement's separatist fervor. Instead of becoming a more revolutionary sect, it is becoming a more "conservative" black self-improvement group, more interested in material advances than in sacrificing the life of the movement for the sake of a black supremacist doctrine. As it increasingly developed its organizational structures--the temples, schools, farms, stores, clothing business--the needs of these structures modified the charismatic and separatist aspects of the sect towards a more accommodationist approach.

The very success of the Muslims in transforming its members from "have-nots" to "haves" undercut their separatist fervor. Litt cites Eric Hoffer's succinct observation that, "We are less ready to die for what we have or are than for what we wish to have and to be. It is a perplexing and unpleasant truth that when men already have something worth fighting for they do not feel like fighting (:85)."

The Black Muslims are showing increasing signs of accommodation since the 1970's. Instead of viciously attacking other black civil rights groups which advocate an integrationist approach, as it had done in the early years of the movement and on up to the mid-1960's, the Muslim press now gives such groups fair coverage. It also decreased emphasis on separatism in its publications. Accounts of integrationist battles are now often treated sympathetically and positively. The movement has even aligned itself with avowedly integrationist groups advocating a full-scale attempt to elect black officials. It has backed black candidates for mayor, and figured prominently in the Reverend Jesse Jackson's campaign for the Democratic Party's Presidential nomination in 1984. Finally, the movement has modified its stance regarding the "white devil." Increasingly, stress is made on "black pride" rather than on "white hatred."

The Politics of Radicalism

A third and final strategy for minorities to employ involves rejecting the value system of the majority society and seeking to replace those values with their own. This radical strategy also exhibits two major tactical approaches: "old-style" and "new-style" radicalism.

In "old-style radicalism" the ideology is very different from the prevailing one of majority society at the time, but the behavior of the minority remains rather standard. Groups following this route attempt to use standard electoral politics to win over the majority to its new ideological value-system. It is the politics of third-party movements.

The American Communist Party, in its attempt to win support among blacks in the 1930's and 1940's, exemplifies this approach. While never very successful in winning electoral support, even among alienated blacks, it did have some indirect impact. Likewise, the American Socialist Party sought to win over a large immigrant following. In a few places with large German-American populations, such as in Milwaukee, Wisconsin, they were able to achieve a short-term local electoral success. The Socialist's influence was strongest in its indirect impact on the trade union movement, especially where Jewish influence in the union was pronounced. The American Alliance of Polish Socialists likewise tried to appeal to the Polish immigrants, although never as successfully as the more accommodationist Polish National Alliance. Those interested in American Socialism joined the Polish section of the American Socialist Party.

A small faction of Italian-Americans flirted briefly with radical politics. A few were attracted to the Communist Party, and another small but slightly larger faction supported the American Fascist Party. Neither group ever achieved much electoral success.

Perhaps the most important reason why none of these third-party ideological movements took hold among the nation's immigrant and minority groups is the difficult nature of the task facing the radical leaders. The radical ideologue had to convince the ethnic masses that attachments based on abstract political principles were more important in the long-run than the short-term satisfactions obtained through membership in ethnic fraternal and social associations. The ideologue's success depended upon a degree of political awareness and sophistication by these ethnic minorities which in reality exhibited low to moderate political interest. The old-style radical leader had to forge a common bond between "blood and believer." They also had to promote the ideological premises themselves (see Litt: 98).

As a result of these obstacles and difficulties, radical ideological politics never really caught on among ethnic groups. The religious beliefs and organizations of many such groups provided them with the emotional and structural support needed to cope with their strange new environment. Their desire for social acceptance was too strong for many to be attracted to the radical political parties. Accommodation-style politics won them sufficient material rewards to undercut the ideological appeal. Ethnic groups simply preferred the immediate gratification and the emotional and psychological ties to their own group rather then the long-range and doubtful rewards of an alien ideology.

The major parties, too, undercut the electoral appeal of the more radical third-party movements whenever such splinter groups seemed to be gaining electoral strength. The major parties would adapt a few aspects of the radical party's platform and bring a few of their more popular ideas into conformity with majority society goals. Thus, the greatest success of this radical ideological tactic was to focus the attention of the majority society on some problems, ideas, or concerns which they stressed. Their greatest impact was indirect, by inducing the major parties to adopt some modified forms of their more radical planks.

Increasingly, today's minorities are following a version of a "new-style radical politics." perhaps best exemplified by the militant black civil rights movement of the late 1950's and the 1960's. Under this approach, the minority espouses somewhat less radical ideological points, but is willing to employ radical behavior, at least what is considered to be radical behavior at the time.

Three converging elements precede new-style radicalism. The first element is a widespread feeling of anomie among a minority group's membership. Because of this personal anomie, such deprived persons, who are united only by a common location and color (i.e. residence in an urban ghetto), are more likely to view normal accommodation politics as ineffective and meaningless.

The second element is the group's weak social base. The anomie becomes political potent when it is built into enduring social relations. When such individual's frustrations are no longer screened nor adequately controlled by social mechanisms, personal anomie is more likely to produce the politics of passion--an expression of rage such as the outbreak of a riot. History shows that isolated social groups are the most susceptible to mass movements and extremely volatile political behavior. Some isolated farm workers developed radical populism. Some isolated factory workers participated in the more violent aspects of the labor movement (e.g. the Molly Mcquires). Some isolated ethnic groups have developed the politics of radical passion.

The third element leading to new-style radicalism is the broad and direct intervention of federal institutions in the core urban areas. The nationalization of ethnic politics led to tactics encouraging passionate political activity. When the ethnic group develops political leadership with mass media skills, each contributing to the effectiveness of the other, than the rise of a national pressure group is possible. The charismatic leadership of a Dr. Martin Luther King, Jr. establishes the style of minority revolt in the federal era. Nationally recognized leaders, no matter how apparently splintered, can develop unified action reaching the federal government. The media play the role in the politics of group passion of publicizing the existence of a "crisis" which triggers federal responses.

The type of radical behavior may range along the full spectrum of volatile behavior from non-violent, direct-action protest on up to full-scale and violent revolution. Figure Six presents such a continuum with some typical types of radical behavior points identified along the continuum.

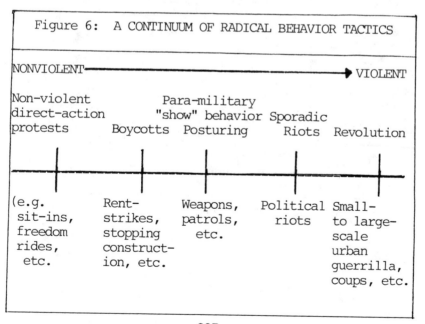

Figure 6: A CONTINUUM OF RADICAL BEHAVIOR TACTICS

NONVIOLENT ──────────────────────────────► VIOLENT

Non-violent direct-action protests		Para-military "show" behavior		
	Boycotts	Posturing	Sporadic	
			Riots	Revolution
(e.g. sit-ins, freedom rides, etc.	Rent-strikes, stopping construct-ion, etc.	Weapons, patrols, etc.	Political riots	Small- to large-scale urban guerrilla, coups, etc.

authoritative decision-makers of society, who would otherwise by unavailable and/or unresponsive to the protestors demands.

Perhaps exemplifying the model will clarify why the tactic sometimes works. A minority group selects some unconventional protest behavior to attract the attention of the media: a lunch-counter sit-in, a "freedom-ride," a "wade-in" of a segregated public pool, a "fish-in" by a local Indian tribe. The Montgomery, Alabama bus boycott was among the first and will serve as a good illustration of the workings of the model.

Figure 7: SCHEMATIC REPRESENTATION OF THE PROCESS OF PROTEST BY RELATIVELY POWERLESS GROUPS

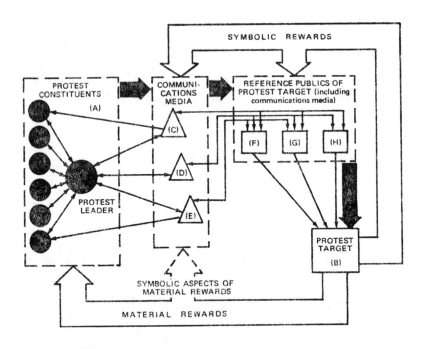

Source: Adapted from Michael Lipsky (1968): 1145.

Michael Lipsky (1968) has developed a useful conceptual framework to explain why peaceful protest is capable of effecting political change--why it can serve as a type of political resource (:1144-1158). As he describes it:

Protest activity is defined as a mode of political action oriented toward objection to one or more policies and conditions, characterized by showmanship or display of an unconventional nature, and undertaken to obtain rewards from political or economic systems while working within the systems. The "problems of the powerless" in protest activity is to activate "third parties" to enter the implicit or explicit bargaining arena in ways favorable to the protestors. This is one of the few ways in which they can "create" bargaining resources. It is intuitively unconvincing to suggest that fifteen people sitting uninvited in the Mayor´s office have the power to move City Hall. A better formulation would suggest that the people sitting in may be able to appeal to a wider public to which the city administration is sensitive. Thus in successful protest activity the <u>reference publics</u> of protest <u>targets</u> may be conceived as explicitly or implicitly reacting to protests in such a way that target groups or individuals respond in ways favorable to the protestors(:1145).

Figure Seven shows Lipsky´s schematic model of how and why such groups can sometimes successfully use protest as a political resource. Such relatively powerless groups--the ethnic have-nots, for example-- lack the traditional power resources of our society: money, prestige, inside access, and knowledge of the political process. The protest situation works like a "credit card" enabling the protestors to "borrow" or use the power and influence of other groups (the reference publics) in the majority society; that is, to play one faction of the majority elite off against the other. The media coverage of their protest activates a portion of the majority by arousing the emotions of fear or of sympathy. The protest group is able to reach and "cash in" on the power resources of the reference public(s) by getting them to apply pressure on the target group--the

Blacks in Montgomery in the mid-1950's were subjected to discrimination in many forms, including a local ordinance segregating the city's public bus system. The city council (the target group) would be the authoritative decision-making body which had the power to change the local segregation law. Blacks lacked access to the city council. They had no voting capacity in the early 1950's. They had no money. They were subject of bigotry, thus lacking prestige, inside connections, or similar power resources. But blacks comprised about 75 percent of the bus company's ridership. By boycotting the bus system, they attracted local and even national media attention: television, radio, newspapers, and national magazines covered the boycott. It was news precisely because it was so unconventional for the time.

Such coverage, and the economic threat implicit in the boycott, aroused fear among several of the city's economic elites (the reference publics). The local bus company executives began to feel the threat to their profits (it hit them in their pocket books where it hurt the most). After a year of losses, they finally responded by putting pressure on the city council to change the law. Downtown businessmen--retail store store owners, theater and restaurant owners, and such-- also began to feel the economic pinch. They were hurt with a drop off in their business caused either directly or indirectly by the boycott and resulting social upheaval and tension. An economic elite trying to attract national business investment to Montgomery was aroused by the fear that all the national publicity about "bad relations with their colored folk" would have a detrimental impact on their efforts to attract new investment to the area. These elites could and did put pressure on the city council to change the law in order to end the boycott. The boycott not only resulted in a positive--the segregation laws were rescinded--but it marked the emergency of Dr. Martin Luther King, Jr. as a national black civil rights leader.

Professor Lipsky discusses some of the typical responses of the target group to a protest situation. He distinguishes six common responses. The target group may offer symbolic satisfaction. In response to a protest over police brutality, for instance, a local police department may hire a single minority member. At that officer's graduation from the police academy the press will be invited, and the department will publically emphasize its hiring of that minority person--symbolically signifying it will end brutality. Such symbolic rewards are easy to give up since they cost the target group virtually nothing. They are really aimed more at the media and the reference public(s) than at the protest group members. If either or both of the former react favorably to the symbolic rewards, than it relieves the target group from the pressure to which it had been subjected by the protest situation. A second common response is to try to "buy-off" the protestors with some token material rewards. The target group dips into some slack resources of its organization. It is a response far "cheaper" than seriously reallocating its benefits in the direction of the protestors goals. Imagine a group of welfare mothers on AFDC protesting the lack of allotments to buy winter clothing in a cold northern city such as New York. The welfare office cannot increase the amounts given to every family on welfare. But it can buy clothing for the children of the few actively protesting mothers. This may end the demonstrations and thus stop the media coverage and/or any resulting pressure on the agency.

A third typical response may be that the target group reorganizes itself to allow it to respond more innovatively in its internal operations in order to blunt the impetus of the protest efforts. By reorganizing to act quickly in the worst cases, the target group can often pre-empt protest efforts by responding to the cases which best dramatize the protestors' demands. The agency may designate all efforts which jeopardize its reputation as "worst" cases and devote special efforts in the most heavily dramatized cases. Such special efforts may wear down the "cutting edge" of the protestors actions.

Many large city agencies have developed informal "crisis" management arrangements which project the publicity that the agency desires and mobilizes their resources for solving "crisis" cases. They may also develop policy innovations allowing them to respond more quickly to a protest situation.

A fourth reaction may be the target group's appearing constrained in their ability to grant the protest goals. They may extend their sympathies but claim they lack the resources and/or authority to respond to the protestor's demands. If successful in this tactical response, the target group takes the heat off itself by diverting the protest group´s attention to some other--usually higher--level of government agency or official. This response is often effective with established civic welfare agencies since they are known often to be financially underfunded or restrained in their policy-making powers by state or federal level agencies and directives. Target groups, therefore, will often attempt to diminish the impact of protest by claiming relative impotence.

A fifth response discussed by Lipsky is that of the target group using their extensive resources to discredit the protest group leader and/or the group itself. The F.B.I.´s attempts to bug Dr. King´s motel rooms in order to blackmail him about his sex life or publish such information to discredit him as a man-of-the-cloth is a classic example of this response. The civil rights movement and many of its leaders were often portrayed as "communists" or "communist dupes." Protestors who were usually local blacks were often shrugged off as responding to the efforts of "outside agitators." The Black Panthers were effectively discredited as violent radicals advocating revolution. Even where there is no validity to such claims, such a response may be effective if it results in the media deciding either to cease its coverage or to change the tone of that coverage in a manner which vindicates the reference public since such a reaction would vitiate any pressures on the target group. The reference publics no longer react to the protest situation--or respond with demands to repress the protest group rather than to grant them their goals or some concessions towards those goals.

The sixth rather classic response to protest is to postpone action. A "blue-ribbon" study commission is appointed to study the situation. Months later their report is issued to gather dust on some shelf. Often the protest situation is time-bound in its effectiveness. If the target group can postpone action, real pressure is removed. Welfare mothers protesting the need for more winter clothes allotments cannot be effectively done in the summer. Protest against inadequate numbers of minority workers on public construction projects cannot effectively be carried out once the job is three-fourths completed. The American Indian Movement´s seizure of Wounded Knee was symbolically effective because it was bound to an anniversary of the massacre. Postponing policy commitments is often an effective way out for the target group since it removes pressure for any real change in the way it allocates its resources.

Any or several of these responses may be used by the target group, sometimes at the same time. They should not be understood as serial responses; that is, try one option first, if that fails move on to the next, and so on. A target group may respond initially with response six, and if that fails, try two or three and so on.

A seventh logical response, although not elaborated upon by Professor Lipsky, is for the target group to grant some or all of the protest group's goals. Often the protest leader purposely includes in a list of goals a few which he/she feels will be relatively easy for the the target group to grant in order to induce a quick favorable response. Such "success" at winning even a few slices of the loaf they are seeking can often then be used by the protest leader to attract new followers, to strengthen the group's cohesion, encourage them to further protest action, help induce the reference publics to keep up the pressure, and thereby increase the pressure on the target group to grant still more of the protest group's goals. The civil rights movement's actions were more successful against "de jure" segregation embodied in Jim Crowism than it has been employed against "de facto" segregation.

The successful use of this approach by blacks has inspired other groups to imitate their tactics. "Black Power" inspired "Red," "Brown," "Grey," and "Gay" Power movements, all of which employed variations of the direct-action protest tactics.

Perhaps one of the best, and certainly among the most eloquent, philosophical justifications of the use of new-style radicalism and the specific employment of the tactics of peaceful direct-action protest is the "Letter from a Birmingham Jail" statement of April, 1963 by the Reverend Dr. Martin Luther King, Jr. in response to a letter sent to him by a number of white southern clergy criticizing him as a minister for advocating such civil disobedience. Dr. King specifies that in any nonviolent campaign there are four basic steps: 1) collection of the facts to determine whether injustices injustices are alive; 2) negotiations; 3) self purification; and 4) direct-action. Nonviolent direct action tries to create such a crisis that a community that has consistently refused to negotiate is forced to do so. Dr. King emphasizes that freedom is never voluntarily given by the oppressor; it must be demanded by the oppressed. He justifies the use of peaceful civil disobedience, the purposive breaking of a law, by distinguishing two types of laws: just and unjust laws. he writes that one has not only a moral responsibility to obey just laws, one also has a moral responsibility to disobey unjust laws. He defines a just law as a man-made code that squares with the moral law or law of God, whereas, an unjust law is a code that is out of harmony with the moral law. He argues that all segregation statutes are unjust since segregation distorts the soul and damages the personality. It gives the segregator a false sense of superiority and the segregated a false sense of inferiority. An unjust law binds a minority but does not bind the majority. It is difference made legal. On the other hand, a just law compels both the majority and a minority to follow it. It is sameness made legal. Dr. King goes on to note that when the black civil rights activists broke an unjust law, they did so openly, lovingly and with a willingness to accept the penalty. He responds to the assertion that the movement´s actions, though peaceful, must be condemned for precipitating violence by likening it to condemning the robbed man because his possession of money precipitated the evil act of robbery. He concludes his eloquent defense of the tactics by stating:

> One day the South will recognize its real heroes. They will be the James Merediths, courageously and with a majestic sense of purpose, facing the jeering and hostile mobs and the agonizing loneliness that characterizes the life of a pioneer. They will be old, oppressed, battered Negro women, symbolized in a 72 year-old woman of Montgomery, Alabama, who rose up with a sense of dignity and with her people decided not to ride the segregated buses, and responded to one who inquired about her tiredness with ungrammatical profundity: "My feets is tired, but my soul is rested." They will be young high school and college students, young ministers of the gospel and a host of the elders, courageously and nonviolently sitting in at lunch counters and willingly going to

jail for conscience sake. One day the South will know that when these disinherited children of God sat down at lunch counters they were in reality standing up for the best in the American dream and the most sacred values of our Judeo-Christian heritage, and thus carrying our whole nation back to the great wells of democracy which were dug deep by the founding fathers in the formulation of the Constitution and the Declaration of Independence (in Dye and Hawkins, 1967: 109).

When such peaceful protest tactics fail to work, however, groups pursuing the new-style radical politics will be attracted to or driven to increasingly more violent radical behavior. Indeed, the need to continue to attract the mass media imposes a pressure or trend towards increasingly radical rhetoric, if not violent behavior. The first few freedom rides and sit-ins were new, unconventional, and thus newsworthy. After a short while, however, such direct-actions become "old-hat." The protest leaders were compelled to use more violent rhetoric, if not behavior, to "keep the cameras rolling." And the use of expressions like "burn, baby, burn" inspires violent reactions among the majority, which in turn instills violent reactions by the minority. The approach almost entails as inevitable trend towards more violent tactics.

The sporadic riots of the late 1960´s are logical extensions of this approach. The targeted political rioting which rocked some 150 American cities in the summers of 1967-1968 was the emotional outburst predicted by the late Dr. Martin Luther King, Jr. The use of sniping, occasional bank heists or kidnapping, such as the actions of the SLA, represent the more violent tactics available to groups who follow this route of new-style radicalism. Such tactics are used by groups when the less violent methods either fail to generate sufficient pressure on the target groups, or bring about results that the violent leadership considers too little too late. Sometimes the two approaches work together. The more radical rhetoric of the Black Panthers causes representatives of the city government to sit down at the bargaining table with a lawyer from the NAACP.

This trend towards increasingly radical behavior is neither inevitable nor non-reversible. The winning of specific goals through unconventional and non-violent protest can bring about sufficient changes in the rules-of-the-game under which standard political behavior is played so that a group which previously rejected accommodation politics as useless might thereafter adopt that approach. After the black civil rights movement, through such direct action protest, won sufficient changes in the South's Jim Crow laws to enable blacks to develop a substantial voting force in southern politics, the movement was able to follow more standard electoral politics in the mid-1970's and win a considerable number of elective offices and appointive positions via the polling booth instead of the streets.

A given minority may pursue any one of these three approaches. It may employ one approach at one time, and another at some other time. Some of the larger minorities may fragment into several factions, each of which is pursuing a different strategy at the same time. Blacks in the 1960's, for example, showed all three approaches were possible. The Urban League followed an accommodationist approach. The Black Muslims were advocating a separatist strategy. And Dr. King and his SCLC preached the new-style direct-action approach. His success inspired others: CORE, SNCC, and even the NAACP began adopting these tactics. The Black Panthers and more radical groups such as the SLA urged or actually practiced still more violent tactics within the new-style radical approach. By the mid-1970's, however, the black civil rights movement changed to a predominantly accommodationist approach. Table Fifteen summarizes these strategies and their tactical approaches citing examples of the various minorities previously discussed who have exhibited one or more of these approaches.

Table 15: STRATEGIES AND TACTICS OF MINORITIES' RESPONSES TO DISCRIMINATION		
STRATEGY:	TACTICS/GROUPS EMPLOYING:	
ACCOM-MODATION	ECONOMIC APPROACH: -Occupational queuing and special niches. Used by Scots, Welsh, Scandinavians, Germans, Dutch, French, Jews, Japanese, Chinese, Greeks, Slavs, Blacks (1800's, e.g. Booker T. Washington, 1980's-- Rev. Jesse Jackson)	POLITICAL APPROACH: -Machine Politics coalitions. Used by Irish, Italians, Jews, Greeks, Slavs, Women (e.g. NOW)
SEPAR-ATISM	PHYSICAL -Chinese (Chinatowns) Mormons (1800's) Amish and Mennonites Blacks (Marcus Garvey's "Back to Africa Movement" Chicanos (barrios) Native-Americans (Reservations)	PSYCHOLOGICAL -Black Muslims Mormons Jehovah's Witnesses Seventh Day Adventists Zionism
RADICAL-ISM	IDEOLOGICAL -"Old-Style Ideological Socialism--Jews, Poles Communism--German Radicals Russians, Slavs, Blacks Radical Agrarianism Utopian Movements Fascism--Italians	BEHAVIORAL -New-Style Direct-Action SCLC, SNCC, CORE, Dr. King, Jr. Chicanos-- Cesear Chavez Indians--AIM Elderly-Grey Panthers, Violent Protest riots, SLA, Black Panthers, etc.

Additional Readings

Blalock, Hubert M. Jr. Race and Ethnic Relations. Englewood Cliffs, N.J.: Prentice-Hall, 1982.

_____. Towards a Theory of Minority Group Relations. New York: Capricorn Books, 1976.

Dye, Thomas R. and Brett Hawkins (eds.). Politics in the Metropolis. Columbus, Ohio: Charles E. Merrill, 1967: 100-109, "Letter from a Birmingham Jail," by Dr. Martin Luther King, Jr.

Fuchs, Lawrence H. (ed.) American Ethnic Politics. New York: Harper, 1968.

Greenstein, Fred I. The American Party System and the American People. Englewood Cliffs, N.J.: Prentice-Hall, 1970.

Kitano, Harry. Race Relations. Englewood Cliffs, N.J.: Prentice-Hall, 1974.

Kurokawa, Minako (ed.) Minority Responses. New York: Random, 1970.

Lieberson, Stanley. A Piece of the Pie. Berkeley: University of California Press, 1980.

Lipsky, Michael. "Protest as a Political Resource," American Political Science Review, 62, 4 (December, 1968): 1144-1158.

Litt, Edgar. Ethnic Politics in America. Glenview, Ill.: Scott, Foresman, 1970.

Parrillo, Vincent. Strangers to These Shores. Boston: Houghton Mifflin, 1980.

Van Der Slik, Jack. Black Conflict With White America. Columbus, Ohio: Charles E. Merrill, 1970.

CHAPTER EIGHT: OTHER BASES OF MINORITY STATUS

The strategies reviewed in Chapter Seven have been employed by other minorities as well. The protest politics model of the black civil rights movement has been especially copied by the more activist minorities emerging into greater prominence during the 1970's and 1980's. This chapter will briefly review a number of other bases for minority status: 1) gender, 2) age, 3) sexual preference, and 4) the "newest" immigrant groups of the post-World War II and Korean War era.

Gender

At just over 51 percent of the total U.S. population, women comprise the nation's largest minority. Their minority status is reflected by a number of indicators of such status: occupational segregation, income gaps, lower political participation until very recently, (see Wassenberg, et al: 181), and various legal limitations. A number of such issues about which women feel there is discrimination against them based upon gender were recently identified by the Commission on the Status of Women [CSW]: employment, lack of child care facilities, rape, battered women, education and training, passage of the equal rights amendment, issuing of credit, legal rights of women especially regarding marriage and family matters, self-assertiveness, treatment of female offenders, issuance of insurance, availability of housing, abortion laws, and tax laws (see Women's Movement in Community Politics in the U.S.: 42).

Sex discrimination in employment is the number-one ranked issue. It is also among the most clearly documented aspects of gender discrimination. It is an area of special concern since more and more women are entering the work force. The number of one-earner households in the United States has declined from 49.6 percent in 1960 to 22.4 percent in 1980. During those same years, the number of married women in the work force rose from 32 percent to over 51 percent, and the number of children with mothers who work outside the home (31.8 million) now exceeds that of the number of children with mothers at home (26.3 million) (Time, July 12, 1982: 22-23).

The remarkably steady increase in the number of women in the work force since World War II is detailed in Table Sixteen. Whereas in 1950 women comprised less than 28 percent of the nation's workforce, today they are over 44 percent. During that same time, men in the work force dropped from 87 percent to 78 percent. Currently, more than 52 percent of women work outside the home, numbering 45.6 million workers. The increase in women working outside the home has raised their awareness of sexual discrimination as greater numbers have experienced the occupational segregation and the pronounced wage gap which characterizes their status in the work force (see Bianchi and Spain, 1983). This segregation into a few fields is highlighted by the following list of jobs in which the percent of working females has been consistently in the high 80 to low 90 percentiles since the 1960's. The fields and the percent of female workers in that field as of 1979 are: 1)registered nurses, 97; 2) elementary school teachers, 84; 3) typists, 97; 4) telephone operators, 92; 5) secretaries, 99; 6) hairdressers, 89; and 7) waiters and waitresses, 89 (The Women's Movement:5).

Table 16: WOMEN IN THE WORK FORCE, SELECTED YEARS, 1947-1982		
YEAR:	NUMBER: (IN THOUSANDS)	PERCENTAGE OF ADULT FEMALES IN THE WORK FORCE
1947	16,683	31.8
1951	19,054	34.7
1956	21,495	36.9
1961	23,838	38.1
1966	27,333	40.3
1971	32,132	43.4
1976	38,520	47.4
1977	39,952	48.4
1978	41,878	50.0
1979	43,391	51.0
1980	44,574	51.6
Source: Based on data in The Women's Movement: Agenda for the '80's: 5.		

Until the mid-1960's such male/female occupational segregation was undoubtedly related to state legislation which was originally enacted to protect women in such matters as long hours, night work, or physically dangerous or strenuous work, although states began expanding such restrictions during the 1940's to fields where such a rationale is puzzling at best.

310

In Pennsylvania, for example, women were prohibited from working as crane operators, welders, truckers, meter readers, or on railroad tracks or in boiler rooms. At least 17 states prohibited women from working in the mines. Ohio had the longest list of occupational restrictions. Women were banned in bowling alleys, pool rooms and shoe shine parlors; they could not handle freight or baggage, operate freight elevators, guard railroad crossings, or operate vehicles for hire (Women's Movement: Agenda for the '80's: 187).

Such state laws, however, were held to be unconstitutional under the sex-discrimination ban of Title VII or the 1964 Civil Rights Act.

One rather immediate result of such gender-based occupational discrimination is the wage gap between men and women. Working women average only 62 percent of the annual pay for men in the category of over-25, college-educated workers. The average earnings of women in relation to men has declined over the past thirty years. In 1955 women earned 65 percent of what men earned. Women now are paid roughly 59 percent of what a man gets (Bianchi and Spain, 1983). In large measure, the wage gap reflects the fact that women have lower-level jobs. Only five percent of the executives among the top fifty U.S. companies are women. Lower earnings can be readily documented for many fields in which pay for women is consistently lower than men's pay in the same field, as can be seen in Table Seventeen, which shows 1981 data on earnings by several occupations.

Table 17: EARNINGS BY OCCUPATION, BY GENDER--1981 WEEKLY MEDIANS		
OCCUPATION:	WOMEN'S PAY:	MEN'S PAY:
1. Lawyers	$ 407	$ 574
2. Physicians	401	495
3. Engineers	371	547
4. Computer Specialists	355	488
5. Nurses	326	344
6. Editors, Reporters	324	382
7. Teachers (Elementary)	311	379
8. Clerical workers	220	328
9. Saleswork	190	366
10. Waiters	144	200
Source: Based on data in Time, 7/12/62:23.		

The following figure and tables illustrate the wage gap across various age-groupings, and while the gap is less among younger workers than older ones, the overall picture is one of pronounced discrimination, a steadily growing wage gap since the 1950´s in both dollar amounts and as a percentage of men´s earnings, and differences which hold across various status groups as well.

Fig. 8: THE GENDER/WAGE GAP BY AGE GROUPS
(Women´s Earnings as Percent of Men´s: 1980)

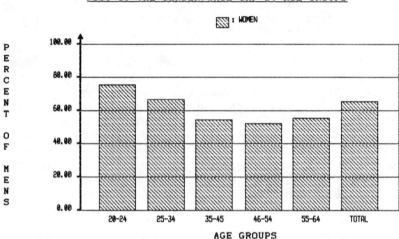

FIG. 8: THE GENDER/WAGE GAP BY AGE GROUPS

Source: Adapted from data in The Women´s Movement: 116.

TABLE 18: THE GENDER/WAGE GAP, 1955-1979				
YEAR:	MEN:	WOMEN:	WOMEN´S EARNINGS AS PERCENT OF MEN´S	EARNINGS GAP IN DOLLARS:
1979	$17,062	$10,168	59.5%	$ 6,894.
1978	15,730	9,350	59.4	6,380.
1977	14,626	8,618	58.9	6,008.
1976	13,455	8,009	60.2	5,356.
1975	12,758	7,504	58.8	5,254.
1970	8,966	5,323	59.4	3,643.
1965	6,375	3,823	60.0	2,552.
1960	5,417	3,293	60.8	2,124.
1955	4,252	2,719	63.9	1,533.
SOURCE: Adapted from data in The Women´s Movement: 10.				

TABLE 19: THE GENDER/WAGE GAP BY STATUS GROUPS: 1980
(Median Weekly Earnings, Males vs. Females)

All Workers	$266
Males	322
Females	204
Whites	273
Blacks	219
Hispanics	214
White Males	329
Black Males	247
Hispanic Males	238
White Females	206
Black Females	190
Hispanic Females	177

Source: Adapted from The Women's Movement: 37.

Nor are these average wage differences only the result of sex discrimination in the job place. Private market pension systems seldom cover women adequately. Currently, only 20 percent of retirement-age women receive either public or private pensions on their own or through their husband's employment record. That means that the female elderly are overwhelmingly reliant on the Social Security System which itself has a few inequities built into it. Over 60 percent of women over 65 years old depend on social security as their sole source of income. In general, women receive their social security benefits as dependents of their husbands. If women work outside the home, they can be covered by their husband's work record or by their own--but not by both, even though both paid into the system. If divorced, a woman loses the social security benefits if the marriage lasted less than ten years. Also, widows over 50 years of age who remarry retain their benefits whereas divorced women of any age forfeit their benefits upon remarriage (The Women's Movement: 117).

The divorced status is a particular problem area for women. Despite myths to the contrary, only about 14 percent of divorced women are awarded alimony, and of those, only 46 percent collect it regularly. Similarly, only 44 percent of divorced mothers are awarded child support and only 47 percent of those collect it regularly. That means, of 100 divorced mothers, fewer than 21 regularly collect child support (Report, National Commission on the Observance of the International Women's Year, 1976: 16).

313

The Reagan Administration's cuts in social welfare have hit elderly women in particular, contributing to what critics such as Tish Summers, President of the Older Women's League, have labelled the "feminization of poverty." OWL estimates that 60 percent of persons affected by these cuts are the elderly poor reporting incomes below $10,000. Some highlights of those cuts and their impact are as follows (Porter: 6):

1) Nearly three-fourths of the over-65 who are below the poverty level are women. In 1980, more than 6 million women over 65 and living alone had an average income under $5,000. Nearly one-third were "officially poor" (that is, had incomes below $3,941) and half were "near poverty" (that is, had incomes below $4,926).

2) Of the more than 4 million recipients of S.S.I., more than half are aged, and of these an overwhelming 73 percent are women.

3) Food stamp cuts have had an extremely serious effect on the elderly poor, of whom seven out of ten are women. It is estimated that food-stamp cuts will effect 92 percent of all elderly.

4) About half of all public housing units and a third of all assisted units are occupied by the elderly; 75 percent of those units are headed by elderly women. Reagan programs impacting the elderly include sharp rent increases, new standards for determining benefits, and reduced operating subsidies to local housing authorities. Of those who participate in both food stamps and housing programs, 85 percent are female-headed households and older women living alone.

5) Of all medicaid recipients, 61 percent are women and 40 percent are over 65.

Another area of obvious discrimination based on gender concerns the political activity of women. Indeed, that men were more likely than women to participate in politics is one of the most thoroughly substantiated patterns in social science (see Milbrath and Goel: 116). Until recently, the voting rate of women in the U.S. had typically been about ten percent less than that of men, although the gap has been closing over the past two decades. In the 1976 election, for instance, the percent of turnout for females was 58.8 while for males it was 59.6, and in the 1980 election female turnout for the first time ever exceeded that of male turnout--59.4 percent female to 59.1 percent male (Statistical Abstract of the U.S., 1981: 500; see also, Wassenberg et al.: 181).

314

The gap between men and women was widest among persons at the lower levels of social status and narrowest among the upper-class population. In any case, men are more likely than women to feel politically efficacious--that is, to feel they are qualified to deal with the complexities of politics and that such participation is likely to bring desired results. Women have apparently closed the turnout gap, but have not yet closed the gap in electoral results. Past lower levels of participation has resulted in a decided under-representation of women in both elected and appointed positions.

A 1975 study by the Center for American Women and Politics at the Eagleton Institute found that in 39 states, 53 percent of the appointed boards and commissions had not a single woman member. This lack of membership was especially pronounced among the more powerful boards and commissions generally composed of fewer members (3-9 member range). The percent of women serving on boards and commissions ranged from a low of 8 percent in Mississippi to a high of 23 percent in Arizona, Hawaii, Iowa and Washington (Report; 44).

The picture is similarly one of great underrepresentation among elected officials. While the gains in recent years have been impressive, the lack of elected women is still striking.

There were 301 women state legislators in 1969, 908 in 1981; 5,765 female elected officials in 1975, 14,225 just four years later. And yet, those 908 legislators are only 12 percent of the membership of state legislative bodies. Only 19 of the 435 members of the United States House of Representatives are women, only two of the 100 Senators (Time, July 12, 1982: 20).

The 1980´s have been marked by a concerted effort by women to close that electoral gap. In 1971 there were only 7 women mayors in cities with populations over 30,000; today there are 76 such mayors. In 1971 women in state legislatures numbered 362, or 5 percent; today the 994 women state legislators are 13 percent of the total. In Congress there are 24 women, 2 in the Senate and 22 in the House, an increase of 60 percent since 1971. As of 1980, there were a total of 16,083 female state and local elected officials (12 percent of the total of such offices). Females numbered 763 (10 percent) of state legislatures, 1,144 (6 percent) of

County Commissioners; 1,333 (1 percent) of the nation's mayors, and 12,843 (3 percent) of the township and local council officials (U.S. Statistical Abstract, 1981: 496). And of course, 1984 saw for the first time in our history a woman nominated for Vice-President by a major political party.

In part, past underrepresentation in elective offices reflects their tradition of underrepresentation in law schools. As recently as 1981, despite nearly a decade of affirmative action efforts to increase the law school enrollments of women, only 30.2 percent of the nation's law school graduates were female (Time, July 12, 1982: 23).

Women have been even more scarce on the nation's judicial benches. As of 1976, of 399 U.S. district judgeships, and 97 U.S. Courts of Appeal seats, only 4 were held by women. The appointment of Justice O'Connor to the Unites States Supreme Court in 1981 was the first time in our history that a female was appointed to that bench. At the state level, as of 1970, only 869 of the 11,380 judges (a mere 7 1/2 percent) were women.

When voting, women tend to split their preferences between the two major parties, at least when measured by their presidential voting habits. As the following table shows, women were consistently within a couple of percentage points of the national vote split for every presidential election since 1952. Of the seven elections, women were slightly more Republican in three, slightly more Democratic in three, and exactly the same as the national vote in one of those seven presidential ballots.

Table 20:   VOTE BY GENDER, IN COMPARISON TO NATIONAL
            VOTE FOR PRESIDENTIAL ELECTIONS, 1952-1980

YEAR:		NATIONAL VOTE:	GENDER/MALES:	GENDER/FEMALES:
1952	%Dem.	44.6%	47%	42%
	%Rep.	55.4	53	58
1956	%Dem.	42.2	45	39
	%Rep.	57.8	55	61
1960	%Dem.	61.3	60	62
	%Rep.	49.9	48	51
1964	%Dem.	61.3	60	62
	%Rep.	43.4	43	43
1968	%Dem.	43.0	41	45
	%Rep.	43.4	43	43
1972	%Dem.	38.0	32	38
	%Rep.	62.0	68	62
1976	%Dem.	51.0	52	52
	%Rep.	49.0	48	48
1980	%Dem.	42.0	37	45
	%Rep.	52.0	54	46
1984	%Dem.	41.0	36	45
	%Rep.	59.0	64	55

Source: Polsby and Wildavsky, Presidential Elections:
        6; updated from Pomper, et al. The Election of
        of 1976: 61, and The Election of 1980: 71; and
        1984 data from initial exit polls as cited in
        Time, November 19, 1984: 45.

That picture, however, may be changing during the 1980's. Traditionally, little if any evidence of differences between the sexes showed up in political party identification or issues stands other than one issue dimension, that of war and peace (see Pomper, Voter's Choice, 1975). Since the 1980 election, gender differences in basic political evaluations have appeared and seemed to be persisting in the polls. Before the 1980 election, public opinion polls indicated that women preferred Reagan far less than did men. More

importantly, on election day itself, all the major polls
reported a 20 point margin in favor of Reagan among men,
to a virtual even split among women. This less
favorable view of President Reagan has persisted in the
way women evaluate the job he is doing Their party
identification and stated voting intentions for the
1982 Congressional elections also showed a trend toward
the Democrats and away from Reagan and the Republican
Party. This trend has also shown up at the state level.
In the 1982 Virginia gubernatorial race, men were evenly
split between Robb, the Democratic nominee and eventual
winner, and Republican Coleman. Women gave Robb a 15-
point margin (Frankovic: 440).

Opinion polling since 1980 has shown women
consistently rating Reagan more negatively than men.
Their disapproval extends beyond simple overall approval
or not. They fear he will get the country into a war;
they are far more likely to disapprove of the way he is
handling foreign policy, and women are less likely than
men to trust Reagan to make the right choice about use
of nuclear weapons. They evaluate his administration
far more negatively than men on his handling of the
economy, and are more likely men to think that
Reagonomics has hurt the country's economy. They are
less likely than men to be optimistic about the
program's eventual success. Differences between the
sexes about the President's economic progress have been
growing over time. It even extends to his personal
life--women saying that the lifestyle at the White House
is too extravagant, while men say it is "appropriate:
(Frankovic: 441).

Table Twenty-One presents the approval ratings for
Presidents Carter and Reagan at roughly comparable times
in their term. It shows the clear difference between
gender.

Table 21: PRESIDENTIAL APPROVAL RATING, BY GENDER				
	Reagan, May of 1982		Carter, April of 1978	
	Men:	Women:	Men:	Women:
Approve	49%	39%	47%	45%
Disapprove	38	48	39	35
No opinion	13	13	14	20
Source: CBS News/New York Times polls, as cited in Frankovic: 441.				

These gender differences remain even after one
controls for age and education (see also, Wassenberg, et
al.: 201). They do not seem to be accounted for by
women's stands on traditional "women's issues." They
hold across women's economic status. In terms of
the best explanation for the more negative view of
President Reagan are the war and peace and the
environment. The gender gap is now showing up in party
party identification and regarding stated intentions for
future Congressional elections. In part, this may
reflect the fact that in women's rights and
discrimination matters there is a substantively
meaningful split between Democratic and Republican
members of Congress, and likewise among Democratic and
Republican jurists (see Stidham, et al.: 212-216).
Table Twenty-Two shows party identification, by gender,
for 1980/1982. The gap is not explained by age and
educational differences. It is clearest among the very
youngest groups. Moreover, polls about intentions of
Congessional votes show them favoring Democrats
significantly above men (Frankovic: 447). The gap did
not widen in the 1984 Presidential election, as we have
seen above, but it seems to have persisted in that
President Reagan won by 59 to 41 percent overall, but he
won only an estimated 55 percent of the female vote (see
Time, November 19, 1984: 45; and Newsweek, Election
Extra Edition, November, 1984: 6).

TABLE 22: PARTY IDENTIFICATION, BY GENDER, 1980/1982				
	1980		1982	
	MEN:	WOMEN:	MEN:	WOMEN:
Democrats	39	42	33	41
Independent	38	36	45	36
Republican	23	22	22	23

Source: Based on data from cbs News/New York Times
Polls, as cited in Frankovic: 447. "All
polls for each year have been aggregated.

Political activities by women go beyond mere
political party and voting involvement and have a long a
venerable tradition in American politics, even if such
activism has been a minority role. During the 1800's
the women's movement was largely a drive for greater
equality of educational opportunity. From the 1830's
throughout the 1850's the movement was concerned with
social issues--prominently the unionization movement,

the Abolition Movement, and battles for legislative reform to ensure greater property rights for women (Burke: 41-43).

The drive for greater political participation began with the women's suffrage movement. That drive formally commenced in 1848 when Elizabeth Cady Stanton and Susan B. Anthony called for the Seneca Falls, New York conference which launched the movement to secure the constitutional right to vote for women. Even during its early days the suffrage movement demonstrated a tendency to fragment which has plagued and weakened the efficacy of the women's rights movement consistently from its birth to today.

During the period of 1860 until World War I, a major split over long-term strategy developed. In 1869 two national organizations formed, based on differing perspectives regarding such strategy. The National Women's Suffrage Association, headed by Stanton and Anthony, felt the cause should be concerned with a wide-range of issues of special concern to women. They advocated more radical tactics. In contrast, the American Women Suffrage Association, headed by Lucy Stone and Antoinette Brown Blackwell wanted to focus on the suffrage issue alone and tended to favor more conservative tactics. These two organizations did manage to merge in 1890 to form the National American Women's Suffrage Association. This loose-knit association worked until the successful passage of the 19th Amendment in August of 1920 (Burke: 43-44).

The very success of that battle led to another major split. The more conservative suffragettes, organizationally the lose-knit coalition of the National American Women's Suffrage Association (NAWSA), felt the battle was over with the successful passage of the right to vote. A more radical group emerged, pushing for passage of a full equal rights amendment. An ERA proposal was first advocated in the early 1920's by Alice Paul and the National Women's Party. The NWP used picketing, hunger strikes, and other radical tactics, starting their ERA campaign in 1921. They did succeed in getting a proposal introduced into Congress in 1923 by Senator Charles Curtis and Representative Daniel R. Anthony, Jr., both Republicans from Kansas (see Goldstein: 3). The proposal languished in Congress from 1923 until the 1940's when there seemed to be little interest in it or the women's movement in general.

320

Indeed, the 1940's were a period of regression for the movement, when 11 states had laws that stated a wife could not hold her own earnings without her husband's consent, 16 states denied a married woman's right to make contracts, 7 states favored the father in custody cases, and over 20 states prohibited women from serving on juries. During the 1940's, 43 states set limits on the daily and weekly hours a woman could work outside the home, and 15 states flatly prohibited night work for women (The Women's Movement: 187).

During the 1940's the movement again exhibited considerable fragmentation, with many groups opposing the ERA. Such opposition included the National League of Women Voters, the National Women's Trade Union League, the Y.W.C.A., the National Association of Catholic Women, Jewish Women, and Negro Women, as well as the American Association of University Women. Liberal and labor groups also opposed the ERA, for example, the AFL-CIO and AFT, the National Farmer's Union, and the ACLU. These groups opposed passage of an ERA fearing it would set back or ban needed "protective" legislation for women working outside the home. They led the coalition which defeated the ERA proposal finally voted on in the Senate in 1946. The movement then went into a decline until the 1960's.

The modern push for the ERA began in the mid-1960's when a number of cultural and socio-economic pressures led to a revival of the women's movement. 1) The 1960's witnessed the development of a cultural setting which was structurally conducive to the rise of the women's movement. These included the increased education of women, a greater awareness of the issue because of the mass media, a greater involvement of women in the workforce outside the home, accompanied by an increased stratification of women in the workforce. 2) A widespread awareness of those conditions led to increased discontent and unrest. 3) This was associated with the spread of a generalized belief in the existence and prevalence of a sexist ideology and practice. Particularly important was the publication, in 1963, of Betty Friedan's best seller, The Feminan Mystique. 4) Also important were the beginnings of a new organizational base. In October of 1966 the National Organization of Women (NOW) was founded. Alice Paul, by then 82 years old, inspired NOW to launch a new campaign for the passage of an ERA in 1967. 5)The social, economic, political, and marital inequities women

321

experienced were being blamed on specific social agents and institutions. This was important since women were no longer accepting the blame themselves for these conditions. It also gave them specific targets for action. 6) They experienced, too, a growing recognition of the effectiveness of organized action. There was a renewed spurt of feminist organizational activity. In addition to NOW, the Women's Equity Action League (WEAL), which started in 1968, and several other groups began pushing for an ERA. These included the New York Radical Women, the Redstockings, the National Women's Political Caucus, and Female Liberation (see Feminism in American Politics: 10-19). These feminist groups employed a variety of tactics: economic boycotts, legal defense and offense, use of the electoral process, lobbying, efforts to increase favorable media coverage, rallying members to political activism, and generally combating gender-role stereotyping. They copied the black civil rights movement by attempting to raise the consciousness of women, and by stressing an ideology of action which politicized women personally. As a recent study of the movement put it:

> Feminist means to achieve equality are diverse, but clear. Almost all organized feminist groups simultaneously pursue a dual-pronged strategy: (1) structural systemic change, and (2) basic attitudinal and value change...Reform feminists advocate greater flexibility in gender roles, shared responsibility in the home, and equally shared power in the political and economic arena. The foremost plank...of NOW, at this writing, is passage of the Equal Rights Amendment (ERA). Other efforts include litigation on as many fronts as possible, the elimination of public school texts that reflect sex bias in roles or language...legislation that recognizes the right of women to control the use of their own bodies...promotion of adequate day-care centers, no-fault divorce, homemakers rights, credit insurance for married women who are employed, economic boycotts of products that reflect sexism and of states that have not yet ratified the ERA, and so forth (Feminism in American Politics: 32-33).

At first the movement seemed to be developing a politically undeniable momentum. The ERA proposal ultimately had the support of some 450 national organizations. At one time, public opinion polls showed that the ERA was favored by 2/3 of the American public (Time, July 12, 1982: 32-33). Liberal groups which had opposed it in the 1940's, such as the ACLU, endorsed it during the 1960's. Organized labor likewise supported it, as did the Department of Labor in 1969.

The House of Representatives first passed a measure proposing such an amendment in 1970 by a vote of 350 to 15. The House again approved the measure in 1971. Finally, the Senate approved a proposal on March 22, 1972. It read simply, "Equality of rights under the law shall not be denied or abridged by the United States or by any state on account of sex" (Time, July 12, 1982: 32).

Hawaii became the first state to ratify the proposed amendment, and twenty-one other states followed its example that year. Its ratification seemed almost assured when 32 of the necessary 38 states ratified the proposal within the first two years. A 1978 Gallop Poll found that 58 percent of all Americans favored it. A Lou Harris Poll of that same year found 55 percent approved it, although his poll noted a significant dropping off of support--to 51 percent--by February. The last state to ratify was Indiana, in 1977. Ultimately, the push for ERA ended three states shy. In 1979 the proponents did win an extension beyond the original seven-year cut off date, to July 30, 1982.

But the organized opposition to ERA developed by the mid-1970's, and their forces carried the day. The opposition groups were mainly conservatives who saw the issue as linked to abortion, government-sponsored day-care centers, sex education, and gay rights--all of which they strenuously opposed. They feared that the amendment would overturn the traditional role of women in society and be fundamentally detrimental to the family, the church, and the nation. Anti-ERA groups argued that the amendment's passage would have:1) ended alimony and child support, 2) required the military conscription of mothers, 3) banned separate bathrooms, and 4) permitted homosexual marriages (The Women's Movement: Agenda for the '80's: 182-183. See also, Goldstein: 2).

Prominent opponents groups included the Ku Klux Klan, the John Birch Society, the American Conservative Union, the Conservative Caucus (founded and financed by Joseph Coors, of Coors Beer fame), and such church groups as the Mormon Church (effective especially in Utah, and Arizona which never ratified the proposal), and the hierarchy of the Catholic Church (for instance, the National Conference of Catholic Bishops). It was also opposed by the Reverend Jerry Falwell and the Moral Majority, plus a host of fundamentalist Christian churches. The American Farm Bureau opposed it. Under-Secretary of State James Buckley was a leading opponent, as was Senator Jesse Helms and Representative Hyde of Illinois, and former Senator Sam Ervin. But perhaps the most prominent opponent was Mrs. Phyllis Schlafly, founder of STOP-ERA, and later the Eagle Forum. As _Time_ described her:

> Feminists might initially have mistaken her for a kind of grandstanding Betty Crocker, but Schlafly and her supporters marshalled all the fear and uncertainty that trails every social revolution, trimmed it and turned it against the opposition. ERA would encourage everything from rampant homosexuality to unisex bathrooms, from women draftees in combat to women victims of some squalid unisex millennium. Cheap and scary, sure, but as they say about such quibbles in Hollywood, "Hey, it worked." (_Time,_ July 12, 1982: 26.)

Ultimately, as the following map shows, thirty-one states ratified the proposal, five states ratified but later rescinded their vote, and fourteen states never ratified the ERA. This latest effort to pass an ERA failed by three states. The reader can easily note the regional aspect of the opposition. The sun-belt, or bible-belt area was solidly anti-ERA.

NOW and related proponent groups have vowed not to give up the fight. The National Women's Caucus has developed its "dirty dozen" list of various state legislators whom it will seek to defeat at the polls. NOW has sponsored an economic boycott of the fourteen states which held out, and over fifty business, political, and professional organizations have agreed to support that boycott by not holding their conventions in those states. Such a boycott means literally the loss of millions of dollars in convention-generated revenues

324

to such traditional convention-site cities as Chicago, Miami, Atlanta, New Orleans, Las Vegas, Reno, and Phoenix. The movement has begun a state-by-state approach to achieving their legislative goals. Fifteen states have already adopted ERA provisions in their state constitutions. Many of the proponents of the Equal Rights Amendment are now pushing for a new "ERA" effort--an Equal Rights Act by Congress (see Goldstein: 18).

FIG. 9: THE ERA RATIFICATION EFFORT: BY STATES

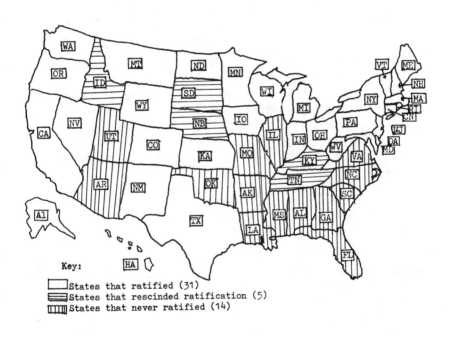

Key:

☐ States that ratified (31)
≡ States that rescinded ratification (5)
▥ States that never ratified (14)

The failure to pass the ERA, coupled with the less than appreciable number of mid- to high-level appointments of women in the Reagan Administration increased talk of the "gender-gap" and has led to a modification in the strategy of feminist groups. The NWPC launched a "Win With Women Campaign" designed to recruit, train, finance, and help elect women to public office, especially at the state level. Since NWPC was formed, women state legislators increased from 5 to 13 percent. The 1982 redistricting throughout much of the nation afforded many new opportunities to increase that share. State legislative experience is often a stepping-stone to higher office. Such efforts are needed as women candidates have traditionally faced tough odds in getting campaign contributions and workers for their uphill battles to win votes. As one observer of this new effort put it:

> The NWPC is not a juggernaut. While it has chapters in all but four states, its active membership is just over 10,000. It has had its internal splits on endorsements, with a good deal of dissatisfaction in 1980 by Republican women who saw it as an automatic ally of the Democrats.
> But Wilson [Kathy Wilson, its head] says 35 percent of the membership is still Republican, and she has begun to use her own Republican credentials to heal the breach that developed in 1980. NWPC now seems pointed on a path that will help, over the next decade, bring more women into elective office at all levels and in both parties (David Broder, "A Feminist Electoral Strategy," The Washington Post, January 24, 1982: D7).

If women could unify into a cohesive and active voting bloc, their potential for power is immense. At more than fifty percent of the population, they are a minority in political power mainly because of their fragmentation. It remains to be seen whether this latest battle over the ERA, and the nomination of Representative Geraldine Ferraro to the Vice-Presidency by the Democratic Party in 1984 will inspire a greater unity of action which will activate them and lead them out of the ranks of minority status.

A similar minority in its potential for power is that of the elderly. Minority status based upon age is the discussion to which we next turn out attention.

Age

Discrimination based on age hits persons at both ends of the age cycle--both the young and the old are subject to it. As Maggie Kuhn (1979), founder and leader of the Gray Panthers, noted:

> Life is a continuum, but we divide it into little segments by chronological age, and thereby violate its essential wholeness. The old and the young have much to share and give to each other. When we get together we realize that growing up is just as hard and stressed as growing old in a technological society. The same ageism that makes old age lonely and despairing, robs youth of a future. To be eliminated, racism, sexism and ageism will require sweeping changes in society as well as in personal attitudes and life-styles, social theories and policies, our national priorities and political processes. I like to think that age may be the unifying force. We are all ageing. Age is the one factor every living thing shares (: 2).

The problems of the aging are significant for society and are increasingly important as the size of this minority grows. Daily, some 5,000 Americans join the ranks of the more than 25.5 million who are 65 years old or more--some 11 percent of the population. That is an increase of 28 percent in the decade of the 1970's.

That growth rate in the elderly is evident world-wide and is an increase substantially greater in overall population growth--which makes the potential impact of the trend all the greater. World-wide population over the age of 60 was, as of 1970, over 291 million. The U.N. estimates that by the year 2,000 that figure will exceed 600 million! There will be a 50 percent increase in that age group in the developed nations, as opposed to an estimated 33 percent increase in the overall population of the world (see Ageing, 1979: 2).

In the United States that trend means that the ratio of those over 65 to those age 20 to 64 will rise from around 20 percent in the near future to nearly 40 percent by the year 2030. In percentage terms, the elderly are now the fastest growing segment of the U.S. population. The 1981 Conference on Ageing noted the demographic impact in their final report. The

327

increasingly aged population, supported by a decreasing working population and coupled with a trend of increased life expectancy, contributes to the sense of crisis about the demographic imbalance. The two factors seem to threaten a seemingly intolerable burden on the social security and pension systems of the nation by early in the next century (Work Life in the '80's: 75-76).

In the year 1900, persons over 65 years old comprised 4 percent of the total population. That figure reached 5 percent by 1925, and 8 percent by 1950. By 1975 it was 11 percent. It is projected to be 16 percent by the year 2030. In 1900 there were ten active workers for every retired one. That ratio is expected to be two to one by the year 2030. When the Social Security System began in 1935, the average person lived 12.8 years in retirement. Today that average person lives sixteen years, and the retirement-life span continues to grow.

Ironically, the very industrialization and modernization processes which have enabled the longer life span and contributed so significantly to the rise in the number of the elderly seems also to have contributed to the majority society's view of the elderly to be a more negative one. In industrial countries where constant and rapid change makes the "new" and the "young" more valued, the elderly are often viewed as nonproductive "burdens" on society, which has contributed to low self-esteem among the elderly. In more traditional societies the elderly are viewed more positively--as repositories of accumulated wisdom. They are accorded higher levels of status and more important positions of power.

The problems faced by the elderly are concentrated in jobs, income, health care, housing, and social services. Job discrimination, especially as evidenced in mandatory retirement laws, has for some time be considered the number one priority for change desired by the organized elderly. The Rights Revolution, for example, notes:

> For years older people have been lobbying for the right to work as long as they are physically able. Under pressure from such groups as the Gray Panthers, the National Council on Aging, and the National Council of Senior Citizens, Congress, on March 23, 1978, cleared legislation which raised the mandatory

retirement age from 65 to 70 in private
industry and removed it altogether for federal
employees (:17).

The most overwhelmingly favored recommendation coming
from the 1981 White House Conference on Aging was for
the ending of mandatory retirement laws altogether,
allowing for a gradual phase-in of retirement plans such
as part-time work or more flexible work schedules for
older workers. Despite the wide-spread support for a
policy which enables or encourages the able-bodied older
worker to chose to continue working, attempts to design
an acceptable and effective policy raises many problems.
Barriers exist due to age discrimination practices by
employers, health or displacement problems, and even the
law--such as the Social Security retirement income test
which entails a disincentive to continue working after
age 65.

The effect of the disincentives built into
retirement pension plans and the Social Security System
is to encourage a marked trend towards early retirement.
Since World War II the labor force participation for men
aged 62 has declined steadily from 80 percent in 1940 to
60 percent in 1979; for men aged 65 that rate fell from
67 percent in 1940 to 37 percent in 1979. That trend is
projected to continue its decline steadily through 1995.
Coupled with this trend is the downward turn in
mortality rates: a man 65 could expect to live 1.8 years
longer in 1977 than his counterpart in 1940; and a 65
year old woman in 1977 could expect to live nearly five
years longer than a woman that age in 1940. If these
trends continue, the current 35 retirees per 100 workers
will rise to more than 50 when the baby boom generation
retires. Even if the benefits are not increased, the
cost per worker to support the retired population would
increase by 50 percent (White House Conference on
Aging,Report; 19).

A problem related to this is the fixed-income
status of most elderly. Inflation effects the elderly
relatively more than younger age groups. The elderly
must spend a large share of their fixed incomes on
precisely those categories where the price increases
during the 1970´s and continuing into the 1980´s were
the most virulent: food, energy, and health care. The
White House Conference noted an almost "Catch 22" aspect
of such inflationary pressures:

The rising costs of entitlement programs--
notably Social Security, Medicare, and
Medicaid--contributed substantially to rising
government expenditures in the 1970´s, and
through its effect on the size of government
deficits, added to the pressure on the Federal
Reserve to increase money growth and thus may
have contributed to worsened inflation (Ibid:
29).

The income problems of the elderly were noted by
Representative Claude Pepper of Florida, then Chairman
of the House Select Committee on Aging. He stated that
some 4 million people, roughly 16 percent of the
elderly, have incomes below the poverty level.
Moreover, an estimated 60 percent of the elderly would
be in those circumstances if not for the Social Security
benefits. He noted that in 1980 more than two-thirds of
all senior citizens had incomes under $6,000. per year
(NY Times Magazine, November 29, 1981: 126).

The White House, however, disputes those figures,
claiming that during the 1960´s and 1970´s the median
family income for the elderly rose from 50 percent of
the national average to 57 percent. From 1959 to 1979,
they assert, the number of officially "poor" elderly
dropped dramatically, from 5.5 million to 3.6 million,
or from 35 percent of the elderly to 15 percent. They
claim that the nation´s elderly are the wealthiest,
best fed, housed, healthiest, and most self-reliant
older population in our nation´s history (White House
Conference on Aging, Report: 8).

Everyone agrees, however, that health problems and
their associated costs are among the most serious
problems facing the elderly. Some two million of the
elderly are estimated to be afflicted with severe health
problems: 38 percent suffer from chronic health
conditions, half of which are serious. Roughly 5
percent are homebound. While Medicare pays an estimated
36 percent of health bills, the costs have been rising
markedly during the past few decades, and the medicare
system has been raising the portion of those bills that
the elderly themselves must pay. The Conference on
Aging noted the alarming trend in national health cost
figures: such expenditures were $42 billion in 1965, had
reached $212.2 billion by 1979, and are projected to be
$821 billion by 1990. The percent of the Gross National
Product devoted to health care was over 6 percent in
1965 and had exceeded 9 percent by 1979 (Report: 77).

These problems have led to "ageism"--inequities, discrimination, and conflict based on age. Ageism spreads when an increasing number of the elderly are viewed as burdens. They are seen as an outgroup and a threat, suffer stereotyping, subordination, prejudice, and discrimination. Their minority status is further indicated by the need for and passage of "protective legislation" on their behalf (Annals: 140).

Recent studies have disputed some of the traditional stereotypes about the political behavior of the elderly. Although they have an image of being more conservative and of becoming increasingly conservative as they age, cohort analysis from sample survey data from the last 30 years disputes that image (Ibid: 185). Likewise, the decline in participation associated with age is in large measure a function of education and sex differences rather than age. When those variables are taken into account, the decline in the voting rate of the elderly largely disappears. Table 23 shows the turnout by age for the 1980 Presidential election. Table 24 presents the 1952 to 1980 election data by various voting age groups as they split between the two major parties. These data illustrate the slight drop-off with retirement age and the slightly more Republican orientation associated with that age group.

Table 23: 1980 PRESIDENTIAL TURNOUT, BY AGE	
AGE GROUP:	PERCENT TURNOUT:
18-20	35.7
21-24	43.1
25-34	54.6
35-44	64.4
45-64	69.3
Over 65	65.1
Source: Statistical Abstract of the U.S., 1981: 500.	

Table 24:	PRESIDENTIAL VOTE, BY AGE, 1952–1980		
ELECTION/AGE:	UNDER 30:	30–49:	50 YEARS OR MORE:
1952 %Dem.	51%	47%	39%
%Rep.	49	53	61
1956 %Dem.	43	45	39
%Rep.	57	55	61
1960 %Dem.	54	54	46
%Rep.	46	46	54
1968 %Dem.	47	44	41
%Rep.	38	41	47
1972 %Dem.	48	33	36
%Rep.	52	67	64
1976 %Dem.	59	49	47
%Rep.	51	49	52
1980 %Dem.	44	37	40
%Rep.	43	54	54

Source: Data from Polsby and Wildavsky, Presidential Elections: 6; updated from Pomper, et al. The Election of 1976:61, and The Election of 1980: 71-72.

Initial exit poll data from the 1984 election indicate that persons over 65 gave 61 percent of their vote to President Reagan (Time, November 19, 1984: 45; Newsweek, Special Election Edition, November, 1984: 4).

Recently there has been some dispute in the literature of political analysis as to the importance of age per se in affecting an individual's political behavior and attitudes. On the one hand, Regan and Dowd maintain the political consciousness manifests itself in the group identification and verbalization of similar interests and in the various forms of political activity such as voting, association in organizations based on age, lobbying and other pressure tactics. It varies among individuals depending on other identifications to which they may be drawn, such as race, social status, region of the country, and political party, but also by age, especially when motivated by organizations such as the Townsend Movement of the 1930's (Annals: 139).

Angus Campbell (1971) has observed that age is not a strong force in American politics at the present time and he feels it is not likely to be so in the future. He doubts the aged will develop into a self-conscious political group with a shared sense of interest and the ability to move as a group to support whichever party they feel best serves their interests. Atchley (1972) basically agrees with Campbell, calling the possibility of a voting bloc of the aged an "illusion," a view to which Schmidhauser (1968) concurs, as do Binstock and Lohman (Ibid:141).

Another consideration they raise as to the difficulty in the development of a group consciousness among the aged concerns the diminished self-esteem resulting from their systematic loss of prestige and meaningful social roles. Their lowered self-esteem, in turn, results in decreased political efficacy. Those over 55 rank lowest of all age strata on a measure of political efficacy (Ibid: 149-150).

Despite all of this, however, there is evidence of a current upswing in aged political consciousness and it is attributed to such factors as the increasing proportion of the aged in the electorate, the poor economic status of the aged, and the earlier retirement trend. While there may be an upswing, it still involves only a proportion of the present aged cohort. The development of an aged group political conscious and of significant numbers is certainly a prerequisite to their effective organization and mobilization of the potential for political power on their own behalf.

In terms of voting, the over 65 group casts about 15 percent of the total vote in national elections. The numbers and propensity for high turnout, however, mean little as long as their vote is fragmented. To date, their vote has not been cast in anything remotely resembling a cohesive bloc. They split their vote along the same sociological and economic lines of class, ethnicity, religion, area of residence and political party affiliation as do other age groups. As Binstock puts it: "The political attitudes and partisan attachments of the aged are diverse and noted for stability" (Ibid: 202).

Even the politically disadvantaged elderly don't necessarily see their socioeconomic problems as being primarily aged-caused, but may instead see them in other contexts. A full life cycle of experiences and attachments presents many sources of group identification and perceptions of special interest.

Each age cohort includes people who differ in many important conditions of life. It is unlikely that any age group will be homogeneous to any significant degree in its attitudes. Evidence from national surveys demonstrates that attitudinal differences between age groups are far less impressive than those within age groups. In addition to voting behavior, however, we need to recognize interest group activity. With respect to age, interest group activity has seen a significant increase in recent years, and has shown greater variety in organizations and tactics than those of the past.

The two most notable movements among the elderly in the past were the Townsend Movement of the 1930's and 1940's, which proposed a $200 per month allocation to every person 60 years or older to be financed by a national sales tax, and the Ham and Eggs Movement in California, a script-issuance scheme that developed during the Great Depression. These movements failed because they were politically unrealistic, inept at lobbying, and torn by internal strife.

Currently, there are eleven different interest groups associated with the problems of the aged engaged in politics at the national level. Four are trade associations: the American Association of Homes for the Aging; American Nursing Home Association, National Council of Health Care Services, and the National Association of State Units on Aging. One is a professional association: the American Gerontological Society. The National Council on Aging is a loose confederation of about 1400 public and private social welfare agencies. The National Caucus of the Black Aged is a recently formed group. There are four mass membership organizations: the National Council of Senior Citizens (NCSC), the National Retired Teachers Association-American Association of Retired Persons (NRTA-AARP), the National Association of Retired Federal Employees (NARFE), and the Gray Panthers. These groups are more successful than past groups since they have found sources of income beyond the members' dues, have created bureaucracies recruited on the basis of performance criteria rather than charisma, and have capitalized on the recent emergence of a more neutral, as opposed to hostile, climate for old aged political activity (Annals: 106).

The NCSC emerged from the 1961 White House Conference on Aging. Its political ability during the years of the Medicare battle was restricted by lack of funds and staff resources. NSCS now claims over 3 million members, although only 250,000 are dues-paying members. Its leadership is dominated by labor unions, with 34 of its 50 member national board from the unions, and about 40 percent of its budget coming from unions.

The NRTA-AARP was formed in two steps. The NRTA, formed in 1947, has always had a political dimension to its goals, but individual uplift and social betterment were its primary goals. The AARP was formed in 1958 to cope with the growing number of non-teachers who sought some of NRTA´s benefits, particularly life-insurance. In late 1973 total NRTA-AARP membership was 6.02 million, making it one of the nation´s largest voluntary associations. Its perspective has been closely linked to that of big business, particularly the insurance industry with which it has developed a symbiotic relationship. The NRTA-AARP neither opposed nor actively promoted the 1965 Medicare bill.

The NARFE is the oldest of the four, having been founded in 1921. The special situation of retired federal employees has enabled this organization to survive in the face of newer, larger, and more comprehensive organizations. NARFE works almost exclusively for better benefits for retired federal employees. Its membership totals about 182,000.

In general, these senior-citizen interest groups have sufficient credentials to participate in most formal and informal national policy processes dealing with problems among the aged. The recognition of them and the solicitation of their views from politicians increases their legitimacy. They rely on three avenues of power. First, they have ready access to public officials, allowing them to put forth proposals they favor and work to block proposals they oppose. Second, they can readily attain access to the mass media, using Congressional hearings, and what Binstock calls "pseudo events" such as the 1971 White House Conference on Aging (Annals: 206-207). From these platforms they can

335

initiate and frame issues for public debate and register public support for or opposition public policy alternatives to meet those issues. Third, they have been able on occasion to employ an electoral bluff. Since the aging can't be swung in a large and cohesive bloc, and since both they and the politicians with whom they deal realize that fact, the groups keep their demands within moderate limits. Politicians are more likely and able to respond to moderate proposals. As long as the groups´ constituencies are satisfied with modest goals, everyone is happy. The group appears to be successful, their constituents get something, and its costs the politicians very little. If and when these interest groups and/or their constituencies ever deem it necessary to take a more radical stance on some issue, the politicians may be forced to call the bluff on the aging vote.

Given this approach, these groups do not vigorously pursue major policy changes which would bring about fundamental changes in their status in American society. Instead, they focus on two basic types of policy: direct income transfer policies and middleman programs. Direct income transfer policies are designed to put additional purchasing power into the hands of the elderly. Though legislation or simply bureaucratic regulations, these interest groups pursue incremental adjustments, some probably inevitable anyway, in existing programs. Examples of direct income transfer policies include Social Security, Old Age Assistance, Rent Supplement, Medicare, and Railroad Retirement Benefits. Middleman programs are those that empower and support public and private organizations to develop and operate properties and carry out multifaceted social, health, recreational, and welfare services. These groups generally seek to create programs to provide themselves with new sources of funds and authority or, with existing programs, to lay claim to as large a share of funds and authority as possible. Examples of this approach include the Hill-Burton Act, the Older Americans Act, Manpower Training and Development, and many other NIH AND NIMH programs.

The Gray Panthers, founded in 1970, exemplifies a more radical approach in its tactics and goals, emulating the black civil rights groups in the use of direct-action tactics to cope with some of the problems they face. It is a loose-knit network of highly vocal older persons dedicated to fighting ageism. They are funded by various church groups and Ralph Nader´s organization. Their name consciously hints at their radicalism.

"We hassled the name for a year and a half," explains Maggie Huhn. "We wanted to show we were taking a stand--not just giving lip service. We decided that if the word ´Panthers´ did turn some people off, we were glad. They weren´t going to do much radical action anyway. Gray is a symbolic color-- everyone gets old, and if you put all the colors of the rainbow together, you get gray" ("How to Fight Age Bias," MS Gazette, June, 1975: 91).

The group originated out of a combined youth/aged church group with which founder Kuhn was associated. Seeking to meet some economic and social needs of both the young and the old, the group was first known as the Consultation of Older and Younger Adults for Social Change. In discussing the affinity between the two age groups, Maggie Kuhn said, "We realized that the young and the old in this society are equally discriminated against. Both have identity crises. Both groups can´t get credit from banks. Both groups are into the drug scene, although there are different drugs and different pushers" (Current Biography, 1978: 241).

Elsewhere she described the "advocate role" she perceived the elderly as being especially able to play.

"Gray Power" doesn´t mean using our large numbers and our growing political awareness for our own self-interest or to build another self-serving group. The national interest is rarely seen beyond contending private interests. Political decisions are at best compromises between conflicting private groups. Old people as "elders of the tribe" should be seeking and safe-guarding the survival of the tribe--the larger public interest. I believe the old people of America have the responsibility to transcend our personal needs and use our freedom to work for a just and humane society that puts people first. We should be advocates of the public interest (Kuhn, Advocacy in This New Age: 3).

Service receivers and service providers are
advocates. I like to think that the old and
the young can be advocates of the people who
are trapped in mid-life careers and
obligations. We who are old have nothing to
lose! We have everything to gain by living
dangerously! We can be the risk-takers,
daring to challenge and change systems,
policies, life-styles, ourselves. We can
build coalitions, and close the ranks between
the disadvantaged groups that have been
contending for small slivers of power and
recognition (Aging: 3).

Since 1971 the Gray Panthers have been pursuing
such goals as ending age discrimination and training
older persons to use their skills in various kinds of
public-interest work. In 1973 they merged with the
Nader group, the Retired Professional Action Group. The
Gray Panthers took over two national projects of that
group: promotion of legislation affecting the hearing
aid industry, and reforms of nursing homes. They
launched a three-year study of the nursing home
industry. With typical straight forwardness, Kuhn
asserted in one newspaper interview that, "The American
Medical Association spent millions lobbying against a
national health program and now the same doctors who
tried to defeat Medicare are getting rich out of the
maladies of the aged. Doctors prey on the infirmities
of the old, and you can quote me." In a later interview
she explained how the Gray Panthers wished to eliminate
the profit motive from health care and advocated a
system much like the British health care program. When
the interviewed pointed out that such "socialized
medicine" is an inflammatory term in the United States,
she replied, "If its so great for the armed forces, and
Congress, and the President and his family, we would
like to have it for everybody" (in Current Biography:
241).

The Gray Panthers are training older people to
monitor banks, insurance companies, and municipal
agencies such as planning and zoning commissions. To
combat negative stereotyping, they watch the way older
people are depicted on TV and in advertising. They
sponsored a group called "Media Watch" which targeted
and protested programs that use insipid dialogue and
erratic behavior to make older people look useless and
helpless. They charged T.V. in particular, and the mass

media in general, with failure to use the opportunity to correct the age bias that they contend contributes to the alienation of the young and old.

In addition to the Gray Panthers, a prominent advocate of elderly rights and increased political clout for the elderly is Congressman Claude Pepper of Florida. His leadership role in elderly-related legislative battles has attracted media attention to his use of the House Select Committee on Aging and his service on the fifteen-member bipartisan Social Security Review Commission to push his views.

He recently relinquished his chairmanship of the House Select Committee on Aging to become Chairman of the powerful House Rules Committee, a position from which he feels he can be even more effectively the "Champion of America's Elderly," as he has been called by Time (April 25, 1983: 21-29).

"Ageism is as odious as racism and sexism," he says, and with the stamina of a man half his age, he scurries about like an octogenarian Paul Revere, calling people of advanced age to their own defense and demanding that the rest of the population recognize their rights and their work.
In recent years he has introduced legislation to abolish mandatory retirement, to help fight crime in housing projects for the elderly, to cut Amtrack rates for senior citizens, to make nutritious meals available to the elderly. His committee on aging has kept up a steady schedule of widely publicized hearings. His newspaper column--"Ask Congressman Pepper"--is circulated to more than 700 newspapers all over the country. "We all look to him," says William R. Hutton, executive director of the National Council of Senior Citizens. "He's the focal point of the older American's interest in Congress. Since his wife died, he has lived completely for his job. He's the nearest thing this country has to a national congressman." (N.Y.Times Magazine, November 29, 1981: 128, 131).

Congressman Pepper led a drive which had the goal to elect as many as 500 delegates to the Democratic National Convention who were 65 or older in order to increase their voice in the choice of the nominee (he strongly backed Mondale) and the platform's stand on issues of great concern to the elderly.

The elderly, then, remain a minority with considerable potential for political power whose present lack of cohesion is the primary basis for that power remaining only "potential." Another group which has also recently exhibited signs of awakening political activism is the "Gay Americans." It is to that group, and its largely "potential political power," we next turn our attention.

Sexual Preference

Like Gray Power, Gay Power is a relatively recent phenomena within the American political scene and another example of a minority adopting the strategy and tactics of the black civil rights movement. Like the aged and women, the gay minority's potential for political power is considerable, but remains largely unfilled due to a lack of visibility and participation. Lack of cohesion is a primary aspect of their power remaining untapped.

A significant aspect of the homosexual movement's political power status is that the vast majority remain "in the closet." Just how large their population is in the United States is a somewhat disputed point. The lack of reliable demographic data contributes to their problem of coping with discrimination. Perhaps the best estimates are still those of the Kinsey report. His study found that approximately 37 percent of the adult male population had at least some homosexual experience to the point of orgasm. Of course, not all of them are, or should be, considered to be true homosexuals. The Kinsey report estimated that roughly ten percent of the adult male and six percent of the adult female population are actively leading a predominately homosexual life. If these estimates are correct, and subsequent studies confirm them to be so, than a reasonable estimate of the size of the homosexual population is eight percent of the total U.S. population or roughly 17 and-a-half million (see Fisher: 193, 254; and Siminoski: 6).

Gays suffer from discrimination like any other minority--in laws, housing, employment, public accommodations, police harassment, and negative stereotyping. One aspect of the gay minority that is unique, however, is that only members of this minority grow up and many often continue to live their lives without the protective benefits of a distinct subculture. Homosexuals are not raised to be homosexuals, in the sense that Jews, Catholics, Poles, Blacks, Asians, etc. are all raised by their families and groups to be members of that subculture. The homosexual has no community with which he or she can share that minority status while growing up. They lack the minority tradition which shapes values, goals, styles of behavior and ways of relating to others in their group and in the world at large. The homosexual generally lacks siblings, peers, and older persons with whom they can relate and who can serve as role models. The homosexual is generally aware of his/her own sexual orientation before being aware of the idea that other homosexuals exist, and thus he/she rarely has an opportunity to meet others and pattern themselves upon those others. They feel sexual feelings which nobody else seems to share, and they quickly learn that it is dangerous to openly acknowledge those feelings (Fisher: 70-71). As one homosexual put it:

> To be homosexual has traditionally meant an invisibility no less destructive for its being, in part, self-imposed. My most humiliating memory is feeling forced to laugh at a fag joke, because I didn´t dare to expose my own homosexuality by objecting to it. Denying one´s own reality is a universal gay experience in our culture, and thus the cycle of invisibility, alienation, and superstition feeds on itself (The Gay Academic: 387).

Gay activists have stressed the disastrous consequences on their psychological development at having no "hero" models to look up to because the majority society expunges all reference to the homosexuality of historical figures who could have served that function.

In terms of their interaction with majority society, the most pervasive problem the gay community faces is their legal status. Virtually everywhere in the United States homosexual behavior is a crime. Sex laws are invariably occasionally enforced, and they are more likely to be enforced against homosexuals than heterosexuals. And if a crime is committed against a homosexual he or she is less likely to get help from the police or justice in court than is a heterosexual in a similar situation (Fisher: 127-128).

The legal tradition against homosexuality goes back as far as 550 B. C. when the ancient Jewish laws called for death by stoning. Following the adoption of Christianity as the official state religion by Rome, homosexuality became punishable by death as the legal policy throughout Christian Europe until the French Revolution and of North and South America as long as they were under European domination. The first Roman edict condemning gay men to death was issued in 342 A.D. In 390 A.D. the imperial edict condemned them to death by burning at the stake. That tradition was carried throughout the middle ages and is the probable source of the term "faggot" as a perjorative word for homosexuals (Fisher: 107; The Gay Academic: 67-69).

In the United States the legal tradition goes back to a 1641 Massachusetts law which was later adopted by Connecticut, New Hampshire, New York, New Jersey, and Pennsylvania. In Europe, hundreds were actually executed under these laws, and the actual number may be far higher. In the U.S. three such executions have been documented, and on the basis of cursory searches of colonial records, one scholar estimates there were over two hundred executions during colonial times (Crompton, in The Gay Academic: 73).

Laws which regulate the sexual relations between consenting adults are by their very nature bound to be discriminatory at least in their enforcement.

Such laws would be laughable were it not for their tragic implications. Traditionally, in Massachusetts, the only legal form of sexual activity has been intercourse between a married husband and wife without contraceptives. It would be impossible and undesirable to apprehend the multitudes of people who have violated 272. Whatever enforcement is made will necessarily be discriminatory, against those few who were unlucky enough to get caught (Kyper, 1978: 401).

Another aspect of the discriminatory impact of those laws is that they enable the police to harass and sometimes to systematically "shake down" persons apprehended for homosexual behavior. As Fisher notes:

> If homosexual relations are a crime, than so are many related possibilities: loitering with intent to commit sodomy, conspiracy to commit sodomy, solicitation to engage in sodomy, etc. As if this were insufficient, vaguely worded state laws against outrageous or disorderly conduct, lewd or lascivious behavior, and conduct offensive to public morality broaden the powers of police even further. Some people consider homosexuals outrageous, lewd and offensive simply because they are homosexuals. Not the sodomy laws, but the broad range of these other laws whose interpretation is left to the discretion of the police, accounts for the numerous homosexuals with arrest records (:131).

In the United States, only five states have repealed laws against consensual sodomy between adults in private: Illinois, Connecticut, Colorado, Idaho, and Oregon. Most states still have numerous anti-homosexual laws with stiff penalties. In some states those penalties are comparable to those given for such crimes as manslaughter and murder. A maximum sentence for life imprisonment is provided for in three states, one of which--Georgia--makes it mandatory unless clemency is recommended. North Carolina reduced it to three years when an unfortunate homosexual was actually sentenced to life. Even the state legislature came to realize such a sentence was cruel and unusual. Yet three-fourths of the states still impose terms ranging from 10 to 20 years as maximum sentences for consensual sodomy. Only a handful of states have reduced the crime to a misdemeanor punishable by a fine or short-term imprisonment. Even fewer have removed such laws from the books altogether.

Even though such laws may be infrequently enforced, the impact of their being on the books is considerable. Police shakedowns have already been alluded to above. Another common practice is to arrest a homosexual, fail to prosecute, but "check with his employer" before releasing the individual. This practice fuels job discrimination and acts as a tremendous societal pressure which keeps many gays "in the closet."

Discriminatory enforcement contributes to the severe problems of police/homosexual relations in most cities. In large cities where a sizable gay ghetto exists, the relations between the police and the gay community range from poor to openly hostile. As the gay liberation movement became more radical, a degree of "straight backlash" surfaced. Violence against homosexuals increased, and the police refusal to protect homosexuals from violent attack--including attacks by roving gangs who randomly beat up homosexuals as a sort of sport--seemingly encouraged such open violence. Large city police departments, and more especially their vice-squads, have been selective and arbitrary in their enforcement of laws governing sexual behavior. The sodomy laws are often sources of police graft and corruption. Anti-homosexual attitudes are sometimes socialized within police systems. Police officers who may not have a strong bias against homosexuals when they first join the force acquire such attitudes during the institutionalized training procedures and the daily operation of the average precinct. It was the police hostility and violence during the Stonewall riots in 1969 that led to the start of the militant gay liberation movement. Homosexual minority members are decidedly second-class citizens in their treatment by the police, juries, judges--the entire judicial system and process.

Discrimination in employment is also pervasive. The fear of losing one's job is one of the most important pressures keeping gays in the closet. Certain jobs have become closely associated with the gay subculture: bookkeeping, dress design, window display, hair dressing, interior decorating, art, music, acting, radio work, religious service, nursing, and social work. Likewise, certain occupations are considered inappropriate or are jobs in which the sentiment is heaviest for immediate firing if one's homosexuality becomes open, and even if the "appearance of homosexuality" leads to a generally accepted if erroneous perception of one being a homosexual: the military, the police, and teaching or other professions which involve working with young children. The law clearly endorses the refusal to hire, or the firing of individuals, in such cases. Whereas groups such as blacks, women and Chicanos are "protected classes" of minorities when it comes to the enforcement of affirmative action programs, such a protective stance is decidedly not present when it comes to gays.

344

As with other minorities, gays suffer from a general discrimination in the mass media involving stereotyping. Many gays have experienced so severe a degree of hostility that they no longer have anything to do with straight society. They often develop as rigid and unappealing a stereotype of straight people as do the latter of gays. In fact, prejudice against gays still remains so pervasive in our society that the straight person who associates with homosexuals too closely runs the risk of becoming subject to the same discrimination as gay people suffer. The experience is akin to whites in the South during the 1940's and 1950's being called "nigger-lovers" if they supported the black minority in any visible way. This pervasive image problem affects gays from their earliest years on. Homosexuals are held up to be the incarnation of what is "queer," and such aberration packs an enormous emotional punch of the growing child so especially vulnerable to societal peer pressures during adolescent years. Deviation from the expected masculine role invites family, peers, and other significant individuals in the child's environment to try to pressure him/her back into more acceptable patterns of behavior. Stereotyping is pervasive in all but a few metropolitan areas where a more tolerant atmosphere has developed: New York, Los Angeles, San Francisco, Chicago, Washington, D.C., Minneapolis, and the like. In smaller cities, suburbs and rural areas of middle-America, the gay is not likely to experience any real integration, mutual acceptance, or even a modicum of respect.

It was this discrimination in jobs, housing, public accommodations and services, and the mass media's treatment of gays as pariahs that finally drove them to open political activism. Organized violence against gays, often including police harassment or police departmental condoning of the violence of others against them, led to the "coming out" of gays. Homosexuals began to leave the closet and join the gay liberation movement. Such "coming out" became a politically conscious act--a declaration to majority society that the gay person had a right to an open and public life free from discrimination and harassment.

Their political activity can be traced to the "homophile" organizations of the 1950's. Occasional outbreaks of anti-homosexual hysteria, such as the 1955-1956 incident in Boise, Idaho, which led to the arrest and imprisonment of a dozen or so men for terms ranging from six months to fifteen years, caused the pre-1969 homophile groups to seek a legalization of homosexuality between consenting adults. That was the only realistic goal the various gay student organizations were able to pursue at that stage of the struggle (Crew: 389-398).

The Mattachine Foundation, begun in Los Angeles in 1950, was the first real homosexual political organization, and in a sense, was the founder of the gay movement. New York's Mattachine organization spun off an action committee whose members formed the nucleus of the New Gay Liberation Front, begun in July of 1969, after the "Stonewall Rebellion." Homosexuals developed a militant interest in politics (Fisher: 186; Siminoski: 13-14).

The Gay Liberation Front spread quickly during 1970-1971, with several hundred chapters appearing in cities and colleges across the country. These chapters showed a typically radical and activist pattern. They split and fragmented over tactical questions, and many changed their emphasis from political action to consciousness raising, borrowed somewhat from the women's liberation movement. A more militant middle of the gay movement also emerged at this time--the Gay Activist Alliance which was first formed in 1969. Confrontation was viewed by this group as the best method to promote change. Members of the Alliance felt that gays had to become politically visible in order to become a meaningful force for change. That meant convincing the millions of gays to come out of the closet if they were to wield any political force for their own advantage. Until the recent activism, gays were effectively barred from public office. Discovery of an officeholder's homosexual tendency was sufficient grounds to demand his resignation or seal his failure to win re-election. That has begun to change somewhat, following the increased political activism of the Alliance.

The Gay Activist Alliance, comprised of numerous local chapters of various gay groups, has a wide agenda. It seeks to repeal all sodomy laws, laws against solicitation, and other laws used to justify police entrapment and enticement procedures. It seeks to end discrimination in jobs, housing, or public accommodations based on sexual orientation. It consciously attempts to manipulate the media--to reduce the negative stereotyped image, to recruit new activists, and to use the media to further its own political goals. Confrontational tactics, moreover, have media appeal.

The Alliance has used confrontation tactics to demonstrate their clout sufficiently to bring about some change. Using public demonstrations they refer to as ZAPS, the Gay Activist Alliance managed to get various bills introduced which extend human rights protections to homosexuals, and prohibition discrimination based on "sexual orientation."

Gays have openly and successfully backed local politicians in Washington, D.C., New York, Boston, and San Francisco. Their endorsement of a candidate is no longer the "kiss of death" in some cities. Indeed, they have been successful in helping to win election of an avowed homosexual. In 1974 Elaine Noble became the first acknowledged homosexual to win an election, in her case, to the Massachusetts House of Representatives. Her candidacy was strongly backed by the Homophile Union of Boston, the Student Homophile League, and the Daughters of Bilitis. The 1974 Massachusetts elections were important in demonstrating that gay support was not the political liability that many politicians feared it to be. Several pro-gay legislators were elected, and opponents were defeated in the primaries--including Attorney General Robert Quinn who was running for the governorship (The Gay Academic: 405). A gay city councilman was elected in San Francisco, and Mayor Barry of Washington, D. C. won both election and re-election with strong and vocal gay support. Generally the gay vote has been liberal Democratic because that party has been more openly supportive of the civil rights movement--including civil rights for gays.

A degree of anti-gay backlash has appeared in the late 1970´s. The Roman Catholic Church and most Protestant fundamentalist sects are adamantly opposed to the Gay Liberation Movement. The Moral Majority has been a leading proponent of campaigns, several of which have been successful, to repeal local gay rights ordinances. Anita Bryant launched a successful one in Florida which, for a time, took on national prominence, the "Save Our Children" Movement. Her campaign led to the repeal of an ordinance barring discrimination against homosexuals in Dade County, Florida, in 1978.

Similar repeals were passed that year in St. Paul, Minnesota, Whichita, Kansas, and Eugene, Oregon. In 1977 Florida passed a state law against homosexual marriages or the adoption of children by homosexuals. In Massachusetts, a bill that would have banned discrimination against homosexuals in public employment was defeated. The United Presbyterian Church voted against sanctioning the ordination of avowed, practicing homosexuals. The New York Supreme Court upheld a law making homosexual acts by consenting adults in private a crime. In California, a law was introduced calling for the firing of teachers, teacher's aids, school administrators, and counselors for "advocating, soliciting, imposing, or encouraging or promoting private or public sexual acts defined in the penal code between persons of the same sex" (C.Q. The Rights Revolution: 3-6). A 1979 Gallop Poll found that 65 percent of the general public favored excluding homosexuals from being elementary school teachers, and 54 percent favored excluding them as members of the clergy. When asked if homosexual acts between consenting adults in private was legal, 43 percent said yes, 43 percent said no, and 14 percent had no opinion (Ibid: 6).

A "Gay Bill of Rights" measure has been introduced into Congress but has been effectively "killed" in committee. The bill would outlaw discrimination against homosexuals in employment, education, housing, and public accommodations. The sponsor's approach to the bill is to argue it would protect the civil rights of gays just as those rights are protected for women, blacks, and religious groups. Sponsored by 52 members of Congress, it has the endorsement of the American Bar Association, the National Council of Churches, and the American Federation of Teachers. It was targeted for defeat by such groups as the Moral Majority, the National Pro-Family Coalition, and the Christian Voice Moral Government Fund. These groups fear that its passage would lead to the "molestations of thousands of children" by sexual deviates, if passed. They argue it would "force" churches to hire gay ministers; and local schools to hire gay teachers, coaches, and counselors, and would "force" every family business to hire sodomites. In testifying against the bill before the House Subcommittee in which it was killed, the National Pro-Family Coalition said:

Mere orientation is not the issue. Overt sexual behavior is the issue...What we are advocating is that our right to privacy must be respected: that the homosexual life-style not be flaunted in our neighborhoods and shouted from the house tops. The public has a right to be protected from the promotion and glamorization of everything that is by its nature antithetical to the social order ("Dying Gay Bill of Rights Stirs Hot Debate on Hill," The Washington Post, January 28, 1982: A-2).

Despite these setbacks and backlash reactions, the 1980's are likely to show increasing militancy and diversity in the gay rights movement. The Gay Activist Alliance will increasingly attempt to use both confrontationist politics (e.g. the demonstrations at the Democratic National Convention in San Francisco in 1984), as well as standard electoral behavior to pursue its goals. At the same time, a rising sentiment for gay separation is growing within the gay movement and the gay population at large. That tactical approach is more likely to be favored by the radical left faction of the Gay Liberation Front (Fisher: 227). In any event, gays are more than ever "coming out" and using political tactics to cope with their everyday lives in which the experience of discrimination is still evident. The recent political awakening and the employment of the various tactical approaches discussed above are also characteristic of the newest wave of immigrant groups, to whom we now turn our attention.

The "Newest" Immigrant Groups

Having previously reviewed minorities based on immigrant status prior to World War II, we will here discuss those groups who are ascribed minority status on the basis of national origin which have migrated here since World War II--our "newest" immigrants. This period is characterized by a new pattern of immigration, comprised of the following mixture in status of persons entering the United States: 1) immigrants, 2) refugees, and 3) temporary or undocumented aliens (more commonly called "wetbacks") [1].

"Refugees" became a distinct status during the period immediately after World War II which continues to the present. These are people who flee in large groups, literally hundreds of thousands, fleeing political or religious persecution. Immigrants come in on an individual basis, within the legal (and previously under the quota) system. The illegal or undocumented aliens are individuals who come for economic reasons, but do so outside the law. These distinctions developed after World War II as our nation struggled with allowing asylum for those fleeing the ravages of a war-torn Europe and/or communism, yet maintaining our more restrictive immigration policy. The illegals, escaping the economic poverty of their native lands, poured across our easily penetrated borders.

In essence, the 1924 immigration laws (and subsequent revisions), by establishing a strict quota system, built up tensions between our traditional value of providing asylum for the oppressed with the desires of domestic economic policy to restrict in influx of cheap labor. In the 1930´s immigration was just over one-half million for the entire decade. That meant a dramatic drop from the more than four million of the previous decade. The Great Depression and the restrictive immigration laws accounted for the precipitous decline.

Our refugee policy began with the persecution by Hitler and continued throughout the decade of the 1930´s as displaced persons from a war-torn Europe sought asylum here. We allowed 250,000 refugees from Nazi persecution to enter the country prior to our involvement in the war in 1941. It was the Displaced Persons Act of 1948, however, that constituted the first specific refugee law enacted by Congress. That law, and its several revisions, admitted nearly one-half million displaced persons in a three-year period by "mortgaging" future immigration quotas. Poles accounted for nearly one-third of that total, followed by Germans. Immigration in the 1940´s virtually doubled the previous decade´s numbers, going from 528,431 to 1,035,039.

In terms of numbers, the "temporary workers" category was far more important and changed the character of the incoming minorities. Countries of the Western Hemisphere sent millions of temporary workers to the United States during the 1940´s and 1950´s. Mexico alone sent between four and five million temporary agricultural workers (the braceros) between 1942 and

1964. Large numbers also came from the Bahamas, Jamaica, Barbados, British Honduras, Canada, and Newfoundland. The World War II and Korean War-influenced economy created a demand for these workers. Strict immigration laws did not allow for sufficient flexibility to permit their entrance as regular immigrants, nor would it provide sufficient numbers to meet the need for laborers.

In 1952 the Immigration and Naturalization Act was passed. It constituted a significant revision of the existing law. It also reflected the "cold-war, anti-communist" atmosphere of the time. While it continued to impose quotas and was still restrictionist in nature, its limitations were governed more by a sense of sociological theory of the time relating to cultural assimilation than to the repudiated theories of racial superiority. The 1952 law relaxed the restrictions against Asian immigration, allowing them a small quota. It maintained the national origin quota system, but also established a selection preference system: 1) 50 percent of each nation's quota was allocated first to aliens with high education or exceptional abilities; and 2) the remaining three categories were allocated among specified relatives of U.S. citizens or permanent resident aliens. This four-point selection system became the antecedent of the current system, which places a higher priority on family reunification than on needed skills. The law still favored Northern and Western European nations. As in the 1920's, the Western Hemisphere was not subject to numerical limitations.

Over two and one-half million immigrants entered during the decade of the 1950's, but less than half of those under the formal quota system. Many of the others entered under special refugee laws, or as nonquota immigrants (that is; from Western Hemisphere nations). This led to the realization that a major revision in the nation's immigration policy was needed.

The Refugee Relief Act of 1953 and its amendments of 1954 authorized the admission of 214,000 refugees from Europe and "escapees" from Communist-dominated nations. Italians comprised 30 percent of those admitted under the act, followed by Germans, Yugoslavs, and Greeks. The inclusion of the category, "escapees," defined as persons fleeing persecution in Communist or Middle-East countries, allowed 29,000 to enter; led by Hungarians, Koreans, Yugoslavs, and Chinese. In addition, this law repealed the quota system deductions previously required by the "mortgages" incurred under the Displaced Persons Act of 1948.

This same trend continued into the early 1960's, and subsequently under the Immigration and Nationality Act of 1965. Nearly 20,000 refugees entered under the provisions of the Fair Share Law of 1960. It enabled the U.S. to share in the international effort to close the refugee camps of Europe which still held persons displaced by World War II. Under this law, the U.S. accepted one-fourth of the total number of refugees resettled.

The Immigration and Nationality Act of 1965 represented the most significant revision of immigration policy since the 1921-1924 quota laws. The 1965 law replaced the quota system based on nationality or ethnic considerations with a system based on the reunification of families or the attraction of persons with needed job skills. This major revision of the law reflected the values of the 1960's civil rights movement just as the 1952 Act had reflected the Cold-War era. Under the 1965 law, total immigration was fixed at 170,000 annually, with a 20,000 limit per country. It developed a seven-category preference system for distribution within those limits. It further provided for a total annual ceiling for Western Hemisphere immigration of 120,000 but without a per country limit or preference system.

A 1976 revision of that law extended the 20,000 per-country limit and a somewhat revised seven-category preference system to the Western Hemisphere, under a separate ceiling of 170,000 for Eastern Hemisphere nations and 120,000 for the Western Hemisphere. In 1978 they were combined into a single total ceiling of 290,000 with a single preference system. The Refugee Act of 1980 eliminated refugees as a separate category within the preference system and reduced the world-wide ceiling to 270,000, exclusive of refugees.

The ups and downs in immigration followed dramatically the various revisions in U.S. policy. Figure 10 shows the trends in the number of immigrants as they shift up and down due to these policy shifts or other significant social and economic forces .

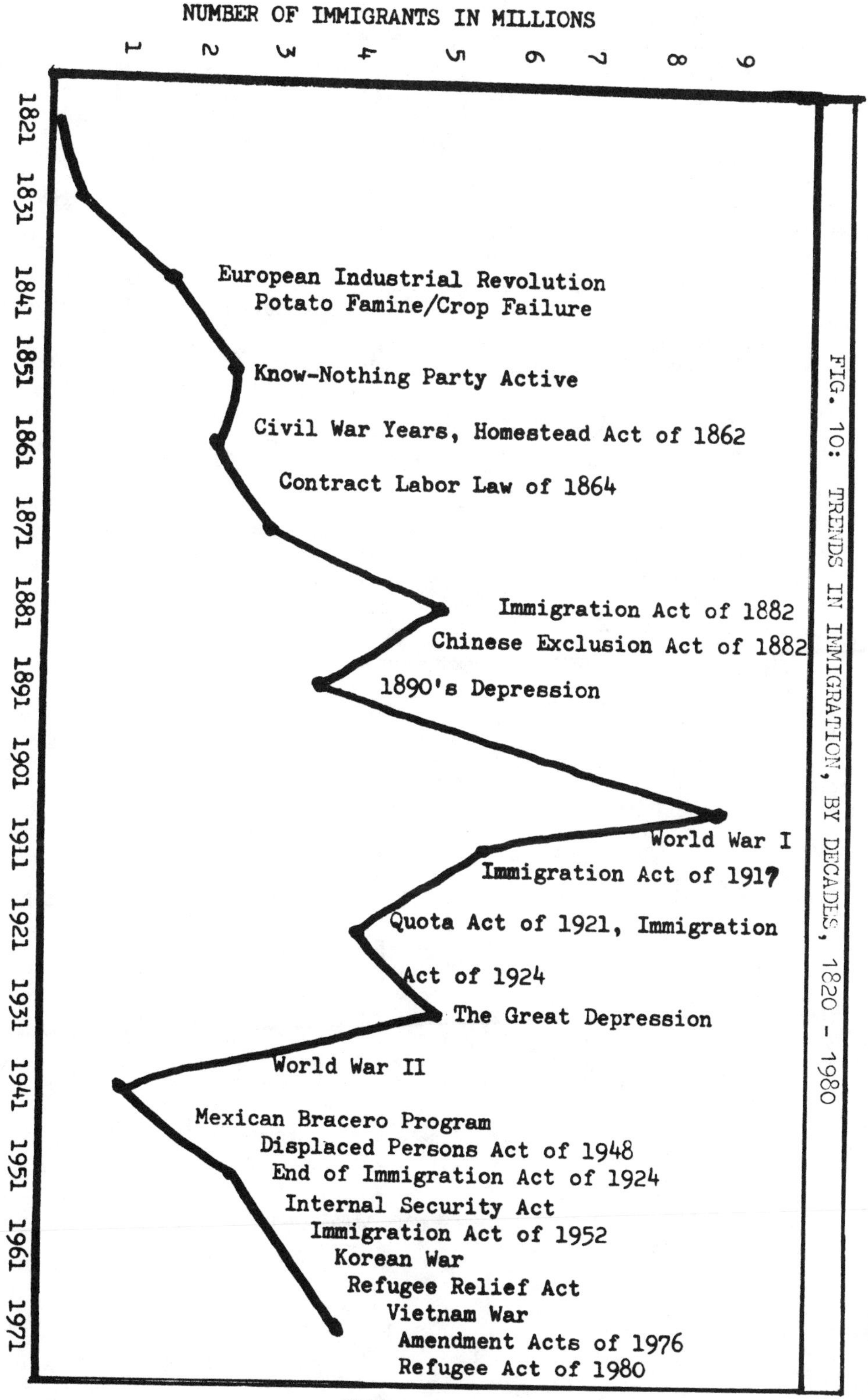

NUMBER OF IMMIGRANTS IN MILLIONS

1 2 3 4 5 6 7 8 9

1821
1831
1841
1851
1861
1871
1881
1891
1901
1911
1921
1931
1941
1951
1961
1971

European Industrial Revolution
Potato Famine/Crop Failure

Know-Nothing Party Active

Civil War Years, Homestead Act of 1862

Contract Labor Law of 1864

Immigration Act of 1882
Chinese Exclusion Act of 1882

1890's Depression

World War I
Immigration Act of 1917
Quota Act of 1921, Immigration
Act of 1924
The Great Depression

World War II

Mexican Bracero Program
Displaced Persons Act of 1948
End of Immigration Act of 1924
Internal Security Act
Immigration Act of 1952
Korean War
Refugee Relief Act
Vietnam War
Amendment Acts of 1976
Refugee Act of 1980

FIG. 10: TRENDS IN IMMIGRATION, BY DECADES, 1820 – 1980

Since the ending of the quota system, immigration to the U.S. has also shifted from Europe to Latin America and Asia. Figure 11 shows the shift from the decade of the mid-1950´s to the mid-1970´s. In the latter decade, North and Central American countries and Asian nations predominate. The North and Central American influx increased by more than 43 percent over the previous decade. The Asian immigration rose spectacularly: an increase of 369 percent (remember, its base was small due to the Asian exclusionary policy prior to 1952). That was from 224,342 immigrants from Asian countries during the 1956-1965 period to 1,052,688 during the 1967-1976 period. This contrasts sharply with a <u>decline</u> in European immigration, which fell by 27 percent. The dominance of North/Central American and of Asian immigration reversed a trend of almost two centuries of immigration to the United States! By the late 1970´s, legal immigration was 34% Asian, 44% Latin American, and only 15% European (McClellan: 28).

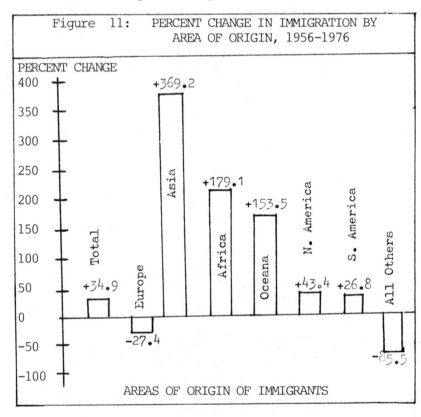

Figure 11: PERCENT CHANGE IN IMMIGRATION BY AREA OF ORIGIN, 1956-1976

The 1970´s and 1980´s have witnessed a continued struggle in U.S. immigration policy to stem the tide of influx into the nation yet to cope with the problem of refugees and illegal aliens. After years of low numbers, the INS began reporting ever-rising numbers of apprehended deportable aliens--over one million in 1978, just under the all-time high of 1,089,583 apprehended in 1954 (U.S. News and World Report, January, 1979: 38).

The number of illegal aliens in the country has been estimated between 3 and 6 million. Their major impact has been an economic one--allegedly affecting the labor market by displacing workers, depressing wages, and deteriorating working conditions. The economic imbalance between the U.S. and the nations of origin (e.g. Mexico, Haiti) is the driving force behind their annual flow into the U.S. by the hundreds of thousands.

The Refugee Act of 1980 repealed the ideological and geographical limitations which had previously favored refugees fleeing from communist countries or from the Middle-East and redefined "refugees" as persons who are unwilling or unable to return to their country of origin because of persecution on account of race, religion, nationality, membership in a particular social group, or political opinion. It revised the ceiling upward to 50,000. An additional 14,000 Indochinese refugees per month were allowed to enter under a separate United Nation´s Conference agreement (McClellan: 23).

The concern over the refugee question was heightened by the new migration of some 117,000 Cuban boat people. The problem was especially depressing since the potential size of the refugee migration was so immense. As of 1980 there were approximately 15 1/2 million refugees world-wide. They were distributed as follows: 7 million Asians, 4 million Africans, 3 million from the Middle-East nations, 1.2 million from various Western Hemisphere nations (Cuba, Haiti, El Salvadore), and about 300,000 Europeans (McClellan: 10). Obviously, the U.S. cannot absorb all those refugees. The Indochinese were entering at a rate of 14,000 per month in 1980, and Cuban and Haitians were coming in at a rate of 3,000 per month. In 1980 an estimated one million persons entered the U.S., some 700,000 of whom did so outside the regular immigration process.

The number of persons formally presenting themselves at all U.S. ports of entry every year--some counted many times on various trips--is a staggering 250 million! That figure exceeds the total population of the U.S. To decide whether to admit each of these 250 million people and then to enforce its rules, the Immigration and Naturalization Service (INS) has a total staff of less than half the number of police officers in New York City (Crewdson: 1983). This massive influx, especially of new immigrants from Asia, the Middle-East, and Latin America has resurrected a renewed anti-immigration movement. Some fear the newcomers and have expressed that fear in new forms of negative invective against them: "rug riders" for the Arabs, "pineapples" for the Somoans, and so on (Newsweek:27). Some of the fear relates simply to the huge numbers and what they will do to our nation's economy, its birth rate, and coping with the population increase of that magnitude. As of 1980, some 375,000 Indochinese, 900,000 Cubans, and 100,000 Haitians entered the U.S. as "refugees"-- including the "Freedom Flotilla" of 123,000 Cubans in 1980 itself. They cost the U.S. government some 1 billion dollars in direct aid. That raised renewed fear and opposition. A 1980 Roper Poll found that 80 percent of the population favored cutbacks in our immigration quotas (McClellan: 45-56).

The Haitian refugees, being "economic" rather than religious or political, caused the greatest political/legal problems and aroused the severest reactions. The Refugee Act of 1980 created a specific legal status to deal with their influx: a new category of parole "entrant status." This provided a way of granting temporary refuge to the Haitians without having to determine whether they are political or economic refugees--and without altering the government's treatment of the Cubans. The "entrant status" enabled the Haitians to be given employment authorization, as well as access to certain federal benefits such as supplementary social security income, Medicaid, aid to dependent children, and emergency assistance (McClellan: 91).

For our purposes, the refugee status distinction is an important one for more than the numbers who may or may not be allowed to enter. Groups which immigrated here under that status received far different treatment and show a different acculturation/assimilation pattern than did the regular immigrants. In general, their experiences here are made far easier on the basis of their special "refugee" status, and they assimilate more rapidly than do other groups.

The Hungarian refugees, for instance, were aided by a special White House Committee to assist their resettlement. Various local government, church, and service organizations and numerous business groups aided them in finding jobs, housing, and adjusting to their new life in America. Several millions of dollars were spent by government and private groups to assist these "Freedom Fighters," who were hailed as hero and warmly welcomed into many communities, concentrating in New York, New Jersey, Pennsylvania, and Ohio where there were already many Hungarian-Americans who settled there during the 1880-1920 era.

The Cuban refugees, as we have seen, were aided by special legislation and government resettlement programs. Those Cubans have been highly successful as a group. In part, their success is due to their middle-class status when first coming here, but also is the result of the special status and aid accorded them because of their being "refugees from communism."

A similar success story emerges with respect to the Soviet Jews who came during the 1970´s. Some 200,000 Soviet Jews emigrated during that decade, about 81,000 of whom came to the United States rather than going to Israel. As political and religious refugees from a communist nation, they received special status and aid in resettlement. In New York City, the Brighton Beach area on the southern tip of Brooklyn next to Coney Island came to be known as the "Odessa on the Atlantic." About one-third of its 50,000 residents are Russian Jews who have settled here in the last five years, a few of whom have already achieved the status of being millionaires.

According to the 1980 census data, New York City is home to some 400,000 Asians. They include Chinese, Koreans, Vietnamese, Cambodians, Laotians, Thais, Filipinos, and some Japanese. They exhibit another aspect of the difference between the "newest" immigrants of the post-World War II era and other older immigrants. They came as refugees from a war-torn or communist country and therefore had no "sojourner" attitude. They had no homes to look back to with the hope of ever returning. This psychologically enables them to bear

357

temporary conditions of an extreme nature in order to achieve the success they are so highly motivated to acquire.

Political and religious refugees, being suddenly faced with emigration, are also more likely, as a group, to be middle-class and upper-class in their occupations. This often gives them an edge in job skills over previous immigrant groups, whom as we have seen were also low in literacy and job skills. The Vietnamese provide an excellent "case study" of this special type of refugee settlement experience.

In 1975 the United States absorbed some 130,000 Vietnamese refugees. An Office of Refugee Resettlement was established within the Department of Health and Human Resources. Congress designed and funded an Indochina Refugee Assistance Program. These refugees fled here because, with the collapse of their American-backed government, they had to flee. Our country was willing to accept them and aid them because we felt an obligation to do so. The influx was generally well-educated persons: two-thirds of them held white-collar status jobs in Vietnam. A breakdown of their occupational status shows that 24 percent had professional, technical, or managerial backgrounds--including over 7 percent medical professionals, 17 percent in transportation, 12 percent from clerical sales backgrounds, and only 5 percent farmers and fishermen (Montero: 23). As with the Hungarians, local groups sponsored the placement and resettlement of Vietnamese. Subsequently, however, they have tended to cluster together in ethnic enclaves, especially in New York, Dallas, New Orleans, San Francisco, and Los Angeles. Forty percent of the Vietnamese now reside in California (Montero: 61).

They have shown a rapid socio-economic improvement in their conditions. Their political awareness and assimilation has also been faster than previous Asian immigrant groups.

The Tai Dam (Vietnamese) are frank about their own belief--which runs to animism and ancestor worship--and pragmatic about their children, enrolling them in Baptist and Methodist churches. They have quickly caught on to the secret of minority political power, which is to place their own people on the public

agencies that serve them: Houng Baccam, one
of the Tai Dam leaders, works for the Iowa
Refugee Center and Des Moines´ Central
Advisory Board. His third job is one of the
managers of Tai Dam Industries, which produces
leather key cases. Other Tai Dam work in
factories and private or government offices.
They may not be members of country clubs yet,
but they have founded the Society of Tai Dam-
American Friendship. "The more I have
materially," says Baccam, who is 39 and
married with three children, "the more
relationships I have with Americans, the
happier I become" (Newsweek: 29-30).

Montero´s (1979) study of the Vietnamese
resettlement stresses the more rapid assimilation of the
refugees than previous Asian groups. He accounts for
that difference by the transition assistance afforded by
the temporary relocation camp experiences followed by a
phase of private sponsorship (:59).

The Haitians offer a decidedly contrasting
experience. Although now given some legal status, they
were first treated as illegal immigrants. Their
motivation for coming is far different than the
"refugees," and their reception here is even more so.
They have been pouring into Florida since 1972. Their
legal status was kept clouded for years as the
Administration grappled with the question of what to do
with them. Since the State Department considered them
to be purely "economic refugees" fleeing dire poverty,
they were not accepted as were the Cubans, Hungarians,
or Vietnamese. Their largely illiterate and unskilled
backgrounds ill-prepared them for assimilation into the
American economy or culture. Even after being released
from their detention camps, the Haitians were not
assisted as other refugee groups had been. Their
illiteracy, poverty, poor work-skills, and language
problems made them easily exploitable, and they have
lived in near slave-like conditions as migrant workers.

The Haitians were often perceived to be a special
threat to the labor market, and their acceptance has
thus been more problematic than other refugee groups.
Just how negative an effect they have on the job market
is a disputed point.

Haitians are but one of several groups of illegal immigrants. They generally work in agriculture, including the Mexican "indocumentados" or "wetbacks," or in restaurants and hotels. Their total number is estimated at 3 to 6 million. In addition to Haiti, they come from Cuba, the Dominican Republic, Hong Kong, the Philippines, and some sixty percent from Mexico. Many scholars argue that the tendency of the illegal immigrants to concentrate at the lower-job levels limits their effects on depressing wages, but they do seem to agree that the migrants tend to lower working conditions by causing a return to the "sweatshop" type of conditions (see McClellan: 31).

John Crewdson (1983) argues that the _real_ threat to U.S. jobs is from _visa abusers_, that is, from the more educated, articulate students, semi-skilled workers and professionals who come in legally to study or vacation, and then overstay their permits. Some remain in the United States permanently. They stay at an estimated rate of one-half million per year. These persons are more likely to take the white-collar and better paying jobs that are more desirable to U.S. workers. Despite this trend, U.S. embassies and consulates grant visas on what Crewdson characterizes as a haphazard basis. The INS, stretched so thin as to approach transparency, simply cannot cope with the situation. He goes on to point out the potential corruptive effect of the situation. The ABSCAM bribery scandal involved fake Arabs seeking special immigration "help" from the members of Congress who were not surprised that their help was worth literally thousands of dollars.

For the millions of illegal immigrants who make it inside our borders, their illegal status poses additional system-corrupting problems. The illegal aliens fall prey to lawyers, dishonest landlords, and phony "immigration consultants." They are sometimes forced into near-slavery in those industries where they are more heavily employed: the clothing, food, and electronic industries which depend on their cheap labor to keep prices down. The exploiters find the illegal immigrants to be easy marks since their fear of deportation keeps them from complaining about being exploited.

Crewdson argues that many of the illegals are providing a useful service. They pay taxes but seldom claim refunds or medical benefits. They work hard in positions few others want to fill, sometimes helping to create higher paid jobs for the native workers, for example becoming the hod carrier for the brickmason. They are providing this generation's human fuel for development, a role traditionally performed by our nation's immigrants.

Their large scale influx during a time of economic recession, as in the early 1980's however, has led to considerable conflict among the various minorities, particularly Asians and blacks. Asians often serve as "middle-man minorities," serving as small business proprietors in black neighborhoods. Others have often served that role--before the Koreans and Vietnamese of today, Jews, Armenians, Greeks, Japanese, and Chinese have all performed that function. But tensions, violence and crime between such middle-man shopowners and the blacks in the neighborhoods they serve have been exacerbated by the recently extraordinarily high rates of black unemployment.

These newest minorities vary and conflict both politically and economically. The "refugee" groups have typically been better educated, organized and equipped to acculturate into the nation's job-market structure. Their special status has meant the majority was more willing to accept them. They received special aid easing their transition into majority society. Their assimilation has been more rapid than the immigrant groups which entered under the old quota system. By contrast, the illegals have been at the mercy of an economic system which exploits them due to their poor education and lack of organization. They remain at the lowest levels of society, living in a social and cultural world largely apart from the majority society. They lack any political voice because of their illegal status. The majority society's members mostly reject them as persons who, at best, will lower wages and depress working conditions, and, at worst, will swell the ranks of criminals and the violent.

The diversity among these newest minorities contributes to their internal conflicts with one another, as well as with the majority. The renewed massiveness of their influx has resurrected nativist sentiment against unrestricted immigration, and raises anew a complex set of questions concerning the issue of immigration policy (2).

1) Do we as a nation have an obligation to accept the oppressed of the entire world?

2) Is there a realistic way of dealing with the problems of so many illegal aliens already in our country?

3) Can we effectively prevent other illegals from entering in the future?

4) Can we guard against illegal entry without compromising our standards of human rights by unconstitutional surveillance, the questionable use of identity cards, or sweeping "raids" on places of employment?

5) If limits are set on the total number allowed to enter, who decides who gets in or who does not? On what basis will those decisions be made?

6) Is it equitable to welcome Cubans who flee a communist regime we oppose and discourage the Haitians who flee a dictatorship with whom we still maintain diplomatic relations?

7) Can we afford to accept all who so desperately want to enter the U.S.?

As of this writing, the Senate and the House of Representatives have each passed somewhat different versions of an Administration-backed bill, the Simpson-Mazzoli Act, to revise the nation's immigration laws. This measure represents the most substantial revision of those laws since 1965. New to the approach in both versions of this bill is the setting of <u>stiff fines and prison terms for employers who knowingly hire illegal aliens</u> (although the administration dropped its original plan to mandate "identity cards."). The new law would also grant amnesty to the millions of illegals already in the country. It sets a new total ceiling of 425,000 immigrants per year, not counting refugees. It retains the limit of no more than 20,000 from any one nation—except Canada and Mexico for which the limit would be 40,000 each. The Democratic Party, at its 1984 National Convention, opposed passage of the law. President Reagan, in an appeal to the Hispanic voters who generally are strongly opposed to the law, has now indicated he would not sign the bill as it is currently written. Whether the conference committee can manage a compromise version of the two bills which would be acceptable to the President and/or to the Democrats is problematic at this time. Nonetheless, the chances are good that after the 1984 Presidential election some type of revised immigration law will be passed and signed into law.

Chapter Endnotes

1. This entire section draws upon "A Brief History of U.S. Immigration Policy," a staff report (80-223-EPW) by Joyce Vialet, dated December 22, 1980 for the Select Commission on Immigration and Refugee Policy. See also, John Crewdson, The Tarnished Door: The New Immigrants and the Transformation of America (New York: Times Books, 1983); and Grant McClellan (ed.), Immigrants, Refugees and U.S. Policy (New York: H. W. Wilson, 1981).

2. See, "Closing the Golden Door," Time, May 18, 1981: 24; "Right Versus Right: Immigration and Refugee Policy in the United States," Foreign Affairs, Fall, 1980; and "The New Immigrants: American Dream, American Nightmare," The New York Times Sound Filmstrip on Current Affairs, (New York: The New York Times, 1981: 12-13).

Additional Readings

Annals of the American Academy of Political and Social Sciences (September, 1974).

Burke, Mary P. Reaching for Justice: The Women's Movement (Washington, D. C.: Center for Concern, 1980).

Crewdson, John. The Tarnished Door (New York: Times Books, 1983).

Congressional Quarterly. The Rights Revolution (Washington, D.C. Congressional Quarterly, 1979).

_____ The Women's Movement: Agenda for the '80's (Washington, D.C., The Congressional Quarterly, 1981).

Fisher, Peter. The Gay Mystique (New York: Stein and Day, 1972).

Karla, Jay and Allen Young (eds.). Out of the Closet: Voices of Gay Liberation (New York: Douglas Books, 1972).

Kyper, John in Louie Crew (ed.). The Gay Academic (Palm Springs, California: ETC Publications, 1978).

McClellan, Grant S. (ed.). Immigrants, Refugees and U.S. Policy (New York: H. W. Wilson, 1981).

Montero, Darell. Vietnamese Americans (Boulder, Colorado: Westview Press, 1979).

"The Graying of America," Newsweek, February 28, 1977: 50-65.

CHAPTER NINE: AREAS OF MINORITY/MAJORITY CONFLICT

Introduction

Whenever a majority and minority culture come into intimate and sustained contact with one another, a degree of conflict is inevitable. Certain public policy areas move to the forefront of relations between the two cultures. A minority group can be seen to be ascribed minority status in a given society because it manifestly lacks the political power to influence certain policy areas to its benefit or by its inability to restrain certain factions of majority society from using public policy to its detriment. Majority society employs public policy to treat the members of the minority in a negatively differential manner. That is, majority society develops a degree of <u>structured</u> and <u>institutionalized</u> <u>discrimination</u> against the minority which is reflected in certain public policies.

Likewise, when a minority group seeks to cope with and change its minority status, whether through accommodation, separatism, or radicalism, it must do so by using these strategies to influence public policies or their impact upon themselves. A number of public policy areas can be viewed as the forefront areas of conflict in minority/majority relations.

While virtually any policy area can be used by the majority society to "keep a minority in its place," and while the minority may seek to influence any number of policy areas as being more likely to respond to its particular needs, capabilities or resources, this chapter will focus on six major policy areas that have traditionally figured most prominently in minority/majority relations. Specifically, it will deal with: 1) education, 2) employment, 3) foreign policy, 4) housing, 5) law enforcement, and 6) political participation.

Each of these policy areas will be discussed briefly. The chapter will highlight how aspects of each area have been used by some faction(s) of the majority society to discriminate against the minority groups prevalent in American society, and how some minority groups have sought to influence those policy areas in such a manner as to redress their minority status and mitigate related problems. Once a portion of majority society becomes convinced that a "problem" exists and change must be forthcoming, they will advocate or support specific proposals for change in one or more of these areas.

365

Since education is one of the most fundamental processes necessary for the assimilation of any group into society, it is to that policy area we will first turn our attention. We will briefly examine past and continuing patterns of discrimination in education and then discuss the policy attempts to integrate education in American schools.

Education

Of all the policy areas of critical import to minority/majority relations, none is more basic nor significant in its impact than the educational one. Discrimination against minorities in educational opportunities is the primary method by which minority status is enforced, since poorer educational background in turn influences occupational and income opportunities, related housing options, and the social status of the individual.

Segregation in schools has been the most pronounced and long standing form of institutionalized discrimination used against minorities. The segregation of the Indians within special reservation schools has already been discussed in Chapter Five. So too, the segregation of Chinese and Japanese students in the 1880's to 1920's in California has been cited. These incidents exemplify de jure segregation; that is, formal segregation based upon law. The most significant example--both in terms of numbers and impact--of de jure segregation in education has been directed against Black Americans.

Despite the Fourteenth Amendment the Reconstruction effort had clearly failed by 1877. The Southern states increasingly enacted "Jim Crow" laws which legally segregated all aspects of life, including education, and effectively kept blacks in second-class citizenship status. Although the Fourteenth Amendment states: "No State shall make or enforce any law which shall abridge the privileges or immunities of citizens of the United States; nor shall any State deprive any person of life, liberty or property, without due process of law; nor any person within its jurisdiction the equal protection of the law..." the Supreme Court had ruled state laws segregating the races were constitutional as long as persons in each of the segregated races were protected equally. This "separate but equal" doctrine became the Court's interpretation of the Fourteenth Amendment with the 1896 case of Plessy v. Ferguson (163 U.S. 537).

In essence, this doctrine gave a constitutional blessing to de jure segregation--Jim Crow laws. It led to extensive segregation of all facilities, especially public schools. Such segregated facilities, particularly the schools, were seldom if ever equal in reality. Black schools (as were the Indian and Asian schools out west) were poorer in physical facilities: dilapidated and overcrowded buildings, smaller libraries and gyms, no pools, less audio-visual equipment, antiquated books, and the like. Moreover, such schools were given fewer supplies; their teachers were paid lower salaries, and their faculties were less qualified. Most such schools were restricted in their curriculum (Dye, 1971: 24).

The following map graphically portrays the status of de jure segregation as of 1954. Seventeen states required segregation of the races by law: Alabama, Arkansas, Delaware, Florida, Georgia, Kentucky, Louisiana, Maryland, Mississippi, Missouri, North Carolina, Oklahoma, South Carolina, Tennessee, Texas, Virginia, and West Virginia. Even Congress required segregation in the public schools of the District of Columbia. Four other states--Arizona, Kansas, New Mexico, and Wyoming--had enabling laws which allowed local schools to impose segregation or not. Only sixteen states prohibited segregation: Colorado, Connecticut, Idaho, Illinois, Indiana, Iowa, Massachusetts, Michigan, Minnesota, New Jersey, New York, Ohio, Pennsylvania, Rhode Island, Washington, and Wisconsin. Eleven other states were simply silent on the matter: California, Maine, Montana, Nebraska, Nevada, New Hampshire, North Dakota, Oregon, South Dakota, Utah, and Vermont.

The NAACP led the fight to overturn Plessy and to end de jure segregation. They attempted to use federal power, via the Supreme Court, to overrule the state laws. Prior to the 1950's they achieved very limited success: two cases in which the Court ruled that blacks must be admitted to white law schools because comparable black law school facilities were not available (Missouri ex rel. Gaines v. Canada, in 1938, and Sepuel v. University of Oklahoma, in 1948).

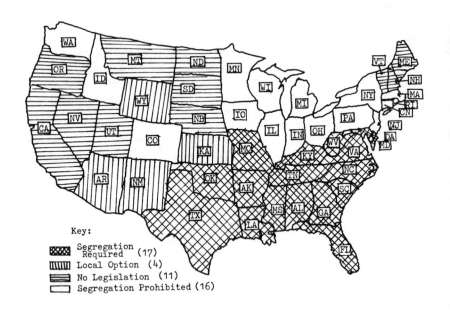

Figure 12: SEGREGATION LAWS IN THE U.S. IN 1954

Key:
- Segregation Required (17)
- Local Option (4)
- No Legislation (11)
- Segregation Prohibited (16)

The first real dent in the separate but equal doctrine´s wall of separation came with the Sweatt v. Painter case of 1950. Although the Court refused to overturn Plessy directly, it ordered the admission of black students to the University of Texas law school on the grounds that the segregated professional school was necessarily unequal. The Court´s test of "true equality" included such factors as the reputation and experience of the faculty and the school´s traditions, prestige, and standing in the community. Nonetheless, the Court stopped short of a full reversal of Plessy. A question remained as to whether such tests--virtually impossible to meet-- would also apply to the primary and secondary school levels. The decision did lead to immediate and significant improvements in black schools in the South, as Southern states scrambled to upgrade their black schools to come closer to apparent equality in conditions and facilities.

The NAACP pressed on seeking a frontal assault on Plessy. They backed litigation in five border area school districts where the conditions were fairly equal (Delaware, D.C., Kansas, South Carolina, Virginia). They were seeking a ruling that would uphold their contention that segregation per se was unconstitutional. On May 17, 1954 the Court so ruled in its famous Brown v. Board of Education of Topeka, Kansas decision. The Brown case case was historic in several respects. Not only was Plessy overturned, but, in arriving at its decision, the Court deliberately underplayed the importance of legal precedent. Instead, the Court used social and psychological evidence to determine the detrimental effects of segregation on black children. The decision stated that in the field of public education, the doctrine of separate but equal had no place. Such facilities were inherently unequal. The Court held that segregation laws deprived those segregated of the equal protection of the laws guaranteed by the Fourteenth Amendment.

The ruling became a watershed case. Just as Plessy gave its constitutional underpinning to segregation based on the "separate but equal doctrine," the Brown ruling that segregation was "inherently unequal" gave the constitutional basis to overturning all such Jim Crow legislation. The Court then moved rather swiftly to end legal segregation in transportation, public parks, playgrounds, golf courses, and bathing beaches.

The ruling, however, did not end segregation in schools. It did strike the death knell for de jure segregation. The victory in the Court, moreover, precipitated the black civil rights movement. It legitimated their concerns and protests over second-class citizenship implicit in a segregated society. It sparked the use of mass political protest actions to seek true equality in public and private life. While the significance of the historic decision was tremendous--in a single blow it struck down the laws of 21 states and the District--its effects were far less immediate or dramatic. In allowing for its implimentation to proceed "with all deliberate speed," the Court opened the door to the use of litigation, obstruction, and delays by those states which chose to resist desegregation.

Nine states and the District of Columbia generally decided not to resist desegregation and progress proceeded fairly well in those places. By 1964 over half the black children in those states--Arizona, Delaware, Kansas, Kentucky, Maryland, Missouri, New Mexico, Oklahoma, and West Virginia--were attending integrated schools (Dye, 1978: 50). The eleven states of the Confederacy, however, chose to resist and were very successful in doing so. In those eleven states only 2 percent of the black children were attending integrated schools by late 1964. These states employed a number of delaying tactics.

Some states passed new laws creating an endless series of litigation. Other states established "private schools" in which the state payed the tuition of white students attending such schools. Still others revised their compulsory attendance laws so that no child was compelled to attend integregated schools. Still others resisted on the grounds of protecting public safety by attempting to "interpose" the state between the schools and federal authority. Most successful of all was the tactic of revising "pupil placement law" such that each child was guaranteed freedom of choice in selecting his or her school. In those cases, most students chose to attend the school they had previously attended-- maintaining a segregated system "de facto" rather than "de jure."

Resistance also took the form of violence. Violent resistance to court-ordered desegregation achieved national prominence in Clinton, Tennessee, in 1956; in Little Rock, Arkansas, in 1957; in New Orleans, in 1960; and at the University of Mississippi at Oxford in 1962. Both Presidents Eisenhower and Kennedy met such resistance with the use of federal troops to ensure compliance with the law.

But real change came about only after the passage of the 1964 Civil Rights Act and the 1965 Elementary and Secondary Education Act. Title VI of the 1964 Act specified the termination of financial assistance to states and communities that resisted compliance with court-ordered desegregation. The 1965 Act provided sufficient funding to make the threat a compelling one. This monetary "club" sped up desegregation faster than all the previous federal court actions. The U.S. Office of Education released "guidelines" for required desegregation plans to which the seventeen states with past histories of de jure segregation had to submit in order to retain federal financial assistance. In three years the desegregation of schools in those states increased eight-fold. By 1970 desegregation in the South actually reached a point where more black pupils were attending integrated schools in the South than in the North--58.3 percent versus 42.6 percent respectively (Dye, 1978: 43).

Perhaps more importantly, this situation demonstrated that the real issue of racial segregation involved "de facto" segregation--that is, where racial isolation in schools was based on housing patterns coupled with neighborhood schools rather than on direct discrimination based on the law. Overcoming "de facto" segregation has proven to be far more difficult than striking down barriers erected by law.

A 1967 U.S. Commission on Civil Rights Report found that 75 percent of the black elementary school children in 75 large cities attended schools whose enrollment was 90 percent or more black. Ending or even reducing de facto segregation was to be no easy task. Attempts to reduce the problem required that school officials classify their students on the basis of race and use race as a category for school placement decisions. Effective reduction of de facto segregation seemed to necessitate busing. Opposition to busing, however, was widespread and often violent. Boston, for instance, was the site of long and violent confrontations over busing. Often black parents opposed forced busing plans as much as did white parents. And the nation witnessed a revival of the Ku Klux Klan and its spread north as cities across the country grappled with busing plans to desegregate school systems of central city and suburb.

The Court ruled that were no present or past actions of state and local government were used to create racial imbalance there was no affirmative duty to correct racial imbalance. Where such imbalance, however, was the result of past discriminatory laws by states or local school districts, than school officials had a duty to eliminate such vestiges of segregation, and that duty may entail busing and deliberate racial balancing to achieve integration of their schools (in Swann v. Charolette-Mecklenburg Board of Education, 402 U.S. 1, 1971). The Swann decision affects mostly Southern schools. In the North, where no history of segregation law is evident, the Court ruled, by a 5-4 vote, that the Fourteenth Amendment does not require busing across city/suburban school district lines to achieve integration (in Milliken v. Bradley, 418 U.S. 717, 1974). In essence, the Court's ruling meant that the nation's largest black central cities surrounded by mostly white suburbs will remain segregated de facto because there are not enough white students living in the central city boundaries to achieve anything nearing a balanced integration.

Nevertheless, significant progress has been made. A 1982 study released by the Joint Center for Political Studies in Washington, D. C. showed a marked drop in intensely segregated schools. Such schools (measured by minority enrollments of 90 to 100 percent) have been cut in half—from 64 percent in 1968 to 33 percent in 1982. As before, the biggest drop occurred in the South. There, black enrollment in nearly all-minority schools fell from 98 percent in 1963 to 23 percent in 1980 (U.S. News and World Report, September 27, 1982: 39).

Public attitudes about integration have shifted dramatically as well. A 1963 Gallop Poll found 61 percent of Southern white parents opposed sending their children to a school with even a few black students enrolled. In 1981 another Gallop Poll found such resistance had dropped to 5 percent. The number of blacks completing high school rose from 42 percent in 1960 to 75 percent in 1979, and in two decades the percentage of black college students rose from 6.1 percent to 10 percent (Ibid: 41).

Many educators attribute the significant rise in achievement levels among blacks, while similar levels for whites have run slightly higher or held steady, to the integration of the schools. Progress has been most dramatic where, in the past, segregation was most deeply rooted. In the North progress has been less marked. In some communities opposition remains intense. Although busing about half of Boston's 57,000 students has been under way since 1974, school vehicles are still stoned, and several empty ones have been overturned and set afire. Many whites simply fled the public school system. White enrollment has dropped from 70 percent to 33 percent in the last decade. More whites are now enrolled in private schools than in Boston's public school system (Ibid: 40).

Proponents of mandatory busing argue that it is the only efficient and effective way to achieve integration since most residential areas remain segregated. Opponents charge that such forced busing is divisive, costly, and counter-productive because it prompts white flight from the public school system, leaving those schools even more segregated.

The Reagan Administration favors voluntary plans, such as those used in Milwaukee and Buffalo. The Justice Department is now leading the anti-busing drive. They argue that the voluntary system which offer special programs, called magnet schools, which provide intensive instruction in subjects like fine arts, will ultimately be more effective. Yet such programs are very costly. The Administration's cuts in federal support for desegregation have been drastic. Buffalo's program was cut from 7 million dollars in 1981-1982 to one million in 1982-1983. Such voluntary plans have not worked in many large cities, and the courts have often dismissed them as ineffective.

Integration, moreover, is no longer solely a black and white issue. Los Angeles is one of many cities where the Hispanic minority is as large or larger than the black. In 1972 the Los Angeles school district was nearly half white, with the remainder being about equally divided between blacks and Hispanics. By 1982 the district had become half Hispanic, with the number of blacks and whites about even. That district recently shifted from a mandatory busing system to a voluntary one. A total of 86 magnet schools have been identified, up from six such schools in the past five years. Yet nearly 300 of the district's 700 schools remain predominantly Hispanic, black, or Asian, up dramatically from 219 such schools in 1979. Widespread resistance to forced busing appears to be growing and the extensive use of that approach to overcome de facto segregation is likely to decline as a result.

A 1982 study of "ethnic voters" found overwhelming opposition to busing, with substantial opposition even among political liberals and moderates. It also found that opponents to busing were more likely to turn out on election day than were proponents (Rothenberg and Licht: 56).

By contrast, the popularity of voluntary plans is growing and is being listened to in the Congress and the White House. The Reagan Administration filed not a single school-desegregation suit in its first two years in office. Federal dollars to support desegregation efforts have been drastically cut. As mentioned above, the Justice Department is now a leading force in the anti-busing movement by pushing voluntary programs and refusing to push for or enforce mandatory ones. In August of 1982 the Department requested a U.S. Court of Appeals to allow reconsideration of a year-old busing plan in East Baton Rouge, Louisiana, after nearly 4,000 white elementary students left the school system during its first year of court-ordered busing (U.S. News and World Report, Op. Cit.: 40).

Gains in educational opportunity, moreover, are closely linked to progress in the employment area. It is to that public policy area we next turn our attention.

Employment

From the days of slave labor, through the era of "No Irish Need Apply" signs, to the present day, discrimination in employment opportunity has been a recurrent aspect of minority/majority relations. Employment discrimination has, on occasion, been institutionalized, manifested in formal policy such as specific laws. Usually, however, it is informally enforced through labor union training practices, educational entrance barriers, and the informal hiring practices of majority-member employers. The "last hired--first fired" norm has always been a problem for the nation´s minorities, and continues to be so today.

The discussion in previous chapters has noted a number of instances of formalized job discrimination. Chapter Two described the Irish experience when they were initially limited to periodic or seasonal work, low pay, and constant job threat explicitly implemented by the common use of the "No Irish" signs. Chapter Four dealt with the Jews, who experienced both the signs and job advertisements labeled "Christians Only," or "Gentiles Only." The use of the padrone constituted a formalized system of occupational discrimination for the Greeks and Italians. Even the Foran Act of 1885, which forbade contract labor and was intended to counteract the padrone system, constituted a formalized pattern of discrimination.   374

Institutionalized racism in the United States was the basis for various formal acts of job discrimination. Blacks were legally enslaved for a time. Even after slavery was abolished, Jim Crow legislation re-inforced informal norms (for example, by segregation of schools with their legally limited curricula blacks were kept out of many jobs) which severely restricted the occupational opportunities of blacks. In California such racism led to the Foreign Miners Tax of 1885 which, when coupled with violence, was used to expel the Chinese from the mining camps. The Chinese and Japanese were likewise the targets of the California Alien Land Act, a legalized attempt to restrict them from certain occupational endeavors where the threat of their competition was feared. That law was upheld as constitutional in 1921 in <u>Ozawa</u> <u>v.</u> <u>the</u> <u>United</u> <u>States.</u> In 1923 California strengthened the legal restrictions by plugging several loopholes in the 1913 Act. Similar laws were passed in Arizona, Idaho, Louisiana, Montana, New Mexico, and Oregon. The reservation policy of the 1870´s legally forced occupational restrictions of the American Indian, another example of formalized job discrimination.

As with race, formal or legal barriers in the job market have been used in the case of gender, age, and sexual preference as cited in the previous chapter. Women and persons over 65 face legal barriers in occupational opportunity in the social security laws. The firing of gays from certain jobs has been legally upheld even though the sole basis for the dismissal was the individual´s sexual preference.

Undoubtedly, however, the greatest degree of job discrimination against the nation´s various minorities has been and continues to be <u>informally</u> enforced. Such informal mechanisms as: 1) restrictions in job training conducted by labor unions, 2) educational barriers which deny certain minorities the opportunity to acquire the formal educational backgrounds required for many jobs, and 3) the informal hiring practices of majority employers have all been used to enforce majority society´s norms by denying equal opportunity in employment. Because these norms are informally enforced, they cannot be directly measured. That they have been and continue to operate, however, cannot be denied. The indirect evidence of such informal discrimination is both pervasive and persuasive. The patterns of employment among minority groups demonstrate such discrimination indirectly, but unmistakably.

375

Whenever exceptionally large percentages of minority group members congregate into specific and limited occupations, as indicated by the occupational niches typical of minority groups, one can conclude that employment discrimination is channeling large numbers of such individuals into those jobs. While many minority members voluntarily enter such occupations, they are jobs which are inordinately attractive to those persons because a pattern of informal discrimination has closed off access to alternative occupations of equal or better opportunity.

Table Twenty-Five shows the types of special occupational niches that were, or are, common for various minorities discussed herein. It is but one indirect indicator of pervasive job discrimination. Subsequent data will show additional evidence which, taken together, comprise persuasive evidence of informal job discrimination which has been and continues to be used against many minority members of our society.

Figure Thirteen shows a similar pattern between male and female and whites and blacks for 1978 across four broad occupational categories, each divided into upper and lower status jobs. The pattern of minorities (blacks, women) congregating in the lower categories or in the lower divisions of the higher status jobs is evident.

A look at unemployment rates presents a similar picture--pervasive discrimination across age, sex, and racial bases. The nation's minorities are clearly still the "last hired, first fired," even in this day of affirmative action. Table Twenty-Six shows teenage unemployment data from 1970 to 1976. When the economy is sluggish, the minority unemployment rate, for both male and female minority members, rises dramatically.

Finally, Figure Fourteen shows comparable data graphically. The split-bar graph presents the unemployment rates for varying age groups for both males and females, comparing the rates of blacks and hispanics with total unemployment rates for selected years between 1973 and 1979. It indicates a bias against the minority worker. Only a pattern of discrimination seems to be able to account for the pattern displayed in Figure Fourteen.

Table 25: EMPLOYMENT DISCRIMINATION: SPECIAL OCCUPATIONAL NICHES	
GROUP:	SPECIAL OCCUPATIONAL NICHE:
National Origin Groups:	
Greeks	Restaurants, Confectionaries, Candy stores, RR, Construction
Hispanics	Migrant farm work, Low-skilled blue-collar urban jobs
Hungarians	Unskilled labor in heavy industries (steel, rubber, mines)
Irish	Unskilled--mines, RR's, police, fire, stevedores
Italians	Restaurants, truck farms, wine, barbers
Poles	Truck gardening, domestics, unskilled--mines, steel
Russians	Unskilled--mines, construction, tailors, furriers
Race	
Blacks	Blue-collar unskilled to low-skilled menial jobs, migrant farm work, tenant farming, domestic service
Chinese	Restaurants, laundry, domestic service, import/export, gift shops
Japanese	Gardening, truck farming, fishing
Religion	
Amish	Agriculture
Jews	Garment and cigar industries, retail sales, theater/music
Mormons	Agriculture
Gender	
Women	Nursing, elementary school teachers, typists, secretaries hairdressers, waitresses, telephone operators
Sexual Preference	
Gays	Bookkeeping, dress design, window display, hairdressing, interior decorating, art, theatre, music

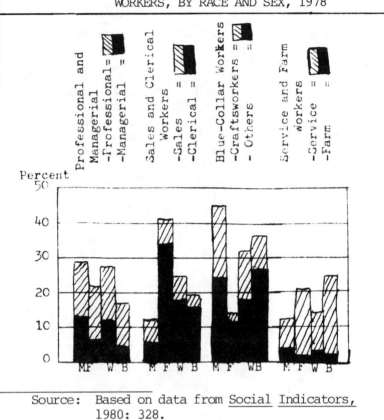

Figure 21: OCCUPATIONAL DISTRIBUTION OF EMPLOYED
WORKERS, BY RACE AND SEX, 1978

Source: Based on data from Social Indicators,
1980: 328.

Table 26:	TEENAGE UNEMPLOYMENT, 1960-1976			
	MALES 1960	FEMALES 1960	MALES 1976	FEMALES 1976
BLACKS	12%	21%	48%	51%
MEXICAN AMERICANS	14	15	24	27
PUERTO RICANS	15	18	55	38
NATIVE AMERICANS	17	18	35	36
WHITES	10	11	15	19

Source: U.S. Commission on Civil Rights, Social
Indicators of Equality for Minorities and
Women, (August, 1978): 32.

The various governmental programs designed to mitigate the systematic discrimination versus minorities apparently have done little to change that picture. During the recession of 1982 when the national unemployment rate reached the highest levels the nation has witness since the end of the Great Depression in 1941 and when more than 12 million workers were unemployed, the nation's minorities again bore the brunt of the unemployment burden. Whereas 8 percent of white adult women and 9.2 percent of white adult men were out of work in November of 1982, both below the national average of 10.8 percent, the minority figures were consistently more than twice the non-minority rates. The unemployment rate among Black adult women was 16.7 percent and among Black adult males was 19.0 percent. The same holds true for teenagers. While the rate for white teenagers was at a "Great Depression"-like level of 21.3 percent, even that figure pales in comparison with the black teenage unemployment rate of 50.1 percent! (Time, December 13, 1982: 54). While the 10.8 percent rate was called a "national disgrace," the white/black portion of the burden clearly reflects the relative status of the two groups. White collar workers faced 5.6 percent rates, while blue-collar workers saw their rates climb to 16.5 percent. Total black unemployment was 20.2 percent (UPI, December 4, 1982).

The nation has taken steps to reverse the effects of occupational discrimination. A series of Congressional actions and Supreme Court decisions have attempted to address the problems engendered by informal but institutionalized job discrimination.

Congress took action with various "War on Poverty" programs of the 1960's, some of which were designed to provide training which would permit the unemployed to develop needed job skills. Examples of this approach would be the Job Corps and the Neighborhood Youth Corps projects conducted by the Office of Economic Opportunity. Other programs encourage employers to do the training, for instance, the Comprehensive Employment Training Act (CETA), and Public Service Employment (PSE) (Cochran, et al:139).

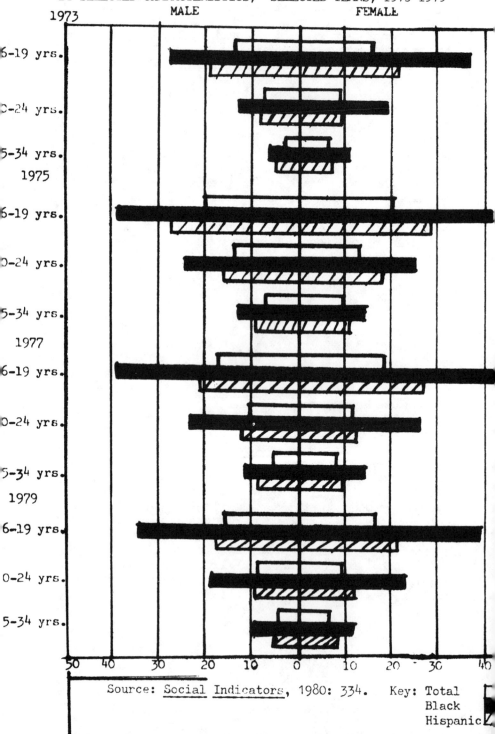

FIG. 14: UNEMPLOYMENT RATES OF PERSONS 16-34 YEARS OLD
BY SELECTED CHARACTERISTICS, SELECTED YEARS, 1973-1979

Source: Social Indicators, 1980: 334.   Key: Total
                                               Black
                                               Hispanic

By far the most significant Congressional action regarding employment discrimination was the passage of the Civil Rights Act of 1964. Title VI of that act states that "No person in the United States shall, on the grounds of race, color, or national origin, be excluded from participation in, be denied the benefits of, or be subject to discrimination under any program of activity receiving federal financial assistance (see Paul and Russo: 247)." The Office of Contract Compliance is charged with the responsibility of implementing that policy.

Title VII of the 1964 Act created the Equal Employment Opportunity Commission (EEOC) which is charged with implementing policy towards ending discrimination by any employer or labor union with 25 or more persons. While the EEOC cannot require specific quotas nor even preferential treatment from the mere fact of racial imbalance, the Commission may use such imbalance as evidence of discrimination. The law assumes that if discrimination were not at work, members of the targeted groups (Blacks, Hispanics, Women) would be present in the various sectors of society in rough proportion to their numbers within society at large.

This "proportionality" criterion, which now serves as the basis for all preferential treatment plans, represents a significant shift in society's conceptualization of what constitutes "equality": from equality under the law to equality of opportunity to equality of well-being.

> The most clearly discernible trend in the struggle for equality is the evolution in the generally understood meaning of the term, which has changed the goals and issues involved. The meaning of the term once referred to the struggle for the eradication of discrimination upon racial, religious, sexual, or ethnic attributes and of laws or social policy that burden and penalize people on the basis of such attributes. It has, in recent decades, come to imply that each identifiable racial or ethnic group and each sex has a right to a proportionate share of the values of society. The legitimacy of an uneven distribution of material well-being and of the dominance of certain groups over others has increasingly come under attack (Cochran: 349).

The policies which attempt to attain this goal of
equality of material well-being are known collectively
as "affirmative action," a search for compensatory
justice   for   the   persisting   effects   of   past
institutionalized   discrimination.   We   may   define
affirmative action as any program designed to get
minority persons past the institutionalized barriers
that would normally stop them.   These programs are
concentrated in educational and employment structures
where such barriers exist.   A minority student, for
instance, who had been placed in a high school terminal
class group and lacks the skills needed to pass a
college entrance exam might be lifted over that barrier
and be given a chance that would otherwise be denied
him/her.   The logic behind affirmative action is that
there exists a cycle of discrimination which affects the
minority individual.   That cycle must be broken.   If
poor education leads to poor jobs, which leads to poor
housing, which leads back to poor education, then one
might be able to improve the whole chain by breaking one
link in it. A better job should lead to better housing,
a more middle-class life style, and better schools.
These in turn should lead to better education and
hopefully a new generation that will not need the
affirmative action programs since the cycle has been
broken. In short, affirmative action is an attempt
to force structural assimilation (Luhman and Gilman:
220).

These programs have led to a number of Supreme
Court   cases   on   the   matter.   Where   "performance
standards" or tests which serve as entrance barriers to
higher   education programs or to certain preferred
occupations have been disproportionately failed   by
members of targeted minority groups, such standards have
been challenged in the Court as discriminatory.   They
are alleged to be in violation of Title VII of the 1964
Civil Rights Act and/or the due process clause of the
Constitution.   The Supreme Court, however, has been
split in its interpretation of the law with respect to
who must prove whether or not such performance standards
are discriminatory.   When the case is argued under the
Title VII provision, the burden of proof is on the
administrator of the test, who must show that the test
is indeed relevant to the job.   Under the Constitution,
however, the burden of the proof has been held to be on
the challenger, who must demonstrate that there is
intent to discriminate in the test.

The attempts to achieve better racial or sexual balance in employment and higher education led to various plans for racial preference. These plans were challenged in a number of cases: DeFunis, Bakke, and Weber (see Cochran: 336-339).

The Office of Federal Contract Compliance and the EEOC began the process of court battles by setting guidelines which held that any test for employment, promotion, or membership (in a union, for example) that disproportionately failed members of a designated group constituted evidence of illegal discrimination, unless the job relevance of the test could be shown. In short, the employer had the burden of proof to show that those who scored higher on their test or selection criteria actually performed better in the roles for which they were being selected.

In 1971 the Supreme Court, in Griggs v. Duke Power (401 U.S. 424), upheld those guidelines, thus threatening the legality of virtually every performance criteria. The job relevance of such tests is nearly impossible to prove since it is so difficult to measure precisely enough subsequent job performance. Three "suspect" categories have been identified by the Court: race, sex, and alienage. In 1976, in Craig v. Boren (429 U.S. 190), the Court set standards for when sex may be used to classify people: the government had to convince the Court that its purpose is an important one and that sex classification is "substantially related" to achieving that purpose.

In yet another case that year, Washington v. Davis (44 LW 4789), the Court muddied the waters still further. This case concerned a Washington, D. C. police officer test. Although four times as many blacks as whites failed to pass the written test, the Court nonetheless decided that this failure rate was not in and of itself sufficient evidence to invalidate the test. Unlike the Griggs case, this one was not argued under Title VII, which did not apply to governmental units. Rather, it was decided under the Fifth Amendment's due process clause. The Court ruled that, under the Constitution, a test is presumed valid unless the intent to discriminate is shown.

The situation is complicated further by several challenges to various racial preference plans. In DeFunis v. Odegaard (416 U.S. 312, 1974), the Court essentially dodged the question by ruling that the DeFunis challenge of the University of Washington's Law School preferential admissions program was a "moot" question since, by the time the case had reached the Court, DeFunis, who had been ordered admitted by the state trial court, was ready to graduate. In the 1978 case of Bakke v. Regents of the University of California (438 U.S. 265), the Court had to decide upon the admission criteria and procedures for the medical school at Davis. Alan Bakke had been denied admission even though he clearly had higher scores on his G.P.A and Medical College Aptitude Test than did a number of minority applicants who were admitted under the school's set-aside quota system of 16 placements out of 100 to be used for non-whites. The Bakke decision, involving a 5-4 split in which the deciding opinion of Justice Power hinged on a different basis than the other four justices comprising the majority, found the school's program invalid on equal protection grounds by objecting to the fixed-quota system.

The cumulative effect of these Court cases is to maintain a modified affirmative action structure. While strict quotas in preferential plans may violate either the Civil Rights Act or the Constitution, other uses of race or sex for the "benign" purposes of achieving racial or sexual balance seems acceptable. Critics of affirmative action, however, continue to press their case on several grounds. They hold such plans to be a denial of meritocracy, inconsistent with the concept of equality under the law, or focusing on groups' rather than individuals. They object to its penalizing of competitive success and its denial of performance standards.

The problem, of course, involves the conflict among rights and the difficulty of pursuing group goals at the expense of specific individuals. Whenever a society seeks a goal of social policy involving the redistribution of material well-being, such "redistribution" inevitably involves a finite value. Such policy involves a "zero-sum" situation. Whatever new benefits are accorded to some must be taken away from others; what one group gains another must lose. Although the history of discrimination against groups clearly establishes an argument for some form of compensatory justice, the confusion between bigotry and discrimination of groups and those of individuals within groups muddles the concept of justice. The white race, in the aggregate, may be guilty of discrimination, but individuals--Brian Weber, Allan Bakke, or Marco DeFunis--pay the debt even though they may not have personally so discriminated. Nor do the benefits of affirmative action necessarily flow to the most disadvantaged individuals in society. The hard-core unemployed seldom get to professional schools under such programs; rather, these programs benefit middle-class members of the designated groups. To change the rules of the game and deny benefits to the Bakkes of society, benefits to which they were entitled under the old rules, is perceived by many as the denial of their rights. Yet minorities do have a right to combat the persisting impact of the history of social discrimination (Cochran: 349).

Similar hesitancy in policy is shown regarding sex discrimination. Title IX of the Educational Amendment Acts of 1972 forbids any institution from receiving federal funds if it engages in sex discrimination. Yet, in 1981, in Rotsker v. Goldberg (66 L.Ed.2nd 611), the Court upheld the right of Congress to exempt women from the draft.

The racial preference issue was further muddied when Angel Luevano challenged, under Title VII of the Civil Rights Act, the use of the Professional and Administrative Career Examination (PACE) by the Office of Personnel Management on the grounds that a disproportionate number of blacks and Hispanics failed the test. The failure rate for all applicants on PACE is about 60 percent, while the failure rate for blacks is around 95 percent. Recall that Griggs held that employers must show the job relevance for any hiring criteria disproportionately failed by targeted groups, while the Davis precedent held that when the due process clause of the Constitution is used, no such requirement exists. Accordingly, the plaintiffs in Luevano v. Campbell (1981) relied on Title VII even though the employer in this case was the federal government. The case was settled out of court by the Reagan Administration with an agreement to phase out the PACE test and replace it with "alternative examining procedures" that have no "adverse impact" on blacks and Hispanics. Yet, in the agreement, adverse impact was defined to mean a failure to be hired at the same rate as whites. Further, the government agreed to hire certain categories of individuals without reference to test scores (for example, Spanish-speaking people when knowledge of Spanish is an asset), and to strive to have blacks and Hispanics comprise at least 20 plus percent of the workforce at the GS-5 level and higher. Clearly, this constitutes a quota or the sort that Bakke seemed to threaten and that has been alleged by some to constitute reverse discrimination against whites in the sense explicitly banned by Title VII. Thus, the image of the Reagan Administration as being less supportive of affirmative action is not consistent with its action in extending affirmative action benefits with this out-of-court settlement.

It is difficult to assess the effectiveness of affirmative action. Undoubtedly, some progress has been made. Almost 25 percent of black families in 1980 had incomes of $25,000 or more, up from 14 percent in 1965. The number of blacks finishing high school rose from 42 percent in 1960 to 75 percent in 1979. And where 6.1 percent of the nation´s college students were black in 1960, that number has risen to nearly 10 percent by 1980. The resulting improvement in education has led to better jobs. In 1980, 2 out of every 5 employed blacks were working in white collar job compared to 1 out of 5 in 1970. From 1970 to 1982 blacks´ income rose from 72 percent of that of whites´ income to 89 percent, in 1980, before falling back to 87 percent in 1982 (see U.S. News and World Report, September 27, 1982).

A study of black employment in municipal jobs in 43 U.S. cities shows that affirmative action programs do show some marked gains where black populations provide a sizable bloc voting power. The research suggests that ethnic politics which involves the distribution of divisible economic goods to a particular group (that is, blacks´ employment in the city´s public personnel system) as a consequence of that group´s political power is still possible in American cities (see Eisinger: 380).

The 1982 recession demonstrates, however, that blacks are still far behind whites. Critics of affirmative action note that such programs seem to help mostly those members of minorities who are already doing fairly well to do still better without having much impact on those minority members who are seemingly locked in the lower class. Such programs have spurred the political opposition by some factions of the majority who counter them with cries of reverse discrimination. Such critics have opened an assault on affirmative action programs in the courts and in the offices of the Reagan Administration.

Critics of the Administration, such as Benjamin Hooks, executive director of the NAACP, charge the administration with an assault on civil rights across the spectrum of areas. Such critics note that, at a time when black unemployment stands at 20 percent and at over 50 percent among black teenagers, more than 300,000 public service jobs have been cut and job-training programs have been drastically reduced. Under the current administration, the EEOC cut by half the number of discrimination suits brought against employers. Administration officials are proposing that small companies no longer be required to file written affirmative action plans. The Justice Department is seeking a Supreme Court ruling that would find it unconstitutional to give minorities and women preference in hiring and promotions. Likewise, the critics note, few minorities have been named to federal posts and that many of those selected were not qualified. Less than 5 percent of the 3,231 presidential appointments are black. In September of 1982 the heads of 33 state civil rights commissions sent a letter to the President raising their concern over a "dangerous deterioration" in civil-rights enforcement. A White House spokesman denied that there was any letup, saying "The President has made it clear on many occasions that he will not permit a civil-rights rollback, and he is proud of his record." They contend that quotas are not acceptable in their efforts to treat all people equally. Their approach is to fight civil rights violations on a case-by-case basis rather than to go for a group remedy. They maintain that the Administration has filed more criminal civil-rights charges than any other. Assistant Attorney General William Bradford Reynolds, Chief of the Justice Department's civil rights division, says that "discrimination will not be used to cure discrimination. Two civil wrongs do not make a civil right" (U.S. News and World Report, September 27, 1982: 41).

As a group of scholars assess the conflict between job discrimination and affirmative action:

> The point is that rights conflict. The intractable difficulty of the equality issue is that it is not a clear case of right and wrong, but one of conflicting rights. Plausible ethical arguments can and have been constructed to support conflicting claims based upon powerful interests. Because of

this conflict among plausible rights, issues concerning equality promise to continue to be among the most intractable and divisive of issues facing the country for the indefinite future (Cochran, et al: 349).

Another issue-area which promises to continue to be amongst the most divisive and intractable of concerns facing the nation is that of foreign policy. The impact of minority groups on U.S. foreign policy has been for a long time, and continues to be today, a significant force. It is to that policy area of minority/majority relations we next turn our attention.

Foreign Policy

The impact of minority groups upon the foreign policy of the United States has a long tradition. From the days of the Founding Fathers to the most recent headlines, a political debate has been waged over the effect and appropriate role that "other-nation" loyalties should be allowed to pay in this nation's conduct of its foreign affairs.

Madison, for example, in The Federalist Papers, warned of dangerous factions. President Washington, in his Farewell Address, warned the country to be on guard against the undue power of artful minorities to do mischief: "At a time when rival factions within the new nation were pulling, one toward England, the other toward France, Washington warned against the twin evils of excessive animosity and excessive attachment to particular foreign nations, especially the latter...´facilitating the illusion of an imaginary common interest, in cases where no real common interest exists...´" (Mathias: 975).

The issue is problematic since: 1) we are a nation of so many diverse ethnic groups; 2) such groups often feel an intense emotional loyalty another country, which colors their judgement and strongly motivates them to participate in politics in order to influence our foreign policy; 3) our political system's structurally dispersed power and decision-making gives them many points of access; and 4) we are now so politically powerful a nation with so many and diverse world-wide interests and relations, that such an impact on foreign policy can have profound effects on our foreign relations and also on domestic policy and our economics (Power: 4).

This section will briefly review some of the major examples of minority-group impact on our foreign policy. In doing so, it will illustrate that such influence is not limited to the "nationality-based" minorities, nor are the effects of the influence limited to foreign policy as such. The domestic reverberations of such influence can be profound.

We should perhaps begin this discussion by making a clear distinction between foreign lobbying activities and American-based ethnic lobbies in the area of U.S. foreign policy. While the activities of foreign agents and their lobbyists have attracted considerable press attention, those agents who lack strong indigenous support affect only very limited and transient influence on our foreign policy. The "Korea-gate" scandal of 1978, for instance, showed that, for all its exertions and expenditures, the South Korean government was unable to acquire a solid base of influence within the Congress. While foreign bribes and gifts may suborn individual legislators or win specific minor favors, they are no substitute for an ethnic interest group of American citizens ready and able to threaten a member's re-election.

The once formidable China lobby is a case in point. President Truman and Secretary of State Dean Acheson wanted to recognize the People's Republic of China in 1950. The China lobby and the Korean War prevented this. Under President Eisenhower and Secretary of State Dulles intransigent support for the Nationalist Chinese and opposition to the People's Republic became embedded in U.S. foreign policy. As a result, the Kennedy and Johnson Administrations found it very difficult to make overtures to the mainland Chinese. It was not until the Nixon Administration, with his impeccable conservative credentials, that an Administration was able to move the nation to recognize the reality of the People's Republic of China. The China lobby failed, however, in its efforts against the Carter Administration's decision late in 1978 to transfer our recognition from the Republic of China on Taiwan to the People's Republic of China on the mainland. They were ultimately ineffective because they lacked the united support of an aroused Chinese-American community.

Likewise, the well-publicized white South African lobby attempted to influence Congress. They, too, had but limited and transient impact. They succeeded in getting adopted the 1971 Byrd Amendment which for some years permitted the import of Rhodesian chrome. Yet, despite their strenuous efforts, supporters of Rhodesia and South Africa have been incapable of reversing the trend in our foreign policy of supporting black majority rule in Zimbabwe and Nambia. The major influences on our foreign policy vis-a-vis Africa have been our tradition of support for self-determination of people and a commitment to racial justice that reflects, in large measure, a respect and responsiveness towards our own black population, which has been demonstrating increasing strength, participation, and sensitivity to the African foreign policy issue.

Arabs have been less successful than an aid-dependent Israel for influence on U.S. foreign policy not for lack of resources, but because Arab-Americans have not been comparable in size, unity, or motivation to the Jewish community in the United States. As Senator Mathias so aptly puts it: "The real powerhouses of foreign influence are homegrown" (Mathias: 979).

A recent study by Professor Spiegel argues persuasively that ethnic interest group attempts to influence U. S. foreign policy have been prominent and particularly active vis-a-vis Congress, but less successfully so upon the President and his close circle of advisers. He argues that the greatest alteration in foreign policy occurs when a new Administration takes office. Ethnic groups have added to the discourse and increased an issue's prominence, but decisions have most often been made within the Administration more in light of global and regional strategies than for reasons related to domestic [that is, ethnic group] political considerations. The greater significance of ethnic group activity relates to their influence on the public discussion of the issues they bring to the fore. As he concludes: "Ethnic lobbies are part of the domestic constraints upon policy-makers, but they do no determine that policy and executives may decide to ignore them" (Spiegel: 30).

The oldest and most redoubtable of such homegrown ethnic interest groups are the Irish-Americans. They showed major exertions, if little success, prior to World War II, in setting the United States at odds with Great Britain. Irish- and German-American opinion strongly resisted and probably caused a delay in our involvement in World War I.

Similarly, prior to our entrance into World War II, President Roosevelt complained privately of Irish-American isolationist opposition to his policies. Their opposition, plus the influence of the large contingent of German-American citizens, undoubtedly tempered Roosevelt's actions and delayed our entrance into that conflict as well (Fuchs: 149; Lieberson: 106). Power ranks the Irish in the third of four tiers of ethnic groups based on their record in the foreign policy arena since 1945 (Power: 6).

Since the 1970's, the Northern Irish conflict has aroused Irish-American sensitivities. The insertion of British troops into Northern Ireland in 1969 and their recurrent failures to resolve the Protestant/Catholic conflict in Ulster has generated considerable concern and indignation among Irish-Americans, including the highly placed "Four Horsemen": Senators Kennedy and Moynihan, Speaker O'Neil and then New York Governor Carey. Although they have been cautious in their suggestions, their call for a united Ireland was less than warmly received in London. Other prominent Irish-American lobbying organizations include the Irish National Caucus, the Ad Hoc Committee for Irish Affairs, and the Ancient Order of Hiberians.

The South/Central/Eastern European groups who came after the Irish have likewise strengthened their ethnic identity while becoming American in other respects-- especially political attitudes and behavior. As they acquired knowledge and influence within American politics, they discovered they could use such influence not only to ease their own situation in this country, but to influence their countries of origin and American policy towards those countries.

Somewhat ironically perhaps, many of them developed their first real sense of ethnic awareness here in the United States. Since most of them were marginal members of their native societies, it was only here in America that they were free to become politically aware and active. Distance in time and customs, moreover, probably softened their memories of the harshness of life in the old country. Many acquired an affection for and awareness of their native land and culture here, where they were free and had the opportunity to practice customs and religions and speak languages that often had been restricted in their native lands. Also, the difficulties associated with making a new life in the United States often forced them to seek the security and solace of their ethnic enclaves--the "Little Italies," "Little Polands," Jewish "ghettos," and "Chinatowns." It was in urban America's ethnic enclaves that very often their awareness of the myths of their native villages were born. These villages came to be "remembered" as safe and serene havens compared to the strange, vast, confusing, and often harsh surroundings of America (Gerson: 3-10).

Native politicians and party organizations, as we have seen in previous chapters, played up to and even aroused that ethnic awareness when they discovered that such appeals enabled them to manipulate large blocs of ethnic voters.

The impact of these nationality groups on U.S. foreign policy is well-exemplified by the adoption of a Congressional resolution calling on the President to proclaim an annual "Captive Nations Week." President Eisenhower's proclamation caused some tensions during then Vice-President Nixon's trip to Russia in 1959. This resolution, and the unforseen consequences that followed its implementation, were more serious than the mere embarrassment of the Vice-President. The resolution calling for a "Captive Nations Week" had been strongly promoted the Assembly of Captive European Nations, a group that had been formed in 1954 to work for the freedom and independence of the nations of Eastern and Central Europe. In July, 1959, it was adopted by Congress verbatim from a draft submitted by Professor Lev Dobriansky of Georgetown University. Each year thereafter, Representatives and Senators have been reminded of the annual observance so they could place appropriate statements in the <u>Congressional</u> <u>Record.</u> In adopting the resolution, Congress responded to interest groups whose goal, although desirable, was practically unattainable. By the time of its adoption, the Administration had already been compelled by political realities to abandon its early, facile statements about "liberating" Eastern Europe from Soviet domination. The inability of the "Free World" to challenge the Soviet Union on its borders without incurring unacceptable risk had been convincingly demonstrated by the events in Poland and Hungary in 1956. The implicit threats of the resolution created an unnecessary element of tension with Russia and, at the same time, cast doubts on the Administration's right to be taken seriously in this foreign policy arena. By encouraging hopes among suppressed populations of Poland, Hungary, and the other East European countries that simply could not be realized Congress, in order to appease an insistent internal domestic pressure group, acted in a manner that led to bitterness, if not to actually inciting the taking of dangerous risks, on the part of people who had looked to America with confidence and hope (see Mathias: 984-985).

American ethnic groups based on Eastern European national origins have been most successful when they sought limited and more specific objectives. In the 1960's, for example, they delayed our extending the "most-favored nation" trade status to communist Yugoslavia. They were also effective with a boycott against Eastern European products, such as Polish hams. In 1964 they forced the cancellation of a sizable manufacturing contract between the Firestone Rubber Company and the government of Romania. Nor were these efforts random in their impact: collectively, along with related lobbying activities, they obstructed the President's stated policy of building bridges to Eastern Europe. Sometimes, however, their effort has been to work in precisely the opposite direction of their intended objectives. Their attempts to pressure the U.S. to use its trade policy to "punish" the communist governments of Eastern Europe, instead of bringing about greater autonomy of those countries from the Soviet Union, have actually driven those governments into greater dependence upon the Soviet Union, and may have contributed to the Soviet paranoia about Eastern Europe which made it act more harshly towards trends for change in the economies of the Eastern block countries. Power ranks them in the third tier, along with the Irish, on the basis of their record of activity in the foreign policy arena (Power: 6).

Another powerful ethnic lobby group is the Greek-American. When the Greeks engineered a coup in Cyprus in 1974, the Turkish military intervention which followed aroused the Greek-Americans to mobilize their powerful lobby. Led by the American Hellenic Institute and supported by Americans of Armenian descent, the Greek-American lobby successfully brought about congressional action for an arms embargo against Turkey on February 5, 1975. They continued their campaign to prevent repeal of the embargo by bombarding Senators and Representatives with letters, telegrams, phone calls, personal visits, and gifts. When the Senate voted in May of 1975 to repeal the arms ban, it aroused the lobby to renewed effort within the House of Representatives. Greek-American rallies were held on the Capital steps and Representatives were flooded with appeals and messages. They succeeded in that in July, by a vote of 223 to 206, the House voted to uphold the embargo. That prompted Turkey to close 26 U.S. bases and listening posts on its territory. The 45,000 Americans of Turkish origin, however, largely politically unacculturated, were simply no match for three million Greek-Americans. When Israel, fearing the consequences of the loss of U.S. listening posts in Turkey, which had proven to be so valuable to Israel during the 1973 Arab-Israeli War, informed its supporters of its opposition to the embargo, the leading Jewish organizations lent quiet but effective support to the Ford Administration's efforts to have the embargo repealed. Intensive efforts by President Ford and Secretary of State Kissinger resulted congressional approval, in October of 1975, of a partial lifting of the arms embargo against Turkey (Mathias: 988). That partial embargo lasted until the summer of 1978 when the Senate finally repealed it. Relations between Turkey and America remained strained, however, and the Turkish government expanded their economic ties with Moscow. The tilt in U.S. policy against Turkey continued even after the embargo was formally lifted (see Spiegel: 27).

Perhaps largely on the basis of such visible exercise of "clout," the Greek-American lobby has been sometimes considered the "number two" lobby in terms of power and influence, second only to the Jewish lobby (Power: 6). There are only three million Greek-Americans, compared to the six million Jewish-Americans. Like Jewish-Americans, they are concentrated in a few areas within which they constitute an important voting bloc. They are both well organized and cohesive, strongly motivated, and well represented in business and the professions. Both groups, while predominately Democratic, are politically active in both major parties. Both groups are generally viewed in the American public opinion as having a favorable case.

Hispanic groups have, on occasion, exercise a similarly visible effort to influence U.S. foreign policy. The Reagan Administration's proposed revisions of the immigration laws were killed, in December 1982, by a coalition of labor, black, and Hispanic groups. The League of Latin American Citizens was the most visible of the Hispanic groups working against the proposed law (Villarreal: 15-17. See also The Washington Post, December 18, 1982: A 12, 15).

Hispanics have also been active in pressuring the U.S. to condemn various Latin American governments for violating basic human rights, particularly in the recent cases of Nicaragua and El Salvador. A recent survey of ethnic voters found that Hispanic respondents displayed a decidedly conservative bent, with over 56 percent agreeing that the "U.S. must get involved in helping stop the spread of communism in South and Central America" (Rothenberg and Licht: 76). Power ranks Hispanics and the Arabs in his fourth tier (Power: 7).

Nationality groups are not the only minorities who attempt to influence our foreign policy. Religious minorities have exerted, and continue to do so, strenuous efforts to see that the U.S. acts in a manner which they perceive to be morally correct. The Quakers, for example, have long opposed our involvement in war. Not only have their own members sought conscientious objector status, the church continues its tradition of aiding draft resisters.

The Roman Catholic hierarchy have recently taken strong, vocal, and somewhat radical stands on nuclear disarmament, opposition to the MX deployment, and related "peace" issues (The Washington Post, May 2, 1982: C 7). They have long opposed the government's policy regarding the support and spreading of the use of contraceptive devices among the populations of the developing nations. They have also been among the most severe critics of nations considered to be violators of human rights, including the political spectrum of South Africa, Israel, Iran, the Soviet Union, Nicaragua, and El Salvadore (Cochran: 420-421).

By far the most effective lobby, in terms of influence on U.S. foreign policy, has been the American Jewish lobby. Although American Jews were not particularly active in politics prior to World War II, they were most effectively galvanized by the Nazi Holocaust and the birth and tribulations of the State of Israel.

President Truman, now revered in Israel for his critically important efforts towards the creation of the Jewish state, was not committed to the cause when he assumed the Presidency in 1945. Dean Acheson, then Undersecretary and later Secretary of State under President Truman, opposed the creation of a Jewish State. General Marshall, Secretary of State in 1948, likewise argued that the decisions regarding "the Palestine question" not be based on U.S. domestic policy. Truman, however, listened to his domestic political advisors who argued a strong case against alienating the domestic Jewish vote. President Truman first publically endorsed the creation of Israel on October 4, 1946--the day of Yom Kippur, and only a month before the congressional elections. Over the next year and a half, pressures for further support increased steadily. In the spring of 1948, with his election looming, the political risks of delaying his recognition of the State of Israel mounted along with the pressure upon him to do so. Those electoral considerations again overrode strong advice from State Department and other advisors (such as Clark Clifford, Special Counsel to the President) to the contrary. The State of Israel was proclaimed at 6:00 p.m., Washington time, on May 14, 1948. The White House announced its recognition of the new state at 6:11 p.m. (Mathias: 992).

That decision stands as a virtual paradigm of our mid-east policy-making since then. Except for President Eisenhower's decision which compelled Israel's withdrawal from the Sinai in 1956, American Presidents and the Congress have been pressured rather successfully by the Jewish lobby.

The American Israel Public Affairs Committee (AIPAC) generally leads the way. One of their major successes in lobbying, the Jackson-Vanick Amendment of 1974, appears to have been, in hindsight, a somewhat pyrrhic victory. This amendment, which won overwhelming Senate support, linked nondiscriminatory trade with Russia with freedom to emigrate. It so angered the

Soviet government that they cancelled the 1972 Soviet-American Trade Agreement and stopped payment of World War II lend-lease debts. Jewish emigration from Russia dropped dramatically from a peak of 35,000 in 1973 to 21,000 in 1974, when the Amendment was adopted. Jewish emigration then fell still further to 13,000 in 1975, 14,000 in 1976, and 17,000 in 1977 (Mathias: 996). The amendment not only failed in terms of its stated purpose, it proved highly consequential for overall U.S.-Soviet relations, straining d´etente in the early 1970´s.

Similarly, the strong influence of the Jewish lobby, and some inadvertent impact on broader issues, are illustrated by the Arab-Israeli conflict of 1973. The Arab oil embargo was a direct result of the pro-Israeli U.S. foreign policy, and had tremendous impact on our domestic and even the world-wide economy.

The Yom Kippur War broke out with a surprise attack on Israel by the Arab states on October 6, 1973. After a few initial setbacks, the Israeli forces repulsed the Arabs and gained the upperhand. On October 17, the Arab oil ministers met in Kuwait and resolved to use oil as a weapon in their struggle against Israel. They announced a 5 percent reduction per month in exports to "unfriendly" nations until Israel withdrew to its 1967 borders and restored the rights of the Palestinians. The basic criterion determining the targets of the embargo was the position of the importing nation on the Arab-Israeli conflict. Nations friendly to the Arab cause were exempt. Unfriendly nations--chiefly, the U.S. and the Netherlands--were hit with oil supply reductions. The embargo included both direct and indirect exports to those targeted countries. The embargo achieved many of its stated objectives. Japan, dependent on the Arab states for 40 percent of its oil, was the first to yield to the pressure. Japan called for Israeli withdrawal and increased its contributions to the U.N. Fund for Palestinian Relief. Except for the Netherlands, similar concessions were wrung from Western Europe. After the U.S. helped establish a cease-fire between Egypt and Israel in January of 1974, the Israeli forces withdrew from parts of the occupied territory. The Arab oil ministers subsequently voted in March of 1974 to lift the embargo.

Although it had limited impact in terms of actually reducing oil imports to the United States, the embargo did achieve a softening of support for Israel in Japan and Western Europe, and a partial withdrawal of Israeli forces. The most significant impact of the embargo, however, was the dramatic example of the power through unified action it gave to the OPEC nations. This period marked the beginning of the rapid escalation in OPEC oil prices and the systematic control on production levels.

The price of Arabian Light crude oil rose from $1.80 a barrel in 1965 to $2.50 in 1972. But from October, 1973 it rose from $3.00 a barrel to $32.00 by 1981 (see Cochran: 67). Only the recession of 1982-1983, which caused a massive decline in the demand for oil, has finally weakened OPEC's ability to control the world-wide oil market's price structure.

The American Israeli Public Affairs Committee (AIPAC) led another campaign in 1975 when the Ford Administration reassessed our mid-east policy to "tilt" a bit more towards the Arab nation's than in previous years. Tremendous pressure was applied to the Congress. A total of 76 Senators signed a letter endorsing more aid to Israel. AIPAC continues to lead the lobby to maintain high levels of military and economic aid to Israel with great success. The letters, telegrams, phone calls, personal visits, and media pressure they are able to generate on any issue touching on Israel has earned them the reputation of being the strongest lobby in Washington. This is not to say that the Administration and Congress support Israel only because of those lobbying pressures, but rather that the debate over this policy area takes place within the context of one side of the issue always being able to generate more pressure when it needs to do so.

Arab-Americans have begun to organize a countering lobby force. There are now about two million Arab Americans, and the National Association of Arab-Americans (NAAA), founded in 1972, has begun to protest and lobby against what they contend is America's "unquestioning" support for Israel. They were a very active lobby countering AIPAC during the debate in the spring of 1978 over the sale of 60 F-15 fighter planes to Saudi Arabia (Spiegel: 10-12).

Ethnic lobbying influences—by Jews, Arabs, Greeks, Hispanics, and blacks—had become so prominent by the mid-1970's that Professors Glazer and Moynihan (1975) plausibly argued that the immigration process could be considered as "the single most important determinent of American policy." As they put it, U.S. policy "responds to other things as well, but probably first of all to the primal facts of ethnicity" (:23-24).

The source of their strength is their ability to galvanize for specific political purposes the strong emotional bonds felt by millions of Americans to their cultural or ancestral homes. The effects of such emotional ties can often be beneficial—alerting broader American public opinion to interests or injustices which might otherwise be ignored or sacrificed to material interests, or simply causing our policy-makers to move slowly and deliberately, asking many tough questions in the internal policy debates of any Administration which might otherwise go unasked. But the effects can also be negative, as Senator Mathias has noted when ethnic groups generate fractious controversy and bitter recrimination:

Public debate becomes charged with accusations of "betrayal" and "sellout," which is to say, of moral turpitude, when in truth the issues that divide us are, with few exceptions, questions of judgement and opinion about what is best for the nation. Ethnic advocacy represents neither a lack of patriotism nor a desire to place foreign interests ahead of American interests; more often it represents a sincere belief that the two coincide. Similarly, resistance to the pressures of a particular group in itself signals neither a sellout nor even a lack of sympathy with a foreign government or cause, but rather a sincere conviction about the national interests of the United States. There is a clear and pressing need for a reintroduction of civility into our public discussions of these matters (:997).

The recent Lebanon crisis and the Reverend Jesse Jackson's bid for the Democratic Presidential nomination has renewed debate over the extent to which our foreign policy reflects too much the impact of one ethnic lobby group or another (see, for example, George Ball: C 8).

Housing

If foreign policy is the area of public policy most influenced by minority group action, then housing appears to be one which has retained the highest degree of discrimination. This pattern is especially pronounced regarding racial minorities and remains despite several federal governmental actions by the Court and Congress designed to end "de jure" segregation in housing. This section will briefly review how such segregation in housing became the established pattern and will discuss governmental policies passed to mitigate such segregation.

Spatial isolation (segregation) is a powerful indicator of a group's general position in a society. As Professor Lieberson notes, "Segregation influences a wide variety of social phenomena such as intermarriage, linguistic assimilation, and even the maintenance of a group's distinctive occupational composition (:253)."

Whether through the informal mechanisms in which minorities largely self-segregate for a degree of security, or through formal and legal segregation, such as the long-standing federal policy to segregate the American Indian on special reservations set aside for that purpose, most minority groups in the United States have experienced at least a period of such housing discrimination. Be it the "Little Italy" or "Little Poland" sections of our East Coast cities, the Chinatowns of New York and San Francisco, or the black ghettos of the nation's major cities, each minority group in its turn has experienced some combination of voluntary and forced segregation in housing. Moreover, housing in America is becoming more segregated, not less.

> In the United States there is a high degree of segregation of the residences of whites and Negroes. This is true for cities in all regions of the country and for all types of cities—large and small, industrial and commercial, metropolitan and suburban. It is true whether there are hundreds of thousands of Negro residents or only a few thousand. Residential segregation prevails regardless of the relative economic status of the white and Negro residents. It occurs regardless of the character of local law and policies, and

regardless of the extent of other forms of segregation or discrimination (Taueber and Taueber: 35-36).

The Tauebers´ study developed a "segregation index" for American cities, the average of which was 86.2, meaning that 86.2 percent of all blacks in America would have to change their place of residence in order to achieve an unsegregated population distribution. Their segregation index for Chicago was 92.6, for New York, 79.3, for Los Angeles, 81.8, for Detroit, 84.5, and for Philadelphia 87.1. These figures, moreover, are increasing with time.

This concentration of minorities into the large central cities of the nation seems to be a product of: 1) the availability of low-priced rental units in the older, run-down sections of the central city, 2) the heavy outflow of the middle-class white populations from those neighborhoods to the surrounding suburbs, and 3) the discriminatory policies of public and private real estate owners and developers.

Black isolation was not always so intense. At the turn of the century, according to Stanley Lieberson´s study (1980), there were higher levels of segregation among the South/Central/Eastern European groups than among blacks in the North. Italians and Russians, for example, were more isolated than blacks (:263-265). He found black isolation to be rather slight in 1890 among the 17 leading cities of the North and West at that time. The average black, frequently working as a domestic servant and living in the white home, lived in a ward where over 90 percent of the population was not black. Although black isolation increased in the next decade, in five or six cities there were actual declines in the degree of black isolation. From 1910 to 1930, however, massive increases in black isolation occurred.

The causes of that sharp increase in black isolation were a rise in anti-black sentiment, corresponding to the massive influx of blacks from the South to the North and the attempts by whites to maintain the degree of isolation previously existing before those new flows from the South began. The new immigrant groups saw a sharp decline in their isolation as their second and third generations were able to move out of the ethnic enclaves. They were replaced in those enclaves by a developing black ghetto (see Lieberson: 11).

This sharp increase in black isolation had severe consequences for them as a group in jobs and education, and indicates that the social position blacks held in the North began to deteriorate drastically at the turn of the century. Historian Allan Spear (1967), in his excellent study of the growth of the black ghetto in Chicago, distinguishes that city's black ghetto from its ethnic enclaves.

> The Chicago experience, therefore, tends to refute any attempt to compare Northern Negroes with European immigrants. Unlike the Irish, Poles, Jews, or Italians, Negroes banded together not to enjoy a common linguistic, cultural, and religious tradition, but because a systematic pattern of discrimination left them no alternative...The persistence of the Chicago Negro ghetto, then, has not been merely the product of a special historical experience. From its inception, the Negro ghetto was unique among the city's ethnic enclaves. It grew in response to an implacable white hostility that has not basically changed. In this sense it has been Chicago's only true ghetto, less the product of voluntary development within than external pressures from without (: 228-229).

Several policy devices were used to ensure black isolation and contributed to the development of the ghetto. One such device, the restrictive covenant, was used by real estate agencies and enforced by the courts. A typical such covenant reads as follows: "No part of the land hereby conveyed shall ever be used or occupied by or sold, demised, transferred, conveyed unto, or in trust for, leased or rented or given to Negroes, or to any person or persons of Negro blood or extraction, or to any person of the Semitic race, blood, or origin which racial description shall be deemed to include Armenians, Jews, Hebrews, Persians and Syrians (cited in Dye, 1971: 61).

Other practices which contributed to ghettoization include large lot zoning, which keeps lower income (i.e. non-white) families out of suburbs; illegal collusion among realtors who refuse to sell to blacks; and the lack of enforcement of housing codes which virtually encourages slum development. Similarly, municipal property tax policies essentially penalize improvements and reward those slumlords who poorly maintain their properties. The use of "earnings power" as a measure of determining the value of a property in condemnation proceedings favor those who overcrowd their buildings. Capital gains taxes and depreciation policies still favor the slum owners. The location of public housing projects concentrated in central city neighborhoods helps maintain the ghetto pattern (Tabb: 18).

From the late 1930's to the mid-1960's, the federal government encouraged the ghettoization process by requiring "homogeneous neighborhoods" in its mortgage policies within F.H.A., Federal National Mortgage Association, and G.I. Bill programs. These programs in essence helped to finance the white flight to the suburbs. Although ghettoization was not an intended impact, it was the direct consequence of this program to subsidize white suburbanization. In 1962 alone, "The federal government spent $820 million to subsidize housing for the poor (this includes public housing, public assistance, and tax deductions). That same year at least an estimated 2.9 billion was spent to subsidize housing for middle and upper income families (Schon, 1968: 208).

Once the ghetto developed, the economics of the situation encouraged their continuation. Segregation was the single-most important factor making slums so profitable. Slum profits depended upon a collusion between city agencies and slum landlords; in return for non-enforcement of the codes, the slumlords took the blame for the slums and enabled the city to evade the political ire of the ghetto residents (Tabb: 15-16). Economist David Gordon (1977) notes the effects of that economic colonization on the conditions of black housing:

> What kind of housing do black people have? One index of the quality of housing available is the completeness of plumbing facilities. In 1910, while 5% of white housing lacked some or all plumbing facilities, 17% of Negro housing was this way. In 1970, the median value of Negro housing was $10,700; for housing occupied by whites, it was $17,400. The degree of overcrowding (defined as more than one person per room) of Negroes varied from 2.5 to 8 times as much as that for non-Negroes (:157).

Professor Rose (1971) distinguishes three types of ghettos. The old or first generation ghetto centers, such as New York, Chicago, Philadelphia, Pittsburgh, and Cincinnati were established prior to 1920. In 1910 there were only 18 first generation ghetto centers, 12 of which were located in the South. The second generation ghettos were those developed between 1920 and 1950. The third generation ghetto areas developed since 1950. They are the most numerous: 28 in number, thirteen of which are located outside the South. By 1970 there were a total of 70 ghettos, over half of which were located outside the South (:17).

The development of the black ghetto reflected the shift of blacks from the rural South to the urban North, where discrimination practices forced them into the central city locations. From 1950 to 1970, black population grew by 25.4 percent, compared to a white growth rate of 17.6 percent. Where 87 percent of the nation's blacks lived in the South in 1900, less than half live there today. Although blacks comprise just over 11 percent of the total population, they make up a much larger share of the nation's large cities. They comprise about two-thirds of the population of D.C., and in excess of 40 percent of the populations of Atlanta, Baltimore, Birmingham, Detroit, Gary, Newark, New Orleans, Oakland, and St. Louis. They exceed one-third of the populations of Chicago, Cincinnati, Cleveland, Columbus, Memphis, and Philadelphia. Black suburban population is concentrated in only ten of the nation's SMSA's: Birmingham, Chicago, Detroit, Miami, Newark, New York, Philadelphia, Pittsburgh, St. Louis, and Washington (Fusfield: 24; Dye, 1971: 61; and Farley: 523).

Professor Lieberson (1980) assesses the results of this segregation into black central cities surrounded by white suburbs as follows:

> We know that black residential segregation is very high, much higher than that experienced by various white ethnic groups in the same cities. This is extremely important because residential isolation is of consequence for a wide variety of other events, such as school isolation, restrictions of opportunities because of minimal contacts with whites, marking the black population as distinctive and different, and the restricted

opportunities to live near all sorts of employment found at great distance from the black ghettos. Through residential isolation blacks also learn over and over again of their differences from whites and the low way in which they are regarded by them--indeed isolation may intensify the ethnic bond (:10-11).

Despite several decades of policy attempts to redress segregation, little real change has taken place. The 1948 Supreme Court case, <u>Shelly</u> <u>v.</u> <u>Kramer,</u> overturned the use of restrictive covenants as unconstitutional. Subsequent court decisions also ended Southern community attempts to legalize zoning for the purpose of racial segregation. But while Jim Crow de jure segregation may have been ended, blacks and whites are still largely segregated "de facto." Our public policy reflects "nondecisions" in behalf of segregated housing and thereby segregated public schools (Dye, 1971: 60).

When blacks attempt to integrate previously all white areas adjacent to predominately black areas they still elicit an accelerated response of white flight. Attempts to generalize this reaction, known as the "tipping mechanism," have led to an uncovering of the principle dimensions of such expected behavior. Attempts to alter the way in which the housing market currently operates to enforce the concentration of blacks into inner-city enclaves is still obviously a politically explosive situation. As Professor Tabb (1970) notes, the basic economics of the ghetto would have to be changed before real change in housing patterns would be affected.

Success in changing living conditions in the ghetto necessitates the rupture of the colonial relationship which now exists between the ghetto and the larger society. "The dark ghettos," as Kenneth Clark has written, "are social, political, educational, and--above all--economic colonies. Their inhabitants are subject peoples, victims of the greed, cruelty, insensitivity, guilt, and fear of their masters." The economic relation is a key one in understanding the ghetto (:3).

In 1966 President Johnson first requested open-housing legislation. Those bills died in the House in 1966 and 1967, in part due to the entrenched opposition of the real estate industry which lobbied against the passage of any fair housing law. The National Association of Real Estate Boards published a "Property Owner's Bill of Rights" which specifically opposed those bills. The Civil Rights Act of 1968 finally established a fair housing law. In large measure this law was passed as a memorial to Dr. Martin Luther King, Jr. The law prohibited the following forms of discrimination:

1) The refusal to sell or rent a dwelling to any person because of race, color, religion, or national origin.
2) Discrimination against a persons in terms, conditions, or privileges of the sale or rental of a dwelling.
3) Indicating a preference or discrimination on the basis of color, race, creed, or national origin in advertising the sale or rental of a dwelling.
4) Inducing "block-busting" techniques of real estate selling.

The law covered all apartments and houses rented or sold by real estate developers or agents. It exempted private homes sold without real estate agents and apartments with less than five rental units where the landlord maintained his own residence in the building (Dye, 1971: 68).

Yet the federal government worked at cross-purposes to this law by concentrating low-rent housing projects in central city locations. Only one of the nation's 24 largest cities--Cincinnati--has permitted public housing authorities to build new units outside the central city. The Department of Transportation spends billions of dollars in its highway program constructing metropolitan expressways which induce urban sprawl and promote white flight to the suburbs, in addition to promoting the outflow of commercial interests which follow the white middle-class exodus. This leads to further racial segregation within the metropolitan areas and reduces the number of jobs available to the minorities trapped in the central cities. That same trend is supported by FHA mortgage programs that encouraged white flight to the suburbs. Yet that same federal government, through the Department of Housing and Urban Development, is

trying to induce the return of the middle-class to the
central city through its urban renewal programs. By
tearing down slum housing and replacing them with civic
centers and upper-middle class developments it also
displaces the poor.

Such contradictory policy actions and the policy of
"nondecision" have resulted, despite a decade or more of
policy efforts supposedly designed to end segregation or
at least to promote "fair housing," in the ghetto areas
remaining virtually untouched. As Allan Spear notes:

> No other ethnic enclave in Chicago has changed
> so little over the past fifty years. While
> the city's Irish, Polish, Jewish, and Italian
> sections have broken down or developed new
> forms in the suburbs, the Negro ghetto
> remained much as it had been--cohesive,
> restrictive, and largely impoverished (:224).

Like Spear, Professor Tabb (1970) is decidedly
pessimistic as he summarizes the various studies
concerning the ghettoization process by concluding that
only a radical--and therefore highly unlikely--change
which essentially ends the colonial economic system
represented by the ghetto would end massive and
pervasive housing discrimination in the United States.

> Three conclusions emerge from these various
> studies. First, black-segregated residential
> patterns can be explained not by low income
> but by the working of the "exclusionary
> interests" (real estate boards, suburban
> governments--that establish and maintain vast
> sanctuaries from Negroes and poor people).
> Second, there is a great variety of available
> suburban housing. Studies show "a large
> supply of older low and moderate income
> housing already existing in many suburban
> communities...The existing suburban housing
> supply, in terms of housing costs, provides
> ample opportunity for desegregation now.
> Third, government policies subsidize slumlords
> through lax or non-existent code enforcement,
> thereby saving them millions of dollars, offer
> them generous tax treatment, and pay them
> handsomely for their property when slums are
> bought under urban renewal. The economics of
> ghetto housing insures that bad housing is

profitable and that good housing cannot be
maintained. There is a sort of Gresham´s Law
at work: bad housing drives out good; as
neighborhoods   deteriorate,   further
deterioration is induced (:13-14. His
italics.).

Thus it is that newer metropolitan areas develop
their ghetto areas in a pattern just like that of the
nation´s older ghettos. First, second, and third
generation ghettos are alike even though the first and
second developed at a time when formal law (such as
restrictive covenants) was used to induce the ghetto,
because the third-generation ghettos follow the same
economic patterns. The inertia of legal and extra-legal
actions of the past have spilled over into the present.
Thus, Denver´s ghetto, which was slightly more than a
neighborhood size in 1948 when the Court issued the
Shelly v. Kramer decision, is just as intensely
segregated today as the Detroit ghetto which included
over 150,000 blacks in its population at the same time
(see Rose: 35).

Law Enforcement

If housing is the most segregated area of
minority/majority relations, and the policy area showing
the least change over the years despite attempts to
mitigate housing discrimination, the area of law
enforcement seems to be a close second to housing in
those respects. As one scholar of the urban police
scene put it:

The relationship between the police and
minority groups in big city ghettos is one of
the sorest spots in American life today. In
the words of a recent report by the
President´s Commission on Law Enforcement and
Administration of Justice, a "wall of
isolation" surrounds the police, blocking
understanding between them and the dwellers in
the slums, permitting the growth of every kind
of misunderstanding and hatred...The
policeman, whose mission is is to guard the
peace, walks uneasy in the ghetto. What
worries him is not so much the ordinary
criminal; usually he feels he can cope with
lawbreakers, whose apprehension is his main
job. He fears, rather, the very people he is

408

there to protect. For many otherwise law-
abiding ghetto dwellers are openly hostile to
him; many refuse to cooperate with him in
maintaining law and order; and on occasion
some may attack him (Edwards: 2).

Increasingly, the relationship between the police
and the nation's minority population, particularly
blacks in the ghettos, is characterized by a hostility
bordering on a "war" mentality on both sides.   One of
the country's leading criminologists, James Q. Wilson,
stated: "The views of many police officers seem to
confirm the "war" theory of police-community relations.
Data gathered at least as far back as 1960 suggests that
most big-city police officers see the citizenry as at
least uncooperative and at worst hostile" (in Stedman:
60).   Wilson goes on to note that although his research
shows that the majority of black and white citizens
evidence positive attitudes toward the police, the most
anti-police groups are young adult males, and especially
young black males.   Another police scholar says simply,
"Hating and mistrusting the police has become a way of
life in the ghetto" (Alexander: 23).

In large measure, the animosity between the two can
be attributed to racial prejudice.   Such prejudice is
two-sided.   It is a force which runs deep in American
society; one that is explosive in nature.   When racial
prejudice breaks out in an uncontrolled manner, such as
a race riot, the racial violence which runs loose in our
city streets unleashes fear and hatred which turns
otherwise good and even warm human beings--both black
and white--into savages. Unfortunately, it is often the
innocent people who are the victims of such outbreaks.
Each such outbreak, moreover, exacerbates the antipathy
between the police and minority groups. Most such riots
have been touched off by an encounter between the police
and ghetto residents.   The police serve as the "flash
point" for black anger, the formation of mobs, and the
outbreak of civil disorder (see Levy: 349).

Minority hostility towards the police reflects our
long history of discrimination.   Blacks remember the
mistreatment of their Southern past where "de jure"
segregation was enforced by the police.   As a former
police chief put it:

Many people living today remember far worse things--the worst being the lynchings which were possible only because law enforcement agencies stood aside and let the mobs work their will. From 1882 to 1959, 2,595 Negroes were lynched in nine Southern states. No white person was ever punished for these offenses (Edwards: 25).

Much of the pervasiveness of the conflict is due to the commonality of anti-minority attitudes among police department personnel. When the civil rights movement first got under way in the late 1950's and early 1960's, that attitude was apparent and engendered a reciprocal feeling, in both the North and the South.

Every time illegal violence is employed against civil rights demonstrations anywhere, it increases animosity against police everywhere. The dogs which Police Chief T. Eugene "Bull" Connor set on young Negroes in Birmingham, Alabama, in 1963, probably caused more physical injury to police officers in other cities in the long run than to the demonstrators they were pictured as attacking (Edwards:17).

Numerous studies have indicated a fairly widespread prejudice among police against minorities, particularly blacks (see several cited in Cooper: 32). Edwards cites the results of the President's Crime Commission Task Force which found 72 percent of the police officers whom it interviewed in three major cities exhibited prejudice against blacks in their responses to Task Force observers (Edwards: 27). Blacks and whites, moreover, manifest sharply different attitudes in their attitudes towards and experience with police, as shown in Table 27, below.

Nor is this study unique. Edwards (1968) cites a number of studies that indicate a widespread problem of police abuse and excessive use of force (:3). Albert Reiss reports a study on police brutality that found it to be not uncommon, and that the lower class bore the brunt of the victimization. Mostly, the police mistreated citizens who were of the same race as the officer: 67 percent of citizens victimized by white police were white, and 71 percent of citizens victimized by black officers were black.

"Some people say that police don't show respect for people and use insulting language. Do you think this happens to people in this neighborhood?"

	BLACKS:		(In Percent)	WHITE:		
	MEN	WOMEN	TOTAL	MEN	WOMEN	TOTAL
YES	43	33	38	17	14	16
NO	38	41	39	75	75	75
Don't Know	19	26	23	8	11	9

"Some people say the police frisk or search people without good reason. Do you think this happens in this neighborhood?"

YES	42	30	36	10	9	11
NO	41	40	41	75	75	76
Don't Know	17	30	23	10	16	13

"Some people say that the police rough up people unnecessarily when they are arresting them or afterwords. Do you think this happens to people in this neighborhood?"

YES	37	32	35	10	9	10
NO	42	41	41	80	76	78
Don't Know	21	27	24	10	15	12
	100	100	100	100	100	100

Source: Adapted from Ruchelman: 137. Data is from National Advisory Commission on Civil Disorders.

Nor were the rates of such abuse found in these studies insignificant:

> In our study, there were 643 white suspects, 27 of whom experienced undue use of force. This yields an abuse rate of 41.9 per 1,000 white suspects. The comparable rate for 751 Negro suspects, of whom 17 experienced undue use of force, is 22.6 per 1,000. If one accepts these rates as reasonably reliable estimates of the undue force against suspects, then there would be little doubt that in major metropolitan areas the sort of behavior called "police brutality" is far from rare (in Lipsky,1970: 74).

Most troubling, in terms of systematic abuse problems was their finding that in a third of the cases were excessive use of force was evident, it took place in the police station after the arrest, in which the police officials should have been able to control the situation. Moreover, incidents like the highly publicized Algier Motel case during the Detroit riots are especially troubling because they confirm the worst fears among the nation´s minorities. In that case, three black youth were executed by police officers. "It was murder. They just murdered them boys. They just happened to be with these white girls, all of them sitting up in the room together. That´s what it was (Ibid: 47)."

The ghetto setting itself virtually assures the development of police/minority conflict. Because of their skin color and the resulting residential segregation and density problems, blacks are more likely than whites to come into adversarial contact with the police. Wilson cites a study of six-hundred police officers in three major cities which had large black populations. Three-fourths of the white officers working in predominately black areas expressed prejudiced or highly prejudiced views of blacks. Moreover, twenty-eight percent of the black officers in the study did so as well (in Stedman: 65). Levy similarly assesses the problem as one not of a few "bad eggs" but rather of a police system which is racist in its recruitment, training, socialization, and assignment patterns (in Ruchelman: 80).

The very existence of the ghetto as a center of intense "crime problems" aggravates the systematic nature of the police/minority conflict. Metropolitan areas have a violent crime rate five times as high and a property crime rate twice as high as the smaller city or rural area.

The adversary relationship is compounded by the role the police must play in the ghetto. The police serve as a sort of buffer. Their job is to minimize crime by inhibiting it where possible, but also to contain it within an area where it is less likely to be a threat to the person or property of the majority members of society. This means that the police officer quite literally personifies "the law." The officer becomes the symbol of authority, empowered to use his gun when necessary. He becomes the symbol and the agent of the sovereign right of the state to take lives if need be (Alexander: 1969; Cooper: 29). Ghetto residents react to that role. Their frustrations and anger are directed towards the police like lightning to the rod. The enmity and animosity so pervasive in the ghetto is transferred to the police officer. It provides for ghetto residents a release for their pent-up frustrations that, if left without an object, seethe and boil over into social eruptions such as riots.

In addition to this adversary role played by the police, the entire judicial system is structured in a manner which tends to exacerbate the problem. The "victimless crimes" policies of society represent an option which enhances the likelihood of police/minority conflict by concentrating many of the resources of the entire judicial system, most especially law enforcement, on the control of such crime. The arrests for prostitution, public intoxication, crimes of "sexual perversions," or drug abuse consume a huge portion of the court time in any large city, time that might otherwise be otherwise devoted to more swiftly prosecute perpetrators of crime against person or property. Add to the court time the use of the resources of the prosecutors office, court-appointed defense attorneys, and the police time spent on "victimless crime," and the total mounts dramatically. Such laws demean law enforcement officers who must consort with prostitutes, homosexuals, gamblers and drug pushers in order to catch them. Such laws are inevitably selectively enforced against social undesirables. Police arrest streetwalkers but rarely arrest expensive call girls. Blacks, Hispanics, and lower-class people in general are arrested for public intoxication, but middle-class people are rarely bothered for such unless when driving. Victimless crimes encourage organized crime which functions to provide such "service." These laws, moreover, fail to prevent the conduct they proscribe; it is arguable whether they even reduce such conduct that much. But the need to enforce these laws puts the police into sustained conflict with minorities. To the police, who almost always witness the ghetto resident or minority member in the context of breaking a law, the anti-minority attitudes are confirmed and reinforced. To the ghetto resident, the police are viewed as "The Man" whose only contact is when they bust somebody for something often not even viewed as "real crime."

What, if anything, can be done to reduce the inherently conflictual relationship? The December, 1982 riots in Miami touched-off by a police/black incident, led Miami Mayor Maurice Ferre to observe, "We live in a community that divides itself on ethnic lines in a stronger way than just about any other community in America...The most affected party in the whole process is the black community (U.S.A. Today, January 5, 1982: 10 A)." This riot led to calls for some suggested reforms that are fairly common:

1) More minority officers. A city's police force should mirror the racial diversity of its citizens.
2) More sensitivity and stress training.
3) More patrolmen to walk neighborhood beats. Foot patrolmen get to know the people they serve, and vice-versa.

There have been some attempts along these lines. Between 1972 and 1981 the share of minority police increased from 7 percent to 13 percent. In cities such as Atlanta, Detroit, Philadelphia, and Newark, fatal police shootings have been sharply reduced. Atlanta Mayor Andrew Young echoed those suggestions when explaining why the situation in Atlanta was so much better than in Miami.

Our long history of integrated leadership has also helped us avoid riots. The first blacks were elected to the Board of Education in 1961; to the City Council in 1965. In 1973, Atlanta elected its first black mayor, Maynard Jackson. He began the process of desegregating our police force; today about half our officers are black. We have a black public safety commissioner, but a white chief of police. In our police zones, if we have a white major, we have a black captain, and vice-versa.
When you desegregate your police department, the attitudes of the rank-and-file officers change. When the officers are under bi-racial command, their attitudes toward the other race change. We worked hard on neighborhood watch and citizen participation programs, to bring police officers close to the people. Once the police and the police officer knew each other, they realized they needed each other to prevent crime (U.S.A. Today, January 5, 1982: 10 A).

Such reforms led Bertram Levine, of the U.S. Community Relations Service, to observe, "Police-community relations have a thousand miles to go before we reach equal justice, but they have come a long way in the last 15 or 20 years (Ibid)." But other scholars of police/community relations are far less optimistic about how much improvement such "reforms" can bring about. They argue that as long as the police must be the buffers, the social brokers and urban colonial guards the conflict will remain. Police departments, moreover, tend to attract "stratiphiles"--that is, individuals who are extraordinarily disposed to the forces and commitments that flow from social stratification. They are also marginal men. Thus, in the ghetto, the police are often viewed as pariahs, judas goats, and sacrificial lambs. This is doubly so for the black cop, who often feels a double marginality, rejected by both blacks and by many white cops, sometimes viewed as traitors to their race (Alexander:14-17; Cooper:61-70). And the cops who regularly work the ghetto, be they black or white, can become ghettoized. They come to feel rejected, abused, exploited, alienated, and even powerless. These feelings are a function of working in the ghetto. Thus, even the black officers sometimes becomes abusive toward ghetto residents.

Another proposal for reform has been the civilian review board. Such boards have not been very successful. Only a few metropolitan areas have established them. New York City had a board. A study of its operation noted that the board had heard a total of 324 complaints, of which twelve resulted in formal charges by the department, seven policemen were reprimanded, and four cases referred to other agencies. Ninety six were thrown out as unsubstantiated, and the remainder were pending at the end of the year (Adams, 1972: 309). Such boards are clearly not panaceas. Several cities which have them--Philadelphia and Rochester, for example--still experienced riots. They have been faulted for being inadequately staffed, relying on the police for the investigation of the police. They often lack control or remedial powers-- being only able to investigate and advise (see Edwards, 1968).

But "self-policing" can also prove to be a sham. Police are rarely convicted and punished on the basis of citizen complaints by internal affairs division investigation or by outside police civilian review boards. The police reform movement has persuaded state, local, and even federal authorities that the responsibility for handling complaints against the police should be handled by them. Yet, out of a deep concern for the reputation of their department, the internal affairs units and other such special squads have on occasion employed reprehensible tactics to discourage citizens from filing complaints against officers. Fogelson (1977) cites a virtual litany of such devices employed in Cleveland, Los Angeles, New York, Philadelphia, and Washington, D.C. These tactics included threatening citizens who sought to lodge complaints with criminal libel; forcing them to take lie detector tests; employing disorderly conduct charges and resisting arrest charges against them; or threatening to do so; intimidating them and their witnesses if they did file; refusing access to counsel or to files; and developing procedures which were often expensive, complicated, and protracted (: 283-284).

The police reform movement has also called for increased police "professionalism." This approach is very expensive. In New York City, to cite but one example, from 1963 to 1973 the police force increased in size by 18 percent--from 26,700 to 31,500 officers. But its costs rose by 96 percent--from $299 million to $587 million. Thus, a variety of police scholars and critics are pessimistic about the value of the "professionalism reforms" (1). Such reforms have not prevented the outbreak of riots, reduced significantly the allegations of brutality, nor improved ghetto resident attitudes towards the police. The major public policy response from the national government was the Crime Control and Safe Streets Act of 1968, which created the Law Enforcement Assistance Administration (LEAA). This law poured millions of federal dollars into local police departments with an approach most critics allege to have been highly inefficient, with most of the money, at least early on, being spent on expensive "hardware" and a repressive response to police/minority relations (2).

Even such an advocate of police reform as James Wilson ultimately assesses such reform tactics as being very limited in their impact upon the central problem of policy/minority relations.

The chief policy implications of this argument is that police/community relations cannot be substantially improved by programs designed to deal with citizens in settings other than encounters with patrolmen; evening meetings, discussion groups, block clubs, police-community councils, and the like will be seen by both officer and citizen as tangential to their central relationship. Nor can the behavior of patrolmen be modified other than by providing him with incentives and instructions relevant to his central task; lecturing him on good behavior, sending him to one-week human relations training institutes, or providing him with materials designed to make him think blacks are just like everybody else will be ignored and even scorned by him. Indeed, seeing the police/ghetto problem in the context of the central police mission and its incompatibility with the freedom of all persons to come and go as they please cannot make one optimistic about how much improvement is possible at all in police relations with blacks. So long as crime and disorder are disproportionately to be found among young lower-class males, and so long as blacks remain over-represented in (though by no means identical with) such groups--blacks--especially young ones--and the police are going to be adversaries (Wilson, in Stedman : 68-69).

Political Participation

If the policy areas of housing and law enforcement continue to be the most racist and show the least amount of change, primarily because of their reliance upon "de facto" types of discrimination, the area of political participation shows the greatest degree of change. This section will briefly trace the changes in American public policy with respect to minority political participation. It will show how we changed from a society which systematically and in various institutionalized ways disenfranchised its minority population to one which now guarantees their basic civil rights of participation.

In earlier chapters we described the varying but consistently lower levels of political participation that is characteristic of minority groups in the United States. Much of that lower level of participation is undoubtedly related to their lower level of socio-economic status. Social science scholars focusing upon political participation have developed the view that socio-economic status (SES) is the most important influence of the level of participation. Indeed, the consensus among scholars as to its importance is such that it is referred to as the "standard SES model" (Verba and Nie, see chapter 8). Simply put, the higher one´s SES the more likely one is to vote, and vice-versa.

But as we shall see, ethnicity can have an independent impact upon political participation quite apart from its association with SES. Moreover, public policy has been consciously used by some factions of the majority society to disenfranchise ethnic minorities and has been instrumental in developing that association between low SES and low levels of participation. As Professor Sigler (1975) so aptly puts it:

> Of all the rights available to democratic citizens, none is more generally significant than the right to vote. Voting is the primal act of democratic citizens. Without the suffrage all other rights become endangered, since a minority could prevent the enjoyment of these other rights by exerting its power upon government disproportionately. The enjoyment of the right to vote is a test of democracy...
> At the core of the right to vote is the opportunity for a group to protect itself against injurious governmental policies. The right is available to individuals, but it is also a safeguard for groups (:111, 113).

Majority society has employed a number of laws and public policy devices, as well as informal measures such as violence and intimidation, to deny participation to minority groups. The poll tax, literacy tests, the white primary, racial gerrymandering, and registration laws are among the more prominent public policy devices used to disenfranchise various minorities.

Women were denied by law the right to vote until the 19th Amendment was passed in 1920. Asian immigrants, denied citizenship by law, were thereby effectively disenfranchised. So too, the American Indian could not vote, except for their tribal leadership, until Congress finally passed the Indian Citizen Act in 1924. Even then, some states limited them from participation in state and local elections until the 1940's. The most extensive use of public policy to disenfranchise minorities, however, were the various Jim Crow laws aimed at blacks. So intense was racial (and sexual) prejudice that, at one time, seventeen American states permitted male aliens to vote but denied women and blacks from doing so (Sigler: 114).

Although immediately after the Civil War three constitutional amendments were passed which abolished slavery and granted citizenship to all persons born or naturalized in the United States, and specifically prohibited the denial of the right to vote to any citizen on the basis of race, the enjoyment of this basic right by blacks was short-lived. As soon as federal troops left the South in the late 1870's, Southern whites began to re-establish political control over the black population in the South, effectively denying their voting rights until the mid-1960's. Although Southern blacks continued to vote, sometimes in fairly large numbers, until well into the 1880's and 1890's, by the 1890's most of the former Confederate states had passed laws which began segregating public facilities. The first objective of the white supremacy movement was to disenfranchise blacks.

At first Congress attempted to deal with the South's efforts to curtail black voting rights. Congress passed the Enforcement Act of 1870 to give clear "teeth" to the Fifteenth Amendment. A hostile Supreme Court, however, effectively scuttled the law in 1876 (in United States v. Reese, 92 U.S. 214). The Court argued that the right to vote was not conferred to anyone by the Fifteenth Amendment, since the right to vote was still derived from the states. In 1894 Congress repealed the Enforcement Act, thereby leaving black voting rights to the mercies of the Court. Despite the clear intent of the Fifteenth Amendment, most of the nation's blacks living in the South were denied the right to vote prior to the twentieth century. Several Supreme Court cases led to that development.

In the Civil Rights Cases of 1883 the Court's interpretation of the Constitution was that Congress had no expressed nor implied powers to pass a law prohibiting discrimination practiced by private individuals. And in Hurtado v. California in 1884, the Court ruled that the Fourteenth Amendment's due process clause did not make the Bill of Rights binding upon state governments. It took forty years before the Court reversed itself on that issue (Dye, 1971: 13).

One of the more common devices used in the South to disenfranchise blacks was the literacy test. These tests originated in the North--in Connecticut and Massachusetts--and only later came to the South. They were first developed in many states to screen out the new immigrants and deny them the vote (Sigler: 114). Southern states soon seized upon them as effective devices against their black population. The tests were upheld by the Supreme Court in 1898 (Williams v. Mississippi, 170 U.S. 218). V. O. Key (1949), in his classic Southern Politics, labels them as "...fraud, and nothing more (:576)."

Another such device was the poll tax, used by eleven Southern states. In several cases, the tax was made retroactive--that is, the citizen desiring to vote not only had to pay the poll tax for that year, but for all past years for which he or she had been eligible to vote. The poll tax was a very effective device which prevented large numbers of poor whites as well as blacks from voting in the South. It was upheld by the Supreme Court in 1937 in Breedlove v. Suttles (302 U.S. 277). It was not until 1966 when the Court finally declared the poll tax as invalid (Harper v. Virginia Board of Elections, 383 U.S. 663).

One of the most blatant forms of legal disenfranchisement of the black was the "grandfather clause," at one time used by seven Southern states. This law allowed a registrant to vote without barriers if one's grandfather could do so. Since the grandfathers of blacks had been slaves legally barred from voting, this device blatantly denied blacks that right. The Supreme Court struck down such laws, based on an Oklahoma case which exempted whites from a literacy test on the basis of a grandfather clause, in Guinn v. United States, (238 U.S. 347), in 1915. Oklahoma quickly passed a new registration law that continued to deny blacks the vote until it, too, was finally overturned in 1939 (Lane v. Wilson, 307 U.S. 268, 275).

Another frequently used device was the white primary. This device was popular in many Southern states, since the domination of the Democratic Party was so solid that an aspiring politician effectively had to win the Democratic Party primary in order to win office. The primary election became the real election, with the general election merely rubber stamping the choice actually made in the primary. By legally banning blacks from voting in the primary, through the use of "white-only" primary election laws, the Southern states could essentially deny blacks an effective vote even if they were allowed to vote in the general election. The Supreme Court first ruled that there was no national authority to regulate primary elections (Newberry v. United States, 256 U.S. 232, 1921). That ruling was modified by the Nixon v. Herndon case of 1927, which invalidated a Texas law which flatly prohibited blacks from voting in the state's Democratic Primary. Texas responded by authorizing the executive committees of the state's parties to prescribe voting qualifications in primary elections. That law, too, was struck down by the Court, in Nixon v. Condon, (286 U.S. 73) in 1932. Texas then set up the Democratic Party as a "private club," whose members could be limited to whites only. At first the Court upheld the law, on the basis of such action being discrimination by a private organization rather than by a state (see Grovey v. Townsend, 295 U.S. 45, 1935; and Breedlove v. Suttles, 302 U.S. 277, 280, 1937). The white primary, however, was finally ruled unconstitutional in any form when the Supreme Court reversed itself in the 1944 case of Smith v. Allwright, (285 U.S. 355).

The use of racial gerrymandering was ruled unconstitutional by the Supreme Court in Gomillion v. Lightfoot, (364 U.S. 339, 1960). This case overturned an Alabama legislative redistricting plan which designed voter districts in a manner which the Court ruled was clearly intended to diffuse black votes. With virtually every Jim Crow law being overturned, the white majority turned increasingly to more indirect methods. Registration laws still remain a hurdle to the poor, and intimidation and footdragging still suppress black registration. As one scholar of black politics in the South noted:

Even in the 1970's, Mississippians utilized economic and physical intimidation, including murder, obstacles to registration, denial of the ballot on election day, legal and extra-legal barriers to candidacy, and other methods to dilute black electoral power (Colby: 16-17).

Such intimidation was successful because of the South's history of violence against blacks who dared to participate. During the late 1880's through the early decades of this century, the Ku Klux Klan used a systematic campaign of violence against blacks to "keep them in their place." As we have seen, from 1889 to 1918, this nation witnessed 3,224 lynchings of black Americans.

In the late 1940's Congress became involved in the process. In 1948 President Truman supported proposals to ensure fair employment, fair elections, the outlawing of poll taxes, crackdown against violence and lynchings, and the elimination of segregation in interstate commerce. He also advocated creating a permanent Civil Rights Commission. The South's power in the Senate was such that none of his proposals were passed, but clearly the pressure was on Congress to act.

In 1962 Congress passed the 24th Amendment outlawing the poll tax in national elections. It was ratified by the states in 1964. In 1966 the Supreme Court, in the Harper v. Virginia Board of Elections case, applied it to state and local elections as well, via the 14th Amendment. This decision brought an end to all poll taxes in the United States.

The civil rights movement, through its direct-action tactics, brought continued pressure on Congress to enact legislation which would end "de jure" discrimination. In 1963 the Birmingham demonstrations ignited protests across the nation, culminating in the March on Washington in August of that year, which saw more than 200,000 blacks and whites participate, and culminated in Dr. Martin Luther King Jr.'s famous "I Have a Dream" speech. In large measure in response to that March, President Kennedy sent a strong civil rights bill to Congress, which was passed after his assassination, the famous Civil Rights Act of 1964. That act was hailed as the most sweeping civil rights law enacted in American history. Its various titles and provisions did much to end all Jim Crow laws and practices in the South. The act contained several provisions which touched directly upon participation. Title I concerned literacy tests, making it unlawful when determining whether an individual was qualified by State law to vote in any Federal election to apply any standard, practice, or procedure different from those applied to other individuals within the same county. It required written literacy tests and stated that any one who had completed sixth grade in any English-speaking school was presumed literate unless proven otherwise.

Title V of the act empowers the U.S. Commission on Civil Rights, first established by the Civil Rights Act of 1957, to investigate deprivations of the right to vote. The law was immediately challenged, but the entire act was upheld as constitutional in the Heart of Atlanta Motel v. the United States, (379 U.S. 241), and Katzenbach v. McClung, (379 U.S. 294), both decided in 1964.

Local registrars in the South were still able to bar blacks by an endless variety of registration barriers. Congress reacted by passing the Voting Rights Act of 1965. This law was the first truly effective tool for protecting the voting rights of minority citizens. Congress extended the Act in 1970, 1975, and 1982. The law has both permanent and temporary provisions (3).

The permanent or General Provisions of the Act: 1) ensure that length-of-residency requirements will not prevent any citizen from voting in presidential elections; 2) prohibit anyone from denying an eligible citizen the right to vote or from interfering with or intimidating anyone from seeking to register or to vote; and 3) forbid the use of literacy tests or other devices as qualifications for voting in any federal, state, local, general or primary election.

The temporary or special "triggering" provisions where applicable to those states or counties where: 1) literacy tests or similar devices were enforced as of November 1, 1964; and 2) where fewer than 50 percent of the voting-age residents either were registered or had cast ballots in the 1964 Presidential election. In such jurisdictions the Attorney General of the United States, upon evidence of voter discrimination determined by him, was empowered to replace the local registrars with federal examiners who were authorized to abolish literacy tests, waive poll taxes, and register voters under simpler federal procedures. Although quickly challenged, the law was upheld in <u>South Carolina v. Katzenbach</u>, (383 U.S. 301). A third triggering provision, added in 1975, concerned minority languages. It was added to ensure that U.S. citizens are not deprived the vote because they cannot speak, read, or write English. A jurisdiction is covered by the language provision if: 1) in November, 1972, more than 5 percent of the voting age population in that jurisdiction were members of a single language minority (specified as American Indian, Asian-Americans--Chinese, Filipino, Japanese, Koreans--Alaskan Natives, or persons of Spanish heritage); <u>and</u> the jurisdiction provided English-only election material <u>and</u> less than 50 percent of the voting age population registered or voted in the 1972 presidential election; or 2) more than 5 percent of the voting age population in a jurisdiction are members of a single language minority <u>and</u> the illiteracy rate for that minority population is higher than the national illiteracy rate, such rate being defined as failure to complete the fifth grade.

The original "trigger" provisions brought under its special coverage the entire states of Alabama, Georgia, Louisiana, Mississippi, South Carolina, and Virginia, and about forty counties in North Carolina, and a scattering of counties in Arizona, Hawaii, and Idaho. Hundreds of observers and federal examiners were sent to these jurisdictions under the original act. The special language provisions affected many more jurisdictions in other parts of the country, including local governments in California, Massachusetts, and Kansas.

Section 5 of the Act requires all jurisdictions covered under its first and second "trigger" provisions to submit <u>in advance</u> any proposed changes in their election laws or procedures to the federal government for approval. The intent of this section is to prevent new discrimination practices from replacing old ones--a common cycle prior to the 1965 Act. This section further places the burden of proof on covered jurisdictions to demonstrate that neither the purpose nor effect of proposed changes in their election system is discriminatory.

The impact of these laws has been dramatic. Whereas only five percent of voting age blacks were registered to vote in the eleven Southern states in 1940, black registration rose to 45 percent in 1964, and to 57 percent by 1968. In Mississippi, before the 1965 Act, only 6.7 percent of the voting-age were registered. By 1972 that figure was up to 60 percent! Georgia's rate jumped from 27 percent in 1965 to nearly 68 percent in 1972. Overall, black registration rates in the South have approached the level of white rates for the first time since Reconstruction days. In the Southwest, after the 1975 language provision was added, Hispanic registration rates rose from 44 percent in 1976 to 59 percent in 1980 (Voter, Spring, 1981: 3-4). In 1962 there were a total of 72 black elected officials in the South; in 1982 there were 2,500 (Citizen Participation, 1982: 4)!

Participation consists of more than just electoral behavior--of voting. Several studies have documented the increased activity and effectiveness of minorities in the use of non-electoral participation. To a large extent, the very success of the civil rights movement during the 1960's was the result of the movement's use of direct action protest tactics. As Parsons and Clark (1966) noted:

> ...the SNCC "kids" in their worn denims brought new verve, drive, daring, and enthusiasm--as well as the brashness and chaos of youth--to sustain the dynamism of direct-action civil rights tactics. They propelled the more orderly and stable groups like the NAACP and the Urban League toward increasing acceptance of direct-action methods not only because some of the older leaders found the ardor of youth contagious but also because, after the manner of experienced leaders, they sensed that bolder programs would be necessary if their own role were not to be undermined. The intervention of youth revitalized CORE and sustained the intensity of the direct involvement of King and SCLC (: 616).

David Colby has recently tested the relative efficacy of electoral, protest, and violent (i.e. riots) tactics on Mississippi welfare policy for the decade 1960-1970. He found that the use of these tactics, rather than the need of the recipients, influenced changes in welfare policy. All three types of tactics

425

were influential, although the relative strength of the tactics and the processes of influence differed.

Colby's study found that the number of applicants was influenced by the tactics of mass insurgency as represented by nonviolent protest and riots. These tactics provided the minority members using them with the political tools, confidence, solidarity, and information to demand and achieve greater economic rights. These tactics were able to <u>directly</u> effect policy changes by influencing those determinants of policy which are "controllable" by the masses and "uncontrollable," in the short run, by the policy makers. Colby's study suggests a modification of the Lipsky model (see Figure 7, Chapter 7), in that his study found that, under certain conditions, protest is able to influence policy without the intervention of the reference public and policy makers.

The change in the approval rate was influenced by black electoral tactics. Policy makers respond to the "normal" tactics of electoral politics because they are socialized to them. In order to appeal to the newest members of the political audience which gradually included greater number of blacks, the policy makers slightly modified the portion of welfare policy which they alone controlled. The expansion of the electorate can cause massive disruptions in the traditional electoral pattern and be a mechanism for change (Colby, 1982: 17-18).

This is consistent with the results of a study by Young and Burstein of the political consequences of American racial demographic change from 1915 to 1982. They argue persuasively that much of the effectiveness of the civil rights movement in the South, using largely protest tactics, was hinged to their increased electoral strength in the North as blacks massively migrated North (Young and Burstein: 23).

Dale Nelson (1982) used multivariate analysis to examine a number of variables which influence political attitudes and communal political participation. He found that both ethnic identity and SES were the strongest predictors. Ethnic identity, however, was the best single predictor, and its impact was independent of SES. His findings support the proposition that while SES and ethnicity share a certain amount of impact due to their statistical inter-correlation, they have substantial independent influence on communal participation. SES was statistically unrelated to ethnic social cohesion and only slightly related to ethnic social consciousness and ethnic political consciousness. In his study, ethnic identity was the best single predictor of variations in political attitudes. It explained 35 percent of the variance, while SES explained only 24 percent (4).

Dale Nelson goes on to make an important observation about the relationship between ethnicity and participation with respect to one ethnic group's ability to dramatically effect the participation of others.

> The argument we have presented on political culture should not be construed as one which points to "fatal flaws" in the cultural makeup of some ethnic groups. One culture is not better or worse than another--it is simply different. If a political system responds to one kind of value system and not another, the problem lies with the system and its inability to respond to the needs of the entire population. But if an individual is born into an ethnic group whose level of participant political culture is low, he is at a disadvantage politically, because his socialization process is unlikely to predispose him to participate.
> Even if cultural differences remain between ethnic groups, cultures do change. Low or high levels of participant political culture are not frozen into a group's existence. But cultural change is slow if such change is the result only of individual adaptation. Dramatic events and increased organizational activity and mobilization can be especially important to increasing levels of participant political culture. Black Americans, for example, may have acted as a prototype for other disadvantaged groups, and there is evidence that the experience of Blacks has had a kind of "demonstration effect" on American Indians, Chicanos, and Puerto Ricans during the 1960's and 1970's. We have provided evidence that a high level of ethnic political consciousness influences the level of participant culture, as does increased social interaction with members of the broader community (:39-40. His italics.).

Changes in political participation among minority groups are increasingly evident in the 1980´s. In the previous chapter we noted the closing of the electoral gap by women. Blacks, Hispanics, Indians and Gay Activists have all launched organized campaigns to increase the political participation of their members. The focus of the 1980´s seems to be primarily upon voting behavior. Formal barriers have been largely overturned. But much still needs to be done before such minorities will reap the electoral benefits of their participation. At-large election districts and gerrymandering are still used to dilute the minority vote. Overcoming those obstacles is the target of this decade´s civil rights movement. A recent study noted the persistence of the at-large election district problem for blacks.

A combination of entrenched political, economic, and social patterns, however, still stacks the deck against black politicians in the South, even when the blacks are a majority of the local population. Of 22 counties in Georgia with a black majority population, for example, 15 have no black commissioners. Only one of the other seven has a black majority on the commission. In South Carolina, only one of 13 black majority counties has a black majority commission.
When blacks are outnumbered by whites, the chances of electing black candidates are almost nil, especially in rural areas. One reason is the acknowledged persistence of racial bloc voting, combined with the widespread use of at-large election systems. In other words, to win even most local elections, black office-seekers must gain some support from white voters--and whites are still rarely willing to vote for a black candidate (Voter, Spring, 1981: 4).

A similar problem confronts Hispanic voters in the Southwest. Recent research reported in Citizen Participation found that at least 66 counties in Texas and 54 in California were racially gerrymandered against Mexican-Americans. Increased registration drives and voter turnout are of little value when gerrymandering dilutes the minority´s voting strength. Such discriminatory re-districting schemes have plagued Hispanic political advancement for some time in the

Southwest, particularly in Texas. One Hispanic interest group, the Southwest Voter Registration Education Project (SVREP) has been involved in 36 lawsuits against racially gerrymandered districts in Colorado, New Mexico and Texas. Most of them were settled out of court (Citizen Participation: 8).

Both Blacks and Hispanics have launched drives to overcome these obstacles. The Voter Education Project (VEP), first begun in 1962 to encourage local black voter registration, has been rejuvenated in 1980. It has targeted special efforts in Alabama, Georgia, and Mississippi where "reindentification programs" have been used to wipe off thousands of blacks from voter registration lists. Another group concentrating its efforts on black voter registration is the A. Phillip Randolph Institute. Also, the Coalition on Black Voter Participation is active. This umbrella group was composed of 50 member organizations in 1976. By 1982 it had expanded to 80 groups concentrating on 50 congressional districts located in 18 states. Likewise, Project Vote, another national voter registration project begun in 1980 has targeted its efforts in Connecticut, Maryland, Michigan, New Jersey, New York, Ohio, and Pennsylvania. Its efforts are concentrated in 22 congressional districts and 35 cities within those states. Its results have been impressive (Citizen Participation: 5). The Reverend Jackson's presidential nomination bid has scored impressive gains in new black registrations with estimates of over two million new voters turning out during the primary elections.

The potential of such programs has inspired the Hispanics to copy them. The Hispanic vote could be the swing vote in states like Texas and California--whose 76 electoral votes constitute 28 percent of all the votes needed to be elected president. The SVREP campaign has also shown considerable success and perhaps foreshadows the efforts and direction that group's minority politics will take throughout the remainder of the decade. The results of their litigation has been remarkable. In Medina County, Texas, for example, reapportionment had not occurred since the turn of the century. When SVREP sued and districts were redrawn, three Mexican Americans were elected to office, the first in the county's history. In Victoria County, where minorities comprise 30 percent of the population, a county commissioner was elected and the city council was forced to go from an "at-large" to a single-member district structure.

Victories such as these set off a chain reaction--when Mexican Americans have a better chance of winning elections, they register and turnout to vote in even greater numbers. The Mexican American Legal Defense Education Fund and the Texas Rural Legal Aid have filed suits challenging the at-large election structures of two Texas school districts. That litigation is moving ahead and may foreshadow future suits in the Southwest.

Chapter Endnotes

1. See the reservations of Gordon Misner and Jerry Wilson in "Reform At A Standstill," in Fogelson, 1971: 269-295; and the criticisms of Burton Levy, Arthur Niederhoffer, and Jerome Skolnick, in Levy, 1968: 348.

2. See Dye, 1978: 91; and Allan Sindler (ed.), America in the Seventies: Problems, Policies and Politics (Boston: Little, Brown, 1977): 207-260.

3. See, "Open Door Policy for Voting Rights," National Voter, Spring, 1981: 1-2; and Dye, 1971: 55-56. See also, the U.S. Commission on Civil Rights, Report of the Commission, 1975 (Washington, D.C.: U.S. Government Printing Office, 1975).

4. Similar conclusions about the independent impact of ethnicity explaining the persistence of ethnic politics are reached using other methods of analysis and based upon a Buffalo study. See, R. Robert Huckfeldt, "The Social Contexts of Ethnic Politics," American Politics Quarterly, 11, 1 (January, 1983): 91-123.

Additional Readings

Alexander, Nicholas. Black in Blue. New York: Appleton-Century-Crofts, 1969.
Ball, George. "American Foreign Policy and American Jews," The Washington Post, Sunday, July 11, 1982, C 8.
Cochran, Clarke, T.R.Carr, Lawrence Mayer, and N. Joseph Cayer. American Public Policy. New York: St. Martin´s Press, 1982.
Dye, Thomas. The Politics of Equality. Indiannapolis: Bobbs-Merrill, 1971.
Fuchs, Lawrence. "Minority Groups and Foreign Policy," in American Ethnic Politics, New York: Harper and Row, 1968.

Lieberson, Stanley. A Piece of the Pie. Berkeley: University of California Press, 1980.

Lipsky, Michael. Law and Order Police Encounters. Chicago: Aldine Publishing, 1970.

Mathias, Charles McC., "Ethnic Groups and Foreign Policy," Foreign Affairs, July 17, 1981: 975-998.

Sigler, Jay A. American Rights Policies. Homewood, Illinois: Dorsey Press, 1975.

Sindler, Alan. Bakke, DeFunis and Minority Admissions. New York: Longman, 1978.

Spear, Allan H. Black Chicago. Chicago: University of Chicago Press, 1967.

Taeuber, Karl and Alma Taeuber. Negroes in Cities. Chicago: Aldine Publishing, 1965.

BIBLIOGRAPHY

"Acts of Violence Accompany State Migrant Workers," Cumberland Sunday Times, September 12, 1982: C-5.

Acuna, Rodolfo. Occupied America: The Chicano's Struggle Toward Liberation. San Francisco: Canfield Press, 1972.

Adam, Barry D. "Inferiorization and Self Esteem," Social Psychology (41, March, 1978): 47-57.

Adams, Thomas F. Criminal Justice Readings. Pacific Palisades, California: Goodyear, 1972.

Adamic, Louis. Nation of Nations. New York: Harper Torchbooks, 1945.

Adorno, T. W.,et al. The Authoritarian Personality. New York: Harper, 1950.

Agresti, Barbara F. "The First Decade of Freedom: Black Families in a Southern County, 1870-1885," Journal of Marriage and the Family. 40 (November, 1978): 697-706.

Alexander, Nicholas. Black in Blue: A Study of the Negro Policeman. New York: Appleton-Century-Crofts, 1969.

Alexander, Shana. State by State Guide to Women's Rights. Los Angeles: Wollstonecraft, Inc., 1975.

Allport, E.S.W. The Nature of Prejudice. New York: Doubleday, 1958.

Alvarez, Rodolfo, "The Psycho-Historical and Socioeconomic Development of the Chicano Community in the U.S.," Social Science Quarterly, 53 (March, 1973): 920-942.

Amir, Yehuda, "Contact Hypothesis in Ethnic Relations," Psychological Bulletin, 71 (May, 1969): 319-342.

Anderson, Arlow W. The Norwegian Americans. Boston: G. K. Hall, 1975.

Annals of the American Academy of Political and Social Sciences. Philadelphia: The Academy of Political and Social Science, 1974.

Appleman, I. "That New Immigration Act: Changes That Were Made in the Nation's Immigration Policy by the Passage Last Year of a New Immigration and Nationality Act," American Bar Association Journal, 52 (August, 1966): 717-722.

Arno Press. Anti-Catholicism in America, 1841-1851: Three Sermons. New York: Arno Press, 1977.

Ash, Roberta. Social Movements in America. Chicago: Markham, 1972.

Asher, Herbert. Presidential Elections and American Politics Homewood, Illinois: Dorsey Press, 1980.

433

Asher, Steven R. and Vernon L. Allen, "Racial Preference and Social Comparison Processes," Journal of Social Issues, 25 (November, 1969): 157-166.

Auerback, T. Immigration Laws of the United States. Indiannapolis: Bobbs-Merrill, 1961.

Babcock, Kendrick C. The Scandinavian Element in the United States. Urbana: The University of Illinois Press, 1914.

Babics, Walter V. Yugoslav Assimilation in Franklin County, Ohio. San Francisco: R. and E. Research Association, 1972.

Bacci, M. Immigration and Assimilation of Italians in the U.S. According to American Population Statistics. Milan: A. Giuffre, 1961.

Bache, R. Meado, "Reaction Time With Reference to Race," Psychological Review, 21 (September, 1895): 475-480.

"Bad Tidings for the Jobless," Time, December 13, 1982: 54-55.

Bahr, Howard M. and Bruce Chadwick, American Ethnicity. Lexington, Mass.: D. C. Heath, 1975.

Bailey, Thomas H. Voices of America. New York: Free Press, 1976.

Balch, Emily Green. Our Slavic Fellow Citizens. New York: Arno Press, 1910.

Ball, George W. "American Foreign Policy and the American Jew," The Washington Post, Sunday, July 11, 1982: C-8.

Banton, Michael. Race Relations. London: Tavistock Publications, 1967.

Baker, Ross K. The Afro-American. New York: Van Nostrand, 1970.

Barker, Lucius J. and Jesse J. McCorry, Jr. Black Americans and the Political System. Cambridge, Mass.: Winthrop Publishers, 1976.

Barron, Milton L. Minorities in a Changing World. New York: Knopf, 1967.

Barth E. and Noel, D. L. "Conceptual Frameworks for the Analysis of Race Relations," Social Forces, 50 (1972): 33-347.

Bayor, Ronald. Neighbors in Conflict. Baltimore: Johns Hopkins Press, 1978.

Beals, Carlton. Brass Knuckle Crusade. New York: Hasting House, 1960.

Bean, Frank D. and W. Parker Fisbie (ed.). The Demography of Racial and Ethnic Groups. New York: Academic Press, 1978.

Becker, Gary S. The Economics of Discrimination. Chicago: University of Chicago Press, 1971.

Bennet, M. R. "The Immigration and Nationality Act of 1952, as Amended to 1965," Annals of the American Academy of Political and Social Sciences, 367 (September, 1966): 127- 136.

Berelson, Bernard and Patricia J. Salter, "Majority and Minority Americans: An Analysis of Magazine Fiction," Public Opinion Quarterly, 10 (Summer, 1946): 168-190.

Berger, M. Equality by Statute. Garden City, N. Y.: Doubleday, 1968.

Berry, Burton. Race and Ethnic Relations. Boston: Houghton Mifflin, 1958.

Billington, Ray Allen. The Origins of Nativism in the United States, 1800-1844. New York: Arno Press, 1974.

Binstock, Robert H. and Katherine Ely (eds.). Politics of the Powerless. Cambridge, Mass.: Winthrop, 1971.

Blair, P. and O.D. Duncan. The American Occupation Structure. New York: Wiley: 1967.

Blalock, Hubert M. Towards a Theory of Minority Group Relations. New York: John Wiley and Sons, 1967.

Blauner, R. "Internal Colonialism and Ghetto Revolt," Social Problems, 16 (1969): 393-408.

_____. Racial Oppression in America. New York: Harper and Row, 1972.

Blegen, Theodore C. Norwegian Migration to America: 1825-1860. New York: Arno Press, 1967.

_____. Grassroots History. Minneapolis: University of Minnesota Press, 1947.

Bloom, Leonard. The Social Psychology of Race Relations. London: G. Allen, 1971.

Bogardus, E. C. "Race Relations Cycle," American Journal of Sociology, 35 (January, 1930): 612-617

_____. The Mexican in the U.S. Los Angeles: Arno Press, 1934.

Bonacich, Edna, "Advanced Capitalism and Black/White Race Relations in the U.S.: A Split Labor Market Interpretation," American Sociological Review, 41 (February, 1976):34-51.

Boque, Allen G. "United States: The ´New´ Political History," Journal of Contemporary History, 11 (January, 1968): 5-27.

Boque, Donald. The Population of the United States. Glencoe, Ill.: Free Press, 1959.

Borrie, W. D. The Cultural Integration of Immigrants. Paris: UNESCO, 1959.

Briggs, Vernon M. Jr. Chicanos and Rural Poverty. Baltimore: Johns Hopkins Press, 1973.

Brodeur, Paul. Expandable America. New York: The Viking Press, 1974.

Brown, Thomas M. Irish-American Nationalism. New York: J. P. Lippencott, 1966.

Brown, W. D. "Cultural Contact and Race Conflict," in E. B. Renter (ed.) Race and Cultural Contacts. New York: McGraw-Hill, 1934.

Bugelski, B. R. "Assimilation Through Intermarriage," Social Forces, 40 (1961): 148-153.

Burke, Mary P. Reaching for Justice: The Women's Movement, Washington, D. C.: Center of Concern, 1980.

Burgess, Thomas. Greeks in America. Boston: Scherman, French and Company, 1913.

Burma, John H. (ed.) Mexican-Americans in the United States. New York: Harper and Row, 1970.

Comprisi, P. "Emmigrants: Italy's Most Profitable Export," Atlas, 10 (October, 1965): 227-228.

Carlson, S. "Some Aspects of Swedish Emmigration to the United States," Swedish Pioneer, 20 (October, 1969): 192-203.

Carmichael, Stokley, and Charles V. Hamilton. Black Power: The Politics of Liberation in America. New York: Vintage Books, 1967.

Carpenter, N. Immigrants and Their Children. New York: Arno Press, 1969.

Carson, Clayborne. In Struggle: SNCC and the Black Awakening of the 1960s. Cambridge, Massachusetts: Harvard University Press, 1981.

Carter, H. and Doster, B. "Social Characteristics of Naturalized Americans from Mexico," Immigration and Naturalization Service, Monthly Review, 8 (September, 1950): 35-39.

_____, "Social Characteristics of Naturalized Americans from Norway," Immigration and Naturalization Service, Monthly Review, 9(November, 1951): 59-64.

Castro, Tony. Chicano Power: The Emergence of Mexican-Americans. New York: E. P. Dutton, 1974.

Cayer, Joseph N. and Sigelman, Lee. "Minorities and Women in State and Local Government: 1973-1975," Public Administration Review, 40 (1980): 443-450.

Centers, Richard. Psychology of Social Class. Princeton: Princeton University Press, 1949.

"Champion of the Elderly," Time, April 25, 1983: 21-29.

Churchill, Charles W. The Italians of Newark: A Community Study. New York: Arno Press, 1975.

Clem, Alan L. American Electoral Politics. New York: Van Nostrand, 1981.

Cochran, Clarke, T.R. Carr, Lawrence Mayer and N. Joseph Cayer, American Public Policy. New York: St. Martin's Press, 1982.

Colby, David C. "A Test of the Relative Efficiency of Political Tactics," (Paper Presented at APSA Convention, Denver, September, 1982).

Collins, Barry. Social Psychology. Reading, Mass.: Addison-Wesley, 1970.

Congressional Quarterly. America in the 1980's. Washington, D.C.: Congressional Quarterly, 1980.

_____. The Rights Revolution. Washington, D.C.: Congressional Quarterly, 1979.

_____. The Woman's Movement: Agenda for the '80's. Washington, D.C.: Congressional Quarterly, 1981.

_____. Work Life in the 1980's. Washington, D.C.: Congressional Quarterly, 1981.

Cooper, John L. The Police and the Ghetto. New York: Kennikat Press, 1980.

Cornwell, Elmer E. "Party Absorption of Ethnic Groups," Social Forces, 38 (March, 1960): 205-216.

Crain, Robert. The Politics of School Desegregation. Chicago: Aldine Press, 1968.

Crew, Louie (ed.) The Gay Academic. Palm Springs, California: ETC Publications, 1978.

Crewdson, John. The Tarnished Door. New York: Times Books, 1983.

Crowell, Susanne (ed.), "Sexism and Racism: Feminist Perspectives," Civil Rights Digest, (Spring, 1974).

Dahrendorf, Ralf. Class Conflict in Industrial Society. Stanford: Stanford University Press, 1939.

D'Angelo, Pascal. Sons of Italy. New York: Arno Press, 1924.

Daniels, Roger and Harry Kitano. American Racism. Englewood Cliffs, N.J.: Prentice-Hall, 1970.

Dashefsky, Arnold (ed.) Ethnic Identity in Society. Chicago: Rand McNally, 1976.

Davis, Jerome. The Russian Immigrant. New York: Arno Press, 1967.

Davisson, William and John J. Uhran, Jr. "Modeling and Simulation: A Systems Science Approach," (Notre Dame University of Notre Dame Mimeographed, 1976).

Deckard, Barbara. The Women's Movement. New York: Harper and Row, 1979.

DeLeon, Shirley. Puerto Ricans in America. Chicago: Claretian Publications, 1974.

Deloria, Vine, Jr. "This Country Was A Lot Better Off When the Indians Were Running It," in Alvin Josephy, Jr. (ed.) Red Power. New York: McGraw-Hill, 1971.

437

Desmond, Humphrey J. The A.P.A. Movement. Washington, D. C.: 1912.

DeVos, George and Lola Romanucci-Ross. Ethnic Identity. Paloalto, California: Mayfield Publishing, 1975.

Dinnerstein, Leonard and Frederick C. Jaher. Uncertain Americans. New York: Oxford University Press, 1977.

Dinnerstein, Leonard and David M. Reimers. Ethnic Americans. New York: Harper and Row, 1975.

Divine, R. A. American Immigration Policy. New Haven: Yale University Press, 1957.

Dolbeare, Kenneth. Political Change in the United States. New York: McGraw-Hill, 1974.

Dollard, John et al. Frustration and Aggression. New Haven: Yale University Press, 1939.

Duncan, B. and D. Duncan, "Minorities and the Process of Stratification," American Sociological Review, 33 (June, 1968): 356-364.

Duran, Livic Isauro and L. Russell Bernard (eds.). Introduction to Chicano Studies. New York: McMillan, 1973.

Dye, Thomas R. The Politics of Equality. Indiannapolis: The Bobbs-Merrill Co., 1971.

_____. Understanding Public Policy. Englewood Cliffs, N.J.: Prentice-Hall, 1978.

"Dying Gay Bill of Rights Stirs Hot Debate on Hill," The Washington Post, January 28, 1982: A-2.

Easton, David. A Framework for Political Analysis. Englewood Cliffs, N. J.: Prentice-Hall, 1965.

Edwards, George. The Politics of the Urban Frontier. New York: Institute of Human Relations Press, 1968.

Ehrlichman, John, "An American Struggle," Parade, March 14, 1982: 4-8.

Eisinger, Peter K., "Black Employment in Municipal Jobs: The Impact of Black Political Power," American Political Science Review, June, 1982: 380-392.

"Evacuation of the Japanese Americans," The Washington Post, December 5, 1982: A-1, 13-14.

"Every Region, Every Age Group, Almost Every Voting Bloc," Time, Election Special Edition, November 19, 1984: 42-45.

Fairchild, H. "Public Opinion and Immigration," Annals of the Academy of Political and Social Sciences. 262 (March, 1949): 185-192.

Farley, Reynolds, "The Changing Distribution of Negroes Within Metropolitan Areas," American Journal of Sociology, January, 1970: 523.

Feaver, G. "Wounded Knee and the New Tribalism," Encounter, March, 1975.

Featherman, David L. "The Socioeconomic Achievement of White Religio-Ethnic Subgroups: Social and Psychological Explanations," American Sociological Review, 36 (April, 1971): 207-222.

Federal Writer's Project. The Italians of New York. New York: Arno Press, 1969.

Feldstein, Stanley and Lawrence Costello (eds.). The Ordeal of Assimilation: A Documentary of the White Working Class, 1830-1970. Garden City, N. Y.: Doubleday, 1975.

Fenton, Edwin. Immigrants and Unions: A Case Study: Italians and American Labor, 1870-1920. New York: Arno Press, 1975.

Fichter, Joseph, S. J. Social Relations in the Urban Parish. Chicago: University of Illinois Press, 1954.

_____. "Intermarriage of Puerto Ricans in New York City," American Journal of Sociology, 71 (1966): 395-406.

Fisher, Peter. The Gay Mystique. New York: Stein and Day, 1972.

Fitzpatrick, Joseph P., "The Importance of Community in the Process of Immigration Assimilation," International Migration Review, January, 1966: 6-16.

Fitzpatrick, Joseph P. Puerto Rican Americans. Englewood Cliffs, N.J.: Prentice-Hall, 1971.

Flanigan, William H. and Nancy H. Zingale. Political Behavior of the American Electorate. 3rd Edition, Boston: Allyn and Bacon, 1975.

Fogelson, Robert M. Big City Police. Cambridge, Mass.: Harvard University Press, 1977.

Forbes, Jack (ed.). The Indians in America's Past. Englewood Cliffs, N.J.: Prentice-Hall, 1964.

Fox-Piven, Frances and Richard A. Cloward. The Politics of Turmoil. New York: Vintage Books, 1975.

_____. Regulating the Poor: The Functions of Public Welfare. New York: Pantheon Books, 1971.

Freedman, Morris and Carolyn Banks. American Mix. New York: J.B. Lippencott, 1972.

Friis, Erik J. (ed.) The Scandinavian Presence in North America. New York: Harper and Row, 1976.

Fleisher, Eric and Jorgen Neibull. Viking Times to Modern. Minneapolis: University of Minnesota Press, 1953.

Frankfort, Ellen. Vaginal Politics. New York: New York Times Books, 1972.

Fuch, Lawrence H. (ed.) American Ethnic Politics. New York: Harper and Row, 1968.

Fullenwider, Claire K. *Feminism in American Politics*. New York: Praeger, 1980.

Fushfield, Daniel R. *The Basic Economics of the Urban Racial Crisis*. New York: Holt, Rinehart and Winston, 1973.

Galloway, L. "Distribution of Immigrant Population in the United States--Economic Analysis," *Explorations in Economic History*, 2 (1974): 213 ff.

Gamson, William H. *The Strategy of Social Protest*. Homewood, Illinois: Dorsey Press, 1975.

Gardner, John W. *No Easy Victories*. New York: Harper and Row, 1968.

_____. *Self-Renewal: The Individual and the Innovative Society*. New York: Harper and Row, 1965.

Garfinkle, Stanley. *The Indians in America*. Chicago: Claretian Publishers, 1974.

Gerson, Louis L. *The Hyphenate in Present American Policy and Diplomacy*. Lawrence, Kansas: University of Kansas Press, 1964.

Glazer, Nathan. *Affirmative Discrimination: Ethnic Inequality and Public Policy*. New York: Basic Books, 1975.

_____. "Blacks and Ethnic Groups: The Difference and the Political Difference It Makes," *Social Problems*, 18 (1971): 444-461.

_____ and Daniel Moynihan. *Beyond the Melting Pot*. Cambridge, Mass.: Harvard University and M.I.T. Press, 1963.

_____ and Daniel Moynihan. *Ethnicity: Theory and Experience*. Cambridge, Mass.: Harvard University Press, 1975.

Glanz, Rudolf. *Jew and Italians: Historic Group Relations and the New Immigration*. New York: Klan, 1970.

Glich, Clarence E. "Social Roles and Types in Race Relations," in A. W. Lind (ed.) *Race Relations in World Perspectives*. Honolulu: University of Hawaii Press, 1955: 239-262.

Goldstein, Leslie Friedman, "The ERA and American Public Policy," Paper Delivered at the 1984 Meeting of the American Political Science Association, Washington, D.C., September, 1984.

Gordon, C. "Racial Limitations in Immigration and Naturalization Laws," *Foreign Policy Reports*, 23 (April, 1947): 20 ff.

_____. "Hardships Under the Immigration Laws," *Annals of the American Academy of Political and Social Sciences*, 367 (September, 1966): 85-92.

Gordon, David M. Problems in Political Economics and Urban Perspectives. Lexington, Mass.: D. C. Heath, 1977.

Gordon, Milton. Assimilation in American Life. New York: Oxford University Press, 1964.

Grant, Joanne. Black Protest History, Documents and Analysis: 1600 to the Present. New York: Fawcett Publications, 1970.

Greely, Andrew M. Ethnicity in the United States. New York: Wiley, 1974.

Greenstein, Frederick. The American Party System and the American People. Englewood Cliffs, N.J.: Prentice-Hall, 1970.

Greer, Edward. Black Liberation Politics: A Reader. Boston: Allyn and Bacon, 1971.

Greer, Germaine. The Female Unich. New York: Bantam Books, 1972.

Guzman, Ralph C., Leo Grebler and Joan Moore. The Mexican-American People. New York: Free Press, 1970.

Hansen, Marcus Lee. The Atlantic Migration: 1607-1860. New York: Harper Torch Books, 1961.

Hanson, M. W. The Immigrant in American History. Cambridge, Mass.: Harvard University Press, 1940.

Haugood, John. The Tragedy of German-Americans. New York: Arno Press, 1940.

Harlich, Wasyl. Ukranians in the United States. Chicago: University of Chicago Press, 1933.

Harlou, Louis R. Separate and Unequal. New York: Atheneum, 1968.

Harris, Fred, "Old People Power," The New Republic, March 23, 1974: 11.

Hennessey, Caroline. The Strategy of Sexual Struggle. New York: Lancer Books, 1971.

Henry, Nicholas. Governing at the Grass Roots. Englewood Cliffs, N.J.: Prentice-Hall, 1980.

Herzog, Stephen J. Minority Group Politics: A Reader. New York: Holt, Rinehart and Winston, 1971.

"Hispanic-Americans: The Fastest Growing Minority," Cumberland Evening Times, July 1, 1982: 12.

Hofstadter, Richard and Michael Wallace. American Violence. New York: Knopf, 1971.

Holmes, Alexander. The Famous Five. New York: Bookmaker, 1958.

Hough, Emerson. The WEB: A History of the American Protective League. Chicago: Arno Press, 1919.

"House Approves Emerging Farm Aid, Kills Revisions of Immigration Law," The Washington Post, December 19, 1982: A-15.

Howard, John R. Awakening Minorities. New York: Aldine, 1970.

Howe, Irving. World of Our Fathers. New York: Simon and Schuster, 1976.

Hueston, Robert F. The Catholic Press and Nativism, 1840-1860. New York: Arno Press, 1976.

"Illegal Aliens: Invasion Out of Control?" U.S. News and World Report, January 29, 1979: 38-42.

"Immigration Law Revised: May Be Derailed in House," The Washington Post, Sunday, December 5, 1982: A-12, 15.

International Catholic Migration Commission, "Japanese Migration, 1868-1968," Migration Facts and Figures, 70 (Sept./Oct.), 1969.

Iarrizzo, Luciano and Salvatore Mondello. The Italian Americans. New York, Twayne Publishers, 1971.

Johnson, Jill. Lesbian Nation: The Feminist Solution. New York: Simon and Schuster, 1974.

Jones, M. American Immigration. Chicago: University of Chicago Press, 1960.

Kallen, Horace, "Democracy vs. the Melting Pot," The Nation, February 18, 1915.

Kanowitz, Leo. Women and the Law. Albequerque: University of New Mexico, 1973.

Karla, Jay and Allen Young (ed.) Out of the Closet: Voices of Gay Liberation. New York: Douglas Books, 1972.

Karsel, H. G. "Selected Factors Directly Associated With Population Growth Due to Net Migration," Annals, Association of American Geographers, 53 (June, 1963): 210- 233.

Katz, Daniel and Kenneth W. Braley, "Verbal Stereotypes and Racial Prejudice," in Eleanor Mausby, Theodore Newcomb, and Eugene Hartley (eds.) Readings in Social Psychology, New York: Holt, Rinehart and Winston, 1958): 40-46.

Kennedy, John. A Nation of Immigrants. New York: Harper Torchbooks, 1964.

Kirby, David J. et al. Political Strategies in Northern School Desegregation. Lexington, Mass.: D. C. Heath, 1973.

Kitano, Harry. Race Relations. Englewood Cliffs, N.J.: Prentice-Hall, 1974.

Kling, Samuel G. Sexual Behavior and the Law. New York: Pocket Books, 1969.

Kinlock, Graham. The Dynamics of Race Relations. New York: McGraw-Hill, 1974.

Komisar, Lucy. The New Feminism. New York: Warner, 1972.

Kurokawa, Minako (ed.) Minority Responses. New York:
    Random House, 1970.
LaGreco, A.   "Class, Race, and Ethnicity as Factors in
    Residential Density," (Doctoral Dissertation,   Ohio
    State University, 1973).
Larson, Lawrence M. The Changing West. New York: Books
    for Libraries Press, 1968.
Laserwitz,   B.   and   N.   Rewitz,   "Three-Generation
    Hypothesis," America Journal of Sociology,   66
    (March, 1964): 528-538.
Lanorette, William J.   "The Many Faces of the Jewish
    Lobby in America," National Journal, May 13, 1978:
    755 ff.
Lenski,   Gerhard.   The Religious Factor.   New York:
    Doubleday, 1961.
Levine, Edward M. The Irish and the Irish Politicians.
    Notre Dame: University of Notre Dame Press, 1966.
Leviton, S. and Barbara Hetrick. Big Brother's Indian
    Program--Without Reservations. New York: McGraw-
    Hill, 1971.
Levy, Burton (ed.) Riots and Rebellion: Civil Violence
    in the Urban Community. Beverly Hills: Sage
    Publications, 1968.
Levy, Mark and Michael S. Kramer. The Ethnic Factor:
    How American Minorities Decide Elections. New York:
    Simon and Schuster, 1973.
Lewis, Oscar. A Study of Slum Culture. New York:
    Random House, 1968.
Lieberson, Stanley, "A Societal Theory of Race and
    Ethnic Relations, American Sociological Review, 26
    (December, 1961): 902-910.
_____. A Piece of the Pie. Berkeley: University
    of California Press, 1980.
_____.Ethnic Patterns in American Cities.   New
    York: Free Press, 1963.
_____,"The Impact of Residential Segregation
    on Ethnic Assimilation," Social Forces, 40 (1961):
    52-57.
Liebman, Lance (ed.) Ethnic Relations in America.
    Englewood Cliffs, N.J.: Prentice-Hall, 1982.
Light, Ivan H. Ethnic Enterprises in America: Business
    and Welfare Among Chinese, Japanese and Blacks. Los
    Angeles: University of California Press, 1972.
Lipsky, Michael. Law and Order Police Encounters.
    Chicago: Aldine Publishing, 1970.
_____,"Protest as a Political Resource,"
    American Political Science Review,   (December,
    1968): 1144-1158.

Litt, Edgar. Ethnic Politics in America. Glenview, Ill.: Scott, Foresman, 1970.

Long, Elton, et al. American Minorities: The Justice Issue. Englewood Cliffs, N.J.: Prentice-Hall, 1975.

"Looking Out for Number One," Time, October 31, 1983: 47.

Lopata, Helen Znamechi. Polish-Americans. Englewood Cliffs, N.J.: Prentice-Hall, 1976.

Lopez y Rivas, Gilberto. The Chicanos. New York: Monthly Review Press, 1973.

Loughborough, J.W. The Great Second Advent Movement. Washington, D.C.: Arno Press, 1905.

Lowi, Theodore J. The Politics of Disorder. New York: Basic Books, 1971.

Luebhe, Frederick. Bonds of Loyalty: German Americans and World War I. DeKalb: 1974.

Luhman, Ried and Stuart Gilman, Race and Ethnic Relations. Belmont, California: Wadsworth, 1980.

Lurie, Nancy, "The American Indian: Historical Background," in Norman Yetman and C. Hoy Steele, Majority and Minority: The Dynamics of Racial and Ethnic Relations. Boston: Allyn and Bacon, 1971.

Maquire, John F. The Irish in America. New York: Arno Press, 1969.

Mann, A. (ed.) Immigrants in American Life. Boston: Houghton Mifflin, 1968.

Marden, Charles and Gladys Meyer. Minorities in American Society. New York: Van Nostrand, 1968.

Marians, John H. The Italian Contribution to American Democracy. Boston: Arno Press, 1922.

Martin, Dell and Phyllis Lyon. Lesbian Women. New York: Bantam, 1972.

Marx, Herbert (ed.) The American Indian: A Rising Ethnic Force. New York: W. H. Wilson, 1973.

Mathews, Tom, "Battle Cry Over Gay Rights," Newsweek, June 6, 1977.

Mathias, Charles McC., "Ethnic Groups and Foreign Policy," Foreign Affairs, July 17, 1981: 975-998.

McClellan, Grant S. (ed.) Immigrants, Refugees, and U.S. Policy. New York: H. W. Wilson, 1981.

McLemore, Dale. Racial and Ethnic Relations in America. Boston: Allyn and Bacon, 1980.

McLennan, Barbara (ed.) Crime in Urban Society. New York: The Dunellen Company, 1970.

McSevery, Samuel I., "Ethnic Groups, Ethnic Conflicts and Recent Quantitative Research in American Political History," The International Migration Review. VII (Spring, 1973): 14-33.

Meier, Matt S. and Feliciano Rivera. The Chicanos. New York: Hill and West, 1972.

Meister, Richard J. Race and Ethnicity in Modern America. Lexington, Mass.: D. C. Heath, 1974.

Merrill, Bruce D., "Partisanship, Ethnicity, and Electoral Change in Texas," Public Service, Lubbock, Texas: Texas Tech University, September, 1976: 1-4.

Milbrath, Lester W. and M.C. Goel. Political Participation. Chicago: Rand McNally, 1977.

Miller, Ruth Ann, Mary Alice Waters and Evely Reed. In Defense of the Women's Movement. New York: Pathfinder Press, 1971.

"Minorities Drive Thrown Into Reverse," U.S. News and World Report, September 27, 1982: 40-42.

Mittelbach, Frank G. and Joan W. Moore, "Ethnic Endogamy--the Case of Mexican Americans," American Journal of Sociology, 7 (1968): 395-406.

Moore, Joan and Harry Pachon. Mexican Americans. Englewood Cliffs, N.J.: Prentice-Hall, 1976.

Mooris, Richard S. Bum Rap on American Cities. Englewood Cliffs, N.J.: Prentice-Hall, 1980.

Moskos, Charles C. Greek-Americans. Englewood Cliffs, N.J.: Prentice-Hall, 1980.

National Geographic Society. We Americans. Washington, D.C.: National Geographic Society, 1979.

Nelli, Humbert S. Italians in Chicago: 1830-1930. New York: Oxford University Press, 1970.

Nelson, Dale C., "Ethnic Sources of Non-Electoral Participation in American Urban Setting," Paper Presented at APSA Convention, Washington, D. C., September, 1977.

Nevins, Allan. Ordeal in the Union: A House Dividing. New York: Charles Scribners Sons, 1947.

Newman, William. American Pluralism. New York: Harper and Row, 1973.

Noel, Donald L., "A Theory of the Origin of Ethnic Stratification," Social Problems, (Fall, 1968): 157-172.

Oakley, Ann. Sex, Gender and Society. New York: Harper and Row, 1972.

O'Connor, Thomas. The Disunited States. New York: Dodd, Mead and Company, 1972.

_____.The German Americans. Boston: Little, Brown, 1968.

O'Grady, Joseph D. How the Irish Became Americans. New York: Twayne, 1973.

"Older Women Hit By Budget Cuts," Cumberland Evening Times, October 5, 1982: 6.

Olson, Mancur. The Logic of Collective Action. Cambridge, Massachusetts: Harvard University Press, 1965.

Orth, Ralph and Alfred Ferguson (eds.). The Journals and Miscellaneous Notebooks of Ralph Waldo Emerson. Cambridge, Mass.: Harvard University Press, 1971.

"Open Door Policy for Voting Rights," League of Women Voters, Washington, D.C.: The League, Spring, 1981.

Palmore, Erdman B., "Ethnophaulism and Ethnocentrism," The American Journal of Sociology, (January, 1962): 492-495.

Panning, William H. "Inequality, Social Comparison, and Relative Deprivation," American Political Science Review, June, 1983: 323-329.

Parenti, Michael J. Ethnic and Political Attitudes: A Depth Study of Italian Americans. New York: Arno Press, 1975.

Park, Robert E. Race and Culture. New York: The Free Press, 1950.

Parsons, Talcott and Clark, Kenneth B. The Negro American. Boston: Beacon Press, 1966.

Parrillo, Vincent. Strangers to These Shores. Boston: Houghton-Mifflin, 1980.

Patterson, S. Immigrants in Industry. New York: Institute of Race Relations, Oxford University Press, 1968.

Paul, Ellen and Philip Russo. Public Policy. Chatham, N.J.: Chatham House, 1982.

Philip Morris, Inc. Guide to Hispanic Organizations. New York: Philip Morris U.S.A., 1983.

Pierce, Richard L. The Polish in America. Chicago: Claretian Press, 1972.

Protestant Evangelism Among Italians in America. New York: Arno Press, 1975.

"Police and Minorities," U.S.A. Today, January 5, 1983: A-10.

Polsby, Nelson and Aaron Wildavsky. Presidential Elections. New York: Charles Scribner's Sons, 1976.

Pomper, Gerald. The Election of 1980. Chatham, N.J.: Chatham House, 1981.

_____.The Election of 1976. New York: David McKay, 1977.

Power, Paul F. "Ethnic Groups and the 'National Interest,'" Paper Delivered at the 1984 Meeting of the American Political Science Association, Washington, D. C., September, 1984.

Price, H. P., "Federal Aid to Education Bill," in The Uses of Power:Seven Cases in American Politics. New York: Harcourt Brace, 1962.
446

Prpic, George. South Slavic Immigration in America. Boston: Twayne, 1978.

"Quaker School Aids Resisters to Draft," The Cumberland Times, October 5, 1982: 2.

Radin, Paul. The Italians of San Francisco: Their Adjustment and Acculturation. San Francisco: Arno Press, 1935.

"Raids Nab High-Pay Aliens, Make Jobs, Outrage Clergy," The Washington Post, May 2, 1982: A-10.

Rainwater, Lee. Behind Ghetto Walls. Chicago: Aldine Publishing, 1970.

"Reagon Courting Hispanics," The Cumberland Evening Times. September 15, 1983: 1.

"Reagonomics, The Continuing Urban Crisis, and Politics of Resistance," William Nelson, Paper Presented to APSA, Atlanta, October, 1982.

Redfield, Robert, "Memorandum for the Study of Acculturation," American Anthropologist, 38 (1936).

Reissman, Leonard. Inequality in American Society. Glenview, Ill.: Scott, Foresman, 1973.

Reuter, E. B. (ed.) Race and Culture Contacts. New York: McGraw-Hill, 1934.

"Right vs. Right: Immigration and Refugee Policy in the United States," Foreign Affairs, Fall, 1980.

Rippley, LaVern. The German Americans. Chicago: Claretian Press, 1976.

Roberts, Peter. Immigrant Races in North America. New York: Association Press, 1912.

Rose, Harold M. The Black Ghetto. New York: McGraw-Hill, 1971.

Rosen, B. C. and H. J. Crochett, Jr. Achievement in American Society. Cambridge: Schenman, 1969.

Rosen, B. C., "Race, Ethnicity and the Achievement Syndrome," American Sociological Review, 24 (February, 1959): 47-60.

Rosenberg, Terry J. Residence, Employment, and Mobility of Puerto Ricans in N.Y.C. Chicago: University of Chicago, Department of Geography Research Paper 151, 1974.

Ross, Ken, "Gay Rights: the Coming Struggle," The Nation, November 19, 1977.

Ross, C. The Rights of Women: The Basic ACLU Guide to Women´s Rights. New York: Aron, 1973.

Rothenberg, Stuart and Eric Licht. Ethnic Voters and National Issues. Washington, D.C.: T. C. Research and Education Foundation, 1982.

Roucek, Joseph S. and Bernard Eisenberg. America´s Ethnic Politics. Westport, Conn.: Greenwood Press, 1982.

Rubin, E. "The Penography of Immigration to the U.S.," Annals of the American Academy of Political and Social Sciences, 367 (September, 1977): 15-22.

Ruchelman, Leonard. Who Rules the Police? New York: New York University Press, 1973.

Saloutos, Theodore. The Greeks in the United States. Cambridge, Mass.: Harvard University Press, 1964.

Schermerhorn, R. A. Comparative Ethnic Relations. New York: Random House, 1970.

_____.These Our People. Boston: D. C. Heath, 1949.

Schiro, George. Americans By Choice: History of the Italians in Utica, New York. Utica: Arno Press, 1940.

Schon, Alvin L. Explorations in Social Policy. New York: Basic Books, 1969.

Scuros, M., "The Southwest Voter Registration Education Project," Citizen Participation, 4, 1 (September, 1982).

Schaffer, Thomas L., "Onward Christian Soldier?," The Washington Post, May 2, 1982.

Segal, Bernard E. (ed.) Racial and Ethnic Politics. New York: Thomas Y. Crowell, 1972.

"Senior Power," Newsweek, September 16, 1974: 41.

Shaughnessey, Gerald. Has the Immigrant Kept the Faith?: A Study of Immigration and Catholic Growth in the U.S., 1790-1920. New York: Arno Press, 1925.

Shibutani, Tomatsu. Ethnic Strategy. New York: MacMillan, 1970.

Shingles, Richard D. "Black Consciousness and Political Participation: The Missing Link,"American Political Science Review, March, 1981: 76-91.

Sigler, Jay A. American Rights Policy. Homewood, Ill.: Dorsey Press, 1975.

"Signs of Hope Rise in Indian Schools," The Washington Post, December 27, 1981:1.

Siminoski, Dan. "Visibility and Interest Group Representation: The Case of the Gay Rights Movement," Paper Presented at the 1984 Meeting of the American Political Science Association, Washington, D. C., September, 1984.

Simpson, George E. and J. M. Yinger. Racial and Cultural Minorities. New York: Harper and Row, 1965.

Sindler, Allan P. (ed.) America in the '70's: Problems, Policies, and Politics. Boston: Little, Brown, 1977.

Smeler, Niel J. Social Structure and Mobility in Economic Development. Chicago: Aldine Publishing, 1966.

Smith, T. Lynn and Vernon J. Parenton, "Acculturation Among the Louisiana French," American Journal of Sociology, 44 (November, 1938): 130 ff.

Smith and Jameson (eds.) The Shaping of American Religion. Princeton: Princeton University Press, 1961.

Smith, Lucy M. Biographical Sketches of Joseph Smith. Liverpool: Arno Press, 1853.

Smith, Theodore. Parties and Slavery. New York: Negro University Press, 1969.

Spear, Allan H. Black Chicago: The Making of a Negro Ghetto. Chicago: University of Chicago Press, 1967.

Speranya, Gina. Race or Nation: A Conflict of Divided Loyalties. New York:Arno Press, 1935.

Spiegel, Steven L. "Ethnic Politics and the Formulation of U.S. Policy Toward the Arab-Israeli Dispute," Paper Presented at the 1984 Meeting of the American Political Science Association, Washington, D. C., September, 1984.

Spiro, M.S., "The Acculturation of American Ethnic Groups," American Anthropologist, 57 (1955): 12-44.

Stanley, Frances. The New World Refugee--The Cuban Exodus. (U.S.A.: Church World Service, 1966).

Stedman, Murry, Jr. Religion and Politics in America. New York: Harcourt, Brace, 1964.

_____.The Police and the Community. Baltimore: Johns Hopkins University Press, 1972.

Steele, C. Hoy and Norman R. Yetman (eds.) Majority and Minority. Boston: Allyn and Bacon, 1971.

Steiner, Stan. LaRaza: The Mexican-Americans. New York: Random House, 1973.

Stephenson, George M. The Religious Aspects of Swedish Immigration, New York: Arno Press, 1964.

Stidhan, Ronald, Robert A. Carp and C. K. Rowland, "Women´s Rights Before the Federal Courts, 1971-1977," American Politics Quarterly, April, 1983: 205-218.

Stoddard, Ellwyn. Mexican-Americans. New York: Random House, 1973.

Tabb, William K. The Political Economy of the Black Ghetto. New York: W. W. Norton, 1970.

Taeuber, Karl E. and Alma F. Taeuber, "The Negro as an Immigrant Group: Recent Trends in Racial and Ethnic Segregation in Chicago," American Journal of Sociology, 69 (1964): 374-382.

_____,"Recent Immigration and Studies of Ethnic Assimilation," Demography, 4 (1967): 798-808.

"The Coming Age of Black Political Power," The Crisis, 90, 7 (Aug./Sept.1983): 30.

"The Graying of America," Newsweek, February 28, 1977: 50-65.

"The New Ellis Island," Time, July 13, 1983: 18-27.

"The New Immigrants," Newsweek, July 7, 1980: 26-31.

"The South Is Still Changing," The Washington Post, October 30, 1983: C-5.

Thernstrom, Stephen. Harvard Encyclopedia of American Ethnic Groups. Cambridge, Mass.: Harvard University Press, 1980.

Thomas, William and Florian Znanicki, "The Polish American Community," in Dinnerstein, and Jaher (eds.) Uncertain Americans. New York: Oxford University Press, 1977.

Thomlison, R. Popular Dynamics. New York: Random House, 1965.

Tremain, Rose The Fight for Freedom for Women. New York: Ballantine Books, 1973.

Truman, David B. The Governmental Process. New York: Alfred A. Knopf, 1951.

U.S. Commission on Civil Rights, Social Indicators for Equal Rights for Minorities and Women. Washington, D. C.: U.S. Government Printing Office, 1970.

U.S. Department of Commerce, Social Indicators. Washington, D.C.: U.S. Government Printing Office, 1980.

_____. We, the American Elderly. Washington, D.C.: U.S. Government Printing Office, 1973.

"U.S. Ethnic Profile Undergoing Marked Change," New York Times, June 14, 1971: 37.

U.S. Equal Opportunity Commission, Minorities and Women in State and Local Government, 1978. Washington, D.C.: U.S. Government Printing Office, 1980.

"U.S. Hispanics--Rising Tide," Parade Magazine, September 4, 1983.

U.S. House of Representatives, The KKK: Hearings Before the Committee on Rules, Washington, D.C.: U.S. Government Printing Office,1921.

U.S. News and World Report, November 26, 1973: 94-95.

U.S. Riot Commission Report, Report of the National Advisory Commission on Civil Disorder. New York: Bantam Books, 1968.

Vallarreal, Roberto E., "Ethnic Leadership in American Foreign Policy: The Hispanic Experience," Paper Delivered at the 1984 Meeting of the American Political Science Association, Washington, D. C., September, 1984.

Valletta, Clement. A Study of Americanization in Carneta: Italian American Identity Through Three Generations. New York: Arno Press, 1975.

Van Den Berghe, P. Race and Racism. New York: John Wiley and Sons, 1967.

Vander Zanden, James. American Minority Relations. New York: Ronald Press, 1983.

Van Der Slik, Jack (ed.) Black Conflict With White America. Columbus, Ohio: Charles E. Merrill, 1980.

Vioal, Mirta. Chicana Speak Out Women: New Voice of La Raza. New York: Pathfinder, 1971.

Viteritti, Joseph. Bureaucracy and Social Justice: Allocation of Jobs and Services to Minority Groups. New York: Kennikat Press, 1979.

Vose, Clement E. Caucasions Only. Berkeley: University of California Press, 1959.

Wakin, Edward. The Scandinavians in America. Chicago: Claretian Publishing, 1970.

Ward, David. Cities and Immigrants. New York: Oxford University Press, 1971.

Warner, Lloyd and Leo Srole. The Social Systems of American Ethnic Groups. Cambridge: Yale University Press, 1945.

Warren, B. L., "Socioeconomic Achievements and Religion: The American Case," Sociological Inquiry, 40 (September, 1970): 130-155.

Wassenberg, Pinky S. et al., "Gender Differences in Political Conceptualization: 1956-1980," American Politics Quarterly, April, 1983: 181-203.

Wax, L. Murray and Robert W. Buchanan (eds.) Solving "The Indian Problem": The White Man's Burdensome Business. New York: New York Times Company, 1975.

Weinberg, Daniel, "Ethnic Identity in Industrial Cleveland, 1900-1920," Ohio History, 86, 13 (Summer, 1977).

Weinstock, S. Alexander, "Role Elements: A Link Between Acculturation and Occupational Status," British Journal of Sociology, 14 (1963): 144-149.

_____, "Some Factors That Retard or Accelerate the Rate of Acculturation," Human Relations, 17 (1964): 321-340.

Whitney, Louisa G. The Burning of the Convent. Cambridge, Mass.: Arno Press, 1965.

"What to Do With Our Parents," Time, June 2, 1975: 45.

Whyte, W. H. Street Corner Society. Chicago: University of Chicago Press, 1965.

"What Americans Think: A Black or A Woman Does Better Today Than A Catholic in '60," The Washington Post Weekly Edition, November 21, 1983: 42.

"What Makes Jesse Run?," Newsweek, November 14, 1983: 50-56.

Williams, R. M., Jr. The Reduction of Intergroup Tensions. New York: Social Science Research Council, 1947.

Wilson, Stephen. Informal Groups. Englewood Cliffs, N.J.: Prentice-Hall, 1978.

Witke, Carl. Refugees of Revolution. Philadelphia: University of Pennsylvania Press, 1952.

_____. We Who Built America. Akron: Case Western University Press, 1967.

Workers of the Writer's Program Work Project, The Italians of Omaha. Omaha: Arno Press, 1941.

"Women Power," The Washington Post, September 11, 1983: 10.

Yancey, William, et al., "Emergent Ethnicity: A Review and Reformulation," American Sociological Review, 41 (June, 1976):391-403.

Ylvisaker, Erling. Emmigrant Pioneers. New York: Books for Libraries Press, 1970.

Young, Donald. Research Memorandum on Minority People in the Depression. New York: Arno Press, 1937.

Young, Richard and Jerome S. Burnstein, "Political Consequences of American Racial Demographic Change: 1915-1982," Paper Presented at the American Political Science Association Convention, Denver, September, 1982.

Zangwill, Israel. The Melting Pot. New York: MacMillan, 1909.

_____. Italians in the United States: A Repository of Rare Facts and Miscellany. New York: Arno Press, 1975.